Orthodox Consensus and Radical Alternative

Orthodox Consensus
and
Radical Alternative

A Study in Sociological Theory

DICK ATKINSON

BASIC BOOKS, INC., PUBLISHERS

New York

First American edition: 1972

© 1971 by Dick Atkinson
Library of Congress Catalog Card Number: 76-189670
SBN 465-05360-2
Printed in the United States of America

Preface

The process of 'moulding of still ductile forms' cannot go on forever. Sooner or later the process of revolt, of abandonment of 'chrysalids' of concept and method, takes place.

Robert Nisbet

For tenured faculty, the University is a realm of congenial and leisured servitude. It is a realm in which the academician is esteemed for his learning but castrated as a political being. Indeed, it is this trade-off, in which the academician has the right to be a tiger in the classroom but the need to be a pussycat in the Dean's office, that contributes so much to the irrational posturings and theatrics of the classroom. Like other academics, the Academic Sociologist learns from the routine experience of his dependency within the University that he can strike terror only into the hearts of the very young – and now they want to strip him of even that privilege – but that he himself is the gelded servant of the very system in which he is, presumably, the vaunted star. He has thus learned with an intuitive conviction that 'society shapes men' because he lives it every day; it is his autobiography objectified.

Alvin W. Gouldner

I began writing this book in 1963 at the London School of Economics. In the subsequent period of conflict between a number of us and the administration at the School, it often seemed that it would never be completed. But this conflict highlighted many important issues which included the uncritical attitude of some of the staff who claimed to be neutral, objective and unbiased. They did not apply their own sociological criteria to themselves. They did not see that they were prey to the same kind of influences and preconceptions which they so easily recognized when studying others, or when teaching their sociology to students for a living. They did not recognize the connection between their living and their work, while we came to realize that a different kind of living implied a different kind of work.

The ensuing debate made student life meaningful, connecting it with less parochial issues. We made the debate in our flats, in our 'demonstrations' and in occupations, despite and against the restricting activities of those in authority. We engaged in it with friends, school teachers, workers, fellow students, tenants; people who had some new vision and were striving to realize it and to live a freer life.

This experience taught us the relationship between social theory and human activity. It demonstrated the fatalistic aspects of sociological theory and of sociologists. Equally, it encouraged the search for alternative

v

approaches which would emphasize that ultimately it was people who were searching for control and choice.

This search for democratic, human control in all areas of life is what both my academic and my political work are about. This book is meant as an academic contribution to these concerns. It has been influenced by many people, including David Alexander, David Adelstein and, above all, Alan Dawe. I have been helped generally by Ralph Miliband, John Rex, Vic and Barbara Belcher and many others.

I am also deeply in debt to Gi Baldamus, Ann Allen, Alan Shuttleworth, Charles Madge, Peter Worsley, Anita Halliday, Roger Pincott and Bill Hodge, all of whom read this work and encouraged me to publish it. I am also indebted to Heinemann themselves for publishing it – especially I am grateful to Paul Richardson, Steve and Alan Hill and Heather Karolyi.

Criticisms of the work will come from Marxists as well as other kinds of sociologist. Such criticism is welcome – it is one way in which scholarship is tested, and develops. The faults which such criticism reveals will, of course, be my responsibility.

The reader will perhaps be aware of the fuss which surrounded the veto of my appointment to the Sociology Department at Birmingham University in summer 1970, and of the subsequent conflict and protest. The whole matter is related to my sociology and to my activities at the L.S.E., Birmingham (1968–9) and Manchester (1969–70).

This book is dedicated to those members of staff at Birmingham who, by inviting and financing me to come to Birmingham and fill the post which was vetoed, are seeking a challenging alternative to reason alone and fatalism. These people are prepared to suffer – and some have already done so – the consequences of their opposition to authority and commitment to an alternative style of education.

I also wish to dedicate the book to the students of the Sociology of Education course and the first year students whom I am currently teaching at Birmingham. They have already learned more from the actions of the authorities than I can hope to teach them. I trust this book will be of use to them in their continuing struggle for freedom.

All the powers that be are inimical to the highest ideals of sociology.
Alvin W. Gouldner

June 1971   DICK ATKINSON

Contents

5. The Convergence of Concepts and Models   105

PART II   THE CONCEPT 'ROLE', THE ACTOR, AND AN ALTERNATIVE

6. Problems and Possibilities   147

7. An Alternative   171

Orthodox Consensus and Radical Alternative

1: Introduction

It is not easy to raise serious objections to the theoretical explanations which modern sociologists suggest for contemporary events. In particular the non-sociologist finds it difficult to articulate his suspicions. He is unschooled in the jargon, concepts and abstract models behind which he feels it is possible for the sociologist to retreat.

The non-sociologist may be forgiven for believing that the sociologist's intellectual reaction to his queries is so obviously defensive as to give further grounds for suspicion, that the arrogant posture of the expert in fact masks a lack of confidence. The sociologist is indeed insecure. He is so for two sets of reasons, one historical, one immediate.

Historically, sociology was not just involved in a struggle for survival once alive. It encountered difficulty – in the academic-political rather than the academic-intellectual sense – at birth. To gain the respectable, established status of an academic discipline (requiring special departments on the campuses of the Western World) it had to compete with the academic weight of long-accepted fields of study. Just as Darwinian biology had to justify its existence against religious dogmatism and the conservatism of academic natural historians, so also the first sociologists encountered the conservative and powerful political opposition of academic philosophers, linguists, historians and lawyers. The battle was painful but it was won. There are few campuses today which do not have sociology departments though most were established very recently (within the last twenty years) and a bitter, defensive memory lingers.

Sociologists have not had much time to relax in their new-found established status. It is true that they are now consulted by the state and industry, and are popularised by the media. But these academic, political, social and financial rewards are part of the trouble and are offset by a new and genuine intellectual doubt.

One source of this doubt is within the ranks of the modern sociologists themselves. The work of Habermas (of the European Frankfurt school) or Cicourel or Garfinkel (in America) provides an illustration of this fact. Yet in criticising established sociology in this book we shall not even have need to refer to these sociologists again. There are others who are equally capable of shaking accepted sociological assumptions. This fact is testified to in the very title of Alvin Gouldner's recent publication, *The Coming Crisis of Western Sociology*.[1]

Another source of doubt is in the rapidly growing ranks of the students. They have been attracted by sociology's popularised image to study under

1

its advocates and teachers in the universities and colleges. Many of these students hope that sociology can help them to understand the turmoil of contemporary social life, and offer human solutions to social problems. They discover that it has difficulty in doing either. They articulate their distress and force their teachers to justify the existence which they fought so hard to win.

In many respects, these complaints are voiced as harshly against the orthodox left, the Marxists, as against the orthodox conservatism of, say, Talcott Parsons. This fact is testified to by Daniel Cohn Bendit's *Obsolete Communism – The Left Wing Alternative*,[2] by a growing interest in the Frankfurt School of thought to which we have already referred and in the related and well publicised work of Herbert Marcuse.

Still more doubt stems from the non-sociologist, the 'man in the street' who does not recognise himself in the sociologists' explanations. He feels, often quite rightly, that he could tell the expert 'a thing or two' about the way people really live and die.

In one sense, this book is only concerned with the first of these dou..ts – the intellectual doubt which is internal to the discipline. In another sense it attempts to articulate the suspicion of the man in the street. Far from expressing an anti-intellectualism, this involves giving intellectual voice to the complaint that in attaining respectability sociology has come increasingly to ignore its critical task and its initial subject matter – the understanding of ordinary, living, people.

These two doubts are related to each other. They are also related to the third – that of this generation's students. Indeed it may be the students rather than the teachers who finally precipitate the crisis which faces sociology into open conflict through the practical rejection of established sociology and the demand for and implementation of alternative approaches. That remains to be seen and encouraged.

The immediate tasks are to understand the intellectual nature of the crisis – why are sociological theories and concepts not capable of explaining contemporary social life? – and to indicate the nature ci an alternative. Alvin Gouldner has gone some way to account for the historical, social and academic context of the crisis of sterility in modern sociological theory. The task of demonstrating the nature and content of that sterility remains. Certainly, the task of outlining alt. natives has not been accomplished. How are these tasks to be achieved?

It is true that 'the extrication of the liberative potential of sociology today cannot be effected by sweeping generalisations that ignore detail; it must proceed by confronting the theories, point by point, and the theorists, man by man. This process, of working through the details of these theories and our own reactions to them, is necessary if we are to transcend them, liberate ourselves from their penetrating conservative influence, and incorporate their viable dimensions in new standpoints'.[3]

This book first looks at three major sociological thinkers, Parsons, Marx and Weber, who may all be thought of as founding fathers of sociology. The purpose is to review critically their contribution to sociological thought, and with special reference to themes which have become established in modern sociology. In turn, the works of modern sociologists are critically reviewed before the second task of this book is undertaken – the construction of one possible alternative kind of sociology.

Of the three major figures chosen for study Talcott Parsons may be regarded as linking the founding fathers and contemporary sociology. In 1937 he produced his first, and perhaps most important, work in the second quarter of the twentieth century, only 17 years after Max Weber's early death. In *The Structure of Social Action* he produced a synthesis of sociological thought by examining the works of four great and creative men. He brought together what he felt to be the common and important strands in their work. Their work, and his interpretation of it, has had a profound effect on the development of modern sociology.

The omission of Marx from the list of founding fathers whom Parsons found most significant has often been the subject of comment. Many still feel that Marx's and Parsons' work are at opposed ends of the sociological spectrum, and cannot be reconciled. Therein lies the reason for the omission of Marx from Parsons' work of synthesis. Nothing could be further from the truth. It is true that the development of sociology has been such that two unevenly balanced camps have stood opposed, beneath the respective banners of cohesion (Parsons) and conflict (Marx) theory. But the structure and content of the concepts current in each camp, their use, even their views of man, contain striking and lasting similarities. Our first task is to examine the similarities and distinctions in Parsons, Marx and Weber, and in contemporary extenders of their work. By suggesting convergence and distinction in this critical interpretation of a selected few, it is hoped that problems will be raised which are of greater significance than the convergence itself.

In one of the most exciting and frustrating books on sociology of this decade, Robert Nisbet has gone some way to showing the origins of this modern convergence by pointing to the work of the 'founding fathers' in which he finds a common reaction to rationalism, on the one hand, and to the revolutionary convolutions of nineteenth-century industrial societies on the other.[4] The modern sociologists' view of order, the formative and patterned structures in society which gave rise to common patterns in men's actions, emerged against this common back-cloth in the works of Marx, Weber, Durkheim and Freud. It was in response to the distinctive problems of the nineteenth century that these men gained their creative insights. Partly through Parsons' critical interpretation of their work modern sociology has inherited a way of seeing the world of men and human relationships which relates not just to these thinkers but also to the climate of thought and action that stimulated them. But what was new to them, what in their day was so original that it had to fight to be born, in modern times has become the accepted, the orthodox, the mundane.

Concepts like role, norm, value, social structure, institution, authority, interaction, systems of order or conflict come so readily to the practising and teaching sociologist that he no longer gives them a second or sceptical thought. With the spread and general acceptance of sociology, with its teaching in so many colleges and universities, a whole generation of sociologists has been taught in such a way that these concepts are uncritically accepted and taught as the very foundation of the subject. While their main relevance is to the century in which they had their origin, such concepts now form the judgements and pattern the sociologist's view of contemporary reality. Yet our world has changed and is changing with astonishing rapidity, a fact which is so painfully recognised by the most recent generation of students.

Marx, Weber, Parsons, Durkheim and Freud attempted to make sense of apparent chaos, to make patterns out of the apparent variety of history, to demonstrate the hidden and distorted subtlety behind pure rationality. In doing so, these founding fathers developed a view that men were held and sustained within the confines of their social environment. The very pattern of men's lives, their most private and apparently arbitrary acts and thoughts had their causal explanation in the structure of society, though the shapes and political implications of the finished models of that structure which each of the founding fathers developed were different.

This view of man, once so original, even heretical and revolutionary, has now become commonplace. But there was another strand in the thought of the founding fathers. Marx, in his way, Weber in another and Freud in yet another, all felt that the determinisms to which they pointed could, if grasped, be used as means by which men could liberate themselves from social constraint. Theirs was a sociology of choice as well as constraint and order. But this theme has been increasingly ignored by contemporary sociologists and we are left, not with the initial originality of sociology, but only with its formal determinism, with an over-socialized view of man. In turn, this view gives intellectual substance to established social orders, governments and parties.

This is the crisis which confronts modern sociological theory. It has not only not escaped from the founding fathers, it has also stripped them of that dissenting, creative imagination which gained the admiration and respect of their students. Though sociology today is intellectually dated and dull, it is established. As such, it would be difficult to rejuvenate in practice even if a satisfactory alternative could be offered. We have already suggested that the dissatisfied students may be the practical agents of the academic-political aspect of that rejuvenation. However, the major task of this book (Parts II and III) is confined to a criticism of the content of the established and an outline of an alternative content which, necessarily, is radical.

The first part of this work (Part I) examines aspects of the work of

Talcott Parsons, Karl Marx and Max Weber. Two separate, unequal, but distinct strands of theoretical insight are found in the work of these major writers. In order to illustrate these twin themes it proved necessary to treat the authors both separately and in slightly different ways.

Parsons' thought is treated developmentally, for while both themes were present in his earlier work, one became dominant in his later work. However, for Marx and Weber it is possible to look at their mature work, where the two themes exist in uneasy relation one with the other; the dominant theme being the same as that which assumes major proportions in Parsons' mature work.

Parsons extended and combined the work of Marshall, Pareto, Durkheim and Weber. Herbert Marcuse extended the work of Marx. John Rex and Ralf Dahrendorf attempted to link aspects of Marx's thought with that of Max Weber. Consequently, the chapters on Marx will contain considerable reference to Marcuse, and Rex and Dahrendorf will figure prominently at the end of the chapter on Weber. The main point to emerge from this treatment is that Marcuse, Rex and Dahrendorf all ensured that distinctive features in the work of Marx and Weber became submerged. A dominant theme emerges which is indistinguishable from Parsons' own mature work. Together such men as these have forged the modern consensus.

These early chapters set the scene for the final chapter of Part I. This chapter draws the threads of the earlier arguments together, then illustrates and discusses the extent to which the convergence has become the major concern of modern sociology, irrespective of whether its advocates come from within the Parsonian (cohesion) or the Marxist (conflict) school of thought. The convergence, the modern consensus, is the crisis in sociology. It is equally fed by Marxism as by Parsonian thought.

Part II starts by pointing more strongly than was possible in earlier chapters to the alternative theme in the sociological tradition, the one concerned with rationality, voluntarism, choice; the way in which the individual shapes his life, and patterns the form of society. This theme can be located not just in the work of the founding fathers and Weber in particular, but also in the work of modern empiricists, such as Erving Goffman, Ronald Laing and Neal Gross. Their work is examined from this point of view (Chapter 6).

It is this theme which has become submerged in the modern consensus. In attempting to resurrect it in the work of the founding fathers and to illustrate it by reference to contemporary writers, the intention is not to advocate it in its traditional form. Rather, it becomes necessary to use it as a starting point to create a radical alternative. This alternative and the modern consensus are mutually exclusive, raise different problems, demand different solutions, and imply opposing views of the activity and morality of the social scientist.

The final chapter of Part II and the whole of Part III are concerned with constructing this alternative. First this necessitates an examination of the individual person, situational logic, and the elements of situational analysis. The sociological view of the individual, his action, the meaning he gives to that action and its significance for other people is reassessed in the light of this analysis. Inevitably, we are forced to explore choice and the extent to which the individual shapes and controls his social situation.

Secondly, this forces us to reconstruct the sociological view of the relationship between the individual and social structure and, indeed, to question the very concept of 'structure' itself. This stage in the argument represents the sharpest break with the orthodox tradition, and demands its rejection. It has implications for change and the means by which it can be achieved as well as for the explanation of the activity of people and social situations. No claim is made that a complete alternative theoretical framework has been constructed. Merely, a possible starting point has been indicated which, perhaps, suggests the kind of work which must be done before sociology can claim to offer significant explanations of contemporary life, or to satisfy the doubts which surround its immediate existence.

Part I The Founding Fathers of the Modern Consensus

2: Talcott Parsons

Introduction

Parsons has been hailed by his followers as a contemporary emperor of sociology, and his critics have tried to show that he wears no clothes. There is still considerable debate about the validity, even the morality of his contribution, though less so in America than in England and Europe. What is clear is that followers and critics alike have accepted portions of his work. Thus such concepts which he develops as role, institution, social structure, social system, are not the subject of violent disagreement. Indeed, they are used by his critics to attack other concepts, such as equilibrium, integration, and order, which are alleged to form the substance of Parsons' work. It is exactly the former set of concepts and the method of analysis they imply which have become accepted, institutionalized, by modern sociologists and to which we will raise objections.

It is necessary to spend some little time showing how these concepts were developed by Parsons. To do so we shall have artificially to highlight certain stages in the development of his thought. By this means we may be able to see how certain possible alternatives in Parsons' early work slowly became excluded, and why his more mature position took the form it did.

The basic problem facing sociology and the voluntaristic theory of action

Parsons produced several works before 1937, on Durkheim, Weber, Pareto, the role of ultimate values, and other topics. Nothing in these early works contradicts his general theory which emerges from the pages of *The Structure of Social Action* published in that year. Indeed they can be read as preparatory essays for this work.

Two allied themes run throughout both this work and his later publications. Firstly, it is an immense and sustained polemic against positivism in the social sciences. Indeed, the very term 'voluntarism', which he applied to the analytical framework he developed, is 'loaded' against the positivists. Secondly, it represents a search for a solution to the problem of order as represented in the political philosophy of Hobbes. This philosophy itself depends on the idea of a voluntary and rational contract cemented by force.

Radical positivism, Parsons argued, on the one hand, omits all reference to an understandable, normative, system of rules and expectations as understood from the subjective point of view of the social actor. Utilitarianism, on the other hand, regards subjective wants and psychological drives as varying at random, as being, in effect, without order. Goals or

9

ends therefore, are omitted from social analysis. Hobbes, in this respect a utilitarian, solved the problem of resultant chaos by imposing a unified and all-powerful, ordering, state. There was no problem in leaving out any normative institutional structure which might mediate between the individual and that power structure of the state. So, for Hobbes, it was power and force which constrained the actor, not norms or beliefs. Such a solution was quite inadequate for Parsons. At this point he found Durkheim of profound assistance in seeking an alternative approach.

Parsons attempted to resolve both of these problems at once by posing what has become known as his voluntaristic theory of social action. He argues:

> Positively a voluntaristic system involves elements of a normative character. Radical positivism eliminates all such elements completely from empirical relevance. A utilitarian system admits them, but only in the status of random ends which are thus only data for the empirical application of the theoretical system. In the voluntaristic theory they have become integral with the system itself, positively interdependent with the other elements in specifically determinate ways.[1]

So, for Parsons, the solution lies in the possession of common ultimate ends, or an integrated belief system, and, on the intermediate level, in an integrated normative social structure. A voluntaristic system is one which, among other things, combines 'elements of a normative character'. In this sense, a norm is a 'verbal description of the concrete course of action which is regarded as desirable' by the actor, combined with a social 'injunction to make certain future actions conform to this course'.[2]

Action, Parsons argues, cannot be thought of without this 'normative' element. If it is removed the concept slides back into radical positivism.[3] So constraint is *not* exercised by force. On the contrary, its very essence becomes 'the moral obligation to obey a [normative] rule – the adherence to it [being seen] as a duty'.[4] Parsons considers Durkheim's work in this respect to be of the greatest significance, for Durkheim avoids the frequent distinction between force and voluntary acceptance. Parsons feels he does so by arguing that 'While, on the one hand, adherence is voluntary, on the other hand, that adherence is binding on the individual. But it is binding not from physical necessity but from moral obligation.'[5]

It is precisely within this context that Parsons' theory of subjective voluntarism gains its meaning. Voluntarism deals with 'things and events as they appear from the point of view of the actors whose notion is being analysed and considered'.[6] The action of the actor is meaningful to the scientist because the norms by which the action is directed can be understood by the scientist, as by the actor, by virtue of their common humanity. But the norms are not chosen by the actor, nor are they external constraints forcing him to act in these ways. Rather, he is integrated with them, accepting them as a part of his own make-up. Only in this sense is action both subjectively meaningful and voluntary. It should be quite clear that the concept of 'voluntarism' that Parsons uses does not imply what we usually mean by 'freedom of choice' in everyday language, for it has quickly become interchangeable with the concept 'norm', and that 'subjective action' which strives to conform to 'norms'.

There is an element of ambiguity in this argument. For Parsons suggests that a range of choice open to the actor with reference to both ends and means, in combination with the concept of normative orientation of action, implies the possibility of 'error', of the failure to attain ends or to make the 'right' choice of means.[7] This does not clearly suggest whether an actor may or may not make a fresh or original choice within his situation. Parsons' examination of the problem is extensive. The actor, it seems, can voluntarily commit 'error'. But there is little freedom in the everyday sense here, even though its potential is implied. For 'sanctions' come into operation wherever a real element of choice exists. The effect of these sanctions is to induce compliance to the norm when, for whatever reason, the norm is not 'voluntarily constraining'.[8]

It is important to leave this ambiguity for the moment and to state clearly the basic units of analysis of social systems of action as Parsons saw them at this stage in his work. Firstly, there exists the *social goal,* the idea which calls the individual to action and which patterns the choice of means. Action takes place in a situation. *Situations* can be seen as comprising elements over which the actor has no control – these are the *conditions* of action – and elements which he can and does control. *Conditions,* may be either social or external physical phenomena. Control over situational elements implies a subjective, *normative* orientation. Action also implies the *social actor*. These elements combine to make the *unit act*.[9] Many such 'unit acts' make up the system of interaction, which becomes a model of society.

How do these unit acts, these actors, acts, goals and norms link up to form the social system as Parsons sees it? He argues that:

> the conception of an integrated system of rational action . . . [involves] the figure of a web of interwoven strands [of unit acts] . . . Means or end relations [are] identifiable only as connecting a given concrete act with one ultimate end through a single sequence of acts leading up to it. In fact, however, the same concrete immediate end may be thought of as a means to a variety of ultimate ends, so that from this point the threads branch out in a number of different directions.[10]

It becomes possible to picture this 'web of interwoven strands', so we may see what sort of image Parsons had of the social structure of acts and interactions at this stage of his thought (see Figure 1).

It is clear that once one has posed this integrated system of connecting unit acts then movement or change in any one area is going to affect other areas. That is, it will have repercussions throughout the interaction system. No one area will remain unaltered, because it is interconnected with many other areas, which in turn will affect others. It must be noticed that there is a possible bias in this idea, which is not made explicit. If no part of this social system can escape affecting or being affected by another, then in a real sense the individual actors who are, after all, 'behind' the act, become the 'playthings' of the overall mechanisms of adjustment of the 'system'.

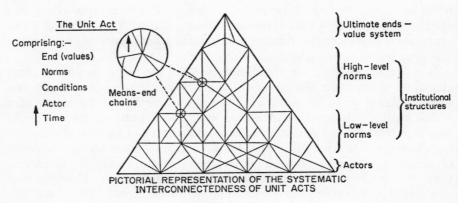

PICTORIAL REPRESENTATION OF THE SYSTEMATIC
INTERCONNECTEDNESS OF UNIT ACTS

Figure 1

This contradicts one aspect of the concept of 'voluntarism' in its admittedly ambiguous formulation.

This objection must not be confused with another complaint, as follows. Parsons refers to unit acts building up into more and more complex phenomena. These complex systems of interaction he calls 'organic'. It has often been charged that this necessarily implies a biological analogy. This is not so. Rather, it refers to the fact that analysis of complexes reduces their meaning or validity. Their significance simply breaks down if their component strands are separated out. In this context Parsons argues that in 'so far as the whole is organic its parts or units are not real entities but abstractions'.[11] Though we might equally ask whether the whole can exist apart from the units, the meaning is clear. Parsons is merely demonstrating the difficulty of isolation in sociology. And he makes the perfectly reasonable point that reification of sections of the whole occurs when units are treated as constant 'real parts through complicated processes of change'.[12]

What has emerged in our discussion so far is the fact that certain ideas of the early Parsons are unclear. In themselves, these ideas may not be very significant. But, if linked together, they could inject a bias into social explanations derived from them. Does the actor have a choice in any real sense? Can he ever avoid reacting to the actions of others, however far removed from him they may be? Can he resist moral obligations or norms? Can he avoid sanctions? In a word, does he exercise any control over the shape of his own life and activities?

At this point it is important to argue against those who, like Finlay Scott, feel that there are dramatic changes in Parsons' work. Thus, it is argued that by 1937 Parsons is already reflecting a swing away from an earlier 'metaphysical' position to one of a 'non-subjective behaviourism'.[13] Scott chooses for his main argument certain passages in an article ('The place of ultimate values in sociological theory') which Parsons wrote several years earlier, and we should do the same.

Parsons argues that 'man stands in significant relations to things other than science . . . The world of science is not itself a closed system but is itself significantly related to other aspects of reality.'[14] From this point of view he goes on to say that '*ultimate empirical* ends are justified to the actor in terms, not of *scientific*, but of *metaphysical* theories'.[15] It is this second quotation upon which Scott has fastened. But the 'metaphysical theories' which guide action refer to the actor, not to the social scientist. In so far as they refer to the task of science it is clear that Parsons means only that assumptions lie behind 'scientific views of the world' which cannot be justified in terms of the science itself. The idea of a mechanical physics, the idea of causality, the idea of determinism, are such assumptions which relate more to 'metaphysical theories' than to any testable hypotheses. Parsons is not in any sense insisting on the idea of an intuitive or non-empirical or metaphysical basis to sociology – themes from which he later switches.

It is clear that even at this stage, Parsons' concern for the analysis of belief systems is crucial. Far from rejecting this point Parsons develops it in increasingly greater detail in all his work. If there is any unfamiliar 'bias' in this earlier work it is, rather, a rational one, which suggests that the actor, though subjectively acting in the world, nevertheless does so as if he were a logical, rational, scientist. He argues that deviation from the rational norm will be explicable in one or more of three sets of terms: 'ignorance' of intrinsic relationships, lack of 'effort' and the 'presence of obstacles beyond the power of the actor to move'.[16] Parsons drops the first of these alternatives by 1937, though, it will be recalled, he is still concerned with the possibility of 'error' of choice in his voluntarism. So the only difference in regard to subjectivity is an earlier bias towards rationality. But this implies a similar determinism to that of 1937, not a greater choice.

For the 'scientific actor' could only ever make one sort of choice, unless constrained, not by clashing ideas, or norms, or originality, but by ignorance or lack of effort. To conclude the argument, it is useful to see that Parsons felt earlier that 'random variations of systems of ends would be incompatible with the most elementary form of social order. In so far as . . . action is determined by ultimate ends the existence of a system of such ends common to the members of a community seems to be the only alternative to a state of chaos'.[17] These ultimate ends are integrated into the institutional sector, and accepted at that level by the actor as norms which he has to pursue rationally. As Parsons sees it, the only alternative to this determining order is chaos, not choice.

It is as well to state at this point that by 1937 Parsons has not developed his analysis of systems of ultimate ends, institutions, or of personality. It is to be our contention that as he gradually does so during the next fifteen years he unintentionally accentuates the existing potential bias in his theory; the external constraint of social systems, and their determination of the action and the very ideas of the actor. In the process of extending his theory, he gradually, and without apparently wishing to do so, cuts off most of the fruitful alternative possibilities. Only one of these is his ability to analyse change. His model of the social system has an *initial* concern with order. But it does not exclude the idea of change. Indeed, we have already seen how he argues that it can spread throughout the 'system', causing action to alter in ways which are determined for the actor.

Parsons feels that the work of Durkheim and Piaget showed that not only 'are already existent systems of ultimate values integrated in a social system, but that the ultimate values of individuals themselves are developed in the processes of social interaction'.[18] For example, he suggests that Durkheim shows that 'most individuals when deprived of a relatively stable system of socially given norms undergo a personal distintegration which destroys the moral quality of their conduct'.[19] And whether we agree with Parsons' interpretation or not, Piaget had suggested that 'not only moral attitudes but even logical thought and morality develop only as an aspect of the process of socialisation of the child.'[20] This helped Parsons to draw the conclusion that the Hobbesian problem of social order is solved when the rules governing social action are both socially *integrated* and *internalized* by the actor. Only then can the individual (and his action) relate cohesively with others. If for some reason social values and norms are not integrated, then this would reflect on the individual, who would revert to pursuing his random, untamed, wants. Indeed, at this stage it would not be reasonable to expect more of Parsons than this. Without additional psychological knowledge (with a different interpretation of Piaget, and the belief that individuals do not suddenly lose their attitudes and values or their personal identity when freed from social constraint), it is difficult to see how else he could have seen society as being organized. To solve the 'problem of order' Parsons shoots right over from the view of chaotic individuality to a subjective but almost totally determinist view of man. 'Voluntarism' has significance only because of man's rational ability to see and choose action to which he must conform in order to survive.

Even so, it is possible to argue that 'the further the immediate ends are removed in the means-end chain from the system of ultimate values sanctioning the system of rules, the more the rules will tend to appear to the individuals subject to them as morally neutral, as mere conditions of action'.[21] A norm which becomes a condition is no longer an aspect of belief, but part of a normative, institutional structure. It may be a norm to one person, but it is a condition to another. Parsons does not recognize a clear distinction between a norm which is believed in and one which is 'morally neutral' from the point of view of the actor. It is exactly at this point that 'norms' can easily be broken. They need not be respected, but can be acted against in relation to alternative values. Conflict is the obvious result if, as is often the case, one section of society regards a norm as morally neutral, while another holds to it with passionate belief. A morally neutral norm implies the possibility of conflict about different values, and not necessarily anomie or chaos. Yet Parsons insists that a slackening of ultimate-end control calls only for the sanction of 'unpleasant, external consequences', or force, so as to give 'a motive of obedience in the place of the internal moral sense of duty'.[22] And, if we take this only a little further, we again have the pure Hobbesian state employing force in order to gain cohesion and order. This is most certainly not the only possible case and a 'slackening of ultimate control' can imply value conflict and, therefore, individual or group conflict. This would imply adherence to or acceptance by the actor of alternative, new, and clashing values. It is at this point that Parsons is attacked for, amongst other things, omitting an analysis of power *within* and *between* institutions.

If we examine Parsons' few comments on Marx we find he was at least partially aware of this point.[23] He feels that Marx can be said to have reintroduced the Hobbesian problem of order. But he solved it not by opposing order to chaos, but by placing conflict between interest groups, not between individuals. Conflict is a consequence of the specific type of social organization which is postulated, the exploitation of one class by another. This suggests the possibility of a theory of the evolution of capitalism in terms of its internal conflict. But Parsons does not seem to recognize the full significance of this alternative.[24] He might have, but did not, develop the idea that two or more internally ordered groupings within the same society would solve the problem of order or integration just as efficiently as Parsons' own single system. Marx does this and, as we shall see, is able to deal with both order and conflict. When Parsons does turn to conflict, at a later stage, he develops it only in terms of his view of order. At this stage he is only able to conceive chaos, rather than conflict, as an alternative to order.

Parsons' vision is of a society whose people are united by 'ultimate common values'. But there is always an element of personal interest in the individual's action. He is not yet sociologically conceived, let us remember, as totally determined. Personal interests balance the advantage of 'obedience and disobedience' and the consequent sanctions of others. This means that

> once a body of rules is firmly established in authority it can remain intact through a considerable shift in [those personal interests and judgments] for there develops an interlocking of interests in the maintenance of the system. But the ultimate source of power behind sanctions is the common sense of moral attachment to norms – and the weaker that becomes, the larger the majority who do not share it, the more precarious is the order in question. For this interlocking of interests is a brittle thing which comparatively slight [change] can shatter at vital points. A social order resting on the interlocking of interests alone and thus ultimately on sanctions.[25]

Simply, the purely Hobbesian state. The ambiguity between the views is clear; one leads to order, the other to chaos.

It is only because of Parsons' peculiar and ill-devised concept of the development of the individual and psychology, combined with a resultant concern for how order can be possible, that we see individual and random wants bursting through the first of these alternatives. Consequently chaos, rather than conflict about values, is a major theoretical concern. This is not to suggest that Parsons completely ignores such conflict, but his interest in it is overwhelmed by these other and prior concerns.

Parsons fails to see that once he has stated the task of sociology to be the study of the subjectively experiencing individual, it is unneccessary to keep on attempting to justify it in later theory. In defending an emergent voluntaristic sociology against positivism he does not realize that the resultant dilemma tends to the exclusion of alternative theoretical perspectives. In fact, a person can be integrated in himself and, of necessity, accepts certain consistent and cohesive relationships with his fellows. But this fact need imply nothing about how society is generally organized. It is not impossible for individuals and groups to conflict or exercise unconstrained choice without resultant chaos. Nor is it even necessary, as we shall see later, to pose a relatively ordered series of social relations to justify the definition of social action in the first place. But, to restate the Hobbesian problems as Parsons does, having already provided a solution – the integration of the actor with others in ordered relations about common norms and values – is to demand a second solution for a problem already accounted for. It is simply not necessary to attempt to resolve it again by suggesting that the whole system of relations in a society has to be ordered. To do so necessitates retaining the idea of a non-social, Hobbesian, actor with subjective but random wants who is prevented from the anomie of chaos only by force and sanction. Parsons feels that this chaos is not possible, so we now have the actor's action doubly determined by the whole network of obligations and sanctions in systems of interaction. This antithesis is both unnecessary and theoretically limiting.

Parsons sees the structure of the social system as external to and determining the actor, in the sense of patterning his 'choices'. The actor's 'choice' is to pursue rationally and normatively his own interests, themselves patterned by the 'social system'. This implies that the 'system', and its tendencies to reinforce itself, will be maintained. This further excludes the possibility of choice, or voluntarism in any ordinary sense. But such analysis still retains the conception of action being subjectively meaningful to actor and scientist alike.

As Parsons is to subsume the economic within the social and belief system, then any occupational or market conflict is going to be localized and contained within wider and more ordered systems of values, both within and between institutions. This, of course, distinguishes Marx from Parsons, but on a subsidiary point. He writes that the Marxian 'system itself is the resultant of the myriad of individual acts. But it also creates for each acting individual a specific situation which compels him to act in certain ways if he is not to go contrary to his interests.' Therefore, the employer was 'placed in a situation where he must act as he did or be eliminated in the competitive struggle . . . The system itself [is to be] thought of as self acting.' Once the individuals involved in it are placed in the situations that are given, their actions are 'determined' (by the normative structure and the rationale of the situation) 'so as to maintain the system as a whole or rather to drive it forward on its evolutionary course'.[26] This is emphatically not materialistic determinism, but poses the idea of a constraining normative structure where the external patterning of choice arises 'out of the innumerable' subjective, but 'rational, acts presupposed by a given situation'. It is crucial to see that there is nothing here with which Parsons wishes to quarrel. But it immediately raises the problem of external and objective social constraint as against conscious interests, of genuine choice against a voluntarism that is socially determined.

The addition of Freud

When he wrote the preface to the second edition of *The Structure of Social Action* in 1949, it might have been supposed that Parsons would fill in some of the gaps hinted at, perhaps by turning to a Marxist model of social interaction. In fact he felt his omission to be psychology. This omission had given a 'major one-sidedness to the book'.[27] Freud had become the fifth 'man of genius' to converge towards a voluntaristic theory of action along with Pareto, Weber, Durkheim and Marshall.

There are two of Parsons' works which are of particular importance in this connection. In March 1947 he wrote an introduction to Weber's *General Theory of Social and Economic Organization*[28] and, secondly, he wrote *The Superego and the Theory of Social Systems*[29] in 1951.

In his introduction to Weber's work he writes that it is 'necessary to clarify the nature of the unit of reference, the "actor",' which

> is the unit of systems of action, and the frame of reference and other categories, in terms of which this unit is treated, are inherently part of the same theoretical system as categories on the level of types of action or social structure. Hence in some sense a 'psychology' is an essential *part of* . . . a theory of social action.[30]

Parsons had previously used a peculiar view of human nature. There are two sides to this view. Firstly, there are these innate interests which, if left to his own devices, the actor will pursue quite irrespective of other people. Chaos is the result. But in order to solve his problem of order Parsons poses against this actor a cohesive set of values and norms, which the actor internalizes. This implies a second view of human nature, which postulates that it is virtually infinitely manipulable by external social pressures. It has to be. How else can the personal interests be entirely subdued or even altered, by the internalization of the 'common values' which make the actor co-operate with others, so pursuing quite different interests? As soon as cracks appear in the ordered system, the personal wants re-emerge – giving an element of choice, which in turn is limited by sanction and force.

While clarifying this view of human nature and its relation to the social system, Parsons was at the same time developing his view of the functional relations of the social system itself. He writes in the same introduction to Weber that 'starting from the frame of reference of subjectively interpreted individual action . . . it [is] possible by functional analysis to develop a generalized outline of social systems of action . . .' Such an outline is 'implicit in the structure of [a] system of ideal types',[31] with which he feels Weber was working. The structural elements which were implied by ideal types are placed in 'their context of a generalized system of social structure'.[32]

The personality system, based on Freud, and its relation to the social system is developed hand in hand with this concern for functional analysis. Indeed, Parsons feels that any systematic ordering of ideal types is not possible 'without the functional point of view'. It 'provides the integrating principles' which mould these categories into a general system.

For Parsons' analysis of the actor to proceed smoothly he must be very clear about what is meant by 'the individual's wishes' in order to relate them more exactly to the levels of structure and culture. In this sense he sees Weber's ideal type actors as types of *motivation* containing both *elements of personality* and *social structure*. So, 'Weber was . . . right that the adequate concrete motive always involves the situational elements which are specifically non-psychological. By doing what Weber failed to do, [by] taking a concrete, in a sense institutional starting point, and then using the resources of modern *psychology* to complete analysis on its *psychological* side, it is undoubtedly possible to develop a far more adequate analysis of concrete motivation than either psychology or sociology have done so far.'[33] Though it does not necessarily follow from this argument, Parsons nevertheless feels that in order to develop this theory of motivation it will be important to get over the problem of the 'tendency to confine . . . the *applicability of subjective* categories to *consciously intended motives*'.[34] The subjective motives and interests are no longer to be seen from the point of view of the actor, but from that of the objective observer, the scientist, who is attempting to relate the personality of the actor to his structural situation. Consequently, wants and motivations can be attributed to the actor about which he knows nothing and which he might well deny.

Parsons takes over and accepts in modified form the least testable aspect of Freud's theory of psychoanalysis: the 'unconscious', and welds it to his own or, rather, Weber's methodological individualism. At the same time, this individualism has become generalized into 'social systems' of action, not separate ideal types as Weber used them.

Parsons was convinced that he could see a 'massive convergence of the fundamental insights of Freud and Durkheim . . . from two quite distinct and independent starting points, [which] deserves to be ranked with the truly fundamental landmarks of modern science'. In making this link Parsons clearly raises the objective-subjective dilemma. By welding the work of others, his task became the 'integration of the psychoanalytic theory of the personality and of the sociological theory of the social system'.[35]

Parsons was convinced that Freud's analysis had been basically correct and yet too narrow. For, 'not only moral but *all* components of the common culture are internalized', mainly by means of identification, 'as part of the personality system'.[36] To summarize too simply, Freud had seen the superego as not just an internalization of the moral standards of close relatives by a process of identification with the culture of a society which they personified. He had also felt it developed as a personal response to and against the culture.

Parsons ignores this feature of Freud's work. He had to, if he was not to contradict his original assumptions. He argues that 'the possibility' exists 'for extending the same fundamental analysis from the internalization of moral standards to the internalization of the cognitive frame of reference for interpersonal relations and for the common system of expressive symbolism'. Relating only the super-ego to culture prevented Freud 'from seeing the extent to which the three elements of the common culture', the personality, the social structure, and the cultural system, 'are integrated with each other'.[37] Parsons is in a sense correct in this critical comment. He argues that Freud did not always or fully recognize the extent to which the person is fundamentally social and must, therefore, be understood in social, inter-personal terms. Yet we may wonder what is lost in altering Freud's idea of introjection by response to that of straight internalization by identification.

As long as Parsons had no social psychology he could not develop a model of conflict and had to see society as structurally integrated. When he did develop one it was not to reopen the problem of order but, rather, to fasten it in its existing position by underpinning it with internalized social values and structural norms. This aspect of Parsons' thought is taken much further in his later work, particularly in his work on the family and social-ization process. There, he sees socialization as the process whereby the unified and collective ultimate ends of his earlier works, now functionally integrated in the 'structural system', are 'internalized'.

This process of internalization during which the child and adult learns and acquires the motives by which he will be driven to act in accord with the structural expectancies of him was, Parsons thought, inadequately worked out by Freud. In developing his own theory of socialization, which he felt Freud lacked, he was providing both a 'systematic analysis of the structure of social relationships' and relating it to a process of learning and socialization by identification.[38] In doing so the distance that Freud main-tained between the individual and those with whom he related became lost. So did any sense of personal, as opposed to social, growth and development of a unique kind.

Social structure as social system
The step which led Parsons to limit the key analytical significance previously given to the conscious actor, directly relates the psychological to the structural and the ultimate-end systems. The step took place concurrently with the development of his functional analysis. Previously Parsons had adhered to a particular type of methodological individualism (hereafter referred to as M.I.). Methodological collectivists (M.C.) see the system or collectivity as having a life, a control, or dynamism of its own in the sense that the individual is powerless against it. The actor's subjective wants are not of key concern. It matters little whether the driving 'system' is seen as social or economic, cultural superstructure or productive base.

Against this position, the usual M.I. argument suggests that the individual is the focal point of analysis. His subjective wants and his goals must apply the dynamic, or the interaction system sustained by it, to action. That is, structure 'just is', whereas the individual injects action into it and determines its shape. However, such a method has often treated the 'social structure' as abstract and hypothetical and the indivi-dual as concrete and indivisible. That is, analysis has been conducted on two different planes. To take the subjective individual on to the same level of abstraction as the structure means taking the actor on to an abstract and hypothetical plane also. That is, the actor must fit no particular concrete person in all his empirical, concrete, detail. Any such hypothetical actor represents a type of action, a type of felt goal. He articulates with a set of external, hypothetical relations on the one hand, and aspects of concrete people on the other. At this level of analysis the structure of the relations of others can in large part be said to 'determine', or at least limit, the alternative choices before the actor. Secondly, whilst the actor is driven by subjective feelings and is analysed as such, these subjective categories are typed in relation to the acts of many concrete actors and fit none of them in particular. They are classifications of types which articulate through the actor with the social structure. As such, it is easy to make the mistake of either regarding this kind of analysis as system-determining (i.e. M.C.), or as non-subjective. But it does not commit either of these errors in its pure form.

Parsons' methodological position, whilst never clearly stated, seemed to be M.I. at the earliest stage of his work, though we saw how he became increasingly ambivalent over the area and degree of choice which he could allow the actor exactly because of the way this choice led to chaos, not conflict. There are new dangers in the position. For, with a little pressure, it could shoot over into the M.C. method. Already we have found that Parsons' analysis of Freud underpins his 'cohesive' bias. Such an integrated theoretical structure, which he developed to deal with order, holds the danger of being further concretized into a position to which its originator would not openly wish to subscribe. This is exactly what Parsons ensures in developing his 'structural system' in terms of 'functional analysis'.

Parsons said of Weber that evidently he 'understood a functional approach to mean . . . either an individualistic form of biological orientation which precluded the use of subjective categories, or the illegitimate reification of collectivities as organisms or as cultural totalities. He did not perceive that starting from the frame of reference of subjectively interpreted individual actions . . . it was possible by functional analysis to develop a generalized outline of social systems of action'.[39] Parsons makes this step at the same time as developing his relation between the personality, structural and cultural systems.

Parsons states that 'the structure of a system is related to its functional needs in such a way that some differentiated parts are particularly important and effective in contributing to one or a related group of functional needs'.[40] We can now see that on the simplest level Parsons is insisting that in order to have a specific type of society, then of necessity we must have certain preconditions for its existence. This is not a generalization, but a statement of a necessary relation. There are obvious and related potential errors in this analysis. Having worked at the system of necessary relations for the existence of a particular form of an actual society, it is tempting to conclude that they will continue to exist. From this point it is easy to search for factors which will ensure its existence:

mechanisms of socialization, of control etc; though the alternative to such a 'system' is not chaos but some other system.

Equally, it is possible to argue that necessary relations do not just cover *some* of the structural features of a particular society, but *all* of them. So, it is possible to argue that if any one feature of a system of necessary relations disappears, or changes, then another must arise, which fulfils the same function as the previous feature. In other words, the 'social system' has specific needs which it must continue to fulfil, and which impinge on every aspect of life in an actual society.

Such errors, sometimes referred to as vulgar functionalism, are not the logical implication of functional analysis. To criticize them is, therefore, not to dismiss, but to miss the point of such analysis. Indeed the early Parsons avoided such errors. Increasingly, however, he came to commit them. One example of the former is in his discussion of system-maintenance and control mechanisms. One of the latter can be found in his and Devereaux's work on gambling in western societies.

It is important to insist again that these mistakes are not built into the logic of 'functional analysis' as Parsons uses it, but that he comes to disregard the more substantial elements in his own methodological base. First, he has a concern for order against chaos and a belief that a common system of ends will involve any alteration to the system being 'felt' throughout the system. This results in Parsons' tendency to argue that the system maintains itself.

Secondly, as the subjective can be used on the level of the unconscious, motives can be expressed in terms of abstract actors, which are not necessarily empirically related to the level of concrete subjective reality. Consequently, we can find actors engaging in action when they are not aware of their 'true' motives.

Thirdly, this gives rise to an objective-subjective dilemma. The actor has an objective place in the social structure, which his personality system encourages him to fulfil, because of the relation of the system to the structure and culture systems. From the point of view of the observer this position is objectively discernible, and can be derived from the model of structure which he has built. But the overtly expressed subjective feelings and beliefs of actual people may depart from this expected reaction. Here lies the objective-subjective problem. That is, real people do not fit the ideal and integrated conceptual model of this action. This is explained by causal factors of which they are unaware. Indeed, it is expected that they will be brought into line by control mechanism and sanctions, of both psychological and structural kinds, which they cannot resist. The alternative is still chaos. Problems for explanation are posed by these people whose action refuses to correspond to such conceptual devices. These are usually related to choice and change. But such action is hardly seen as problematic, and is difficult to conceptualize and explain because systems of interactions have independent constraining powers over individual action.

Such action is to be explained in terms of the system, not by searching for the meaning the actor gives to his action.

The significance of the 'value system' and conflict

The crucial concept which Parsons develops at this stage of the development of his theory is that of role. Before turning to it, however, we must note the final major addition to Parsons' work. The idea itself originated in the late thirties, but it only gained ordered expression in the late forties. It is the 'pattern variable' scheme of social ends or values. Parsons argues that there are a limited number of possible logical combinations of potential ultimate values. A system which adheres to one will find its institutional structure reflecting these values at a lower, normative, level, and the socialization process will result in the actors' internalization of these formal or common values.

In such works as *The Social System*, and *The Family, Socialization and Interaction Process*, these ideas are developed extensively. By this means the ends of the actor of which Parsons spoke at the beginning of his work have become fixed at a quite separate level (that of culture) from that of either the actor or even the normative structure. But they are respectively related to these systems by institutionalization and internalization. At the same time, the actor's ends have become, as it were, summarized. So, for example, America and England are thought to be classified by the pattern variable of 'universalistic achievement'. In terms of this, all action is explained as either integrated, or 'malintegrated' (deviant). We must note that Parsons has finally located and fixed the main position of the values, or subjective element, which we have hitherto tried to analyse as ambiguous, at the level of culture and the personality system, not at the level of the conscious actor. These pattern variables of culture are institutionalized at the lower level of social structure and are then seen as institutionalized in the 'structure system' and internalized in the socialization process into the evaluative aspect of the action of the 'ego'. Ego's motives and need-dispositions relate the actor towards other actors and the social structure as a functional system. In general they provide 'ego' with subjective expectations and motives, which are discernible to the scientist, but not necessarily to the actor. It is the concept 'motive' which is furnished with most of the subjective and yet non-conscious aspects of the actor. The point of view of the individual concrete actor and that of the hypothetical actor, so important at the early stage of Parsons' work, are not now important to a 'functional' analysis of social systems. Thus Parsons is able to state in the concluding section of *The Social System* that the subjective point of view as earlier developed 'is *not essential* to the frame of reference of action in its most elementary form. It is however necessarily involved at the levels of elaboration of systems of action at which *culture*, that is shared symbolic patterns become involved.' [41]

It seems it is only at this point that Parsons finally, and without being aware of it, moves over into the methodological collectivist position which was only ambiguously implied in his first major work. Once the individual as a reference point is removed, once subjectivity is fixed at the levels of culture and personality systems, there remain only the pressures and forces of these systems to move him to action. Their 'dynamic' certainly still comes from within the actor, but it emerges in terms of a 'role' over which he has no conscious choice. Action adjusts to, but does not form or control society. On the contrary, action is controlled by the 'system'.

This is a feature of analysis which gives Parsons many problems, for the level of abstraction at which he works is variable. In speaking of the family he can at one moment relate it to the socialization process and the pattern variables and, at the next, to concrete examples which endanger his whole abstract edifice. It is in this context that his contribution to conflict theory might be thought of.

We must recall that in an earlier stage in the development of his theory Parsons spoke of the possibility of 'norms' fracturing due to structural stress. At this point actors might become attached to clashing values and form into opposed groups. Parsons took this analysis of conflict further in 1948 in a paper given to mark the centenary of the publication of the Communist Manifesto.[42] He separated the Marxist unit of the factory into its component parts of structurally defined hierarchies of status roles. Parsons argues that in such a social network certain clashes would occur. These may be summarized as follows:

1. Interests will diverge as roles diverge.
2. Organization involving division of labour will make for differentiation of leadership and authority.
3. These will combine to give a degree of competitive individualism, and antagonism to authority and sanction-wielding.
4. This will lead to the powerful exploiting the weaker.
5. Thus interests will diverge so much as to 'develop different cultures'.
6. This will 'impede' lines of communication and therefore will accentuate hostilities.
7. There will follow clashes about access to educational opportunity and job mobility.

If we combine these specific empirical points with his analysis of the Fascist movement (written in 1942), his study of McCarthyism in America, and a discussion of the Russian revolution (contained in two formidable chapters of *The Social System*), we can see a continuing concern for aspects of conflict. They stand, however, as fairly separate and relatively empirical works, and are not integrated into any overall theoretical scheme. They are not used as checks to his existing one. The single polar alternatives of order and chaos, of social and non-social (anomic) action could, even at this stage, have been enlarged to take in the alternative of conflicting social groups. Yet, immediately after referring to 'different cultures' in 1948 Parsons' terminology slips back into the narrow perspective, and he refers to these as 'sub-cultures' within the social whole.

It seems important to emphasize that there is nothing in his theory, as we have so far seen it develop, which precludes the possibility of offering an explanatory model of conflict. It is quite reasonable to imagine two or more opposed groups, each integrated in exactly the way we have discussed, in place of the assumption of a single, unified system.

As it is, Parsons is not concerned with a conflict between classes engendered in the economic sphere. Rather, he is concerned with the stress which is constantly posed by technological development. This resembles Weber's concern with the development of a rational scientific and organizational bureaucracy. It is the 'strains' which are engendered by the 'lack of fit' between this technology and the family and other institutions with which Parsons is concerned. Here, of course, power and authority are important concepts, but we only have need to refer to the way Parsons used them in our final comments. At this point we must turn to one final feature in the development of his thought which is of importance to our argument.

The addition of the concept 'role'

In his second preface to *The Structure of Social Action*, Parsons points to an important development with which he had not previously had the space, or the knowledge, to deal. Anthropology and its attempts to relate 'social action' to the 'structure of culture' was what Parsons had in mind. To see how he uses it, we must recall how Parsons first viewed the actor and the social act. Secondly, we shall examine the source of his concept 'role'. Thirdly, we shall spell out the way in which he develops this new concept and fits it into his developing theoretical work.

The first question requires us to look at Parsons' 1937 work, the second to examine two works of Ralph Linton, the third to discover how role theory is designed to articulate with structural and functional, or systems analysis.

By 1937 Parsons had developed his concept of the unit act. The unit act, it will be remembered, was made up of social actor, both physical and social conditions for action, the norms by which action is guided, and the goal towards which the actor is striving and which initially had meaning for the actor within the terms of his wider beliefs. Parsons insisted towards the end of the book that the social system is made up of a myriad of such unit acts, all interlocking with one another into an organic interdependent whole, each section not only being related to each other, but also affecting and being affected by the others.

The conception of the unit act implied the existence of a concrete actor. Such an actor, a model of a real individual, assessed and co-ordinated events, and ranged morals according to the priorities of the belief system as he saw them. Analysis was always conducted so as to build models of the meaning attached to situations from the conscious point of view of the individual. In this sense the actor was used as a unit in social analysis as well as in the atomized sense in the unit act. The actor, his beliefs, and his particular acts were of crucial importance. However, in so far as conditions and normative means were given, the actor's own values were thought to be a reflection of the common culture. The actor was seen as necessarily trapped in a controlling structure. To put it another way – through the actor, life and meaning were given to the social structure. Yet the actor was nevertheless constrained to act within strict limits set by the expectations and actions of others; that is of social structure. The implication was that a harmony existed between the actor and the social structure. How exactly was this harmony achieved? And, what kind of concept could now properly contain it?

The concept 'role' was not used by Parsons at this stage of his work. It does not even appear in the index of *The Structure of Social Action*, and is used as a term in the text only in relation to the way Durkheim and Weber regarded broad fields of action of specific occupations, never as a tight, clearly defined, analytical concept.

There is a sudden and dramatic switch in the way Parsons uses his analysis of the unit act in his later work. The significance of this change might be missed if we were watching the development of his work as a whole, for there is no intentional break or change in what Parsons himself is trying to do. The significance of the change in his analysis of the unit act must therefore be highlighted artificially in a way that Parsons at the time would have felt unnecessary. The point we have to make is related to the diminishing significance that Parsons placed on the actor, and the heightened place he gave to the unconscious personality system on the one hand, and the functional social system on the other.

In 1936 Ralph Linton published a remarkable little work in the field of anthropology called *The Study of Man*.[43] Parsons read the book and by the early 1940s had incorporated certain ideas from it in a series of essays which culminated in his publication of *The Social System*. It is important to examine those ideas of Linton which are concerned with the concepts status and role, and which Parsons adopts in only slightly altered form in *The Social System*.

Linton's main concern, as he himself readily admits, was to describe cultures by defining the 'group norms of action' and not to refer in this process to 'either deviations or individuals'. Status is a concept which he refers to as 'distinct from the individual who may occupy it . . . [It] is simply a collection of rights and duties'.[44] 'Role' is a concept which he defines as 'the dynamic aspect of status' and is the result of the actor putting 'the rights and duties which constitute the status into effect'.[45]

These two concepts respectively define the structural position and the abstract action of the actor. Their definition is tailored to fit Linton's main concern: that of explaining culture and relating it to group norms. That is, Linton is more concerned to understand the normative relationship within and between groups of fairly similar actual individuals and the values and norms of society, than to question the relationships and differences between actual individuals. Empirical variety is not his concern. In order to facilitate his investigations he uses the concepts 'role' and 'status' in the way delineated above. Whilst he was by no means the first person to use the concepts, he was the first recognized sociologist to use them precisely and with this particular methodological aim. We must examine more closely what he understood by them.

Linton's assumption of a complementarity between group norms and the culture implied that there must be a similar mesh between the action of the actor and his position, which is itself defined by the culture and the expectation of other actors. This is why it follows quite logically for him that role, the action of the actor, is only the 'dynamic aspect of status', and not something clearly distinguishable from it. 'Role and status are quite inseparable' and any analytical distinction is 'only of academic interest'. It follows that empirical, individual 'deviations are not significantly analytical features'.[46] Variety and subjective intention is ignored – in the interests of the explanation of a hypothetical integration between the actors and the culture.

Nine years later, in 1945, Linton published a second important book dealing with these same problems. It was, significantly enough, called *The Cultural Background of Personality*.[47] In it he again defines role as 'the sum total of culture patterns associated with a particular status'. The role, he argues, is made up of '. . . attitudes, values, and behaviour ascribed by the society to any or all persons occupying this status'. As in 1936, and 'in so far as [role] represents overt behaviour, [it] is the dynamic aspect of status, what the individual has to do in order to validate his occupation of that status'.[48]

The arguments that emerge from these two books have been selected to show that there is no significant difference in content between them. In *Explorations in Role Analysis*, Neal Gross takes a different view.[49] However, it seems that there are two strands running through them both. The one insists that the concept of 'role' articulates exactly with the structural demands of status. The other, and far less emphasized, idea, indicates that the role represents not just the dynamic aspect of status but also the full range of action of the actor. Those writers who, like Linton, almost overlook the second aspect and concentrate on the first aspect, limit the kind of way we may look at action, curtailing its empirical variety.

Gross' argument, based on his interpretation of the difference between Linton's two books, was that later sociologists have concentrated on the first interpretation of 'role' rather than the second as a result of their having read and been influenced by the first book alone. But it seems more likely that these sociologists' own theoretical preconceptions led them to select the one rather than the other concept as the more profitable for the development of their view of sociology. Before we look at the ways in which

Parsons and others have taken up the first definition, it is important to be a little more precise about what we mean by 'status'.

Unlike the everyday word, the sociological concept 'status' refers to the position or location of the actor in the social structure as it is ascribed to him by other actors and, through them, by the functional social system. It is meant in a very precise way and does not involve vague notions about, say, privilege or social eminence. A beggar and a criminal have 'status'. That is, those expectations which society or 'others' have of them constitute their status position. We must ask, however, whether Linton's definition is adequate. Let us take, for example, the 'status' of 'delinquent adolescent'. Far from there being one societal expectation of him, there must be a variety of different ones; those of the magistrate, the police, the parents, the teacher, the boy's friends, those boys belonging to different sections of society, and so on. It is common empirical sense to see that the expectations of these groups mentioned will not only differ but clash radically. This is a problem that Linton briefly refers to in terms of role conflict – where an actor feels he has to play two clashing roles at the same time. However, an alternative interpretation includes this possibility but also allows for institutional conflict. Thus the actor can identify with some of the status expectations, but only perform the others if forced to do so by sanctions. In this latter sense no role conflict is presented to the actor.

The concept of status is more complex and problematic than Linton supposed. Yet we will find that Linton's basic idea was taken over by Parsons, despite (or because of) the fact that, in effect, he had already built a theory of 'status' into his complex institutional analysis. The concept of 'status' is taken over, but extended into a general analysis of structure.

The concept 'role', however, is usually left very much in the form in which Linton first defined it. But the implication of an empirical variety of clashing expectations held out to the same actor is that some expectations will not be fulfilled by him. Thus, while the actor does perform in relation to others he does not reciprocate the action which all groups would prefer from him. There would seem to be no logical necessity that there should be a complementarity between role and status. But these problems are of 'academic interest only'. What have others had to say?

In his book *Social Psychology*, Sprott argues that 'there is appropriate behaviour for children . . . adult men . . . adult women' and other actors who occupy social positions. 'These positions are statuses, and the appropriate conduct to each is the role'.[50] This suggests that Sprott is in almost complete agreement with Linton. The choice of the term 'appropriate', however, seems particularly unwise as it implies a moral agreement with action which conforms to expectancies. Equally, Gerth and Mills have insisted that the role 'is a conduct pattern of a person which is typically expected by other persons'.[51] There is no suggestion of a moral bias here. Yet we would expect Mills to object to conformist action.

Nevertheless he does accept, largely unquestioningly, Linton's formulation.

K. Davis is an example of those few who have taken up the other side of Linton's concept. In *Human Society*, he maintained that the way an actor 'actually *performs* in a given position' is 'distinct from how he is *supposed* to act' in his 'role'. But how he performs is an empirical phenomenon, and cannot be prejudged by relating performance to an abstract system of complementarity between 'role' and 'status'. Indeed, 'role' is 'the manner in which a person carries out the requirements' of his status. 'It is the dynamic aspect of status . . ., and as such is always influenced by factors *other than* the stipulations of the "status" position.'[52] It should be clear that this formulation is capable of accounting for the empirical objections raised against the method of dealing with the concept of role and its direct fit with the expectations of status. The actual action is considered or, rather, a model of that action, instead of the action logically expected and derived from the scientist's abstract view of the status position and the structural system into which it logically fits. The alternative view expects that role and status may often fail to coincide and that conflict and change may follow. These are, of course, two social phenomena which the ortho-dox method would have great difficulty in explaining. In practice they are often ignored and Davis does not develop that concept which relates to the second theme in Linton's work. Nor does he attempt actual analysis by means of it. Nor has any other theoretical sociologist, as we shall see in a later section.

In returning to Parsons, we find that when he first begins to use 'role' as an analytical concept he accepts only that aspect of Linton's work which was also taken up by Sprott, Mills and others. It is quite clear how it fits exactly into those developments in his work which we have previously specified. In 1945, he maintained that 'from the point of view of the actor, his role is defined by the normative expectations of the members of the group as formulated in its social traditions' and as derived from the social system.[53] It follows that 'in most relationships the actor does not partici-pate as a total entity, but only by virtue of a given differentiated "sector" of his total action'; that is, his 'role'.[54] We find, then, that the actor has become a segmentalized concept made up of a series of roles pinned together only at the point of underlying and unconscious psychological dispositions. Whilst, evidently, some aspects of the actor's action are retained, we might expect them to be omitted from Parsons' later analysis. For, remember, the actor and the unit act have become absorbed into the 'non-conscious' area of Freudian personality. Should this omission of actual action take place, it would seem no longer possible to attach to the actor the possibility of forming action of his own, or apart from that defined for him at a non-conscious level, socialized into him from the 'cultural norms' of the system. Equally, as on a concrete level the actor has become a segmentalized concept, valid only in terms of separate roles, it may become difficult to see how the goals and aims of the actor become ordered in terms of his priorities. Rather, they can only be ordered at the dictates of the external cultural, structural, and internalized personality systems. This becomes quite clear when Parsons argues that 'the essential aspect of social structure lies in a system of patterned expectancies defining the *proper* behaviour of persons playing certain roles, enforced both by his own internalized 'motives for conformity, and by the sanctions of others'.[55] Given this point of view, it can only be that 'role is the concept which links the sub-system of the actor as a psychological behaving entity to the distinctively *social* structure'.[56]

Thus the ultimate ends or values, which Parsons developed into the pattern variables, and their institutionalization at the level of structure, are internalized into the actor's character. It is in this sense that values contribute to the formation of roles, which then in turn mesh exactly with structural expectations which are held out to a person by his status position.

By this reasoning Parsons came to see that it might be important to develop a theory of motivation. This meant that it became vital to introduce psychological analysis and somehow to link the social sphere with the personality one. The fact that this 'internalization' must occur mainly in childhood, led Parsons to what, in later works, he calls, the theory of socialization. He suggests that light is thrown on the 'relationship between the psychological level of behaviour in social systems . . . in terms of the psychological implications of the conception of role'.[57]

It seems likely that Parsons had also come under the influence of Kardiner and Mead who, in their anthropological work, were attempting to relate culture to personality types. At this stage Parsons was rapidly forming the opinion that not only does role have psychological, as well as structural, aspects to it, but also that the link between the social and the psychological systems must be fairly direct. That is, by logical necessity the concepts of role and status must complement one another. Yet, even at this stage, he is still able to argue that 'the limits of' the idea of 'a character structure appropriate to a given role structure are by no means clear'.[58]

It would appear that Parsons was still uncertain that there was any clear or direct relationship between structure and personality. However, given his view of the cohesion between structure and action, such congruence must exist between status and role. What is certain is that he had become committed to the idea that psychological factors must be treated as more than a set of mere conditions for the actor, in contradiction to his and Weber's earlier standpoint. That is, they must now be dealt with on the level of motivation. Throughout this intermediary period Parsons read and came to accept Freud. He even underwent analysis. So it is no surprise to have found the influence of this great thinker in the way Parsons works out the detail of his theoretical preconceptions. He is now quite clear that his own revision of his earliest work could not be logically complete without extending his analysis of the actor to include precise psychological factors and, in so doing, replacing the concept 'actor' or, rather, that of the 'unit act' with that of 'role'.

It is exactly at this point that Parsons, following his interpretation of Freud, argues that it is not necessary to retain 'meaning' from the point of view of the conscious actor. We saw earlier how he criticized Weber for this 'omission'.[59] For Parsons, it followed that 'the structure of social systems cannot be derived directly from the actor-situation frame of reference', but only from a 'functional analysis' of society.[60] Here, Parsons takes that step from methodological individualism to collectivism which he showed was not logically implied in his earlier position. Simply, the way his work developed, particularly in connection with 'role' and, at the same time, with 'status' and 'social system', required this methodological shift.

Several points must be remarked upon in a final commentary on this brief and selective account of the development of Parsons' thought up to the early fifties.

Conclusion

We recognized first of all that Parsons was faced with a particular kind of problem because of his initial view of human nature. Derived from Hobbes and Durkheim, and at that time unqualified by any modern psychological theory, it was seen as being compiled from a random set of interests, which often conflicted with each other, and certainly with those of other people. Parsons was then faced with the task of seeing how any kind of social order could be possible. The only solution was to use the insights, in particular of Durkheim but also of Weber, and pose against this Hobbesian individual an integrated normative and value structure. The individual accepted this structure through moral obligation, in an ill-defined process of internalization, and was consequently harmoniously related to others. This implies two views of human nature, the one Hobbesian, the other infinitely manipulable, where the individual's social action is determined by the external structure of the social system.

In all Parsons' later work the initial opposition between chaos and order was retained. It was as if Parsons was constantly trying to solve the same problem whilst having already solved it (in one of the possible ways) in his first major work. There, under the influence of Weber, the concept 'actor' was used as an element in the explanation of the actual action of people. So also was the subjective viewpoint which Weber used to give meaning to action from the point of view of the actor. And though we recognized that Parsons had a highly novel definition of 'voluntarism', the actor was nevertheless 'offered' an ambiguous margin of real choice.

As each subsequent layer of his initial theoretical framework was developed, Parsons' position gradually, but perceptibly, shifted. The developments of Freud, their incorporation at the level of personality, and their subsequent integration with structure, occurred at the same time as that of functionalism, which integrated the personality, structure and culture into systems. But the addition of Freud did not re-open the question of individuality and choice. Rather, it closed it by an eccentric use of Freud's view of identification and learning. This, at a still later stage, became developed into a full-blown theory of socialization. Similarly, functionalism led to an even more integrated view of the way norms and values were related in the general structure of society. With the final addition of the pattern variables at the level of culture, we saw the emergence of three related systems: personality, structure and culture.

The place of subjectivity had been removed through these developments and replaced at the level of personality and culture. Though this subjectivity still had meaning to the scientist, the actor was no longer of key significance. When action 'deviated' from that expected by derivation from the overall model, this was not thought to be problematic for the model. Thus, both an objective-subjective dilemma arose, and the question of the empirical reference of the model became problematic. If the actor did not have the beliefs and hence the actions which he 'should', then clearly sanctions would operate against him at both a personality and structural level. He would consequently become aware of his 'true' interests in that position. In a word, he would adjust and step back into line.

If our point of reference is no longer the actor, how is our model to be built? How may it be checked or falsified? How may new events cause us to amend it? There are no answers to these questions. It is not that the model of society is so abstract, which it is, but that it has lost its subjective, empirical, grounding in its rejection of the concept of the actor.

At the same time as these problems and features arose, Parsons came under the influence of anthropologists and developed the concept 'role' in terms that harmonized with his theory. He used it to show how the position of the actor, his 'status', was related to and made congruent with his activity, his 'role'. In this way the concept contained both unconscious elements of the personality system, and normative as well as value elements from the structural and cultural system. The three systems were, more or less, finally integrated and given their dynamic. But the individual and his choice had finally disappeared along with his subjectivity. He had become an entirely determinate being, and the methodological framework within which he was analysed took the form of collectivism.

None of this is to argue that Parsons failed to deal with change. But he did have a particular view of it, and he did fail to deal with it even to his own satisfaction. To extend the problem of order, once a certain cohesiveness has been noted between people, to the level of complete societies, is to ignore, or underestimate the effect of group conflict. The view of social integration at the societal level is fostered not least by the idea of a common value system, the pattern variables, and the way these values are institutionalized and internalized. We have seen that Parsons is ready to accept the idea of social strain, which leads to conflict, even conflict about values. Indeed, he engaged in several important empirical studies that may be thought of as contradicting his overall model, or at least as extending it.[61] But the concepts of power and authority which he developed at this point are of great significance. Though they will be more fully discussed in later chapters, we may indicate here the clear moral bias which is necessarily injected into Parsons' mature work.

'Power' he argues, 'is an attribute of the *total system* [of society] and is a function of several variables. These . . . are the *support* that can be mobilized by *those exercising power*, the facilities they have access to [notably the control of the productivity of the economy], the *legitimation* that can be accorded to the *positions of the holders of power*, and the relatively *unconditional loyalties* of the *population* to the *society* . . .'[62]

Because Parsons has no exact method of empirical reference, he systematically confuses his abstract model, and the diffuse idea of power and authority which is built into it, with the power, authority and action of particular groups of men. As such, his model 'takes sides' in social conflicts, and renders him prone to the attack of conservative bias. This is quite justified, but we have not been so concerned with this overtly conservative aspect of Parsons' work. We can only note that Parsons' model of a social system can equally take account of such conflict situations as the Russian Revolution. That is, a group of people quite different from the rulers of western societies may be conceptually 'offered' the power which this analysis also 'offers' to, say, the rulers of America: first in a period of conflict, then in the subsequent period of cohesive communist rule.

The point to be made is that *whoever* rules, a society also reflects the dominant social values and, thereby is 'given' a total legitimacy in the sociological terms of this type of explanation. This would also seem to hold in those instances where Parsons examines a society in conflict, where two or more groups are competing for authority and power. The social system of each opposed sub-group is analysed in terms of diffused authority and an implied stability. Each conflicting group consequently socializes its actors in terms of its respective values. When 'fully socialized' in this 'system of interaction' the actor would not merely have or play a series of roles. The roles would be 'something that he *is*'.[63] This, and not the overt political conservatism, marks the exact nature of the value position of the kind of analysis developed and represented by Parsons. It implies a sociological view of man as the plaything of social constraint, without choice and without the ability to gain control of his life. It projects a whole range of subsequent sociological problems for analysis and research in terms of its value position, which are equally value-laden. As long as only the overt conservatism in Parsons' work is recognized, a full criticism of his work is not possible. Nor can its similarities with other sociological theories be acknowledged.

3: Karl Marx

Introduction

We have looked at Parsons from the point of view of major developments in his work. Now we must examine the sociological dimensions of Marx's work. However, we will not look at Marx from the point of view of the development of his thought. That has been done often enough before. Rather, we must attempt to discern what his mature sociological view was concerning human nature, socialization, class and social structure, conflict, change, power and authority, in order to understand his more general model of the social system of capitalist societies. To help us in this task we shall also take aspects of the work of a major modern Marxist scholar. Marcuse has not seen his vocation in terms of interpreting Marx, but rather in extending his concepts and explanations in the light of contemporary conceptual and empirical developments. Thus, Marcuse will help us in our discussion of Marx's and the Marxists' conceptual view of socialization, psychology, and explanatory models of advanced industrial societies. Only in this sense will we treat Marxian thought developmentally.

Human nature and social structure

Marx felt that in the earliest stages of history man was able to live a natural, self-fulfilling and co-operative life, but at a primitive stage of development. Such men were unfettered in their relations with their fellows. Yet, with the first division in this communal society, as one tribe captured members of another tribe and used them as slaves, there arose the first structural feature which cut men off from this 'true' spontaneous self. In a word, 'true' man was divided against himself through opposing interests and, thus, relations of conflict.

Marx wrote that 'every alienation of man from himself and from nature appears in the relations which he postulates between other men and himself'.[1] Indeed, the whole history of society came to be seen as the history of alienated man. It was merely possible to differentiate various stages or types of alienation as social revolution followed social revolution. The various divisions of labour, the various forms of exploitation of man by man constrained, twisted, and thwarted the true or fundamental nature of man from being expressed in social form. Man would only be able to express himself in this true way when he no longer stood over and against other men in a class-divided society. This would only become possible in the final stage of classless communist society where, as in primitive society, everyone had the same relations to the means of production and of livelihood; the same, not divided, interests and aims.

34

Marx felt that man lived by his active labour, by work. It is that labour, and distinctions between different types of labour that result from different social relations to the means of production, on which Marx focuses his attention. He sought to explain how different societal structures, and in particular, capitalist societies, constrain men to act differently and in conflict with one another. He also felt that if the changes in men's relations to the means of production could only be uncovered they would be the key to understanding social change. What does Marx mean by alienation?

He wrote that 'the alienation of the worker in his product means not only that his labour becomes an object, takes on its own existence, but that it exists outside him . . . and that it stands opposed to him as an autonomous power. The life which he has given to the object sets itself against him as an alien and hostile force'.[2] Men's relations to other men constrain and form their action, for these relations are not entered into freely. They are not a consequence of spontaneous action. So, 'in the social production which men carry on they enter into definite relations that are independent of their will . . . The totality of these relations of production constitute the economic structure of society – the real foundation on which legal, political superstructures' and therefore legal and political relations 'arise, and to which definite forms of social consciousness correspond . . . It is not the consciousness of men that determines their being, but, on the contrary, their social being that determines their consciousness . . . With the change of the economic foundation', as a consequence of contradictions in men's relations to the means of production, 'the entire immense superstructure is more or less rapidly transformed'.[3]

Marx is arguing that the position into which man is born, that is, his social position in the structure of relationships, determines his relations to other men and, in particular, to the means of production. In turn, his relations and thoughts about legal, political and religious life are equally and similarly determined. Consequently, 'upon the different forms of property, upon the social conditions of existence, rises an entire superstructure of distinct and peculiarly formed sentiments, illusions, modes of thought and views of life'. It may be that 'the single individual who derives [these] through tradition and upbringing, may imagine that they form the real motives and the starting point of his activity'. In fact it is 'the entire class' in which he is situated which 'creates and forms them out of its material foundations and out of the corresponding social relations'.[4]

Later, we shall have to discuss the reasons for and consequences of Marx's argument that economic relations tend to shape relations in all other spheres of activity. Here, it is only important to recognize the general point that every sphere of activity into which men enter, and their consciousness of that activity, is entirely determined by those structural relations between men which already exist. These relations and ideas may change, but they do so as a consequence of changes in the structure of society. Marx merely emphasizes this point when he argues that man's 'activity is not voluntary, but naturally divided, man's own act becomes an alien power opposed to him, which enslaves him instead of being controlled by him . . . Each man has a particular, exclusive sphere of activity, which is forced on him and from which he cannot escape'.[5] Why should Marx feel that man's activity and consciousness has to be entirely constrained by the prevailing structure of relationships?

Marx started with the initial assumption that human nature was basically creative and co-operative. At the same time he was faced with the apparent empirical evidence which suggested that contemporary society was in conflict. How could co-operative men come into a competitive struggle against their fellows? Marx had to pose the idea of an externally-determining system of relationships between men. So, despite his nature, man had to act in conflict with other men. The conflicting patterns or social norms were bound together by different sets of interests or goals. They gave meaning to and further bound or institutionalized the normative relations. Marx did not start from the Hobbesian problem of order, solving it by placing conflict between competing classes. Rather, he started with the 'problem of conflict', and solved it by dividing man's co-operative relations, which seemed to him no problem, so inducing competing norms, interests, and values between classes and within a generalized social system.

This means that Marx had to work with two contradictory views of human nature. On the one hand, that nature was self-fulfilling and communally spirited. As such, it was to be revealed again in ideal, communistic society. On the other hand, each stage in the development of an alienated, class-divided, society required that nature to be twisted or manipulated by social structure. Therefore it must take many different forms. At once we recognize the two problems: do actors and action make society or does society control action?

Contradictorily, as long as Marx retained his original view of human nature, it was equally vital for him to retain the view that social structure acted as an absolute constraint over and against that nature. He could not for a moment permit that structure to relax, to open up in a way which might allow individual men a free choice. For in this eventuality man would immediately revert to expressing his true nature, that of co-operation, which would not allow Marx even to begin an explanation of the many conflicts between men, and the evident injustices which man perpetrated against his fellow man. The ambiguity of this dual position exists throughout Marx's work. It is reminiscent of Parsons' struggle to suppress the Weberian formulation of social action, the principle of subjectivity entailed in it, and that margin of 'choice' which he allowed in his earliest work.

The extension of Marx by the addition of Freud: Herbert Marcuse

A number of Marxist scholars have added Freud to Marx, attempting to expand the body of his work in much the way we might have expected from Marx himself had he not died before Freud made his singular contribution to social thought. We shall look briefly at the way in which Herbert Marcuse has merged Marx's implications and assertions about human nature with the elaborate theories of Freud.

We have already argued that Marx has two views of men's actions. The one relates to the activities of alienated man in which man's true, rational, co-operative nature is repressed. The other constitutes the free expression of that true nature under conditions which do not involve its manipulation and domination. The latter form can only arise from the experience and contradictions of the former. The two views are, therefore, not contradictory, but placed in an historical perspective. Marcuse accepts this formula and expands it in detail. In the process, he leans heavily on important themes in Freud's work, but, like Parsons, ignores others.

In contrast to such 'Freudian revisionists' as Erich Fromm, Marcuse believes 'that Freud's theory is in its very substance "sociological", and that no new culture or sociological orientation is needed to reveal this substance'.[6]

Human relationships in this society are seen at one and the same time as a means through which the actor's personality expresses itself and the means by which his basic instincts and nature are repressed. Freud argued that such forms of repression or suppression were essential for the existence of society. In allegorical or metapsychological form he developed these arguments in *Totem and Taboo, Civilization and its Discontents*, and other works. Marcuse agrees in one respect, finding this to have been the case in historical and present societies. He does not, however, find it to be necessary in principle for future societies, where the co-operative, loving, instincts of an actor could mould and develop potentially destructive instincts, thus controlling his own destiny, rather than having it controlled for him by the structure and form of society. We should look at the psychological processes by which, it is argued, society represses or conditions the individual.

We must first recognize that adult people are 'no tabulae rasae, they are indoctrinated by the conditions under which they live and think and which they do not transcend'.[7] But this process of conditioning is not recognized as indoctrination by them, for the people voluntarily accept the values which they internalize as 'what is'. They happily abide by the normative, consensual means of achieving those values. Marcuse, borrowing heavily on the one hand from Marx, suggests the class nature of social structure through which repression occurs and, on the other hand, uses Freud to suggest how the personality responds to and accepts that repression in the course of development.

Marcuse argues that Freud's latent sociology only requires extension, not contradiction. So, he finds that in society generally,

the productive apparatus tends to become totalitarian to the extent to which it determines not only the socially needed occupations, skills, and attitudes, but also individual needs and aspirations. It thus obliterates the opposition between the private and public existence, between individual and social needs. [In modern societies in particular] technology serves to institute new, more effective, and more pleasant forms of social control and social cohesion.[8]

But we need not worry at this stage about the form or model of society for which Marcuse argues. Having gained this general idea, we now need to see how that structure determines and manipulates human nature so as to sustain the structure itself.

Freud is used with increasing emphasis to solve this problem. The actual form which the structure of society takes is not problematical. It may involve either social conflict or cohesion. In each case, however, the effect on the individual is the same. He is patterned in his private as well as in his public needs and aspirations in a way which makes his activities mesh with the social structure.

The family is seen as a crucial agent of socialization, which encourages this congruence between action and the needs of 'the system'. The basic drives or instincts of the child are moulded and influenced by his or her mother and father in much the same way as it is felt Freud himself outlined. In the process, 'parental influence' becomes 'the core of the super-ego' of the developing child. Subsequently, a number of societal and cultural influences are taken in by the super-ego until it 'coagulates into the powerful representative of established morality . . . Now the "external restrictions" which first the parents and then other societal agencies have imposed upon the individual are "intro-jected" into the ego and become its "conscience".'[9] Basic drives are repressed, diverted and developed in such a way that the child comes to act in accord with the structural needs of the family, then of other institutional situations into which he is placed. This means that the ego, as well as the super-ego, is deeply related to the external, socially constraining environment. It channels and affects the otherwise random and socially unco-ordinated drives of the id. The super-ego, an introjection of social values through the family, is the conscious dimension of the personality. It affects the ego which mediates between it and the id. Both super-ego and ego are, therefore, key sociological concepts, linking the personality system with the social system.

Marcuse's interpretation of Freud is more accurate than that of Parsons, who he felt injected an otherwise non-existent sociological dimension into Freud's work. But, like Parsons, Marcuse goes on to use such psycho-analytic concepts as sublimation, identification and introjection in order to understand the socialization process and the means by which basic instincts are moulded and harmonized by social interaction.[10]

These basic instinctual but socially patterned drives are often completely fastened within the unconscious areas of the ego and id. The particular individual is consequently not aware of them, though they can be subjectively expressed by the social scientist. He is able to recognize that there is no accidental correspondence between these drives and the general, structural, expectancies in terms of which action takes place. For the personality has been formed and key instincts repressed or divided in terms of the dominant norms and values of institutionalized society.

As with Freud, this process can be defined allegorically, or in terms of metapsychology. At this level, Marcuse suggests that Freud's theory of the Oedipus complex (as expounded in *Totem and Taboo*), can be argued more elaborately.

> The revolt against the primal father eliminated an individual person who could be [and was] replaced by other persons; but when the domination of the father had expanded into the domination of society, no such replacement seemed possible, and the guilt becomes fatal . . . The father, restrained in the family and in his individual biological authority, is resurrected, far more powerful, in the administration which preserves the life of society and in the laws which preserve its administration.

However, these laws 'appear as the ultimate guarantors of liberty'. To revolt against them would, therefore, be as great a crime as the original revolt against the father.[11] The individual *wants* to conform with them because he has internalized the values that legitimize them. But he also *has* to conform with them, for to break them would involve the powerful psychological constraint of guilt.

It is only in this sense that the individual is seen as determined and his nature as being infinitely manipulable by the structure of pre-existing society. The individual does not know he is determined, openly coming to want to behave in ways demanded of him. His basic instincts are, in the process, manipulated and repressed to the extent that he may actually disown or fail to recognize them. Should he consciously wish to act at variance with himself, mechanisms inside his personality make sure that such action fails.

To understand human action therefore, we have to examine features of a person's character and motivation of which he is not aware. At the same time, we can only understand his character if we understand the mechanism of socialization by which the fabric of society enters into the conscious and unconscious dimensions of personality. This means it is essential to recognize that personality and society are not separate, but are crucially linked, not just through such psychological concepts as the ego and superego or by sociological concepts such as structure and value, but by the very idea of social action itself.

In one sense, all this implies a stable or conservative view of human action and the social order.[12] Marcuse is only able to inject a critical dimension into his work by expanding his idea of repression. Only by postulating the 'regression' behind the mystifying forms of the mature individual and his private and public existences did Freud discover their basis negatively in the foundation on which they rest. 'Only by pushing his critical regression back to the deepest biological layer could Freud elucidate the explosive content of the mystifying forms and, at the same time, the full scope of civilized repression.'[13]

Even at the point of attempting to free man from constraint Marcuse ignores exactly that dimension of Freud's work which related to the way both the 'normal' individual (by himself) and the sick individual (with the help of the analyst) could establish a degree of rational control over his own life situation. Unlike Parsons, Marcuse resurrects this dimension. He does so by placing it within the potentialities of a future, not present, society. Marcuse contradicts Freud's assertion that any individual can potentially exercise differing degrees of rational control over his situation. Rather, he feels, this is only possible when man is freed from the conditioning, repressive, constraints of the class structure of society.

In any real sense, it follows that in such class-ridden society this would mean curing the patient to become a rebel or (which is saying the same thing) a martyr.[14] Firstly, such an argument involves criticising much of the established goal of therapy. For, 'while psychoanalytic theory recognizes that the sickness of the individual is ultimately caused and sustained by the sickness of his civilization, psychoanalytic therapy aims at curing the individual so that he can function as part of a sick civilization without surrendering to it altogether'.[15]

Freud believed that 'repression' and 'unhappiness *must be* if civilization is to prevail'.[16] On the contrary, and secondly, Marcuse maintains that by rebellion and revolution, the constructive instincts, the rational, self-fulfilling, and co-operative nature of man can be given free rein. This will mean that a new kind of society will emerge which has almost no repressive structure to it. Each man will control his own destiny and shape his own life.

For Marx, choice or voluntarism in the everyday sense was an attribute of men in primitive and advanced communist societies. The implied analysis involved reference to the subjective meaning of action and the deliberate exertion of human control over social situations. Between these stages it seemed that man was controlled by the social system. This implied an analysis which need not pay reference to meaning, in which action need only be seen in terms of forced adaptation. We shall, however, come to recognize that the distinction between these two themes was not so clear-cut in Marx's sociological thought. On the contrary, Marcuse used Freud in a way which demands only the latter kind of analysis for contemporary social systems. The possibility, let alone the analysis, of individual control and choice is placed in the future. Here and now, man is unfree and 'the system' determines his action.

Marx and the structure of society
Marx felt that the structure of all alienated societies was basically divided

into two main classes. Slave-owner was opposed to slave, feudal lord to serf, bourgeois to proletarian. We shall only be concerned with the opposition in more modern industrial societies between the bourgeois class and the proletarian class.

The first questions we must ask are: what, for Marx, were the factors which make up the class situation or structure for each of the two types of persons who occupy these class situations, and why do they make people act so differently?

It is often assumed that Marx defined class situations in entirely objective terms; that is, ignoring the subjective considerations of those who occupied those positions. Indeed, it is assumed, even by some Marxists, that it was simply a question of a person's ownership or lack of ownership of property which determined the class situation and, through this, the consciousness of the individual who occupied that situation.

Marx wrote that 'in every historical epoch property has developed differently and under different social conditions.' Thus 'to define bourgeois property means no less than to describe all the social conditions of bourgeois production'.[17] But man produces by the act of labour, and labour is divided in society into different forms. The factory-owner, the priest, the educator, the mother are all part of the general division of labour. Their combined labours create bourgeois production. Therefore, it would seem that to talk of simple ownership, or its lack, is not sufficient to define a common situation for a class. To do so we have to look not at the particular relations to production alone; we must include the meanings which actors give to property in a particular period. So, 'the attempt to define property as an independent relation, a special category, an abstract and eternal idea, can be nothing but an illusion of metaphysics or jurisprudence'.[18] Class situation only partly depends on how property is used by people at any given historical period. For how property is used must depend on how men feel about it, what they understand by it, and what subjective significance it has for them.

On occasion, we can be more specific. 'It is always the immediate relations of the owners of the conditions of production to the immediate producers – a relation whose specific pattern of course always corresponds to a certain stage in the development of labour and its social force of production – in which we find the final secret, the hidden basis of the whole construction of society.'[19] Is it, then, the common *relations*, which involve the common understandings men have of the means of production, which defines their common class situation? Unfortunately, class situations are not quite as easily defined as this. For Marx talks at the same time of the possibility of an objective way of distinguishing class situations which are quite separate from the subjective feelings of those in the class. The significance of this ambiguity will become more clear when we turn to a discussion of 'class interests'.

Class interests and classes-for-themselves

We must now ask what relation Marx sees between a class situation which is shared in common between people and the aims or goals which people express in that class situation. In a word, what are 'class interests', and how are they formed?

Firstly, it is important to note that it is by no means necessary that a class situation will produce what Marx called a 'class-for-itself'. Even when in a common situation men may well not pursue a common interest or set of values. The French peasantry were a case in point. 'The small-holding peasants form a vast mass, the members of which live in similar conditions but without entering into manifold relations with one another.'[20] Their method of production and their relations to one another tend to keep them in isolated family units. There is no great division of labour, no means of communication from farm to farm and certainly not from village to village. 'In this way, the great mass [of the nation] is formed by simple addition of homologous magnitudes, much as potatoes in a sack form a sack of potatoes.'[21] It must be noted that this is more an objective description of the peasants' class situation than one which refers to their subjective ideas or action.

The same can be said of the 'proletariat' when it is newly formed. When factories are small, when communications between towns are still intermittent, when the pressure of exploitation has not forced the members of the class to organize together, when their numbers have not yet been swollen by the growth of towns and factories, there is no overall or binding conscious unity between the people in the class situation. But there is a common situation in which the proletariat, like the peasantry, exists as an inert class-in-itself.

Marx is not arguing that people in these identical class situations have no interests or aims which they feel subjectively and in terms of which they act. Indeed they do. But these interests drive them only to individual or family, not to corporate action. They do not act together as a class and they make no attempt to exert control over their class situation in a corporate way by political action. This is important, for 'individuals form a class only in so far as they are engaged in a common struggle with another class'.[22]

The vital point is that Marx is 'not concerned with what this or that proletariat or even the whole proletariat' as a whole class 'visualizes as a goal for the time being. Its goal and its historic action are obviously and irrevocably predetermined by its own life situation as by the whole organization of contemporary society'.[23] The same is the case for other classes, in particular the bourgeois class.

Marx makes a theoretical leap from purely individual actions and interests to those of a whole social group or class. The former may take many intermediate stages as the class struggle develops and takes on new forms. Marx is predominantly concerned with the latter form of class action, which has a very special goal. We are distinguishing, just as we do 'in private . . . between what a man thinks and says of himself and what he really says and does, so in historical struggles we must distinguish even more carefully the phrases and fantasies of parties' and people who represent classes 'from their real organism and their real interests, their conception of themselves, from their reality'.[24]

In the course of this discussion, we have revealed the distinction between 'class-in-itself' and 'class-for-itself'. In both cases, there are common class relations and ideas between people that distinguish them from other groups in society. So do the actions of those other groups in society that affect their relations. But classes-in-themselves have no tangible or common interests which they express and which would unite the class of people, forcing them to act as a unit, or as if they were one person. Classes only come to act for themselves like this when they do develop such common goals.

We have already noted that both objective (usually economic) conditions and subjective relations play a part in defining the common class situation of those individuals who make up a class. It was, in part, the domination by the capitalists which formed this common situation for the workers. At this stage 'this mass is already a class in relation to capital, but not yet a class for itself'. In the struggle, resulting from opposed and felt interests which pass through many phases, 'this mass unites', through a developing ideology and an emerging common understanding of their situation.[25] The mass slowly 'forms itself into a class-for-itself'. The interests which it defends become 'class interests' of a 'pure form'.[26] These 'pure interests' correspond to the Weberian ideal type which Marx himself rationally deduces from the objective or common class situation.

There are two important points that we must note. Firstly, in connection with the concept 'class-for-itself'. Marx is again arguing that men's 'class situation' is formed by men's relations, activity and subjective understanding of their class relations to the means of production. Indeed, their class situation is partly formed by the consequences of their ideas and activity. Any objective economic factors independent of man's subjective understanding are, therefore, only one dimension of what is involved in the concept of 'class situation'. Yet, it remains true that Marx feels these relations, understandings, and activities are rigid phenomena which cannot be affected by the 'illusions or fantasies' of any individual. Man is determined by his social position and, in this sense, his relations to the means of production are predetermined. Therefore they are objective to him, determining also his relations and consciousness in other spheres of his activity.

Secondly, there are two kinds of interests which are analytically distinct. Marx argues that the common 'class situation' need not give rise to common interests based on that situation. Nevertheless, in those situations men act in terms of interests. These can only be empirically determined and are not class interests. But they are certainly understandable in subjective terms as the goals or aims which real men have and express in various activities.

The second type of interest can be theoretically determined. This is a 'pure' or rational interest. It can be rationally derived by the scientist from his objective understanding of the 'class situation', even before the actual people who make up the class-in-itself come to express that common interest. At this stage these people will only express the first kind of interest.

For varying historical and other reasons, men may never come to express the 'pure' kind of interest. But they always express some individual group aims. For example, the peasants may support Napoleon or the proletariat may support the political party of the bourgeoisie. In this way they express an interest which fails both to understand their 'true' situation and to recognize their 'true' or 'pure' interest. Their action is based on 'false consciousness', or a false understanding of their 'real' or objective class position in society. As such, they do not act as a class and do not form a class-for-themselves.

Marx is saying two quite separate things concerning men's interests. On the one hand interests are to be analysed in terms of what actual men say their interests are in particular situations. These interests are then easily accessible to subjective observation by the scientist. But, on the other hand, and ambiguously, Marx is saying that these actual interests may not be true or pure interests of the class. However, these 'ideal' interests will eventually correspond to 'real' or 'actual' interests which are yet to be developed by the class. While reference is paid to actual interest, the major concern is with the 'ideal' interest.

Marx clearly feels that these pure interests can be derived by the scientist from his own objective understanding of class situation before men in that class come to understand that situation fully or see the destiny of their class. This is not surprising. For, once a clear understanding of class situations is obtained, there can only be one rational way of acting in that situation. Sooner or later the actual occupants of these class situations will be pressed by developing social circumstances and the political struggle of their class into recognizing what that pure, rational interest is likely, even certain, to be. But, to understand that, Marx had to be quite certain that the real 'class situation' was objectively definable. Because of this he was, ambiguously, led to define both it and ideal interest now in objective and external, now in both objective and subjective terms.

At this point, we must note that Marx is often very hesitant to say in substance what men's interests will be before they come to articulate them themselves. He paints the picture in outline, not in detail. Thus, while discussing the French peasantry, which, he felt, was incapable of becoming a 'class-for-itself', he quite clearly saw why at one stage, they might act only as separate individuals, at another, that they might support Napoleon and, at a later stage, that they might support the proletariat.²⁷ These interests were of the non-pure kind, and were discovered only on empirical observation. As such, Marx analysed them with historical precision, but he did not dare to predict their development.

Marx even hesitated to discuss in detail the 'pure' interests of the proletariat. 'As long as the proletariat has not sufficiently developed to organize itself as a class, as long as therefore the struggle of the proletariat with the bourgeoisie as yet has no political character, these theoreticians are merely Utopians who invent systems in order to satisfy the needs of the oppressed classes.'²⁸ This argument confirms Marx's view that a class only really becomes a class when its struggle with the class opposed to it forces it into political activity. Only at that point will it come to defend and articulate its 'pure' interests. Its interests can only be understood if we observe the goals and aims of the political and ideological spokesmen of a class when it is actually engaged in struggle. We may predict these in outline, but it would be rash to fill in the detail before the actual situation developed in its full complexity.

Yet, ambiguously and at the same time, we are told by Marx that we must be wary of the 'catchwords and fantasies' of individuals and even class spokesmen. For it is possible for the scientist to understand the objective class situation more correctly than this or that class leader, and to deduce the general outline of the 'pure' interests which other leaders will later come to articulate for that class. Once the objective structure of relations is laid bare in the actual process of the class struggle, when the class situation develops in extreme or 'pure' form, when the classes themselves polarize and when the proletariat become utterly immiserated, then most of them may see as rationally as the scientist what their pure interests really are. At that stage the class will be acting for itself and will have developed its own theory of society and change. At that moment Marx himself would be superseded by such a theory of action and human control.

We can perhaps now see that there are two deeply related but very distinct themes in Marx's structural thought. One concerns his activity as an abstract theoretician. Its concern is with social systems in conflict and which shape men's actions. It is clearly visible in particular works, such as the *Communist Manifesto*, the Preface to the *Critique of Political Economy* and *Das Kapital* itself. But this side of his work is often hidden in his detailed political and historical analyses of actual events in the history of France, Germany and England. Here, the theory of social systems forms more of a guide-line than a set dogma or model of how society and classes really are at any one stage of their development. His concern with action supplants his concern with constraint.

It is at the level of abstract theory, designed to illuminate trends or laws of inevitable social development, that Marx makes the assertions and predictions which people sometimes regard as having been falsified. But we should stress that Marx was virtually concerned with the explanation of development, conflict, change and human control. His ideas, concepts and theories, and especially the explanatory models of society which he constructed were also changing. This, partly, is why it is so difficult for us to tease out with precision what he 'really' meant by any one concept, why they are so often ambiguous, and why the two themes are so often inter-woven.

Authority and power

So far, we have only discussed Marx's use of the concept of authority by implication. We must now refer to it directly before discussing his concept of power. The historically primitive and the advanced, future, communist social systems are consensual and are not driven by conflict. The same is true of the most advanced types of both the proletarian and bourgeois classes as social systems in themselves. Each of these social systems is cohesive, because the actors within them share ultimate values, or an ideology. These values have either been internalized through a process of repressive socialization, as in the cases of the bourgeoisie and those falsely conscious members of the proletariat, or they reflect the unrepressed, rational, and socially co-operative instincts of basic human nature which are encouraged by the social structure of a fully conscious proletariat, and a future communist society.

In both cases, the values are not only consensual, but are voluntarily accepted by those who act in terms of them. That is, people act in relation to them because they have come to want to do so, and not because they are forced to do so. This applies irrespective of the fact that the values and the means of achieving them were defined and determined for the individual even before he was born.

In this sense, the individual does what others expect of him because he wants to comply with them. Though hardly explicit, Marx's view of authority is seen as a social relationship between two or more people which is to be found diffused throughout the social system of each class. It is not focused in any one area.

Power is regarded quite differently by Marx and it is most explicitly central to his sociology. It is not only concentrated in the hands of parti-cular groups or classes at particular times, but also involves people being made to act in ways which they do not voluntarily accept. Power involves forcing people to act against their interests.

Classes-in-themselves only come to act fully for themselves when they enter the arena of politics, for that is where they experience power and open conflict; and a conscious class wishing to conserve or extend its ability to shape the situation is forced to gravitate to the centre of power. It does so in order to curtail by force the action of other, competing, classes. In rare instances in social democracies the proletariat will use the weight and force of its numerical superiority to overthrow these democracies by parliamentary means. Typically, however, it will have to force the ruling bourgeois class to abdicate after a revolutionary struggle in the streets and at the barricades.

Before the proletariat have reached the level of consciousness necessary to engage in that type of action, they will be repressed by the ruling class mainly by authority and not by power. The bourgeois institutions of say, the family, education and religion will legitimize the status quo in countless ways. The extent to which the bourgeoisie succeed, both by accident and design, will be a measure of the depth of false-consciousness in the proletariat. But false-consciousness involves the acceptance of the authority and rightness of norms, ideas and values which emanate and are internalized from the opposed class. And this involves a voluntary acceptance of their fitness to rule. Marx was convinced that ultimately such fitness, and the values which supported it and make it seem to be legitimate, would be exposed in the developing class struggle. At that moment, the true values of the proletariat would be developed and accepted. The rational means to implement these revolutionary values would involve the acceptance of a new internal authority and the use of power against the previous authority. The power of a class-for-itself was, therefore, dependent on the degree of its independent, internal, authority and cohesiveness.

Even in the fairly advanced stages of capitalism, and certainly for all previous forms of society, the State has been the consequence of class struggle and not its cause. Its authority merely indicates the extent to which the lack of consciousness and of alienation penetrates throughout society. Men make their history, but in irrational, non-conscious, ways.

The only class which, by the logic of its exploited situation, can become truly conscious of the function of the State and the ruling class is the proletariat of advanced capitalist societies. At this stage of societal development this class is pressured to develop not only a true understanding of its own situation, but also a true understanding of the whole of society.

The relations between Marx's concepts and his overall model or explanatory view of society were constantly changing. He was not so concerned with society as it was as with the historical forces and tendencies which were only momentarily frozen in the present and which would take on new forms and significance next week, next year, and even in the next century.

We are trying to arrest the fervour of Marx's writing, to resist that sense of process and activity in order to become more clear about the nature of the sociological concepts he was using. We are, perhaps, now at the stage when we can be clear about why Marx was so certain that the development of capitalist society would proceed in the way he predicted.

Inevitability, laws, the rational logic of situations, and the model of capitalism

Marx thought of himself as a scientist. He even compared himself with a natural scientist.[29] Indeed, he felt sure that the science of man would, one day, become completely integrated with the sciences of nature.[30] There was, however, one vital difference which he recognized between the science of nature and the science of man. A physicist in his laboratory can use instruments to isolate his variables the one from the other. He can create a pure experiment in the isolation of the laboratory to reveal the relations between elements which in the reality and variety of nature seem to be inextricably bound up with many other phenomena.

The scientist of man and society can only copy this method if he mentally abstracts the different elements which make up society. For they cannot be separated in any actual laboratory. It is in this sense that Marx refers to the 'pure form' of a class, its situation, its interests and the way they relate into the different stages of an overall developmental model through which society must pass, and in terms of which it may be explained. It is in this sense that he says of the structure of English society that 'even here the stratification of classes does not appear in a pure form. Middle and intermediate strata even have obliterated lines of demarcation everywhere. However, this is immaterial for our analysis'.[31] That is to say, it is immaterial for Marx's abstracted hypothetical analysis of those classes and their development. When the particular influences of local variations and particular men or transitional strata are artificially removed in the only laboratory available to Marx or any sociologist – his own mind – then the 'pure' form is conceptually revealed. It does not exist in reality. No more do atoms or electrons.

We have seen that Marx developed a pure, abstract type of the class situation for the proletariat and the bourgeoisie. He also had a pure type of the subjective interests or goals which the bourgeoisie and the proletariat would have in those situations.

The rational action of the 'pure' type of bourgeois man was to accumulate capital, to invest in plant, to employ more labour. This follows quite rationally from the pure interest or goal of attaining the maximum profit from his product on the market and from the productive process within his plant.

The early stages of this style of life and method of production led to two developments in the form of society. Firstly, it meant that the interests of this developing bourgeois class would clash, inevitably, with the traditional interests of the aristocracy, with the rule of kings. The bourgeois revolution in France, which Marx almost witnessed himself, was for him the closest approximation at the level of concrete reality to this pure form of class struggle and the inevitable revolutionary consequences of that struggle. Other societies, he was sure, would have to go through a development and a revolution which, despite local differences, would fit that pure form or, at least, would be explicable in terms of it.

The second consequence of the activity of the growing bourgeois class, which would take over the state apparatus so as to further its interests, was the gradual creation of the class of the proletariat. At first, this class would be small in numbers. Its members would be relatively isolated from one another, would not recognize its relation to other groups in the productive processes, and would be content to sell their product on the labour market.

Yet, in rationally furthering its interests in its situation, members of the bourgeois class would build larger factories, would employ more and more labourers, would pay those labourers smaller and smaller wages so as to maximize their profits. The accumulating consequences of this process would further create two great and developing class situations in society: those of the bourgeoisie and the proletariat. These would form the objective class conditions from which class interests could be derived, and from which it would make rational sense for members of each class to act only in certain particular ways. Again, these actions and their consequences could be abstracted by the scientist into 'pure types' which, at any one stage, need not correspond precisely with reality.

It is not some obscure economic law which makes each individual proletarian sell his labour for a particular price on the market. Rather, it is in part the consequence of the capitalist acting through his own constraining class situation in which he competes with others like himself, while attempting to maximize his profit by reducing his labourers' wages. This external, objective factor in the situation of the proletariat combines with that created by the many individual members of the proletariat who are all attempting to sell their labour for the highest price within their common situation. The combination and accumulation of these human relations and activities, which encourage different actual and 'ideal' interests and actual and 'ideal' actors, *creates*, sustains, and even *changes* the economic laws of production: profit and price. Because he felt this to be true, Marx attempted both to expose bourgeois economics, which he argued abstracted real men from their real activity, and to introduce the real situations, actions and interests which created those economic conditions.

In the 'pure' situations of clashing 'class interests', Marx was sure that his hypothetically 'pure' proletarian man would inevitably be forced to see connections between the activity of the class to which he was opposed in the factory, in the State and even in the sphere of religion. From this full understanding (a scientist's understanding) of his own class situation, the interests of proletarian man would come to approach their ideal or purely rational form. In order to be free, in order fully to control his own interests, he would not only have to demand higher wages, to organize amongst his fellows who occupied the same class situation, he would also have to enter into the arena of political struggle. The class struggle, previously hidden to all but the scientist, would become quite open and revealed to everyone.

Marx observed the attempted revolutions in France in 1848 and 1871.

He was certain that they approximated very closely to the 'pure' form of the development of society which he was posing on the abstract level. He was sure that all capitalist societies would have to go through exactly the same 'pure' stages of development. Simply, his concepts combined into systems of interaction of such an abstraction to cover all these concrete societies. Measured against such 'systems' individual action is irrelevant.

Of course, it is 'quite possible that a man's actions will not always be determined by the class to which he belongs; but these individual cases are . . . irrelevant to the analysis of the pure form of the class struggle and to the general explanation of particular events in particular societies'.[32] The same is even true of groupings and strata within classes, but not for capitalist societies. Sooner or later they *must* pass through certain stages of development.

The bourgeoisie were successful, in 1848 and 1871, in repelling the organized assault of the workers. Marx expected this because the pure forms of the productive processes, class relations and class ideology or interests had not developed in French society. The situation had not yet arisen in which the proletariat had the ideology, numbers, or power to overthrow the ruling class.

Acting in a pure interest, derived from its pure situation, the bourgeois class was bound to continue to produce the conditions (through new technological inventions, larger factories, even more repressive acts, etc.) which would inevitably create a proletarian situation that approached that of Marx's ideal model. Only then could the proletariat develop the organization and the consciousness through which later political and revolutionary assaults on the fabric of bourgeois society would be successful. From this future standpoint, the incidents of 1848 and 1871 had only been preliminary political skirmishes. The next clash (or the one after) would inevitably result in the overthrow of the bourgeois class, and the introduction of the communist society. This would be created in the interests of the proletariat by the proletariat, and would ultimately represent man in general. At that point the co-operative man of primitive society, alienated for so long, would be liberated from the constraints of a class-divided, alienated society.

Though Marx thought this development was inevitable, it is also very clearly the determinate outcome of men's semi-rational, class-situated actions even though, at the early stages of the development of classes and their interests, it was largely due to the unintended consequences of these actions. The action of the proletariat was to become *increasingly* rational as its understanding of its situation increased.

The argument can be summarized as follows. Human nature is co-operative and rational. In class-divided society different men are placed into different situations which force them to pursue different interests or values. While they still pursue these interests rationally their rationality is proscribed by the limitations of their situation and a false awareness of that situation. As life is defined by labour and as labour is focused in the factory, those relativistically rational interests which are located there are pursued by men into every other aspect of their life-situation. So there is a rational, if situationally located, explanation for why the interests of economic activity link with those of family, religion, politics and leisure. As both bourgeois and proletarian men act in these rational ways, the two main classes of capitalist society oppose each other at every point. But the rational activity of bourgeois man unintentionally creates the proletarian situation that leads to his own downfall and the development of a revolutionary situation.

Society is made by man. But it is unintentionally made by him. These unintended structures of society in turn force man to act in ways which sustain it or, rather, drive it on its revolutionary course. Marx has resolved the dilemma between rationality and choice on the one hand as external social constraint. Society now controls man, not man society. Action adapts, albeit in rational ways, to externally given circumstances and values. This resolution is cemented by Marcuse's adaptation of Freud to explain more fully why men 'voluntarily' accept the constraints of their class-situationed activity.

On the other hand, the dilemma is resolved because of the precise way in which Marx's range of pure types (of actor, situation, interest, class, power, state etc.) combine into specific developmental systems of interaction. Such systems have lives of their own. Analysis of them proceeds in terms of their inner dynamism and their needs. Whilst they are sustained and changed by class action, that action itself is predetermined in terms of the logic of the system itself and not that of those who are situated within classes at any one time.

The tension so far present in Marx's thought is removed. For, in terms of Marx's formulation, relations in the factory only condition or determine the superstructure, including the state and ideology, in so far as people rationally pursue their 'material' interests in all other spheres of their productive activity. That is, the economic base only determines the superstructure in its pure form and not in every stage of actual social development.

This complex relationship is objectively predetermined and conditioning for the individual, in so far as these relations already exist as the product of other men. They are, therefore, given entities, into which that particular individual enters and over which he has no individual or subjective control.

In this way alone (both in general and in particular), man's, say proletarian man's, activity and consciousness is formed by his social condition. In this sense, man's consciousness does not determine his condition or situation. Rather, his social situation creates his awareness for him. But it is this awareness which drives his social action. This action interacts with that of other men, and slowly drives and divides society into two great and conflicting classes. Man's actual interests slowly come to coincide with the pure interests of his class in, say, the institutions of politics and education. These are formed by and are logically related to his pure interests at the basic level of his work situation. But these new interests (of education and politics) extend and develop those which relate solely to his work situation. They lead him to want to control his general life situation and, to do that, he has to change his actual life situation. In this sense, man's conscious awareness does shape his social and, even, his economic circumstances.

This is Marx's pure, developmental, model. With its help we can be more clear about what Marx means when he says that the next stage of development and conflict will be revolutionary. The overall model of society develops with the changing and developing class situation, interests, power and authority of the two main classes. So, any empirical or historical analysis which is conducted in terms of the model is bound to contradict features of that model. For it will have been constructed to explain a previous situation. A present or future model must, therefore, take into account the latest empirical developments. Empirical and historical analysis will always tend to run ahead of theoretical analysis, and the construction of models. It will also have to take great account of men's actual beliefs at that stage in their development, measuring them against their 'pure' interest derived from the model. For this reason, the ambiguity of the exact link between the real and the ideal, the empirical and theoretical, remains unresolved.

Marx's historical and empirical analysis

Marx was engaged in two distinct activities. Firstly, he was creating and developing those abstract, theoretical concepts which we have been discussing. At the same time, he was engaged in analysing in great detail, economic, social and political events as they unfurled before him. In this second activity, the theory was only a guideline, a sociological imagination as it were, by which he directed his attention to certain empirical features rather than others. Yet he was writing far more than a history of his time. He was selecting groups, classes, intuiting their interests and their coming struggles and the causes of present conflicts and alliances in a way which allowed him to construct explanatory models of action and situations.

Such explanations in fact criticized or contradicted his overall, more abstract, theory. It was only because he was writing most crucially as a committed politician himself that he never bothered, or found the time, to amend that theory in order to bring it into precise alignment with his more detailed observation and analysis. Had he done so, he would have noted the theoretical significance of some of those more empirical insights to which we shall now refer.

The bourgeoisie was not simply one class with one pure interest, except as an abstract type. There were many divisions of interest on the level of 'reality' within that class. These divisions were crucial to any understanding of conflict and clashing action within that overall class. This class was divided into at least two great interest groups of landed property and capital. Each of these groups sought to 'restore its own supremacy and the subordination of the other'.[33] Similarly, within the class of peasants there are 'conservative' peasants 'who want to consolidate' their small-holding, and there are also 'country folk who, linked up with the town, want to overthrow the old order'. The former support Napoleon, the latter find the expression of their interest in the organized proletariat.[34] It was to the group of conservative peasants that Napoleon, as the Head of State, appealed for support against the interests of the whole bourgeois class. In this sense, it was evidently quite possible for divisions *within* 'objective' classes to be as significant for explaining situations as divisions between them. It was also possible for the State to become quite indepen-dent of, and opposed to, the bourgeois class. This, of course, contradicts Marx's abstract 'pure' model in which the State acts as the 'executive committee of the bourgeoisie'. Under these circumstances, it follows that the 'super-structure' of politics and ideas is not raised simply on the economic and class division of the social structure but, on the contrary, helps to form these divisions. We have already offered some explanation of why Marx thought this possible.

Similarly, those groups who support 'social democracy', the political system of the bourgeoisie, may be made up from people outside this class. 'What makes (workers or peasants) representatives of the petty bourgeoisie is the fact that *in their minds* they do not get beyond the limits which the latter do not get beyond in life, that they are consequently driven, *theoretically*, to the same problems and solutions to which material interest and social position drive the latter practically.'[35] So also, the petty bourgeois intellectual whose father owns his small shop may, at times of revolutionary crisis, join the revolutionary class out of theoretical and moral reasons, because of what he *feels* in his head, not what he feels in his pocket.[36] Thus, classes and the ideas or ideology which those who claim to represent those classes profess are not just made up of people who have similar objective or even subjective relations to the means of production. On the contrary, they depend just as much on what happens in a person's mind, on what his theoretical position is, on what he believes his class interest to be.

It was in this context that Marx was to write in his incomplete last chapter of *Das Kapital* that even in England 'the stratification of classes does not appear in its pure form', that is, in the most highly rationally developed form which we see in Marx's model of class structure. 'Middle and intermediate strata . . . obliterate lines of demarcation everywhere. However, this is immaterial for our analysis' of that pure model, though not for our analysis of particular situations. And so Marx goes on to discuss the 'infinite fragmentation of interest and rank into which the division of social labour splits labourers as well as capitalists and landlords – the latter, e.g. into owners of vineyards, farm owners, owners of forests, mine owners and owners of fisheries'.[37]

Marx draws a crucial distinction between those who actually own the means of production and who, as an apparent consequence, once took the crucial decisions in the factory, and those who, in the joint stock company, come to take those decisions yet do not actually own the plant. Marx defines the joint stock company as 'private production' or control 'without the control of private property' or as 'the elimination of capital as private property within the capitalist mode of production itself'.[38] But what consequence has this for Marx's general theory, which ambiguously links ownership not only with economic control, but also with political and educational control, and even control of religious affairs? Marx does not see the problem in this way.

It is fitting, perhaps, to take a further example by reference to Marx's opinions concerning the political system which his model predicted would reflect the class interests of the bourgeoisie.

> The parliamentary regime lives by discussion; how shall it forbid discussion? Every interest, every social institution is here transformed into general ideas, debated as ideas; how shall any interest, any institution, sustain itself above thought and impose itself as an article of faith . . . The parliamentary regime leaves everything to the decision of majorities; how shall the great majorities outside parliament not want to decide?[39]

Marx is placing his faith in a strict form of rationality. Acting in their 'pure interests' the workers, who form the majority of society, will come to express that interest and their power through parliamentary democracy. The power of debate, of independent ideas, is destined to transform the state and political system from one which acts in the interests of the ruling class, to one which acts in the interests of the proletariat. Marx states this quite explicitly. 'We know that the institutions, the manners and customs of the various countries must be considered, and we do not deny that there are countries, like England and America . . . where the worker may attain his object by peaceful means.'[40] Through this argument Marx is setting loose the formative controlling power of manners and customs, and, beyond this, ideas and values by which different countries organize their political life. Yet he had built an abstract, theoretical model which, he argued, could be equally applied to each capitalist country. That model only allowed the proletariat to grasp power by a revolutionary and armed struggle against the State apparatus. A State built on the economic interests of the owning class would be used by the bourgeoisie to defend the interests of that class. Yet, as with Napoleon, we find that the State is quite voluntarily dissociating itself from that class and is handing potential power to the oppressed class.

At such points as these the 'inevitable laws' of development seem to be closer to the 'tendencies' with which Marx once equated them.[41] And, fundamentally, this involves a connection with the driving idea that classes are formed as men make their own history through their own action. They form and control their classes irrespective of their 'objective', 'true' or economic relations to the means of production as described by the scientist. These are crucial but unresolved dilemmas and ambiguities between opposed themes of analysis, which Marx did not have the time or the inclination to resolve.

Nor did Engels when he commented on developments in England in the late nineteenth century. 'History', he argued, 'has proved us and all who thought like us wrong . . .' It has proved 'once and for all how impossible it was in 1848 to win social transformation by a simple surprise attack' in France or elsewhere.[42]

With the universal suffrage, and social or liberal democracy, 'an entirely new method of proletarian struggle came into operation . . .' Marx had seen something of this with the Ten-hour Bill in England. 'Rebellion in the old style, street fighting with barricades, which decided the issue everywhere up to 1848 [has become] to a considerable extent obsolete.'[43]

Because Engels, with Marx, felt that social democracy might allow the working class to vote itself into power, he was to write of a current English election that the proletariat had 'discredited itself terribly'. He was bitterly disappointed. But he did not question his general, rational, assumption of action or his general theory of class. So, he wrote and worked on: 'In order that the masses may understand what is to be done, long, persistent work is required, and it is just this work that we are now pursuing.' Both 'slow propaganda work and parliamentary activity are recognized' as important in this respect.[44] He did recognize in this 'the irony of world history [which] turns everything upside down. We, the "revolutionaries", the "overthrowers" – we are thriving far better on legal methods than on illegal methods . . . The parties of Order . . . are perishing under the legal conditions created by themselves'.[45] But he did not recognize the contradiction between this statement and his general assumptions and theory. Nor did Marx.[46]

So there were two empirical ways by which the model of revolution could be achieved. Through the extension of the franchise and social democracy the bourgeois class might unintentionally open the parliamentary and peaceful road to revolutionary socialism. This might happen in the most advanced and sophisticated societies, such as England and America. In other societies, the parliamentary system and State would remain aligned with the power and situation of the bourgeoisie. It would therefore have to be overthrown by street fighting and violent revolution. Either way, Marx thought, the result would be the same: ideal communism.

This later area of Marx's thought is, perhaps, the one most usually fastened upon by critics. They argue that it provides the falsification of Marx's whole approach. Nowhere have such revolutions taken place in industrial societies. The Russian revolution took place in the least ad-vanced of capitalist societies. The Chinese, Cuban and African revolutions have occurred in quite different conditions and types of society. We might argue as a consequence that these revolutions, including the one in Russia, have not been communist ones, and, therefore, present new social prob-lems to us. But this argument leaves aside the question of advanced capitalist societies. For they may still undergo the revolutions which Marx predicted for them. Marx, then, still has a chance of being vindicated – better late than never.

The social structure of modern, western, technological societies: Herbert Marcuse
There has been a huge and often bitter argument amongst people who consider themselves the inheritors of Marx's ideas about the true road to socialism. We are not interested in these arguments here. They are to do with tactics and, through them, the theory of political action. Our concern is with the underlying sociological explanations offered by Marxists of why revolutions have not yet occurred in the advanced capitalist countries.

Herbert Marcuse is strictly in line with the Marxist sociological tradition. As such, his theories are not a revision but, rather, an extension of Marx's method and theory which relates them to the changed empirical circumstances of the mid-twentieth century. Marx himself would certainly have made a similar attempt. Just as his analyses of contemporary developments and situations were amended with changed situations, even to the point of suggesting a model by which revolution could be achieved peacefully, so, in the twentieth century, he would certainly have faced new situations bravely and constructed even more ingenious models to explain them. Why, as Engels stated, has 'the proletariat discredited itself terribly'? What implications has this fact for structural concepts and analysis?

Marcuse works with a dual and, at first glance, self-contradictory thesis. On the one hand he recognizes that 'advanced industrial society is capable of containing qualitative change for the foreseeable future'.[47] On the other hand, he believes that 'forces and tendencies exist which may break this containment and explode society'.[48]

We shall concentrate predominantly on the first of these assertions. To understand it in detail, we must first accept the weight which Marcuse attaches to it.

The 'containment of social change is perhaps the most singular achieve-ment of advanced industrial society; the general acceptance of the National Purpose, bipartisan policy, the decline of pluralism, the collusion of Business and Labour within the strong State testify to the integration of opposites which is the result as well as the prerequisite of this achieve-ment'.[49]

In the hands of other writers these empirical developments are seen as support for an ordered view of social structure. Marcuse is not convinced of the validity of this view, feeling that the ruling class has been rather more subtle than Marx could have foretold. These developments are regarded as evidence of the increased flexibility of the ruling class and the political parties of conservation. They have recognized the conflict which Marx discussed, believed that it was essential to contain it, and developed the ideology of social democracy; that is, the kind of political and social action which made this containment possible. We must try to explain why this change has taken place.

Partly it was because the bourgeois State and the bourgeois political parties offered the agents of change (proletarian unions and parties) the opportunity of entering into the bourgeois parliamentary institutions. This very opportunity was to some extent presented by the developing power of radical ideology and action of the proletariat. The parties of order could not afford to ignore such a development. They did not choose to ignore it or, in the end, to fight it openly as they had in 1848. Rather, they were driven by their own ideology of 'liberty, equality and fraternity' to open their own state and political institutions to the proletarian movements.

The revolutionaries responded by accepting the opportunity. Their actions in doing so were legitimized precisely by those features in Marx's thought which saw the possibility of peaceful, revolutionary, change. They felt the need for 'street fighting' had passed and that entry into, say, parliamentary activity and negotiations between union and management would lead to the quiet defeat of the bourgeois class.

What happened at this stage was not foreseen by Marx, for an unexpected situation had clearly developed. To enter parliament involved the radicals in accepting the bourgeois rules and procedures of political activity. This meant severing or changing the relations between the radical leaders and those whose 'pure' interests they intended to serve. Engaging in negotiation and parliamentary reform determined the need for temporary compromise. The original interests were not served immediately. Yet unintentionally, and over a period of time, the revolutionaries were drawn into, and accepted, a set of institutions which were not of their intention or making. They might still pay lip-service to their old interests. Despite this, their real actions had departed significantly from them.

Thus, it was not so much the parties of order which had opened the path to peaceful revolution. Rather, the parties of revolution slowly became the parties of order. For, still unintentionally, they now supported the rules and so legitimized the complex liberal ideology of the dominant class. They did so precisely by strengthening and extending the power and function of the State. In the process, they actually contributed to changing the rules and developing that liberal ideology, again in unintended ways. What significance does this have for Marx's explanation of society and the relations between concepts which helped him to build a model of that society?

Firstly, Marcuse makes explicit the theoretical point which Marx himself indicated: that the 'universal function of the State [in industrial society] is itself determined by the base, but contains [for modern capitalist and communist societies alike] factors transcending and even antagonistic to the base factors which may become semi-independent forces, in turn actively affecting the base in various ways'.[50]

In early capitalist society, the State was almost entirely the product of the ruling class. Therefore it acted in the exclusive interests of that class. With the assimilation of the working-class trade unions and political parties, with the development of national plans, with the mammoth financial needs of technological progress, the State not only increased in terms of power, but also developed certain interests of its own. Indeed, it has partly grown at the expense of the earlier and more crude interests of the bourgeoisie. Extreme right-wing ideologies are now often opposed to the State as openly as they are to those of the left. The State's interests are still predominantly those of the bourgeoisie, but it develops them and presents them as the values of the whole of society. In the process the 'interests' of the bourgeois class have undergone a transformation in form but not in substance.

Secondly, Marcuse argues that the State has become more powerful as a consequence of these developments. Precisely because the power and ideology has a degree of autonomy from and conflicts with some groupings within the bourgeois class, it has developed new, objective interests and has acted in terms of them. In turn this ideology has extended the power of the State and made it more stable.

Thirdly, through such devices as national plans and the co-ordination of opposed interest-groups the State has gained a financial reserve and interest which is far greater than that which is at the disposal of any traditional capitalist enterprise. Therefore, it has become able to encourage new forms of production. These include the development of rationalized technological innovations and practices. In turn, these encourage the need to develop a consumer market of hitherto unimagined proportions. Such investment and sponsorship, and the developing ideology that accompanies them, expand, strengthen, and further legitimize the newly found power of the State. The parties of change are, as a consequence, drawn even further into an acceptance of this new situation and, thereby, help to extend it even more.

Fourthly, these developments have helped to create institutions and ideas which purport to serve the whole of society. Marcuse is not merely thinking of political consensus at this point but also of, say, the institutions of education. The point to recognize is that:

> no society is a mere aggregate of functions. Over and above the social and economic functions and the form they take as a whole, another set of forms is required to keep them in existence and regularize them – rules, norms, 'values', juridical principles. This is true of every society . . .[51]

The State orders many of these forms in modern society. So, in order to understand how the forces of revolution have been 'incorporated' in advanced capitalist society, we must turn in detail to the emergent ideology of the State. For we must recognize that in one sense it is acting both in its interests and in those of the bourgeois class. At one and the same time, Marcuse argues,

> the State, being and remaining the State of the ruling class, sustains *universal* law and order and thereby guarantees at least a modicum of equality and security for the whole of society. Only by virtue of these elements can the class State fulfil the function of 'moderating' and keeping within the bounds of 'order' the class conflicts generated by the production relations.[52]

The State, and through it the bourgeoisie, appealing to the whole of society, seeks to gain approval for its interests. Expressing these through its ideology it attempts to repress the interests of the class whose interests are objectively opposed to it. To see how this happens we must recognize that for

> every society, every authority has to be accepted. A given social structure, with its specific social and juridical relations, must obtain the consensus of the majority, if not the totality of its members. No social group, no constituted society is possible without such adherence, and sociologists are justified in stressing this consensus.[53]

The point is that Marx saw two distinct, emerging and internally cohesive classes which were separated by a conflict of aims and power. Marcuse still sees the same objective structure of class situations. But the consciousness, values, and institutional norms of the dominant class have been legitimized and extended by the State in such a way that the subject class also voluntarily accepts them. Order no longer exists only within two independent classes, but within the whole of society. This means that

> the labourer whose real interest conflicts with that of the producer, the intellectual whose vocation conflicts with that of his employer, the common consumer whose real interest conflicts with that of management, find themselves submitting to a system against which they are powerless and appear unreasonable.[54]

There are still those who do protest, whether it is in the form of criminal or sexual deviance or in the retention of the original Marxian ideas. But there is an aspect of the ideology of social democratic societies – their 'repressive tolerance' – which ensures that such critical activity is denigrated, ridiculed and, therefore, controlled by the majority of society.

In any society the whole 'determines the truth . . . in the sense that its structure and function determine every particular condition and relation. Thus, with a repressive society, even progressive movements threaten to turn into their opposite to the degree to which they accept the rules of the game'.[55] All ideas, values and concepts are therefore structurally related to the part they play in the social system. Some concepts, originally critical ones, have thereby become redefined and have the function of maintaining order and cohesion. For example, equality, freedom, truth, objectivity are 'loaded'; they are 'determined and defined by the institutionalized inequality . . . i.e. by the class structure of society'.[56] They are emptied of their critical value and transformed to defend the status quo.

Other values which were, initially, patently destructive have become redefined as virtues. So, for example, 'in the unfolding of capitalist rationality, irrationality becomes reason: reason as frantic development of productivity, conquest of nature . . .; irrational because higher productivity, domination of nature, and social wealth become destructive forces'.[57]

The State now controls the means by which these ideas and interests are communicated. Radio, television, the press and art, are all geared to the expression of these interests. For, 'under the rule of monopolistic media – themselves the mere instruments of economic and political power – a mentality is created for which right and wrong, true and false are predefined wherever they affect the vital interests of the society'.[58] But these interests are not, of course, the 'pure' interests of the whole of society. They are identifiable as those of the ruling class alone. It is precisely the political and social success of this class which has enabled them to gain and even strengthen their dominant and repressive grip over the whole of society.

Minorities may speak and protest. But they will be rendered harmless by the acquiescence of the 'overwhelming majority, which militates against qualitative social change'.[59] And this majority, which includes the proletariat, has developed a series of values and styles of action radically different from and in conflict with their 'true' or 'pure' interests. This majority, therefore, is 'firmly grounded in the increasing satisfaction of needs, and technological and mental co-ordination, which testify to the general helplessness of radical groups in a well-functioning social system'.[60]

We have accounted for Marcuse's pessimism. He sees almost no way of breaking the legitimate authority which advanced societies command over all their members. Most people may be acting irrationally, conforming with a repressive, determining system. But then, 'every ideology . . . is a collection of errors, illusions, mystifications, which can be accounted for by reference to the historical reality it distorts and transposes'.[61]

Marcuse and Marx

The first point to note is that Marcuse has made Marx's concepts less ambiguous. He has filled out some of the empirically difficult concepts by applying them to an explanatory model of modern societies which, not surprisingly, Marx failed to envisage. These extended concepts relate together rather evenly; the overall model of the social system is more complete than Marx's. Precisely because of this, it is less flexible in application than Marx himself would have liked. But we must turn to the concepts themselves.

Marcuse has retained Marx's assumption concerning rationality. It is still related both to the scientist's conception of pure interests and to the action of actors who become aware of their pure interests through a full, scientist's understanding of their situation. However, far from the proletariat coming to realize their 'rational' interests, it is the bourgeois class which has become more rational and sophisticated. This is not caused so much by the explicit intentions of that class, but as a consequence of political mistakes and the false consciousness of the radical parties which lead them to support social democracy and, in the East, to create and accept a rigidly bureaucratic State apparatus.

The concept of the State had to be extended to deal with these changes. It became less partisan and more nationalistic in appearance, but it still serves the interests of the dominant class. The rational and tolerant ideas which it has developed in extending its powers are a key feature of its ideology, and are an approximation to the 'pure' rational interests of the bourgeoisie. But this 'reason' is a very peculiar form of reason. It is, if you like, an inverted form of rationality which, of necessity, robs true reason of its significance.

The social transformations which we are discussing have occurred in particular in the '*consciousness* and in the *political action* of the two great classes which faced each other in society . . . In the capitalist world they are still the basic classes. However, the capitalist development has altered the structure and function of these two classes in such a way that they no longer appear to be agents of historical transformation'.[62]

These changes, and 'the fact that the vast majority of the population accepts, and is made to accept [them] does not render [society] less irrational and less reprehensible'.[63] Any explanation of this fact crucially turns on the concept of 'alienation' and 'false-consciousness'. An unpredictable new situation has arisen in which the proletarian class is prevented from recognizing its objective class situation and the rational or 'pure' class interests which are still vested in that situation. It misunderstands its real position in relation to the other main class in society, and the new features of the modern State. Consequently, as the class structure has remained unchanged, so also the distinction between 'true and false-consciousness, real and immediate interests still is meaningful'.[64]

Exactly because Marx does operate with a theoretically rational view of man, because at that level he did not fully constrain his original optimistic view of man, his own analysis of the social relationships and peculiarities which constrain action is ill-developed. It rides uneasily beside the rational self-controlling dimension of his thought. If the actor has a 'pure interest' which is tied to a situation, and if the actor in that situation acts cooperatively and rationally, then there is no obvious need to pose a rigid normative structure between the goal and the actor. When Marx considers rational, aware action, these 'norms' and institutions which Parsons, following Durkheim, and Marcuse, extending Marx, place between the actor and his goal are placed by him in the situation itself. It is for this reason that we found his definition of class situations to be ambiguous, part subjective and part objective. They included, as it were, the end and the rational means to that end. In this sense, Marx does work with an embryonic view of normative rational action. Only where action seemed obviously 'irrational' or 'falsely-conscious' was there a need to develop an extended view of normative structure beyond that contained in the 'objective' class situation. For, in such circumstances, there is a positive need to offer an explanation for that irrational action simply because it deviates from the expected rationality of the theoretical model.

At that point Marx discussed those cultural traditions and standards, the myths and fantasies, which prevented rational understanding and action. These were merely aspects of the more general concept of alienation. But, more particularly, false-consciousness is related to specific classes, and the failure of people in such class situations to transform themselves into a 'class-for-itself'. Like rational action, it remains related to the objective class situation. But, in addition, it contains specifically normative and cultural elements.

The point to recognize here is that class situations themselves are constantly changing and developing as a consequence of class activity. This happens irrespective of whether that activity is rational or irrational. As class situations change, so a full rational understanding and the rational interest must also change.

In fact, the scientist can only predict pure interests if he can also predict future situations and their development. As Marx was fairly confident about the latter, he was also happy to discuss the former, though reality was not expected to conform exactly with these pure types. Rather, reality was destined to approach them through social change and development in late capitalist and communist societies. Similarly, the more we move back in history, and away from the proletariat, so the more Marx's rational types fail to coincide with reality. The lack of correspondence was not used, as we shall see when turning to Weber, as an explanatory device, or, as some have suggested, as a falsification of theory, but involved the need for a new and more complex theoretical concept. This concept, 'false-consciousness', was used to explain the deviations of the empirical reality from the 'pure' rational model of consciousness. However, while Marx felt the need to use it as an explanatory tool for certain periods in history, and felt its significance would diminish as the situation of the proletariat developed and its action became more rational, Marcuse relied on it more and more. He was forced to do so precisely because of the failure of active reality to correspond to predictions based on the rational aspects of the structural concept of class-situation, the State and, finally, the social system. Consequently, Marcuse had to develop and refine the concept in the face of empirical changes which did not exist in Marx's day. The 'catchwords', 'fantasies' and 'traditional myths' which sufficed for Marx's purposes were no longer sufficient when Marcuse found himself faced with the apparent irrationality of advanced industrial society.

Because Marcuse felt that the 'objective' class situations of proletariat and bourgeoisie had remained in the form familiar to Marx, he had to look at the State and its developing institutions and ideology on the one hand and whole socialization process on the other, to explain why proletarian man became so 'falsely-conscious' and irrational as to accept bourgeois values rather than the 'pure' interest of his own class situation. That is to say, Marcuse had to extend those concepts concerning a normative, constraining, social order. Nevertheless, the norms and values which Marx had placed in his objective analysis of class situations were, contradictorily, left at that level of analysis. A whole new, normative institutional and value system had to be created on top of them, so mediating action between that rationally indicated by the objective situation and that encouraged by falsely conceived internalized and repressive ends. Consequently, Marcuse finds it difficult to envisage the means by which the pure interests derived from the basic class situation will ever gain actual expression. For, to do so not only implies the destruction of a whole normative edifice but also the very motivations which people have internalized from that edifice. Like Marx, Marcuse is not arguing that actors who are fastened in such situations are not motivated by subjectively discernible ideas. Rather, such ideas do not serve or coincide with their 'pure' interests. Indeed, they serve those of another class. Such ideas and 'ideologies impose certain obligations on individuals, but these obligations are voluntarily accepted. The inner and outer penalties imposed by ideologies are expected, demanded by the individuals concerned'.[65] But these sanctions which determine the activity of the subject class are no longer the naked force and power of the State, the army or the economic conditions of Marx's day. Rather, they are the internal ones of guilt and the internalized need to conform to the norms and values of advanced capitalism. Without the practical, visible, demonstration of class conflict, how can people free themselves from this voluntary constraint?

At this point, Marcuse's analysis links with his psychological insights through which he accounts for repressive socialization and internalization of external and objectively given values and styles of action. The needs of repressed instincts have a societal content which are determined by external powers over which the individual has no control. Ultimately, this external power resides in the hands of one class. But that power has become transformed into authority now that the subject class has internalized the values of the ruling class and has thus repressed its own instincts. Those new needs which emerge are both men's actual needs and the pure interests of the ruling class. This means that the realm of the subjective is placed by Marcuse more firmly than by Marx into both the personality system, where much of it resides at the level of the unconscious, and into an ideology that legitimates the authority of the State and other areas of the institutional system, which stand 'over and against' man. Henri Lefebvre puts the point in one form when he supposed that 'the very existence of the State presupposes that men make their history without knowing how or why, implies a certain lack of consciousness, of rationality' in the organization of society.[66]

In making these adjustments in conception and theory, Marcuse has faced and explained what Marx and Engels only fearfully indicated: 'the proletariat has discredited itself terribly', 'history has proved us . . . wrong'. The ill-developed concept of false-consciousness was sufficient at that stage to accommodate these desperate comments. But a whole world is contained in the traumatic statement with which Marx concluded his devastating criticism of the Marxist-inspired Gotha Programme: 'I have spoken and saved my soul'.[67] These were the last words he intended to have published, and he died shortly afterwards.

Many questions survive his death. Firstly, we do not have to ask why Marx's predictions failed to coincide with social events as they developed, but what was at fault in the construction of concepts or their relationship in his model of society from which he made these predictions. Secondly, we must ask if there was a difference between the kind of analysis that led him to the empirical insights we have discussed, and that which led him to the creation of an abstract model explaining the whole development of society. Thirdly, are the ambiguities between Marx's concepts of control and rational action and of normative, falsely-conscious action adequately resolved in Marcuse's extension of these later concepts at the expense of the former? For, though the point remains: 'true and false consciousness, real and immediate interests [are] still . . . meaningful'.[68] Nevertheless this distinction can only be 'validated' if men come to recognize it as valid. This will only happen if men 'find their way from false to true consciousness, from their immediate to their real interest'. To do so they must need to change 'their way of life'. But 'it is precisely this need which the established society manages to repress to the degree to which it is capable of "delivering the goods" on an increasingly large scale, and using the scientific conquest of nature for the scientific conquest of man'.[69]

In a word, Marcuse's legitimate extension of Marx removes all immediate prospect of rational actions and choice. As such, the conception of a social system (comprising the three systems of personality, normative institutions, and cultural ideology) also totally fastens, determines, and controls the actor for all explanatory purposes. This may be a good thing for sociological purposes, for it marks a pronounced agreement between Marxian and non-Marxian sociology. After all, 'true consciousness' is a less acceptable notion than 'false consciousness' which, if refined and developed in the way indicated gives rise to a conception of man and society which is positively Durkheimian, let alone Parsonian, and finally excludes analysis based on action and choice.

Finally and consequently, does the new conception of the State in conjunction with a normative and ordered view of society mean that Marcuse's retention of Marx's concepts of class structure is no longer relevant even for Marcuse's explanatory purposes? Can it be replaced by the status analysis which Marcuse's structural interpretation of advanced industrial society seems to imply?

4: Max Weber

Introduction

The sociology of Max Weber takes its starting point from the activity of individual people. He insists that even such sociological concepts as 'the state' or 'association' merely 'designate certain categories of human interaction. Hence it is the task of sociology to reduce these concepts to "understandable" action, that is, without exception to the actions of participating individual men'.[1] This standpoint forms the basis of a sociology of human choice and human control.

At the same time, important aspects of Weber's sociology point in the direction of the dominant theme which we have recognized in Parsons's, Marx's and Marcuse's thought. Indeed, we have already noted (Chapter 2) how Parsons interpreted and was influenced by Weber. Our concern is to emphasize this Parsonian aspect of Weber's thought, only turning more fully to the other theme in Chapter 6.

We shall be helped in the immediate task of demonstrating the convergence in sociological thought by examining the work of two contemporary sociologists, John Rex and Ralf Dahrendorf, whose work was profoundly influenced by Weber's concern with action. But they are not uncritical and have also been influenced by Marx. So, in discussing Weber, Rex, and Dahrendorf together we must not confuse their contributions. Rex and Dahrendorf have not extended Weber's work in the way Marcuse extended Marx. They have fashioned independent approaches, and there are distinct points to make about each of them. But the overriding questions are, which of the two themes do they develop, and what kind of sociology do they finally advocate?

Social action and human nature

In discussing social action and social structure Weber did not have the same problem concerning human nature which confronted both Marx and Parsons. He had no explicit view of human nature apart from the actual action in which men engaged and which he analysed. Consequently, he felt no prior need to pose any particular form of unified or conflicting social structure which had to constrain that human nature in particular ways in order to fit a problem either of conflict or of order. This is not to say that Weber had no equivalent problem. He did, and it will emerge in our discussions.

Weber considered social action to include all 'human behaviour when and in so far as the acting individual attaches a subjective meaning to it'.[2] The key to any form of sociological analysis for Weber is the fact that the social scientist, by virtue of his own humanity, is capable of understanding the subjective meaning of the social action of the people he studies. Yet it is crucial for an understanding of Weber's analysis to realize that he operated with two quite different conceptions of 'subjective meaning'.

The one kind refers to the 'actual existing meaning in the given concrete case of a particular actor'. The other refers to the 'theoretically conceived pure type of subjective meaning attributed to the hypothetical actor or actors in a given "hypothetical type of action" by the scientist'.[3] Not concerned so much with the particular ideas, interests, or indeed actions of certain individuals, Weber felt it vital to create 'pure types' of situation, of 'pure' actors in these situations, and of the 'pure', or 'true', or 'ideal' interests which these 'pure' actors had in these situations. By this kind of hypothetical and theoretical construction, Weber argued, it became possible to build an abstract model of action. This would be subjectively understandable to the scientist. Yet actual men in actual situations would only more or less correspond with that pure model.

Weber distinguished carefully between four pure types of action. Two of these types of action were 'affectual' – where the action was driven by motives of passion, love, hate, devotion – and 'traditional' – where he felt the action was largely formed by habit or routinized practice. These types he regarded as 'irrational' forms of action.

The other two types concerned '*rational*' action. Here, action was either geared to absolute religious or ethical ends which were themselves 'irrational' (*wertrational*), or to rationally calculable ends, where the ends themselves and the means to them were all calculated and taken into account by the actor (*zweckrational*).[4]

Having analytically distinguished these four types, Weber takes an important methodological step. For it is only in the case of the last two, and, more correctly, only the latter of these, that Weber formulated his means of scientifically explaining all action at the level of abstract or 'pure' meaning. Firstly, Weber argued, the scientist should build an ideal model of the ends or goals of the actor. While this takes into account what the real person himself says, we must not expect the model to correspond fully with reality. Then, quite irrespective of how the actual person sees his situation, it is essential to construct a full, scientifically objective, picture of the situation in which the actor is placed.[5] It then becomes 'indispensable, . . . given full [scientific] knowledge'[6] of the situation, to derive how the pure actor would act in that pure situation. We do this by assuming the actor will pursue his end by using a 'purely rational course of action'.[7]

All actual social action must then be treated as 'irrational' and 'deviant' as judged against this pure type which the scientist had created and which had full subjective meaning to him.[8] The deviations of reality from the pure type would, Weber thought, help the scientist to see the causal significance of 'irrational factors' on actual conduct.

Thus, 'the construction of a purely rational course of action' based on full, objective, understanding of the situation 'serves the scientist as a type . . . which has the clear merit of understandability and lack of ambiguity. By comparison with this it is possible to understand the ways in which action is influenced by such irrational factors of all sorts, such as *affects* [that is, passion, hate, intuition], and *errors*', in failing to understand the situation as objectively as the scientist.[9]

Weber felt that only the type of actual action which he called *zweck-rational* would correspond to the scientist's model of that action. All others, affectual, traditional and even *wertrational*, would differ in varying degrees from the abstract scientist's model and the meaning contained in that model. So economic action or, say, that of a mathematician, will only infrequently require explanation in terms of irrational factors, whilst that of priest, worker or peasant will be mostly governed by irrational factors. It is within this context of abstract meaning and explanation (from the point of view of the scientist and from the point of view of the actual person) that we must examine the concepts with which Weber builds up a view of social structure. Before moving to a consideration of social structure, we must note three points.

The first of these concerns a danger implicit in Weber's methodology. Though crucially focusing on the individual, his goals and reasons for *choosing* which action to undertake, Weber's means of constructing a pure model of action in any given objective situation is highly rational. That is, there is only one way that a purely rational person may behave in that situation. Certainly real people are not like that, and Weber is the first to realize this. His whole reason for giving his explanation this emphasis is to distinguish reality from his model in order to understand those distinctions and, therefore, the real action of real people.

Here lies the danger. If the model becomes confused with the reality, or if a view of structure is developed which reinforces the rational model of actor and action, then the sociological men constructed by Weber's method may become trapped within its abstract confines. They will have no choice but to be rational, to pursue particular ends and therefore to act in pre-determined ways. We must wait to see whether Weber's sociology develops in this way.

Weber was quite certain that any form of psychology or social psychology must be excluded from and was not implied by the kind of sociological explanation which he developed. The reason for so thinking is forcefully expressed:

Action in the sense of a subjectively understandable orientation of behaviour exists only as the behaviour of one or more *individual* human beings. For other cognitive purposes, it may be convenient or necessary to consider the individual, for instance, as a collection of cells, as a complex of biological reactions, or to conceive his 'psychic' life as made up of a variety of different elements, however these may be defined. Undoubtedly such procedures yield valuable knowledge of causal relationships. But the behaviour of these elements, as expressed in such uniformities, is not subjectively understandable ... Both for sociology in the present sense, and for history, the object of cognition is the subjective meaning-complex of action.[10]

Though Freud was very much alive at the time Weber was working, he was ignored by Weber for those sociological purposes. Others have criticized Weber for the omission, and distinguished features in his work which indicated the need for psychological concepts in relation to motivation and the selection of values.

Whilst appearing neutral on the question of human nature, both John Rex and Ralf Dahrendorf, working in a post-Freudian era, seem to have accepted many psychological assumptions shared by Weber's critics. In particular, these relate to the mechanisms of socialization of the child by which he gains the values which drive him. Because Weber does not build such concerns into the starting point of his analysis he seems not only to avoid their deterministic implications but also to stress the features of individual action and control. A key consideration for any interpretation of Weber's work becomes: are these features overwhelmed or complemented by his analysis of the way social structures articulate with individual action.

Social structure

It is commonly thought, as a consequence of Weber's major studies of religions, that he was exclusively concerned with the part which ideas play in the formation of social action and structure. It is assumed that his study of the effect of religious ideas, particularly those of Luther and Calvin, on the development of that kind of rational economic activity which gave birth to capitalism, was directly contradicting the Marxist assumption that consciousness was determined by material conditions.

Nothing could be further from the truth. Even in his study of Protestantism, Weber insisted that he was interested in 'only one side of the causal chain'.[11] In order to counter what he incorrectly felt was Marx's almost exclusive bias in favour of material conditions, he pointed to the effect and importance of certain ideas and beliefs. He was only trying to show that both had causal and related effects on social structure and action.[12] He was not arguing for the determination of the one by the other. However, it is in one sense true that his writing on religion was a careful polemic against what he thought the structural relations were between material factors and ideas and, indeed, between actors generally. For the studies of religions and, say, the city, were only empirical extensions of these concepts and theoretical formulations.

To recognize what Weber meant by structure, we must first turn to his understanding of those elements which he believed to be involved in human relationships, of whatever kind.

Social relationships denote the action of 'a plurality of actors in so far as, in its meaningful content, the action of each takes account of that of the others and is oriented in these terms'.[13] This remains the case, irrespective of the content or quality of the relationship. So, the relationship may be one of 'conflict or hostility' or 'friendship or loyalty' or, say, of economic exchange.[14] The relationship only ceases when the plurality of actors no longer take one another into account in deciding on how they should behave.

Weber was confident that people do not constantly take decisions on how they should behave. They often follow courses of conduct which have already been set down before they entered the relationship. Because of this, there is a great deal of regularity and conformity in human relationships. These regularities in social interaction and relationships are what Weber calls social structure. In this sense, social structure exists where 'courses of actions . . . are repeated by the actor or (simultaneously) occur among numerous actors since the subjective meaning' of the action is the same for each of them.[15]

Such courses of action may be repeated for various reasons. They may be repeated because all those in a particular social situation are motivated by the same ends and respect the same customary or traditional means of attaining those ends. The repetition of traditional action, therefore, does not necessarily imply that it is structurally determined or that no other choice is possible. Surprisingly, when choice is apparently more fully involved the regularity may be all the greater. For, 'the more strictly rational [*zweckrational*] their action is, the more [will people] tend to react similarly to the same (or a similar situation). In this way there arise similarities, uniformities and continuities in their attitudes and actions which are often far more stable than they would be if action were orientated to a system of norms and duties which were considered binding on the members of a group'.[16]

It is more than useful to distinguish a series of concepts, pure or ideal types, by which to recognize and analyse different features of social structure. These include the concepts of class, work and market situation, and status. These help Weber to distinguish respectively between material or economic and ideal or social areas of social structure.

Two different kinds of concept, power and authority, are structural, but relate to both class and status. In this initial discussion it is only important to describe in a little more detail what is meant by authority or, as Weber also calls it, domination.

'Action, especially social action, which involves a social relationship, may be guided by the belief in the existence of a legitimate order'.[17] There are three main kinds of order which can usefully be distinguished in terms of the kind of authority which commands the respect of all these actors within that order. They are called charismatic, traditional, and rational-legal orders or authorities. It is difficult, though possible, to think of actual social relationships which are not categorized by the one or other of these pure types of order, or by a combination of them.

It is equally possible for two 'contradictory systems of order to exist at the same time' in a society.[18] There is no necessary reason why this should not be so. Indeed, it will be recalled that social relationships may involve either consensus or conflict. Conflict and change in society usually follow from the juxtaposition within one society of two or more different kinds of order. Thus 'conflict' and 'change' are two further concepts of a general kind which are important in understanding social structure. Here, the more general point must be stressed again. Authority or domination 'in the most general sense is one of the most important elements of social action . . . In most of the varieties of social action domination plays a considerable role, even where it is not obvious at first sight . . . Without exception every sphere of social action is profoundly influenced by structures of domination'.[19] In this context, we can maintain in the broader sense that authority can be produced not only by the exchange relationships of the market, but also by those of 'society'.[20]

Having discussed Weber's conception of social structure in general, it is now possible to examine the component concepts of that general view in greater detail.

The structural concept of class

Though deeply concerned with status, Weber carefully distinguished between what he calls the social order and the economic order.[21] The social order is predominantly concerned with the distribution of honour or prestige; that is, with beliefs and subjective factors. The economic order is predominantly concerned with the distribution of goods and services; that is, evidently, with economic or objective factors. In looking first of all at how Weber treats these economic factors, we must note that his writings on class as a concept were, like those of Marx, unfinished at the time of his death. They are fragmentary and, on occasions, we must guess at what might have been said had he lived.

Class situations

Property and lack of property, writes Weber, are 'the basic categories of all class situations'.[22] Irrespective of people's ideas, actions or feelings, Weber seems to feel it important to distinguish between classes on this simply measured and objective basis.

Whilst making the same fundamental division as Marx, he sees at the same time that class situations are further differentiated. This differentiation occurs 'on the one hand, according to the kind of property that is usable for returns; and, on the other hand, according to the kind of services that can be offered on the market'.[23] There can be ownership of mines, of cattle, of rural or urban land, of slaves or of shops. All these kinds of distinction 'differentiate the class situation of the properties'.

Those who own no property are similarly further differentiated according to the kind of service which they can offer, such as skilled or unskilled
labour. This means that the kind of opportunities which are open to an
individual 'in the market' form 'the decisive moment which presents a
common condition' for his fate and for that of others in common situations.
'Class situation' is in this sense 'market situation'.[24]

The confusion contained in this formulation becomes explicit in Weber's
more particular discussion of class. He feels that class situation should be
defined not just by the actor's objective or external conditions of life, his
type of property and the services which he has available, but also by the
actor's 'subjective satisfaction or frustration'.[25] The explicit intention is to
combine objective and subjective factors in conceptualizing class situation.
Unfortunately Weber does not develop, or, apparently, see the need to ask
how this might be done in any detail, or what its consequences might be
for class analysis or for individual choice. Indeed, he seems unaware of
these problems when he suggests that only 'persons who are completely
unskilled, without property and dependent on employment without
regular occupation, are in a strictly identical class "situation" '.[26] Do
itinerant, unskilled and unemployed labourers share an identical class
situation? Certainly their subjective assessment of their situation is not the
same. Are there really no other class divisions based partly on subjective
criteria within this 'objective' situation? Are objective conditions more or
less important than subjective ones? If so, in what way?

Weber used the term 'social class' for groupings of classes between
which social mobility is possible. He thought Marx's concept of the
proletariat should be an example of such a social class. However, unlike
Marx, he saw this cohesive grouping of men being slowly eroded as the
availability and need for skilled technical tasks increased in technological,
bureaucratic, societies. He saw a 'middle class' developing, which would
recruit from the working class as society modernized and as the division
of labour became ever more complex. But, if this is so, what is the point of
the original distinction by means of the external factor of property? Do
such distinctions still exist alongside occupational and market differentiation or not?

There is another confusion which Weber did not make explicit. It is not
clear in what sense a market situation is a purely objective phenomenon if
defined in terms of distinctions within property, skilled services or
occupations, when those distinctions can only be assessed and clarified
in subjective terms. Indeed, when Weber talks of occupational groups he
talks of them as 'status' and not as 'class' groups at all. We must assume
that he does this precisely because of the subjective element attached to
the distinctions between them.

The equivocation between subjective and objective criteria in discussions of economic class situation is no less marked in Weber than it was
in Marx. However, by quite explicitly introducing the subjective element

Weber, at the very least, seems to have raised a series of important questions.

Class interests

When talking about the interests which those people form who occupy a 'common class situation', Weber is again unclear in his analysis. He writes: 'The factor which creates class is unambiguously economic interest, and indeed only those interests involved in the existence of the "market".'[27] He now seems to be saying that it is *interest* which determines the class situation. That is, subjective feelings determine objective and economic or, rather, market position. If this were so, Weber would have recovered some of the ground he had lost when discussing class situation in objective-economic terms. Yet what he means by the market and market interests are entirely rational claims which are not necessarily identified with any particular group of individuals. He recognizes that 'the direction in which the individual worker . . . is likely to pursue his interests may vary widely'.[28] These variations, Weber ambiguously argues, will depend on the ability of the person, the level of communal action in his industry, the general cultural conditions, and the degree of '*transparency* of the connections between the causes and the consequences of the "class situation" '.[29]

Weber is suggesting that interests will not vary according to strict economic criteria, but according to subjective ones: say, of the kind of culture, the level of co-operative feelings, and organizational relationships. It allows him to argue that action in single class situations may take a great variety of forms, from isolated individual action to those forms of class struggle and revolution which Marx discussed, yet without these forms being in any way economically determined. If this is the case, then it is not economic criteria that determine *either* class situation *or* class interest. Weber, however, remains equivocal. For he argues that co-operative class action, based on interest, can occur *only* if the causal and external connections between classes are 'transparent'. These transparent 'connections' would seem to be exactly those objective economic causal connections to which he refers in the formation of class situations.

In this light, Weber insists that only if the class situation is clearly seen as either resultant from the distribution of property or 'the structure of the economic order', then its true or objective cause may force people to rise against that class structure by forming a 'rational association'.[30] Only if workers understand (from the scientist's point of view) that 'true' situation can they organize rationally to overcome that situation. On such occasions they are presumably responding to the same rationally derivable interests attached to that situation that the objective scientist can discern. There is real and consistent confusion in this argument. If action does not take into account the 'real' class situation, then it is 'irrational' and 'deviant' from the pure model of interest and action. If the actor does see the 'true' class situation in economic terms, then he may respond by acting rationally in accord with the 'true' interest of that situation. Weber is at pains to show that Marx's conception of the workers as a class involved an over-simplification of the divisions of class situations within it (which may make it impossible to speak of all the workers as a class). Nevertheless, he too falls back into precisely this position by citing as an example of rational class action the workers' revolt. [31]

Weber has not escaped the position of arguing two separate points, both of which relate to his method of explanation. First, he suggests that the class situation is objective, and that such a situation has an objectively discernible rational interest, irrespective of the subjective beliefs of the people in that situation. This is his scientist's pure model. But, secondly, the subjectivity of actual people is also important to him. Action based on this subjectivity creates groups within these 'objective' classes, and other interests are developed. However, these interests and action based on them must be seen as 'deviant' and 'irrational' when measured against the scientist's 'pure' model.

This problem becomes even more clear when we see that Weber goes to great lengths to entirely separate most subjective factors from class and class position. To do so he uses the concept of 'status'.

The structural concept of 'status'
In contrast to the purely economically determined class situation, Weber wishes to 'designate as status situation every typical component of the life fate of men that is determined by a specific, positive or negative, social estimation of honour'. [32]

Status situations are determined in terms of the subjective feelings which men have concerning their own and other people's position in society. These subjective feelings are related to 'positive and negative' feelings or values by which the status of actors is to be judged. This allows Weber to discuss status stratification in terms of the social hierarchies which are implied by this estimation of honour.

This excludes a number of groups that could be classified in terms of different kinds of ideas that do not happen to suggest a social hierarchy of the sort that Weber pictured. Secondly, he runs into a major problem when he suggests that occupations are status groups. [33] This, perhaps, partly explains why he feels that the different categories of classes and status groups may in reality frequently overlap. [34]

Light is cast on this point by a third consideration. The status situation which people occupy is determined by the subjective expectations and actions of other actors. But the subjective interest of the person who occupies that status situation is to conform to, or live up to, these expectations of other people. In a word, his activity or role in that situation is determined by the external situation itself. Despite the apparent clarity and unquestionable consistency of use of the term 'status situation', there is a hidden ambiguity which again relates to the objective-subjective dilemma we found in discussing 'class'. If the status situation is externally defined and determined, albeit by the subjective attitudes of other people, then occupancy of that position is thought to carry with it an interest which, though subjectively felt and recognized by the occupant, is equally objectively discernible. That is, we can discover it by asking others apart from the occupant, who then has no other way to act in that situation, and no other interest to assume.

It is difficult to see what the difference might be between Weber's subtle and manifold distinctions between classes, offering their various services on the market, and the way such groups often organize in terms of occupations, defined by status, so as to ensure the best economic and social consequences in their work and status situations. Indeed, Weber goes on to argue that 'stratification by status goes hand in hand with a monopoliz-ation of ideal and *material* goods and opportunities'.[35]

In fact we know this is the way occupational groups often do react, thus in part *forming* their own situation, for the consequence of this action is to affect the terms and conditions for the sale of their services on the market. Weber does not recognize this explicitly. The reason lies partly in the purely rational and independent way in which he sees the market operating. It is this artificial and contradictory view which seems to account for much of his highly formal distinction between class and status. But, when we look more closely at his work, we see that his formal use of the distinction often dissolves, and he himself admits that this is so.

The distinction would seem to be maintained only by a focus on entirely objective, rationally deduced, action in class situations, and by subjective, rational and non-rational, action in status situations. However, Weber insists that 'class situations only emerge on the basis of communalization', and that communal action *brings forth* class situation.[36] This completely contradicts his main and formal distinction between 'class situation', which he sees as being objectively determined prior to any interest which may be rationally deduced from it, and 'status situations', which *are* the subjective estimations and actions of these actors who, thereby, form their status situation. If both class and status situations are formed only by virtue of the action of men in relations with other men, then there can be no prior, objectively independent analysis of class situation. If this were so, the distinction between class and status might seem entirely arbitrary, related only to Weber's highly abstract and artificially rational means of explanation and to his critical acceptance of Marx's own formulation of the concept of class.

Further light is shed on this confusion when Weber argues that the convergence between class and status occurs in particular in periods of economic and technological change, which 'threatens stratification by status and pushes the class situation into the foreground'.[37] Is status (that is, subjective consciousness) determined in the final analysis by objective class situations? When there is identity of class and status position, and of interests related to them, there seems to be a complete fusion of subjective feelings and activity in the two otherwise distinct categories. Yet, if the method of analysis involving subjective factors is applicable to both status and class in periods of identity, should not class analysis equally retain the subjective factor in periods of non-identity? Weber does not draw this conclusion although, at the same time, he operates with an entirely subjective approach to class interests and, indeed, to class formation *following* communal, subjective, action. The problems raised by these confusions are manifold. But no immediate solution to these problems is contained in Weber's work. So, also, the final place of the individual and choice in Weber's work has been obscured rather than made distinct.

Power and authority: Weber's ideal types as a model of society
We must now discuss the concepts of party, bureaucracy, authority and power within the context of Weber's concepts of class and status and his sociological view of modern industrial societies. We are primarily concerned with the extent to which these ideal types do or do not mesh together, thus potentially forming an overall model of a 'social system'. If we find they do so, then the correctness of Parsons' interpretation of Weber, and Weber's convergence with Marx and Parsons will have been demonstrated.

Though the author of a work is not necessarily the best interpreter of the significance of that work, it is only right to start with Weber's own view of the possibility of forming such models.

Weber was in fact quite convinced of the 'futility of the idea . . . that it could be the goal of the cultural sciences, no matter how distant, to construct a closed system of concepts which can encompass and classify reality in some definite manner and from which it can be deduced again'.[38] Here, Weber's concern with the actor and subjective meaning is reasserted. But was Weber correct, and did he stand by his opinion in his own work?

Weber used his concepts of class and status as analytical tools in the study of both ancient and modern society. Though the formal nature of ideal types remained the same, he found that the relations between them were constantly changing. With copious examples, he showed that this was also the case in his studies of advanced industrial society. But we must look at both the concepts and any regularity in their relations within this qualifying context.

We must first of all recall that 'the factor that creates "class" is unambiguously economic interest and, indeed, only those interests involved in the existence of the market'.[39] Basing his arguments on the concepts of class situation and class interest, Weber goes on to discuss the generation of class struggle, relating it to both facilities for organization and a recognition and revelation of the objective class situation.[40] He then combines class associations and status groups which, of course, express a specific style of life and interweave with one another.[41]

On the one hand, the pure market, which creates class, is impersonal, for rational interests dominate it. On the other hand, status works in the opposite direction. Stratification by status considers styles of life, prestige and honour.[42] The one therefore threatens the other's existence, unless we look at them from a slightly different point of view. 'With some over-simplification, one might . . . say that classes are stratified according to their relations to the production and acquisition of goods; whereas status groups are stratified according to the principles of their consumption of goods as represented in their styles of life.'[43]

'As to the general economic conditions making for the predominance of stratification by status', the following can be asserted: 'When the bases of the acquisition and distribution of goods are relatively stable, stratification by status is favoured. Every technological repercussion and economic transformation threatens stratification by status and pushes class situation into the foreground . . . And every slowing down of the change in economic stratification leads, in due course, to the growth of status structures and makes for a resuscitation of the important role of social honour'.[44]

Under capitalism, the market is at first hindered, because the State militates against its full, rational operation by favouring one set of related class and status groups.[45] Class conflict is severe. Though status groups may align themselves with different classes in order to extend their situation by political means, the status structure is, ultimately, preserved in society by the all-pervasive influence of authority.

In advancing capitalist societies, this authority takes a particular form. It relates to class as well as status and, at another level, defines the structure of the political parties which represent class and status interests.

Weber is forced to consider 'political parties', which may in fact represent the interests of either or both classes and status groups, in this light.[46] He suggests that the 'structure of parties differs in a basic way according to the kind of social action which they struggle to influence'. They differ, that is, according to 'whether or not the community is stratified by status or class', or by a combination of the two. But 'above all else, they vary according to the structure of domination'[47] which exists in the society.

Weber, therefore, discusses the different forms of domination before returning to discuss the structure of parties. We must do the same before gaining a more complete understanding of Weber's views of industrial society.

Perhaps the first and most important point concerning domination is to recognize that it transforms amorphous and intermittent social action into permanent associations. That is to say, domination creates, encourages and cements the relationships which men have with one another. In a word, it shapes and patterns their action just as surely as do the common ends which they have and to which the structure of authority is related. The most significant association for our purposes is the modern State and its bureaucratic apparatus. Before discussing this, we must first recognize that there are two quite distinct ideal types of domination. The first of these may be called power.

Power is defined by Weber as the 'probability that one actor within a social relationship will be in a position to carry out his own will despite resistance, regardless of the basis on which this probability rests'.[48]

The second form of domination with which Weber is primarily concerned is domination by *authority*. This form of domination is defined as 'the probability that a command with a given specific content will be obeyed by a given group of persons'.[49] Having defined authority, and basing his argument on his historical knowledge, Weber distinguishes three key ideal types of domination by authority.

The first of these types is 'rational authority'. It rests 'on a belief in the legality of enacted rules and the right of those elevated to authority under such rules to issue commands'.

The second type is 'traditional authority'. It rests 'on an established belief in the sanctity of immemorial traditions and the legitimacy of those exercising authority under them'.

The third, but not least, type is 'charismatic authority'. It rests 'on devotion to the exceptional sanctity, heroism or exemplary character of an individual person, and of the normative patterns or order revealed or ordained by him'.[50]

For the purpose of our discussions of advanced society, we are more concerned with the first of these types, for Weber measures and contrasts the others in terms of it. Further, this type is almost the defining feature of modern society, and is crucially involved in any understanding of the State apparatus.

Weber spends a great deal of energy in elaborating his definition. Once again he gives copious examples.[51] Though these are mainly drawn from his native Germany, they are also drawn widely from Europe and America.

Weber considers the causal factors leading to the development of the institutional form of 'rational legal authority': bureaucracy. He takes into account the way bureaucracy develops through its own logic and from external economic and political determinants. He also considers what the economic consequences of rational administrative structures are.

In trying to answer these questions, he insists that one must 'keep one's eye on the fluidity and the overlapping of all these ideal types'. They are 'after all . . . to be considered merely border cases which are of special and indispensable analytic value and bracket historical reality which almost always appears in mixed forms'. However, it can in general be asserted that 'bureaucratic structure is everywhere a late product of historical development'. Since it has a rational 'character, with rules, means-ends calculus, and matter-of-factness predominating, its rise and expansion has everywhere had "revolutionary" results'. It has consequently 'destroyed structures of domination which were not rational'.[52] Examples of charismatic and traditional authority do co-exist in modern society with rational legal authority, and any full explanation of an actual society would have to take all three types into account. However, Weber concentrates on the rational legal form. Having examined the factors which lead to its development, he goes on to specify the unintended repercussions of its development throughout the form and structure of modern society. He finds that it is spreading into most areas of social and economic life. In order to understand the extent of its penetration, we must first recognize that the 'modern state' is the most significant rational, bureaucratic, organization in any one society.

Weber argues that rational legal authority is established 'with a claim to obedience at least on the part of the members of the corporate group' which issues those rational commands. But this control is typically 'extended to include all persons within the sphere of authority or power in question'.[53] In a society this applies to all 'who stand in certain social relationships or carry out forms of social action which in the order governing the corporate group have been declared to be relevant'.[54] It is in this context, and with these assumptions, that Weber regards the State as that rational grouping of individuals which successfully upholds 'a claim to the monopoly of the legitimate use of physical force (and authority) in the enforcement of its order' for those who constitute the society.[55]

Weber clearly feels that in its 'pure' form and as rationally organized, the State itself is legitimated in the eyes of those who come under its sphere of command; that is, all those who constitute the society which the State governs. In this sense, not only are the dominant rational values of those who constitute the State legitimate in the eyes of all members of society, but they are legitimately encapsulated in rational norms which govern action in organized interaction situations. By virtue of this legitimacy in the eyes of those in society, the State and its officials are enabled to use force. Force involves the second kind of domination, *power*, under which people are forced to act against their inclinations.

The political community, therefore, engages in action which includes 'coercion through jeopardy and destruction of life and freedom of movement . . . The individual is expected ultimately to face death in the group interest'.[56] This standpoint enables Weber to define a 'political community': 'The term . . . shall apply to a community whose social action is aimed at subordinating to orderly domination by the participants or "territory" and the conduct of the persons within it, through the readiness to resort to physical force, including normally force of arms'.[57]

In a sense, Weber finds the western medieval city to be made up of an oath-bound community of armed men. As such it was a precursor of the modern State. He studied the city, its development and different forms in great empirical detail, in order to shed further light on the development and origin of the rational legal state with its huge bureaucratic, central, and local civil services.[58] He finds that in a modern society, 'the basic functions of the "state" are: the enactment of law . . . the protection of personal safety and public order . . . the protection of vested rights . . . the cultivation of . . . educational, social-welfare, and other cultural interests . . . and, last but not least, that attack . . .' on those who deviate to which we have just referred.[59]

It is crucial to recognize that the state and bureaucratic organization encourages, in those spheres which it affects and promotes, a rationalist 'way of life . . . The bureaucratization of all domination very strongly furthers the development of "rational matter-of-factness" and the personality type of the professional expert', whether in government, medicine, or, say, education.[60]

This has far-reaching consequences. For example the educational institutions of modern Europe are 'dominated and influenced by the need for the kind of "education" which is bred by the system of specialized examinations or tests of expertise . . . increasingly indispensable for modern bureaucracies'.[61] Rational, legal organization, therefore, feeds on itself and expands as a consequence of its activities into most spheres of social life. As a further consequence, it develops a status hierarchy which affects and limits the class struggles of earlier periods in the history of modern society. However, because it encourages the rational organization of the market and introduces technological changes, it also may create new class and status conflicts.

This last point is a digression, for we must stress that Weber's ideal type of rationality and his empirical findings lead him to suppose that 'the whole pattern of everyday life is cut to fit this framework' of bureaucratic organization. Indeed, it even 'makes no difference whether the economic system is organized on a capitalistic or a socialistic basis'. In fact the structural organization of socialist societies is even more efficient and rationally perfect than is the capitalist system. For, the key 'question is always who controls the existing bureaucratic machinery [for] such control is possible only in a very limited degree to persons who are not technical specialists'.[62]

A political struggle for the control of the State bureaucracy is minimized in socialism. The fluctuating extent of that struggle in different stages of capitalism is based on competing status, class and party interest. This struggle and competition limits the power of the State. Unlike socialism, 'social democracy is opposed to the rule of bureaucracy in spite and because of its unavoidable, yet unintended promotion of bureaucratization'. The point to recognize is that 'under certain conditions, democracy creates palpable breaks in the bureaucratic pattern and impediments to bureaucratic organizations. Hence, one must in every individual historical case analyse in which of the special directions bureaucratization has developed.

For these reasons, it is also extremely important to note that it remains an 'open question whether the *power* of bureaucracy is increasing in the modern states in which it is spreading'.[63] The fact that it is indispensable does not mean it is all-powerful any more than the fact that slaves were indispensable, to their masters, led the slaves to a position of mastery.

At this stage, Weber returns to a study of political parties and the way they influence and are influenced by the State. We need not discuss this in detail. But it is pertinent to our argument that Weber only criticized his friend Robert Michels for reifying an 'ideal type' of modern political party organization into an 'iron law'.[64] Political parties which seek to control the State bureaucracy merely tend to come to reflect its organization in their own ranks. Similarly, just as social democratic parties of right and left demand education for all in order to overthrow aristocratic status, so they also fear it, as it will create a new privileged status-hierarchy which is based on merit and which will come to dispute their power. Such a hierarchy would merely extend the influence of bureaucracy and the power of the State.[65]

These studies lead Weber to an intense interest in revolution and change. No one with his encyclopaedic historical knowledge and sensitivity could have excluded such a concern from his work. All three types of domination figure importantly in this connection. Charismatic and rational legal authority are dynamic, revolutionary forces. Traditional authority is one means by which both – in particular, charismatic revolution – may be transformed or routinized into the conformity of the day. We should understand these points in a little detail by first of all comparing and noting the difference between charismatic and rational authority as forces for revolution.

The 'revolutionary force of "reason"' works from *without*: by *altering the situations* of life and hence its problems, finally in this way changing men's attitudes towards them'.[66] This argument can be reinforced by putting it a little differently. Thus, we can see that bureaucratic rationalization 'revolutionizes with *technical means* . . . from without'. It *first* changes the material and social orders and *through* them the people, by changing the *conditions* of *adaptation* . . .[67]

On the contrary, 'charismatic' belief revolutionizes man from *within* and shapes material and social conditions according to its *revolutionary will*. It is, of course, the case that 'in traditionalistic periods, charisma is *the* great revolutionary force'. It may 'effect a subjective or *internal* reorientation torn out of suffering, conflicts or enthusiasm'. It creates new attitudes which can create new situations.[68] Yet, it is rational authority which vitally helps to create modern society. Unlike charisma, however, the 'bureaucratic order merely replaces the belief in the sanctity of traditional norms by compliance with rationally determined rules and by the knowledge that these rules can be superseded by others, if one has the necessary power, and hence are not sacred'. Different forms of bureaucratic order can replace one another as, in practice, socialism may replace capitalism. In this sense, the change to rationality leads to further developments within the way rationality is institutionalized.

'But charisma, in its most potent forms, disrupts rational rules as well as tradition altogether and overturns all notions of sanctity. Instead of reverence for customs that are ancient and hence sacred' or rational and hence obligatory, 'it enforces the inner subjection to the unprecedented and absolutely unique and, therefore, divine – in this purely empirical and value free sense, charisma is indeed the specifically creative revolutionary force of history'.[69] It is the form of authority which most directly concerns individual action and choice: 'It has been written . . . but I say unto you . . .'

The style of analysis implied by charismatic authority indeed offers scope for the development of new forms of activity, the creation of new situations and the means by which men may control aspects of their destiny. It is partly because of these qualities that the concept is also a concept of revolution and change.

These features of the concept most exactly link with Weber's original definition of social action as individual and meaningful, suggesting that any explanation of complex situations and groupings must ultimately depend on a reduction to the separate individuals involved and not on group or societal structures. It is, perhaps, precisely for this reason that many sociologists regard the concept of charisma as the least disciplined and least sociological of Weber's concepts, so ignoring the method of analysis on which it is founded.

Weber used the concept liberally, not only to explain the action of prophets and the prophecy of the Old Testament, but also the part which Calvin and Luther played in creating and developing the Protestant ethic and so, also, the spirit of capitalism. Though applied to many historical figures, the number of people in any one society bestowed with such 'grace' were few. Most did not possess it. They either followed, because of their relation with the charismatic leader or were to be explained in terms of their mutual involvement in relations of traditional authority, where choice and control were minimized and action was routinized.

As we have seen, relations of rational legal authority, like those of charisma, were themselves revolutionary. But they replaced traditional and charismatic authority alike with structures of domination in which no person could exercise choice and which slowly influenced all areas of society.

At this point, we must artificially freeze Weber's argument in order to comment further on a point which we raised at the beginning of this chapter. We note that Weber had no overt view of fundamental human nature and so needed no particular view of social structure. Nor, as a consequence, was it logically necessary at this level of analysis for him to develop the idea of the infinite manipulatability of man by such a structure or through a socialization process.

Despite this we have noted, at the abstract conceptual level, the very real emergence of a particular view of man in industrial society. Unlike the charismatic leader, this man has rationally ordered and rational ends which were legitimized by the State. He comprehends with the fullness and objectivity of the scientist the class, status, party power and authority situation which he occupies. Within these two contexts, of ends and situation, he rationally adjusts the course of his action. This action is in this sense determined, for there is only one course which can be followed in strictly normative, rational, terms. This whole emphasis is reinforced by the ideal type of State and bureaucratic organization and rational domination from which there is no individual escape. Abstract man, though not concrete man, is in this sense fully determined in the course of action which he must follow. Concrete man 'deviates' from this course only as a consequence of 'irrationality', 'error' and 'psychological effects', and only so far as he and the structures around him do not coincide with the ideal type of rationality. Such 'deviations' are an intentional feature of Weber's method of explanation and he has no need to suggest further concepts, such as false-consciousness, by which to explain them in structural terms.

We can now, perhaps, see how Weber's discussion of the development of the 'pure' type of rationality spreads into music, education, industrial as well as political and state bureaucracies, and relates to an abstract vision of a 'social system' of complex interactivity in society. It is with this interrelated structure of different rationally ordered situations that the ideal action of the rational actor and Weber's entire methodology, which is based on that concept, *zweckrational*, links and finds its expression. But this is true only for industrial society.

These elements in Weber's work strongly indicate the *possibility* of analyzing the whole of industrial society in terms of an abstract model. Such a model would be built up of integrated ideal-type concepts by which common ends are institutionalized and legitimized at the level of the common 'state' as well as in other normatively rational institutions, encouraging, motivating and determining the rational types of action of the actor. Such a model is, indeed, most aptly described as a 'social system', and the style of analysis ensures that the component conceptual parts are defined as interdependent.

A combination of Weber's rational methodology, the structural concepts by which he analyses contemporary society and the type of individual who fits that society, therefore, pushes him *almost* to the position of methodological collectivism when discussing complex modern societies.

It is decisive, for those who misinterpret Weber, that at exactly this point he gestures in the direction of psychology. In discussing the origin of the goals which drive men to act, he argues that ideas have 'essentially the same psychological roots whether they are religious, artistic, ethical, scientific or whatever else; this also applies to ideas about political and social organization'. In this sense, 'the imagination of a mathematician is 'intuition' in the same sense as is that of the prophet'. The 'decisive difference' between two such men 'and this is important for understanding the meaning of "rationalism" – is not inherent in the *creator* of ideas . . . or of his inner experience; rather, the difference is noted in the manner in which the ruled and led experience and internalize these "ideas".'[70]

This encourages the implication that Weber had a view, a position, with regard to human nature. But that position referred only to man in a particular kind of society. In modern societies, that nature was rational, conformist and dispassionate, and the action which it motivated was determined in the way that the steps taken in the solution of a geometric equation are determined. In an objective class or status position, given a particular value or goal, and the intervention of a constraining situational or normative network of relationships, there is only one course of action which can be pursued. In one sense, sociological man is free to choose his course of action. But there is only one choice, only one path. Real men may well choose differently. But they are then in error, or acting on an irrational understanding of their situation and of their true goal. We noted how very close Weber came to alleging this in connection with class association following from class situation and interests. For while he asserted that men could not be mistaken about their interests, he insisted that association and community could only follow once the 'true' situation had been 'transparently' revealed. This ambiguity is now explained. It is due to the tension between different concerns in Weber's sociology, that he was unable to give any precise or ambiguous definition of class, or to distinguish it exactly from status. He did not escape from his formulation of class action precisely because he had both a rational assumption about sociological man in advanced society and an ambiguously objective definition of class and status situation. Only a combination of the two concepts could make class association possible in any other circumstances but those in which the rational actor oriented his action in terms of a full and rational understanding of his objective situation.

Weber's own position of 'methodological individualism' is not ensured by his own assertions that he is using it. But, to illustrate the force of these assertions, it is fitting to push into motion that analysis which we momentarily froze in order to make the preceding comments.

In doing so, it is helpful first to recognize Weber's own moral and political position, which on occasions has been ridiculed by suggestions that he approved the uneven movement towards a rational society which he analysed and which we have discussed. Though as a person Weber feared such developments in capitalism, their potential for socialist states haunted him. The concept of rational, central planning in the Socialist State (where contending parties could not hinder the spread of bureaucracy) seemed to be raised as the ultimate rational value in terms of which the whole society would be dominated and organized and from which the individual had no escape or margin of choice.

Marcuse is very critical of Weber's sociology. But he gestures in the direction of Weber's concern with rational legal authority when he argues that 'it is difficult to see *reason* at all in the ever more solid "shell of bondage" ', which Weber constructs for socialism and capitalism alike. 'Or is there perhaps already in Max Weber's concept of reason the irony that understands and disavows? Does he by any chance mean to say: And this you call "reason"?'[71]

This is an incredible understatement. Weber was never, even for a moment, happy with what he felt was an actual, empirical, movement in modern societies towards his pure formulation. He felt it was 'horrible to think that the world could one day be filled with nothing but little cogs, little men clinging to little jobs and striving towards bigger ones . . . It is as if . . . we were deliberately to become men who need "order" and nothing but order, who became nervous and cowardly if for one moment this order wavers, and helpless if they are torn away from their total incorporation in it'.[72] Weber felt with a liberal and humane terror that modern reality was steadily approaching towards his pure type of 'social system' model.

He saw little with which to oppose 'this machine . . . this parcelling out of the soul'.[73] So, '"summer's bloom" does not lie ahead of us, but rather a polar night of icy darkness and hardness'.[74]

We must recall not only that Weber set himself at a moral distance from these tendencies, but also that he himself stoically refused to make that final link between his pure structures of state bureaucracy, rational legal authority, party, class and rational action. He did not in fact combine them in any integrated pure-type concept of a 'social system'. Even in his analysis of modern societies, Weber was several steps removed from that position. This shows up dramatically in his empirical work. It was not simply on theoretical grounds that 'the idea that the whole of concrete historical reality can be exhausted in the conceptual scheme' was as far from his thoughts 'as anything could be'.[75] His detailed historical interpretations by means of his ideal types (say, those involving the relationship between the Protestant ethic and the developing spirit of capitalism) invariably overwhelmed the kind of study we might have expected had we first concentrated on his more precise and rational methodological and theoretically ideal statements.

Secondly, and despite this, Weber was certain on methodological grounds that his models of different types of actor and different aspects of social structure could not adequately explain the great wealth of empirical diversity solely in terms of the irrational deviation from those models of that diversity. There was no logical way in which these types necessarily had to relate to one another, and there was no way of deducing empirical reality from them.

Thirdly, and crucially, major concepts in his theoretical scheme ensured that any temporary empirical juxtaposition of them would also be empirically unstable. The alignment of them would change, and they would change in quite unpredictable ways despite his bias towards rationality. Not only are class and status examples of such concepts, but so also is one of his types of authority.

Charismatic authority would be an obvious response to and hope for the kind of rational society which Weber saw developing. Of all his concepts, it is the one which most vitally embodies the notion of individual creativity. In one sense it was true that 'it is the fate of charisma whenever it comes into the permanent institutions of a community, to give way to powers of tradition and of rational socialization. This waning of charisma generally indicates the diminishing importance of individual action. And of all those powers that lessen the importance of individual action, the most inevitable is *rational discipline*'.[76]

But, equally, the increasing power of the modern State, and the spread of rational authority into every domain of social life, is not completely inevitable. People may return to traditional religions in one sphere of their lives in order to escape from the routine of work. Politicians and, say, academics may look for charismatic solutions to the encroaching impersonality of their society. Yet, 'if one tries intellectually to construct new religions without a new and genuine prophecy, then, in an inner sense, only monstrosities will result. And academic prophecy, finally, will create only fanatical sects but never a genuine community'.[77]

It was precisely such prophecy which led Sorel to the 'myth', Michels to Mussolini, and many academics to support Hitler or Stalin. But, in the end, Weber freely admitted he had no solution. This was precisely because he had no theoretical solution. The future was open, but the struggles to oppose rational, technocratic tendencies would have to be almost superhuman if they were to succeed. Nevertheless the point remained. Even the State could only be explained by reduction to the activity of 'participating individuals'. And the key question was not how does the State or social system control man, but 'who controls' the State.

We have found two themes, one explicit, one implicit, in Weber's work and we have concentrated on that implicit theme which led to the control of man by networks of domination. Whilst noting that Weber did not make the final link, for example, by refusing to develop a concept of the 'social system', we recognized his analysis came closest to that point in relation to exactly those modern industrial societies with which Parsons and other interpreters have been concerned. It is little wonder that they have fastened onto this emergent theme in Weber's work, with which they were predisposed to agree, and ignored or criticized as non-sociological the other theme which seemed less significant to them.

Introducing John Rex and Ralf Dahrendorf

It has already been stated that there are no Weberians in the same sense that there are Marxists or Parsonians. Two contemporary sociologists, John Rex and Ralf Dahrendorf, have been chosen for discussion at this stage, partly because they have been as much influenced by Marx as by Weber. Indeed, they have qualified their Weberian standpoint in the light of their sociological understanding of, and political sympathy with, Marx and a Marxian view of conflict. But, just as they are not Weberians, so also they are not Marxists. Rather, they are usually thought of as 'conflict theoreticians'. This certainly distinguishes them from Parsons and the functionalists to whom they are bitterly opposed. Indeed, their sociology was in some respects developed as a contribution to a critical, non-Marxist but conflict-oriented alternative to the contemporary domination of functionalism in the world of sociology. They felt that they, along with such contemporaries as Herbert Marcuse and C. Wright Mills, could prove that the claim of Kingsley Davis – that functionalism *was* sociology – had no foundation. After interpreting their work we must ask whether it achieves this end.

Social structure : Rex

John Rex's central concern is with social conflict. Against Parsons, he argues that this concern need not 'take us back to Hobbes' war of all against all'. Rather, it 'assumes the existence of a very large measure of social co-operation on each side of the conflict situation taken separately'.[78] Analysis of structure within each of the conflict groups is identical, and crucially involves *cohesion*.

Person or Group A is integrated with B, and C with D, each instance involving a normative, patterned, set of expectations ordered in terms of a common culture or set of ends. Rex develops this view of order, but places the possibility of conflict between these groups. So, A and B may clash with B and C about the cultural ends which they wish to achieve. Rex, therefore, hopes that his analysis 'not only explains structure and process within a closed system, but . . . also explains the changes from one system to another'.[79] Rex is, in effect, working with two models of social inter-action. It is important to see how these two models, the one of order and the other of conflict, differ.

The starting point for the model of order is the notion of the unit act, as employed by the early Parsons and as derived from Weber's conception of meaningful, but rational, action. The actor intentionally and rationally attempts to achieve particular relationships and outcomes to his action. In a word, he tries to control his action. Other actors are taken into account to this end. One possibility is that A and B will have mutual expectancies and ends. But, for Rex, a 'sociological explanation of the behaviour of [these] other persons consists in showing that it has a place in terms of the model of A's unit act.[80] That is, the relevant feature for the scientist is 'the role which their behaviour plays in terms of the scheme of action of A, and from which the model starts'.[81] Rex then extends the model to take into account other people, C, D, E and so on, whose conduct and actions are important as a means to A's end. The relationships so established on the initial complementarity of A and B's actions then helps to explain the development of the 'various norms, controls and sanctions which induce C, D and E to behave' in the required ways.[82]

From this initial scheme, Rex feels that he can explain any system of economic allocation, of power distribution, of ultimate values, of religious beliefs and rituals, which support in their respective ways that pattern of interaction which it established.[83] This is an ordered system of interaction.

In systems of interaction where B does not act as A would like him to, Rex argues that the explanation of conflict in the systems of economic allocation, of power, of ultimate values and religious beliefs, is sufficient when it is related to the clash between A and B.

The major difference, Rex feels, between his models of order and conflict and that of Parsons lies in their relation to the unit act of A, and B's reaction to it. This empirical reference to one actor introduces the criterion of falsifiability. It is not the system, but the individual, or group, in whose terms interaction is explained. Rex stresses this point. Like Weber, he insists that this reference to the individual and his aims does not involve a resort to psychological explanation. But, at the same time, he rejects the organic or functional approach, 'which treated social systems as wholes, apart from the motivation of individuals'.[84] There is no psychological determination in this. Rather, action is explained for A in terms of rationality. But, for B, C, D and so on, it is 'determined by the pattern' of A's needs and expectations.[85] This introduces a major problem.

If we have to regard the whole system of interaction as functional only in so far as it is related to the aims and actions of A, then the whole system has to be related deliberately and directly to A's needs. This ignores the factor of unintended consequences. The whole system is intentionally maintained in terms of the ends and actions of one hypothetical individual. This also assumes that A's action is quite rationally geared to these ends. It is as if the ordered 'system' of interaction is functionally related around a set of values in terms of which power, facilities, religious ideas, are developed. But instead of these being the values of the 'system', they are the values of one hypothetical individual, who, as it turns out, may symbolize a class. Whilst in this very particular sense A may not be determined, those with whom he relates are. For it is as if they were part of a system of interaction over which they have no control. In so far as 'A' does not exist in reality, the combination of his hypothetical rationality and the determinism of B, C and D, creates the idea of the 'social system'. Contrary to Rex's assertion, this is by no means unlike Parsons' later models of action and 'social system'.

Rex was acutely aware of the richness and variety of values and ways of acting which were a lively feature of Weber's work. In trying to retain this dimension, he feels his own approach is further differentiated from that of 'system' analysis. Yet we can hardly detect this ambivalent tension between the Weberian and 'systems' approaches in Rex's analysis of order. Indeed, he argues that the action of the one individual 'may be integrated with that of another throughout the cultural patterning' of the elements of action. He even suggests that whether 'action is rational or non-rational, the ends which the individual seeks may be set for him by his cultural conditioning'.[86] We will find that Rex's departure from Weber's basic account of social integration becomes more pronounced in his later work.

Rex's account of conflict, however, remains Weberian. 'What we want,' he argues, 'is a theory which finds a place for both normatively oriented action and action which can be understood as governed by something like scientific knowledge of the relations between means and ends . . . If there is a conflict of ends, the behaviour of actors towards one another may not be determined by shared norms but by the success which each has in compelling the other to act in accordance with his interest. Power then becomes a crucial variable in the study of social system'.[87]

Not all interests are basically integrated through any overall normative structure or by the values of 'the system'. They are only integrated within each of the competing groups. It is only between these groups that explanatory analysis must use the concept of 'power' and the idea of 'rational logic', using the assumption of 'the scientists' knowledge' for the actor.

How Rex resolves the tension between the two themes will be of crucial importance, especially when he turns to the concept of class and its relation to his conflict model of society.

Social structure: Dahrendorf

Dahrendorf works with two models, or sets of assumptions, by which he tries to analyse social structures. The one involves the theory of integration 'as displayed by the work of Parsons and other structural functionalists'.[88] Dahrendorf feels that, say, the East German rising of June 1953 would not be open to such analysis. For such instances of conflict, a different set of tenets become necessary. Collectively he calls these the 'coercion theory of society'.[89]

Dahrendorf has drawn the outlines of two approaches, the one originating in Parsons' work, the other in that of Marx, which he feels to be irreconcilable polar opposites. We are not interested here in the extent to which each approach differs from its parent school of thought. Rather, we must note that Dahrendorf feels them to be mutually incompatible. He feels that a theory or model which combines order and change has not yet been put forward. 'So far as I can see', he maintains, 'there is no such general model; as to its possibility, I have to reserve judgment'.[90]

We will not be in a position to comment on the value of these two sets of structures until we have discussed other features of Dahrendorf's work which are specifically influenced by Weber.

Class structure: Rex

To understand Rex's view of class, we must see how he views the development of class situations and class aims in the context of his understanding of social conflict.

Conflict develops because a 'number of separate individuals [find] themselves in similar conflict situations and thus develop like interests'.[91] The explanation of class action, however, lies 'in relating' the 'behaviour, *not* to the *like interests* of the members, but to the *group's aims* or interests' which develop on a *conscious* level in relation to the political situation. These 'aims' may relate to 'interests', but discrepancy is quite possible.[92]

We seem to be faced with the problem of objective class situations whose linked rational interests may or may not be in accord with those interests which actual people develop. Weber insists that though there can be incorrect definition of situations, there cannot be 'incorrect' aims. For the subjective intentions of a person are always significant for his action. Rex takes note of this distinction between Marx and Weber and finds common ground. He insists that Marx does 'recognize that new aims are introduced into a situation when individuals not only pursue their like interests but also engage in "political struggle". It would therefore seem entirely consistent with the Marxist theory for us to look very closely at the possible class situations, and at the development of class aims in the course of political struggle'.[93] It is not certain at this stage what Rex means. It could be one of two things.

In the course of development a group may develop aims which do not accord with their 'true interests'. They will none the less base their actions on what they feel. This action would then help to create and impose a new class situation. This in turn will lead to fresh aims developing in terms of the new situation. To pursue this analysis could lead to the redundancy of true and false class interests as conceptual tools.

On the other hand, Rex may be recognizing the actual class aims and each succeeding situation as stages en route to the final realization of the 'true interests'. In any intermediate situation, these would presumably be the creation of a revolutionary situation.

Rex looks at the middle class, tacitly accepting the Marxist assumption that the working class is more united. The question he poses is whether the interests of the 'middle class' really rest with those of the workers or whether their aims are significant distinguishing features in their situation. Arguing that the objective situation of the worker and the middle-class bureaucrat are similar – they both have no property, rely on earned income, work is separated from home life – Rex asks what the practical difference might be. The key feature which he sees is that 'the bureaucrat *believes* that he has a career for life, whereas the proletarian may be discharged at very short notice'.[94]

Is the bureaucrat correct in this belief? If he is, perhaps he constitutes a separate class. If he is not, perhaps he is merely a proletarian labouring under false-consciousness of his true interests. In attempting to resolve these problems, Rex argues that the 'expectations' or beliefs of the bureaucrat 'are relevant to the description of his class position'.[95] But what significance does Rex place on this subjective feature?

Firstly, he argues that if the bureaucrat has 'valid' expectations then, clearly, he must be distinguished from the workers and, as such, he must be placed in a separate class. Lockwood reaches exactly the same ambiguous conclusion in his important empirical discussion of clerks.[96]

Rex then looks at the case where the person does not have a 'correct' definition of his 'objective' position. On the one hand Rex argues that this is merely 'false consciousness which . . . may . . . be swept away as the "real" factors of the situation become operative'.[97] On the other hand, he argues, in 'marginal' cases – say that of the clerk whom Lockwood discusses – the group may have in fact no clear objective position.[98] In such instances the competing definitions or legitimations which the organized representatives of the proletariat and bourgeoisie place on the position of the clerk (in an attempt to recruit him as an ally) will be a crucial variable. For whichever definition the clerk accepts will determine his class position.

This is at once an exciting and a disappointing conclusion. Rex seemed poised to break out of Weber's objective-subjective dilemma. But he only did so when it seemed impossibly difficult to define 'objective' situations in terms of orthodox Marxism. Had he pushed his argument further and applied people's subjective definitions and aims to their class situation, irrespective of the 'validity' of these definitions and aims, he might have developed a radically new means of thinking about class.

Class structure: Dahrendorf

If we are to mean by class anything like Marx, Weber or Rex mean by it then Dahrendorf's view of social structure cannot be discussed at this point. He argues that Marx was in error concerning his concept of class and its relation to property and the economy. He feels that social structure can be analysed adequately and exclusively by his use of the concept 'authority'. Though he refers to 'groups' within the authority structure of society as 'classes', they are more properly referred to as 'status groups'. As such, we shall discuss them under the heading of 'status'.

Status structure: Rex

When Rex turns to the concept of status, we might expect his use of Weber's concept to reassert the important place of subjectivity. But his 'Marxist' position is, on the contrary, only reinforced. Despite an illuminating interpretation of Lloyd Warner's six status positions within the general status hierarchy of an American city, he sees 'status' as determined by, rather than affecting, people's class position.[99] Though he accepts the emergence and variability of these six subjectively distinct groupings within society, he argues that the 'lower upper' group, which wields economic power, creates the whole status system in its interests. This is 'not something which emerges . . . from the general will'. Rather, it 'fits in well with the [lower upper's] need to maintain its own power'.[100] Similarly, the 'upper lowers', the large majority of the workers, dispute the legitimacy of the status system as supported by the industrialists. They develop, at least in embryo, a rival status system based on a social ideology which asserts their claim to economic independence and security.

In inventing their status system, the lower uppers are trying 'to seek some means of legitimating' their position.[101] That is, they are offering to such people as clerks a means of defining and understanding their situation. A few such groups may be captured only for a period of time (exhibiting 'false-consciousness') until they recognize that their class interest and status are being defined more correctly by those who assert a different view of reality. In this sense status applies to 'a situation in which there is a ruling class whose interests may conflict with those of the class whom they rule, and whose position rests in the first place on the power, rather than the authority, which they exercise'.[102]

Rex, therefore, sees Weber's concept of status as merely an extension of his own and Marx's concept of class. The two concepts are not distinct. Consequently his discussion of status does not raise the ambiguities and tensions which we found in Weber's work.

Status structure: Dahrendorf

Dahrendorf is mainly concerned with an explanation of structure and conflict in industrial societies. Consequently he bases his argument on only one of the two paradigms by which he felt an explanation of social structure can be attempted. He ignores the one derived from Parsons and chooses the one derived from Marx. But he discards many of Marx's own assumptions; argues that the form of industrial society has changed rapidly; and chooses Weber's concept of authority and control as the key variable for explanation.[103] It 'pervades the structure of all industrial societies and provides both the determinant and the substance of most conflicts and clashes'.[104]

The theory of status and the structure of status groups becomes 'the systematic explanation of that particular form of structure-changing conflict which is carried on by aggregates or groups growing out of the authority structure of social organizations'.[105] For this 'differential distribution of authority becomes the determining factor of systematic social conflicts'.[106] Authority relations are always relations of 'super- and subordination and, as they are relatively permanent social positions, . . . they are . . . legitimate'. Authority always involves this simple division into 'domination and subjection'.[107] Because it is a 'universal element of social structure', it is, therefore, more general than either property or status as defined by Marx and Weber.[108]

Dahrendorf is predominantly concerned with the generation of conflict groups by the authority relations obtaining in imperatively co-ordinated associations. It follows that domination and subjection 'is a common feature of all possible types of authority and indeed of all types of association and organization'.[109]

However, an actual person may play a dominant role in one group and a subordinate role in another. Membership of one group and his relationship in it does not imply the same relation in all the others.[110] Indeed, these conflicts are separated out, and society is best seen as segmentalized, though the superimposition of conflict is on occasions possible. Put more precisely, and without previous ambiguity, this means that 'the distribution of authority in associations is the ultimate "cause" of the formation of conflict groups, and, being dichotomous, it is, in any given association, the cause of the formation of two and only two conflict groups'.[111]

Nevertheless 'among the positions of domination there may be, and often is, considerable differentiation'. However, this observable empirical fact 'leaves unaffected the existence of a border line', or theoretical demarcation between the two main conflict groups.[112]

So, for Dahrendorf, there are two, and only two, kinds of class situations. There may be differentiations within the classes. But these do not basically affect the initial conceptual division. Dahrendorf argues that there are merely as many 'dominant and subject classes' as there are general institutions.

In different social situations the conflict division created by an inequality of authority will occur at different levels. The conflict in any one situation will be 'caused' only by the distribution of authority in that situation. Not only need conflict in education not occur at the same level as it does at work, but different kinds of people will occupy dominant positions in education than those who do so at work. So it may well be the case that a manager at work will be in a subordinate position to the teacher of his child in a school. This gives a flexibility to Dahrendorf's theory when applied to empirical reality.

We must, first of all, recall the peculiarity of Dahrendorf's definition of authority, for its distinction from Weber's concept is now more apparent. Because Dahrendorf sees it is fundamentally concerned with inequality, he assumes that it must also engender conflict. That is, any authority relation implies two objectives and opposed authority situations. Unlike Weber, this removes or downgrades the significance of subjective ideas and, at the same time, introduces conflict at the point where Weber was concerned with legitimacy and shared values. Later we shall discuss the reasons for Dahrendorf's definition. Here we are only concerned with its consequences.

The interests which actors have and which are implied by the theoretically drawn situations of domination and of subjection are present in the common situation and in the role of each actor who makes up the group. They may not be conscious or realized. As such, they are 'latent'. When they become conscious they are 'manifest'. This implies the possibility of actual subjective interest failing to fit with the group's 'objective' or 'latent interest'.[113]

'Quasi-groups' are groups which occupy identical 'latent interest' positions. As such, they are not aware of their common interest. An 'interest group' is one which has realized these interests and is already organized, or is organizing, towards their achievement. In this sense, interest groups are always conflict groups and, it seems, must therefore enter the political realm. Society is basically segmentalized into a great range of these latent and manifest interest groups, though only some will be manifest at any one time. Further, they may remain quite separate, though there may be a tendency for one conflict to be so severe as to superimpose on to the other ones.[114]

'Quasi-groups' would seem equivalent to Marx's concept of 'class-in-itself'. Both concepts, being defined by the scientist without reference to the subjective ideas of the actors contained 'in' them, involve the development of a further concept. This is necessary so as to accommodate those people whose subjective beliefs approach those which the scientist rationally derives from his theoretically drawn objective situation. These concepts are respectively 'interest group' and 'group', or 'class' and 'classes-for-themselves'. But Dahrendorf feels that the active group or class must rarely, if ever, be seen as constituting all the members of the 'quasi-group'. The remainder have then to be seen either in terms of 'false-consciousness' or by recognising that some people in 'quasi-groups' must be seen as never developing any interests at all.[115]

Having distinguished quasi- and interest-groups, the next outstanding theoretical problem is to analyse how the members within the former come to occupy the latter. Dahrendorf argues that certain conditions are necessary for a group 'in-itself' to become organized 'for-itself'.[116] Leaders, and a latent interest group from which the leaders can recruit, are vital. There must be an open political structure in which the merging group-for-itself can pursue its aims. It must have an ideology and an organization. Unfortunately all these features are seen as 'structural conditions' conducive to the formation of manifest interests and so to an interest group or class.[117] But the objective quasi-group could not have formed these 'structural conditions' in its conceptually drawn situation.[118] How these conditions do arise is not analysed. It is never suggested, for example, that people may make those 'conditions' through their own interaction. So, as with Marx, the peasants are seen as a latent group whose interests cannot be realized, because there are no 'structural conditions' present by which they may become organized around their manifest interests.

Much of the difficulty we are meeting follows once the class or group has

been designated both by its initial objective situation (without consideration of the actors' subjectivity) and by its objective interests (again without
reference to the actors' opinions). Dahrendorf is quite explicit about this
formulation. 'People's self-evaluation and [their] ranking of others is . . .
useless for our problem. They substitute for the effort of theoretical
derivation'.[119] Indeed, he seems to equate people's ideas with 'psychological phenomena'.[120] When the group has been predetermined or
prescribed at a theoretical level by the objective considerations of structure
it will always be found at an empirical level that the 'manifest interests'
which some people in the group developed do not fit the 'obvious' or
'rational' or 'objective' or 'ideal' interests and inter-relationships which
might 'logically' derive from such a situation. Dahrendorf readily admits
this.

Having attacked Parsons for his inability to cope with change, he now
sees him as an ally. He uses him (in conjunction with Marx) to defend his
category of objective, true, or 'latent' interests.[121] He says, 'no assumption
is implied about the substance' of a group's 'interests . . . and the articulate
orientations of the occupants of these conditions'.[122] Yet, having predefined his groups and their structure, he is later forced to admit that the
position of the dominant group is 'characterized by an interest in the
maintenance of a social structure that for them conveys authority, whereas . . . that of subjection . . . involves an interest in changing a social
condition that deprives its incumbents of authority. The two interests are
in conflict'.[123] Given his prior definition of both the situation and the
internal structure of the group in that situation, he is forced to ascribe, in
however general a way, an 'objective' interest to it by which the later,
actual, action of the group may be measured and explained. He is then
forced to define these actors in groups who form interests counter to those
theoretically expected as 'deviant' or 'falsely-conscious'. As such, he has to
take their ideas and expressed interests into account. The problem is then
to explain these ideas and false-definitions. It is at this point that Dahrendorf resorts to arguing that their explanation falls within the province
of psychology, not sociology. In other words, he removes the problem
altogether.

Structural concepts as a model of society: Rex
Our immediate question is, do Rex and Dahrendorf retain or submerge
the dominant theme in Weber's work? We must ask first if Rex's concepts
of class, status and power link to form a model of a social system and,
subsequently, whether he has a distinct view of human nature.

Rex suggests that conflicts do spread from one institutional context to
another. '[This is] because the separate institutions are related to one another as "means to ends" in the life situation of the hypothetical actor.'[124]

The general assumption is that education, politics or leisure may be
related to the dominant work institutions as means to ends, apart from

the actual actors' ends in each of these situations. For example, 'the British two party system . . . reflects the fact that British people find that the enemy on one front is also the enemy on the other'.[125] So, Rex develops his model by suggesting that 'instead of one set of institutions embracing all the members of the society, we have two' sets, separated by a conflict about ends, and competing by the use of power.[126] His model then 'starts by assuming sub-systems organized around a clearly defined end or aim for the "sub-system" as a whole'.[127]

Rex argues that his two action models (of order and of conflict) when combined allow him to deal with social change, and he feels that his theory of conflict 'is a theory of change'.[128] This is precisely because it envisages the possibility of conflicting ends within a society.

The precise outcome of rationally pursued conflict cannot be predicted in terms of the combined model. Certain definite stages will be reached and transcended in this conflict. For, 'even if we understand the social system of a subject class during the phase of conflict we do not know how it will organize society in a post-revolutionary situation'.[129] Consequently, Rex suggests three models in order to help him to account for different stages of structural development.

'The most basic conflicts' between each of the two contending sub-systems will develop around the issue of access to the 'means of life'.[130] The conflict may take various forms of intensity and spread to other social situations. On the other hand, Rex feels that conflict may 'only indirectly' relate to access to the means of life. It can occur in education or religion. But the extent to which Rex ignores such alternatives is significant when he comes to outline the three possible types of conflict model which may arise in modern societies.

The ruling class situation[131]

One class may dominate the other through an unequal distribution of power. In this model, there are, in effect, two sets of parallel institutions of education, economics, distinct ideologies and so on. But those of the one class overshadow those of the other class, which has little or no power.

The ruling class uses its dominant power as a means to legitimize its position in relation to the other class. To this end, it attempts to use its institutions of religion and education to persuade individual members or groups within the subject class that its position is just. To the extent that they succeed they can be seen as legitimate rulers not just in their own eyes, but also by sections of the subject class.

Through its own institutions and leaders the subject class will attempt to dispute this claim to legitimacy and, through various forms of resistance, it tries to challenge the power of the ruling class.

The extent to which the ruling class actually succeeds in persuading the subject class that its rule is legitimate is conceptualized in terms of false-consciousness. That is, the ruled do not understand the true nature of their situation. Social order may predominate, but the two-class situation still objectively exists, however small and distorted the actual conflict and dispute within society may be.

Rex feels that the ruling-class situation is not stable because the class structure remains the same and because the factor of power by which rule is maintained is itself unstable. It can change, because of the strength of people's aspirations, their leadership, or because their ability to co-operate and the physical or technological means which are at their disposal can also change. Power, then, like class, seems to be an objective quantity, changing irrespective of men's subjective definitions of it. When that balance of power changes, there are two possible alternative ways in which the relations between the two classes may develop. In this sense, Rex actually does predict how the ruling-class situation may develop. The two alternatives are those of 'truce' and 'revolution'.

The revolutionary situation[132]

The subject class may accumulate enough power to overthrow the previous ruling class. Rex recognizes that new conflicts may arise in the wake of a classless society, say, between controllers and controlled, as in such communist states as East Germany, Hungary or Czechoslovakia which have experienced revolutionary situations. It is for this reason that he argues it is not possible to predict the exact form which such a society will take if only the ideas of the successful revolutionary class are con-sidered. The new power situation would also have to be considered. Rex does not develop the reasons for such developments. This is unfortunate, for it might have forced him to examine further the nature of class and power. As it is, these comments actually contradict much of what he says about class and status.

The truce situation[133]

More time is spent on considering the second of the two possible alternatives to the ruling-class situation. It is Rex's attempt to understand the structure of modern industrial societies, with special reference to England. Rex feels that the subject class accumulates enough power to challenge, but not to overthrow the ruling class. Something of a truce or a balance of power develops between the classes. While each struggles to attain the final means of domination, they begin to adjust to the new or 'balance of power' situation.

The compromises which each class is able to extract from the other in fact lead to the development of 'a value system and of social institutions' which belong to neither class.[134] They are features peculiar to the truce, and straddle the institutions and values of the two competing classes.

This stage is in itself precarious, for it can break down into open conflict again. On the other hand, it could form in such a way that the institutions and values of the truce become the basis of a new and cohesive society.[135]

The crucial variable which determines these alternatives is again that of power.

If the unstable balance of power is maintained for very long the new generation of people who are born into it will know the previous conflict only as a 'folk memory'. Through the socialization process, they will 'internalize' the institutions and values of the truce situation, so solidifying its precarious existence. Despite this, Rex argues that 'the co-operation of the truce can only be prolonged if the balance of power on which it depended in the first place is in some measure maintained'.[136] For this to become the basis of a new order 'exceptionally favourable' circumstances would have to develop.[137]

It is within the more precarious form of the truce situation that Rex frames most of his discussion of class and power. We must return to the significant part which power and rationality play in distinguishing the view of order and conflict in Rex's models at this point. Power changes are vital in studying how one situation moves into the other, yet, as we noted, Rex says hardly anything about the process by which it does actually change.

Secondly, the rational logic, derived from the three basic power situations for each of the two classes, certainly makes sense in terms of the situations as Rex draws them, and the hypothetical actors he places in them. Given a certain goal, and the desire to implement it through the political setting, then the action and rational logic which he ascribes to the two hypothetical actors, representing each class, will certainly follow. But, in accordance with Rex's methodological standpoint, this action is taken in full scientists' knowledge of the situation, and it is explicable only in a Weberian sense. Whether real people placed in those theoretically defined situations will develop those ends and follow that logic is, it would seem, not just an empirical question, but also one of necessary 'deviance' from that or any other kind of model. But Rex does not check the empirical detail, and has no awareness of the extent to which 'deviance' from the rational model exists in practice in modern Britain.

This reliance on rationality has already developed in a rather peculiar way in Rex's work. It will be recalled, first of all, that order was discussed in terms of the rational action of a hypothetical actor with a particular end. But all those who shared this end had their action determined, as it were, by the system of relations which this actor required. Very quickly this rationality was replaced by the idea of normative and value systems, which conditioned the actors' ends and actions. At this point Rex's explanation turned entirely on a structural discussion of order.

Rex only retains his initial view of rationality and the place of the subjective by positing the opposition of two, ordered, class systems in a combined, overall, situation of competition and power. He does so by introducing the concept of conflict into the two-class model, where it is placed between the classes, and by relating subjective rationality only to this sphere of action. So, rational action is confined to an explanation of competition and conflict. The structure and explanation of interaction is quite different *within* each of the two class systems. Though combining these views of ordered and conflicting relations within the same model, the extent to which they are kept separate creates many of the problems which we suggested arose in the developmental aspect of this model, in particular that of 'the truce'.

Such problems do not exist in Rex's second work, for this rational view of conflict becomes subsumed within an overall collectivist view, in which the element of 'rationality' and rational action is finally and completely replaced by 'norms' induced and institutionalized by the 'system'.

Returning to the truce situation, we must recall that the power of the contending forces in it is roughly balanced. Both sides will in fact make concessions. If this does not appear on the level of their charters, then, in practice, their goals will be lowered from what might originally and ideally have been hoped for. Such compromises may well lead to the development of a new value system which legitimizes the institutions of the truce. This value system will belong to neither side, but will specifically relate to the balance of power. On both sides there are some who will cling to the previous goals and values. But a new generation can emerge for which the old, fierce, clashes are merely a 'folk memory'. The institutions and values of the truce will be the ones they have 'internalized'. However, in terms of Rex's initial model, the truce must remain unstable or break down, revealing the old conflicts between the two social systems, for 'the co-operation of the truce can only be prolonged if the balance of power on which it depended in the first place is . . . maintained'.[138] There are no other concepts contained within the model by which 'the truce' can be extended.

There is some contradiction here. Having shown how a new generation will arise which believes in a new set of values, Rex persists in saying that the truce depends on the previous balance of power and that the old conflicts could break out once more. This carries the implications that the old divisions of interests and the balance of power which gave rise to the conflict somehow remain, despite the new situation and the new beliefs formed in it. These old interests will, nevertheless, become 'revealed' again as society develops and when the balance of power is upset. Had those who gained the new ideas, and for whom the original conflict was merely a folk memory, found that 'new order' under such threat, we could in practice well imagine them wishing to defend it against any such regression. Perhaps a discussion of the State would have helped at this point. The power struggle which followed would then not involve cleavage along the original lines but along new ones. We might expect Rex to depart at this point from an orthodox class analysis. Unfortunately, he does not do so.

It is partly because of a concentration on subjective but ideal, rational, action, and the objective use of power, that the new order which may follow from the truce situation is so difficult for Rex to envisage. But the internal stability of the deterministic models of the two social systems is a further impediment here. Had Rex, at this point, not maintained a joint view of rational action and the implied social system which determined the logic of class action, but extended the alternative based on subjective meaning, a solution to this problem might have emerged. That he was prevented from doing this depends partly on his original use of the rational actor, but also on the other key feature of his analysis of situations: class.

In conclusion, we must first of all remark on the singular nature of change in this model. It is determined by power. Not only is the sense of action removed, but also change can only move in one kind of direction. It is a uni-causal and uni-directional model of change. In this sense, it is more helpful as a model of order than it is of change. As such, it is a collectivist model.

Secondly, we must note that those ambiguities which we have raised while discussing Rex's first major work are all resolved in his second work. This theoretically informed empirical study of race sets out to explain the 'social structure', conflicts, 'and the constellations of interests and roles which have "become" built into Birmingham society'. The racialism which Rex found people expressed was a product of 'the social system of which they were part'.[139] In this context, people were 'often acting in contradiction of their own ideals and sometimes of their own interests'.[140] Whilst retaining some aspects of his earlier view of conflict, he recognizes the existence of 'some overall social system'.[141] His perspective inevitably draws 'upon some of the insights of functionalism', such as that conflict as well as cohesion has to be explained in its terms.[142]

It would seem that the variety, as well as the individual, rational and empirical focus that Rex learned from Weber is omitted in his later work. The explanation of this would seem to lie in the extent to which the earlier work had already approached a collectivist view of action and interaction theory.

Finally, we must note that within the context of this position a concept of human nature becomes explicit. Despite his Weberian point of departure, this was already implied in the first work, where Rex discusses the problem of social action and integration in a manner that involves the use of concepts of a normative structure and culture system. He argued that 'the relevance of emphasizing normative elements . . . lies in the fact that they help us to explain how individuals subordinate their own private interests to those of the group or class or society'.[143]

The point is only more explicit and exclusive in Rex's later work: man becomes whatever the values and normative structure of the 'social system' requires of him. His action is contained within the concept of 'role' and the assumptions of a social-psychological determinism are accepted. Man is infinitely manipulable, and it is social structure and the concepts that constitute it which do the manipulating.

Structural concepts as a model of society – Dahrendorf

In considering Dahrendorf's view or model of society we must return to the concepts of power and authority. 'The important difference between power and authority,' he argues, 'consists in the fact that whereas power is essentially tied to the personality of the individual, authority is always associated with social positions or roles'.[144]

'The demagogue,' Dahrendorf argues, 'has power over the crowd he addresses and whose actions he controls, but the officer over his men and the manager over the workers has authority', because it exists 'as an expectation independent of the specific person occupying the position'.[145] In this sense, authority is seen as 'structure', as 'institutionalized power', while power is a non-social or psychological variable.[146]

Dahrendorf also seems to use a definition of power and 'authority' which makes the two concepts overlap. Indeed at times he seems to use authority not as he originally defined it, but as others have defined power.[147] Quite without hesitation, he talks of 'power or – as I should prefer to say – authority'.[148] This uncertainty concerning two quite different concepts is, perhaps, the key to a fundamental and general confusion between Dahrendorf's paradigms of cohesion and conflict.

The cohesion theory which Dahrendorf developed insists that a social structure exists where normative (situational) and value (cultural) elements are analytically separate. This 'structure' forms the 'role' expectancies in terms of which the person is determined and acts irrespective of his own feelings and ideas. Dahrendorf is still aware at this stage of his work on the problems which this approach involves. For he recognizes (in his separate conflict-model) that people may never act in terms of, or realize, their role interests. Whenever this is the case, however, he designates the actual beliefs and actions as 'false-consciousness', within a latent group. Like 'power', this is to be explained in terms of social psychology.

The problem remains, or rather assumes a new form, and we are left with no explanations of the significance, presence and consequences of the relations of real people. If people, or groups or classes of people, are to be 'given' objectively structured interests in the authority situations in which they are objectively placed by the scientist, then the scientist must have some independent means of deciding what that situation is and what the person's interests are without consulting the person.

The problem of false-consciousness and empirical reference may be disguised by embedding meaning, and the significance of other people and groups, at the level of norm and value, which are analytically separated from the actual people. So Dahrendorf argues that objective interests 'are in fact role interests, i.e., expected orientations of behaviour'.[149] The assumption in Dahrendorf's work is that they are patterned by the normative structure, which is formed in relation to the crucial variable of authority and which is internalized to become the role orientations of the actor. The argument is circular, and so fails to solve the problem. Nor does it come near to solving the problems contained in the concept of role, which Dahrendorf had earlier criticized as portraying the 'human individual in the fullness of his expression . . . only as a . . . player of roles [in] structural analysis'. In such analysis, 'the structure of society presents itself in its most formal aspect as a functional system the units of which are social roles or role sets'.[150]

Dahrendorf is forced to accept exactly this view of role, because of the way he views structure. Consequently he equates the concept of 'role interests' with his own concept of 'latent interests' and defines them as being 'undercurrents of behaviour which are *predetermined* for' the person and which are '*independent* of his *conscious* orientations'.[151] This means that order as well as conflict are structurally maintained, and the concept of false consciousness is needed to explain empirical instances where 'manifest interests . . . are not adapted to the latent interests underlying them'.[152] For example, 'the worker who behaves as if he is not in a position of subjection is . . . a "deviant" . . . whose behaviour requires a psychological examination [and becomes] a matter [for] social psychological research'.[153]

In Dahrendorf's model of conflict and authority the structure of society is seen as segmentalized. Actors may be on different sides of the conflict situation in different organizations. They therefore experience role conflict. But, so long as there is no superimposition, this conflict remains latent. Dahrendorf does not examine the way this conflict, or, for that matter, cohesion may spread from one institution to another or from one situation to another. Had he not conceptually taken the person to the abstract level of role, itself therefore segmentalized, we might have seen the possibility of a more thorough analysis of how situations do change in practice. In fact the only way change and process can enter into Dahrendorf's emerging theory is by the quite arbitrary alteration of authority as a consequence of unexplained 'structural conditions'. In this sense, the theory of conflict is as fundamentally static as we found Rex's to be.

Dahrendorf only replaces other uni-causal theories of conflict and change with one of his own. It is 'authority' that shapes the main structural divisions and forms the groups and interests in industrial society. But in Dahrendorf's hands the definition of authority is unusual. For him, authority creates conflict, not order.

Given his association of inequality and conflict with any authority relationship, Dahrendorf recognizes the inevitable formation of two conflict groups in any situation. Each of these groups then organize amongst themselves. To be logically consistent, Dahrendorf should insist that each of these two new associations should divide in terms of their authority relations, and so on, and so on . . . Thus, we have a logical and infinite regress to the point where every individual is competing with every other individual. This, of course, constitutes the Hobbesian dilemma. Dahrendorf is saved from this dilemma only by abandoning his original definition of authority and inserting the concept of structural constraints within these conflict groups, binding them together rather than inducing further conflict. But this solution itself creates problems for Dahrendorf's general and entirely separate models of cohesion and conflict.

The concepts he developed in connection with his structural model of conflict necessitate the structural concepts of order, organization, and role-status congruence. It is only these normative features which help to prevent him from pursuing his 'conflict' definition of authority to the point of infinite regress. He is therefore only able to construct a model of conflict which contains both conflict between groups and order within them. There are however two main problems involved in this formulation.

Firstly, the new model contains the assumption of a single form of cohesion within groups or classes. It involves complete role-status congruence. There are no shades or different forms of cohesion. Similarly, it involves a single form of conflict. There is a simple and open clash between two classes. No other alternatives are envisaged. It is only because these two related classes may occur in all institutions that a fairly complicated model may be constructed.

Secondly, and contradictorily, this model in fact has logical implications for complete social consensus. The explanation of this lies in the confusion between power and authority to which we have referred. For authority (or is it power?) 'both realises and symbolises the functional integration of social systems'.[154] This involves contradicting Dahrendorf's own view of authority, pushing it into a completely integrative structural framwork. Recognition of this contradiction is avoided by only using this particular view of authority when cohesion within any one single conflict group is examined. When conflicts between groups in imperatively co-ordinated associations are examined, Dahrendorf quite arbitrarily uses a different definition of authority. He rationalizes this by arguing that 'authority has two faces'.[155] But we find that the new face of authority involves what is really a psychological definition of power. On the one hand, Dahrendorf separates the two faces out, using the former in his cohesion model and the latter in his conflict model, asserting that neither model is capable of incorporation in the other. On the other hand, he uses both faces within the same model, placing the former within a single group, the latter between conflict groups.

In his later, unambiguous position, the face of authority which involves power is finally displaced by the cohesive view of authority which involves role-status congruence. That is, authority is finally defined as 'a facility for the performance of function in and on behalf of the society as a system.'[156]

A consistent use of the main concepts which Dahrendorf develops to explain a structure of conflict therefore implies the total integration of society. In a word, Dahrendorf has no explanation of conflict, except that which involves power. And power involves personal subjective qualities for which, he still feels, there are only psychological explanations, not sociological ones. As a consequence, the static and cohesive nature of the merging structural model is reinforced.

Finally, in a later work, entitled *Homo Sociologicus,* Dahrendorf elaborates clearly and exactly that analysis of order and consensus which finally broke through his model of conflict.[157] In it, society is not only seen in terms of 'structural functionalism' but man is seen as quite 'plastic'. So Dahrendorf is eventually forced to a position of adapting a particular psycho-sociological view of human nature. It is not one which he likes or, indeed, regards as equivalent to the natures of real men. But then neither did Weber like his rational cogs in his rational State apparatus.

Conclusion

In some respects it was impudent to try to generalize about Max Weber. Even those who have taken important features of his work as their starting point have not succeeded in maintaining them or in emulating his rigorous and sensitive concern for the people he hoped to understand a little more fully. Unfortunately, it has been necessary for our argument to generalize about the work of a man who was suspicious to the point of methodological obsession about such generalizations. The problem is not as great when we consider those whom he influenced.

We have been predominantly concerned with those features in Weber's work which influenced later sociological theory and which were open to a 'Parsonian' interpretation. We noted in passing (and will specify in greater detail in Chapter 6), other, major concerns which directly relate to the (by now) submerged sociological tradition; submerged precisely because such writers as Rex and Dahrendorf have extended and transformed his work in such highly one-sided ways under the influence of Marxian thought and the 'Parsonian' interpretation of Weber himself. That this interpretation is possible is partly Weber's own fault. Elements of his work contained implications of collectivism and involved the reduction of action, meaning, and human control. It was left to others to draw these implications together and develop a sociology of the total domination of man by the social system.

5: The Convergence of Concepts and Models

Introduction

The argument in this chapter is divided into two parts. The first part draws the separate discussions of Parsons, Marx and Weber together. It emphasises the dominant theme in their work and shows how it contains a unified theoretical standpoint.

The second part shows how this theme has been adopted in the work of very many contemporary sociologists of both left and right, Marxian and Parsonian, conflict and cohesion schools of thought.

Convergence: Parsons, Marx and Weber

Marx was most influenced by personalities, events, and problems posed during the early and middle half of the nineteenth century; Weber, by the last quarter of it and the first quarter of the twentieth century.

It was not possible for either of these men to escape the traumas, social upheavals, the ferment of ideas and social problems which were generated in and helped to transform the periods before and through which they lived.

They both wrote prodigious and encyclopaedic works in response to events around them. Whilst Marx concentrated almost exclusively on European problems, he examined history to illuminate the present; Weber examined Middle-Eastern and Oriental societies in order to understand his own more fully. Both during their life and after their deaths they influenced the way men thought and acted. Consequently they helped to shape social life.

Of the events which influenced them, the French revolutions of 1789 and 1848 were vital social features. But they are not to be encapsulated as dates. Another sequence of events, the industrial revolution, had its roots deep in the preceding period and gathered pace during the whole of the nineteenth century.

The same point applies, of course, to Emile Durkheim and Sigmund Freud and, for that matter, to Talcott Parsons. Once we have asked what problems these men were responding to we must ask why their solutions and explanations so influence subsequent social thought. To do so we have to ask a third question: what were their answers to the problems which so excited them that they devoted their lives to their solutions?

Marx made one possible response to the two revolutions. It was a radical, even revolutionary response. The ferment of activity should, indeed would, be pushed into a further revolution. He was excited by the break with the traditional, orderly past, by the power and productive forces being unleashed in his time. The liberal cry of 'liberty, equality, fraternity' should be extended to all men. And man, being rational and able to control and fulfil himself, would be capable of doing just that. But this meant harnessing reason to power and power to a further exhilarating leap into the unknown future.

Weber made another possible response. It too was radical, but deeply coloured by the ideas of liberalism. Like Marx, he saw a potential in the rationality of man. But, living at a later moment in the epoch he had a different and pessimistic vision. The very rationality which Marx felt would liberate man would, in Weber's eyes, trap him in an all embracing and determining machine. The individualism, the utilitarian calculation of liberalism would become denuded of choice and creativity, except for sporadic and charismatic revolts against the unintended consequences of the age of rationality and reason.

Durkheim's response, though politically radical in a way (he was a Guild Socialist), involved an overwhelming concern with order. How was it possible in an age of change, conflict, and turmoil? How was it possible when he started with a crude, Hobbesian view of man's nature? His massive concern with organic and mechanical solidarity testify to a dimension of conservatism in his thought. Yet these concepts were, in themselves, radical solutions.

Freud was also influenced by the rationality of his age and of the liberal response. Equally, conflict and destruction, especially that of the first world war, made him as pessimistic as Weber. Could man gain a rational control over his own inner drives through a greater understanding of them, or would they destroy him? Freud delved into secret ideas which no man had faced before in an attempt to find solutions.

Parsons grew up before these men, except Marx, had died. He too was at first influenced by the liberal strand in their thought of reason and rationality. But this was overpowered by the force of a different problem and argument which was similar to that which Durkheim recognized. From this standpoint he interpreted great, systematic, and converging strands in the thought of each of his predecessors. His contribution was to pull these strands together and to establish once and for all the validity of the discipline: the science of the explanation of social action – sociology.

Each of these men made revolutionary responses to their social environment. They developed concepts and models, ideas, which no other man had used before in attempting to understand society. Perhaps Marx and Freud are better known than the others. Durkheim and Weber are just as important in the field of social understanding. Of these two, we have chosen to look closely at Weber, partly because he influenced and was interpreted by Parsons. We chose Marx because many think he stands outside the convergence which Parsons synthesized and to which he gave the title: 'A voluntaristic theory of action.' One of our questions concerning Marx was, therefore: had Parsons discussed Marx in detail, would he have found him to be a further major figure in the convergence? We chose Parsons quite simply because his work was a major turning point in the development of modern sociology.

In one aspect of their work Marx and, later, Parsons, like Freud, were trying to argue against the liberal utilitarian strand of thought which gave man a free, rational choice. It is not like that, they said. Rather, man is crucially formed in and through the network of relationships which he experiences. While Marx was doing this for man in society, Darwin was making the same attempt for man in biology, by developing his thesis of natural selection and evolution. They were each trying to put the individual man in his place. He was not independent and autonomous. That thesis was an ideological myth. The individual was bound by and deeply dependent on his surroundings. He was formed by biological and social circumstance. Such a thesis now seems fairly unexceptional. The only remaining questions are 'how'? and 'by what mechanisms'? But is the thesis really so unquestionable?

Freud did not think so. More than anyone else he argued that the adult is formed by instinct and early social experience. Even so, the mature, liberated adult could gain a measure of control over his destiny. Freud spent his life in the cause of such liberation.

Marx did not think so. He is renowned for his determinism. But he was quite convinced that the rational element in man could lead to his eventual and future liberation. This was the essence of his conception of the action of the proletarian class and its potential understanding of and development within capitalist society.

Weber did not think so. However renowned for his 'methodological individualism' and the popularized concept of 'charisma', he was at the same time as pessimistic about the future as Freud. Man was free, but in modern society he had unintentionally created an edifice of relationships which seemed to fasten him in a gruesome and regimented deterministic framework. Nevertheless, his methodology and such pure types of action as the charismatic held out a kind of hope.

Parsons, at the beginning of his work, and under the influence of Weber and the rational economists, did not think so. Yet, by the time his work had matured under the influence of that convergence which he identified in the work of Durkheim, Weber, Freud and others, he had come to the theoretical conclusion that such choice was not possible.

Which writer, if any, was correct in this belief? Clearly it relates to an important theme in the social thought of Western society – that of choice, free will, the ways and means by which man exercises control over his social situation, the way in which he shapes and controls his own life, rather than submits to its control over him. Further recognition of this theme in the work of these writers is left to the next chapter, when we consider the possibility of alternative explanations to those offered by the other, dominant, theme. This latter tradition, its convergences in the thought of Weber, Marx and Parsons, are of immediate concern.

The critical interpretation of the work of the three writers given earlier showed that they were driven to and fastened increasingly on the explanatory problems posed by this convergence. They adopted aspects of its emerging assumptions and sometimes reluctantly attempted to chase it to its logical conclusion. Perhaps Parsons took it further than Marx or Weber, but he did so only with the benefit of their experience and the implications of their work. Similarly, Marcuse extended and made Marx's work more consistent. So, also, Rex and Dahrendorf were influenced by Weber's assumption, but also by those of Marx. In the process they drove both Weber and Marx further towards the position which Parsons himself had been forced to adopt. But the fact of convergence is an unpopular one. Parsonians have often come to regard functionalism as synonymous with sociology. Equally, Marxists usually dismiss Parsonian thought as 'bourgeois sociology' and see Marxism as the only true sociology.

In the face of such disagreement it is as well to stress and explain some of the reasons for the convergent strands in the sociology of Marx, Parsons, Weber and their extenders.

The definition of the key sociological problem
It is helpful to note the logical implications of the way Marx, Parsons and Weber saw the basic problem which they felt they faced at the outset of their sociological work. An aspect of the problem is formed by the way each sociologist defined the nature of the social life of their day. Did the facts which confronted them indicate that social life was orderly, or was it torn by conflict? Depending on the answer to this question, a particular kind of new problem arises.

A second question turns on the view, if indeed there is such a view, of the form that human nature takes. If there is a basic human nature or if a particular nature is thought to exist generally in a particular society, then that nature is likely to influence or be influenced by the form of social relations which make up that society. So the answer to the first and second problem must be related, because the problems are related.

As it turns out, Marx and Parsons define the key problems which face the explanation of society very differently. In the revolutionary nineteenth century Marx was empirically confronted by a society in conflict and tension. In twentieth-century America, Parsons felt society was basically orderly.

Each man started with an assumption, albeit a very different assumption, concerning human nature. Marx felt it was basically co-operative, rational, self-controlling. Parsons, following Hobbes and Durkheim, felt it was in competition with itself and implied conflict in social relationships generally.

Starting with these different assumptions, and different empirical views of the different societies in which they lived, Parsons and Marx were consequently faced with a similar problem. For Marx, the question became: how is conflict possible when man is rational and co-operative? For Parsons the question became: how is order possible when man is basically destructive and competitive?

It should not be a source of surprise that each man arrived at similar solutions, especially when we know that Parsons was basing his solution on the benefit of the work of others, and when each was reacting against the nineteenth-century liberal and utilitarian idea of free and rational choice.

Simply, the individual was constrained away from his basic nature by the fabric of social relations and his location or social position within these relations, into which he was born and through which he learned to be social. In a word, man had no choice but to live in order (for Parsons) or conflict (for Marx). The question then becomes: what kinds of analytical concepts might best be used to explain these social relations and positions which constrain man away from his true nature?

Particular structural concepts

In a very real sense Marx prescribed his analysis of choice by situating it at a point towards which society was developing. That is, the possibility of rational activity and choice were placed within the fully developed working-class situation. Only that situation could encourage men to see and understand the way members of the whole society worked, were divided, and constrained their lives. It followed rationally and logically that they should come to see the possibility of shaping their own destiny beyond the dreams of other men in other situations.

This process of dawning realization and liberation from constraint was to be slow and painful, and could eventually come to fruition only within classless society. At that point man would be fully free to develop in terms of his inner and basic nature.

The fully developed working-class situation, and that of communist society, are those situations with the least social or cultural constraints. No normative structural or constraining concepts are required to explain action in them, precisely because men will recognize their true, rational interests. Therefore, the concept of, say, alienation is hardly applicable to analysis of the 'working class for itself' and is completely irrelevant for an understanding of communist society. Simply, if the actor is tied to an objective situation which objectively implies a rational goal, there is no need for a normative explanation of his rational activity.

This view of rationality is in some ways equivalent to that of Weber's. It implies a co-operative and ordered system of relations. It is free from conflict, because all accept the same goals in life and strive to achieve them with a full awareness of the implications of action. In a real sense, social relations are structured by the rational integration of norms which all men accept as legitimate.

Marx's embryonic view of communist society can thus be viewed as highly integrated and ordered. Marx did not see the possibility that such social relations would eliminate choice, as Weber did. But Weber lived in the twentieth century, witnessed the first communist revolution, and studied in a period when both bureaucracy and the State had become more complex and more powerful. They dominated society in a way that Marx had failed to envisage. Weber's view of rationality partly stemmed from his interpretation of complex social organizations and he applied structural concepts derived from it to advanced industrial societies of both a capitalist and a communist nature.

His concepts of rational legal authority, and of status positions within such an authority structure, were detailed and specifically prevented precisely that freedom which Marx felt rationality implied. In this sense, Marx naively retained the standpoint of a nineteenth-century liberal, though relativistically locating the potential for its realization in specific and future social situations.

Parsons was under the joint influence of Durkheim's concept of moral authority and Weber's concept of rational legal authority. His view of social conduct and actual action is an amalgam of the normative structure and the voluntary acceptance of that structure by the actors situated within its confines. This acceptance stems from the actor's belief in a particular system of values which is reflected in the institutional norm. Whilst Parsons' concepts moved away from the bias towards rationality which characterized Weber's position, they none the less implied exactly the same form of normative constraint that Weber's did. Indeed, by closing the circle on Weber's separate ideal types, the constraint was deepened.

It is useful to examine specific concepts within the overall and convergent concept of social structure which these writers shared.

Class
Weber's conception of 'life style' was contained within Marx's more general structural conception of 'class'. This concept was active and contained a greater sense of process, change and development in Marx's hands than it did in Weber's.

Class, for Marx, like rational order for Weber, contained intentional, subjective activity as a vital feature. But this was sharply distinguished and derived from another feature of class: class situation.

Both Marx and Weber were at pains to define class situation. They included in it both objective and subjective factors. These were distinguished from the class aims or interest which people might or might not come to accept in that situation.

On the one hand, Weber was more crude than Marx in his definition of class. It related simply to external economic conditions which were apparently outside the control of men. As such, it was quite distinct from status, which depended on what style of life the person had, and what estimations others had of him. But, on the other hand, Weber was also forced to place the quality of subjectivity into class situation, into the interests of individuals in common class situations, and into the common aims of a class of actor. As such, class aims could take any form. But again we run up against the crude formulation, for these aims could not succeed unless they were based on a 'true' awareness of the 'real' conditions of the 'class situation'. In this sense, for class association to take place the class aims had to be rational in the same way that Marx's had to be rational. Both Weber and Marx were aware at the empirical level that the actual interests which men articulate and follow are widely divergent. They both saw several active groupings of men within any one class, despite their theoretical location in an identical, objective, class situation. But neither made the step, which might be thought to be the reasonable one, of relating the interests which actual men articulate to the way they, as scientists, defined the pure class situation and pure interests of these men. To do this Weber would have had to equate the concept of class far more directly with that of status and, in the process, revise both concepts. Yet he had assigned class to the realm of economic activity, and there, in all its ambiguity, it remained distinct.

An important difference between the work of these main figures might seem to be the emphasis they place on subjectivity, and the clearly rational bias in Marx's and Weber's work. These distinctions are not as evident if we compare Marx and Weber with the early Parsons. But, by 1952, we saw that Parsons had placed subjectivity in the personality and the culture system. The 'unit act' had been replaced by 'role', which was the person, and Parsons' initial bias towards 'rationality' had long since been displaced.

Marx, on the contrary, maintained a view of the actor which, though determined in different respects, is quite conscious of the ends or interests for which he is striving, and applies a more or less rational logic in order to attain them.

The actor's structural position (for Parsons the 'status' position, for Marx his class position, and for Weber his class and status position) is fixed because of the surrounding social relations. This position is objectively discernible apart from what the person who occupies it may do or think.

Similarly, it has an objective interest or goal which may be irrational or rational and which may, for Marx and Parsons, be derived from it. It is independent of the occupant and so can ignore what the actual person may do or think. Weber disagrees, arguing that the actor cannot be mistaken about his interests, but at the same time maintains that classes only form when the 'true' situation is revealed.

Partly because of his Durkheimian development of normative constraints, partly because of his view of socialization and role, Parsons' view of social action comes to omit a conscious or a rational view of action. Exactly because Marx does operate with a rational view of man, his own development of the social relationships and peculiarities which constrain action is not fully developed. If the actor has a goal which is tied to a situation, and if the actor in that situation acts rationally, then there is no need to pose a normative structure between the goal and the actor. These 'norms' which Parsons, following Weber and Durkheim, at first placed between actor and the goal internalized within the actor are predominantly placed by Marx in the external situation itself. It is for this reason that situations are defined by him as being part subjective and part objective. The same is true of Weber's analysis of class. It means that Marx and Weber are only forced to begin to offer an explicitly normative explanation at the theoretical level when action is not based on full awareness or when rationality is seen as constraint. Marx, therefore, poses a more rigid and overtly normative structure between the actor and his false, irrational values as a means of explaining those 'false' values and rational actions than he does in cases where action and values are both rational.

False-consciousness and the situational and cultural factors which encourage it are all sub-concepts of the over-arching idea of alienation. This is Marx's structural conception *par excellence*. It is the means by which all hitherto existing societies, not just capitalist society, are to be explained. It enables Marx to argue that though man's activity makes society, any particular man's contribution is entirely unaware of its consequences. It is socially determined, the product of structural circumstances, not their creator. Marx does not spell out the consequences of this approach in full sociological detail. Those who followed him were forced to do so for particular reasons.

Anyone who accepts Marx's basic position is faced with a major empirical problem by modern industrial society. Firstly, Russia does not seem to approximate to the kind of communism implied by Marx's ideal type of such a society. Secondly, such societies as those of America and Western Europe do not seem to have developed fully conscious working classes. How are Marx's concepts to be used to explain these apparent empirical facts?

The answer follows, once it is decided to retain Marx's concept of the structure of class-situations, and the view upheld that Western societies are all structured explicably in terms of these concepts. The lack of class conflict, of working-class consciousness, and the consequent social order is to be explained in terms of false-consciousness and, more generally, alienation. The concept is crucial, and must be spelled out in the kind of sociological detail which Marx avoided. This is precisely what Marcuse does. He extends Marx's concept by examining the process whereby the institutional and cultural superstructure of the working class has become incorporated into that of the bourgeois class. This involves developing the notion of the voluntary acceptance of alien norms and values, the whole structural and cultural edifice that constrains the working class to act blindly against its own true, rational, interests. John Rex is forced into undertaking exactly the same conceptual elaboration, though he arrives at the same position as Marcuse by relying as much on Weber and Parsons as on Marx's own concepts.

Such analysis of the concepts entailed in explaining an irrational and constraining 'superstructure' of norms and values involves diminishing the significance of a specifically class analysis. For such an understanding of social interaction relies more heavily on an explanation of the normative institutionalization of particular values than on an explanation of the underlying objective class structure. Indeed, we noted that the logical position entailed by the concepts which Marcuse, Rex and Dahrendorf used all lead directly to an explanation of social order and social cohesion. Their explanation of conflict then had to assume particular forms, which either had to rely on mono-causal explanations (Rex, Dahrendorf) or had to be pushed into a hypothetical future (Marcuse). Indeed their explanation of the structure of relations within any one class, or of the structure of orderly Western industrial societies, implied either rejection of the analysis of conflict (Dahrendorf), or a static view of conflict (Rex and Marcuse). Simply, their analysis involved a view of the normative integration of institutions, of dominant values, their voluntary acceptance by the actors, and the integration of all three levels of analysis in the concept of the 'social system'. At this point the Marxian position became identical with that of Parsons. Interestingly enough, Marcuse's own analysis of bureaucratic rationality, in both Western and communist industrial society, also accepted Weber's own view of 'rationality as constraint' from which Parsons' view is derived. Man, in such societies, was 'one-dimensional' and his action became fully determined for him by the needs of the 'social system' of capitalism.

Status

If Weber and Marx were confused, but almost identical, in their concept of class, Weber was apparently quite opposed to Marx in feeling that the implications of class were confined, and that the concept of status was required to explain much of social life. Marx felt that the influence of class extended to all spheres of life. So, bourgeois man would have the same interests in the spheres of home life, politics, religion, and so on, as his fellows had. In so far as he had a definition of man's subjective status, it was one that was entailed in the idea of institutionalized class-consciousness. So, there seemed to him no need to develop a distinct concept. Yet his concept of class was made ambiguous exactly because he did incorporate subjectivity into it. For there was a constant tension between men's actual beliefs and the beliefs he supposed they must come to have, given that his class categorization of them was correct. So, at the same time as retaining his basic model of class, he was forced by empirical circumstances to divide it up in order to cater for local historical variations. Weber's and Marx's concepts of class and status may be summarized as follows:

*A tabular summary of the Marxist and Weberian
structural account of subjective/objective factors*

Marx – structure of society

	Class situation		*Class interest*
Class	*objective* economic factors from viewpoint of individual or group, which circumscribe the position of the two main classes in society.	1	true *subjective* interests related to the objective class situation of class in a direct, one-to-one, manner.
	subjective relations both within and between classes in connection with production in all spheres of life activity. } ambiguous	2	false *subjective* interests, which do not see objective class situations and whose aims are not rational.
Power	stems from class situation.		defends and extends class interests.

Weber – structure of society

		Class situation	*Class interest*
Class	market situation	*objective* economic factors, which circumscribe the position of several classes in society.	does not necessarily relate to or determine subjective feelings except in case of the unskilled property-less.
	work situation	*subjective* – relations at work, cultural ideas } ambiguous	

	Status situation	*Status interest*
Status	*subjective* factors in style of life and expectations of others.	1 can, in part, determine the form of class structure, especially in relation to work situation.
		2 can also be formed by true, objective market situation.
Power	relates to interests of *Parties*, which may relate to either class or status, or both. Therefore, it also relates to class and status.	Parties and the State may develop autonomous interests of their own.

On close examination the distinction between class and status breaks down. The analysis of false-consciousness, of subjectivity, is the analysis of status. So the analysis of complex divisions within one class, let alone the incorporation of the subjectivity of one class by another, must of necessity proceed in terms of analysis similar to that adopted by Weber's consideration of status.

Distinctions which exist within a class cannot be due to the objective class situation, because that is identical for all actors. It can only be due to subjective status distinctions which, in turn, create role distinctions. The analysis of any one class taken separately or of a total, integrated or bourgeois society specifically assumes the need for concepts which are equivalent to those required by Parsons for the analysis of the whole of society. They include role, status, status structure, authority and, finally, their relation together in a social system of unintended consequences. Marcuse, Dahrendorf and Rex all converged towards this Parsonian position.

Even those analysts who retain the concept of class (Marx, Marcuse, Rex) rely on analysis that incorporates concepts which may differ from that of status in name only (Marx). In particular, they involve the idea of a voluntary acceptance of a status hierarchy, which is the direct equivalent of Weber's ideal type of rational legal authority. They are only distinct in having a different view of the implications of a class-situated rationality.

Sociology: the explanation of unintended consequences

The formation of these structural concepts we have discussed imply and were in some way dependent upon the development of a particular methodological position. This position was itself indicated in the discussion of the original problem facing sociology. Though the action of the actor is intentional, and subjectively understandable (whether rational or not), the consequences of social action are unintended. Society and the structure of social relations are not the intended creation of any one actor or status or class grouping of actors. The possible exceptions to this are Marx's view of the rational action of the fully conscious proletariat and communist society and Weber's concepts of rational action and charisma. We have already noted that Marx and Marxists have paid little attention to these modes of action and that Weber's concept of rational action, whilst equivalent to a normative structure of rationality, is encouraged by rational authority, and does not create it. To this extent both Marx and Weber come to concentrate on a view of social structure as the unintended creation of activity. Whilst social action sustains the unintended structure of relations, it is itself formed by that structure.

Despite an almost positivistic dimension to the analysis of class, Marx was certain that history and social circumstances were created by the subjective activity of men. Similarly, Parsons recognized that once Durkheim had emerged from his positivistic influences his argument implied that man created the normative patterns and moral obligations which forced his action to be co-operative and society to be organic and cohesive.

For Marx, the consequence of a multitude of rational acts elevates 'the whole structure of the economic order into a great control mechanism, a compulsive system . . . [it] creates for each acting individual a specific situation which compels him to act in certain ways if he is not to go contrary to his interests . . . [He] stressed the compulsive aspect and through this the total structure of the system'.[1] Marcuse merely emphasized the normative element which guided the relativistic rationality of such structurally situated activity within the context of advanced industrial society. This is precisely the task which Parsons undertook when revising Weber's view of the same kind of society. At this stage in the development of the argument the determinism of the theory lies not on an individual-psychological but on a social level. It is the situation and the norms governing action which dictate a given course of action; in a different situation 'and with different norms' all would be changed.[2]

The interpretation of social action could now become solely the explanation of unintended consequences and their constraining effect on man. The edifice which man creates takes on something of a life of its own. for it was created by no one individual and no one group or class of individuals.

The position of such analysis has departed from positivism on the one hand and idealism on the other. Weber and Marx reached it by different paths, but they reached it incompletely. Neither Marcuse, extending Marx, nor Rex, extending Weber, reached it fully in so far as they retained a positivistic dimension to their view of class and power. To the extent to which they escaped with the help of their Weberian view of the normative organization and the contemporary significance of the State, bureaucracy, etc., they also approached the position which Dahrendorf and Parsons arrived at by abandoning class analysis. The logic of this position demands the analysis of subjective action alone. But such subjective factors can only be treated by:

1. Placing subjectivity in common class or societal values divorced from any one actor.
2. The subjective, but normative, structure of relations is seen as objective and external to any one actor. It is, therefore, to be analysed by the concepts of class (Marx) or status (Weber, Parsons) or class and status (Rex, Marcuse).
3. The actual action of the actor is, therefore, determined by a combination of the first two features of analysis, which are independent of the actors, but voluntarily accepted by them.
4. It is the structure of relations, themselves the unintended creation of individual action, which creates and sustains action. So, the understanding of social action turns entirely on the explanation of the unintended consequences of that action, i.e. their power of constraint over man.

Such systems of interaction are not only independent of the will of particular men, but have 'properties that are emergent only on a level of complexity . . . They cannot be derived by a process of direct generalization of the properties of particular action'.[3] Indeed, they are functioning, self-sustaining, wholes 'in the sense that they have structurally and analytically important emergent properties which disappear when the breakdown of systems into units or parts is carried far enough'.[4]

This means that in order to understand such systems we are obliged to ignore the catchwords and fantasies of particular men, for they tell us nothing of the system of unintended consequences which create those illusory activities. At this point, any empirical grounding which such theory has is obliterated. Class interests (Marx), ideal types (Weber), roles, norms, values (Parsons, Rex, etc.), are properties of the abstract social system and do not correspond with social 'reality' for specific methodological and explanatory reasons. This peculiar standpoint, which rejects empirical grounding or, at least, makes it ambiguous, will shortly be taken up again.

What must immediately be noted is that this 'social system' of 'unintended consequences' *controls* and orders the activity of each particular man. Social circumstance is in the saddle and rides consciousness and action where it will. This approach is ultimately based on those views of man which see his nature as cohesive or conflictful, and opposed to an empirical picture of society which is, respectively, chaotic or orderly. That is, it is based on a view of external constraint. These parallel equations, personified by the Hobbesian problem and its solution, logically force the rejection of any view of choice and autonomy of the individual.

This view of society, which conceives the social system as external constraint, also removes subjectivity from the province of the actor, placing it at the analytical level of class ideology (Marx, Marcuse), or the central value-system (Weber, Parsons), or a merging of the two (Rex and Dahrendorf).

Such controlling systems of action may take different forms. We will shortly discuss the detail of these systems and the form which different models of them may take. But it is immediately necessary to point out that while their form and the shape of a model of them may change, they are equally explicable in terms of the concepts we have discussed so far, irrespective of whether they are thought of as largely cohesive (Durkheim, Parsons), or evolutionary (Weber and, to some extent, Parsons), or revolutionary (Marx).

Elements in the thoughts of Marx and, most particularly, Weber avoided drawing all the implications of such self-functioning systems to the same logical conclusion that Parsons and Marcuse, Rex and Dahrendorf took them. However, it is precisely the addition of a particular series of socio-psychological concepts, which are implied by the concept of the 'social system', that makes that conclusion finally possible. The elimination of pre-existing views of human nature and rationality demands a sociological view of man which is infinitely manipulable.

The sociological view of man: Freud and the role concept

If the pervading concern with rationality is a common theme in Marx and Weber and, through Weber's influence, the early Parsons (as in the concept of the unit act, etc.), so also was the related theme of choice and individuality, the way men shape rather than are shaped by their social environment.

There was no obvious or immediate fit between human nature and the structural condition which shaped that nature into new forms and minimized free choice. The same is true of the relation between rationality and structural constraint.

Marx was to retain his view of man, choice, and rationality, by placing them within the province of the working class, and future communist society. Weber made use of rationality by developing a view of a totally but voluntarily constraining rational, legal authority-structure.

It was left to Marcuse to develop Marx, and Parsons, Rex and Dahrendorf to develop Weber in ways which ultimately removed rationality and choice from their structural analysis of modern industrial society, so making the congruence between the original actor and structural and value or interest concepts more exactly related to one another, in the 'social system'.

In so doing, they also took the Marxian and Hobbesian view of human nature to their logical sociological conclusion. The very conception of the actor had to change. It became fully determined, without rationality, control or choice. So, Marcuse extending Marx, and Dahrendorf and

Rex extending Weber, are forced to the same logical position as Parsons in extending Durkheim and Weber. The steady progress of conceptual convergence was assured, given the initial assumptions and the contradictions between these assumptions. It was assisted by the empirical emergence of a welfare state, mixed economy, technological development, and the failure of working-class radicalism. Such empirical factors forced Marcuse, Rex, and Dahrendorf to search for psychological as well as normative concepts in seeking explanations for the failure of the working class to develop its projected rational awareness and revolutionary potential. The subjective was placed on the one hand into the ultimate value and normative systems and, on the other, into the unconscious level of motivation within the actor.

Marcuse's addition of aspects of Freud to Marx and Parsons' addition of similar aspects of Freud to Weber and Durkheim only made the convergence of these streams of thought more certain. For we now had a precise set of adaptive and 'deterministic' (Parsons) or 'repressive' (Marcuse) and, often, unconscious psychological concepts explaining why men should conform to the external, objective, normative and cultural systems. There was no longer any possibility of a genuine voluntarism or, even, an empirical escape-route from such concepts. Under similar influences the same concepts became added to Rex's and Dahrendorf's revision of Weber and Marx. Consequently, Parsons' interpretation of Weber's sociology and his relation to Durkheim and Pareto were reinforced within the sociological tradition.

Thus the crucial step is taken which removes subjective and conscious intentionality from the analysis of the activity of man. It is no longer necessary to know why men do things from their point of view. This means that the very concept of action has to be rejected. As a consequence of the internalization of external constraint, the actor's action is merely adapted and oriented to these external constraints in a ceaseless process of interaction.[5]

A new and linking concept is required to cement the relationship between the personality, normative and cultural systems. For neither the actor nor action can be seen as figuring significantly in the analysis of such social systems. The actor must either be conceived in a 'one-dimensional' sense (Marcuse) or replaced by the concept 'role' (Parsons). Once the social system is conceived, the concept of the actor as well as the reasons for his actions become largely irrelevant. So does any concern with human control.

The process by which the internalization of external constraint takes place becomes a proper subject for study. Both Parsons and Marcuse assume that Freud's own psycho-sociological insights and concepts imply the basic means for a study of socialization which links the personality and social system.

In developing similar theories about the mechanism of the socialization of the child, crucial aspects of Freud's contribution are ignored. These concern Freud's own involvement with rationality and the extent to which the normal individual develops resistance to external social pressure. He was as concerned with choice as Marx. He felt that only the neurotic person was compliant. It is, therefore, significant that while Marcuse omits these aspects of Freud's work in his analysis of western industrial society, he resurrects them in his projected analysis of ideal communism.

If the sociological view of human nature which develops with the view of the 'social system' sees man as fully manipulable, this forces us to return to the empirical question: what is the grounding of such a conception of the actor and of social action?

Despite Weber's methodological distinction, he none-the-less approaches the Marxian position in the way his ideal-type concepts tend to relate into an interlocking, logically consistent whole in his explanation of advanced industrial society. He saw empirical deviance between his ideal types and reality being gradually eliminated by the rationalization of all social life in advanced technological society. Deviance exists only because life does not yet approximate to the ideal type. While the same was true for Marx's consideration of the proletariat in particular, Marcuse had to extend Marx's emphasis on the concept of 'false-consciousness'.

In ignoring key aspects of Weber's work and extending his conceptual analysis of industrial society, Parsons pushes Weber into exactly the same methodological position which Marx arrives at with the crucial aid of 'false-consciousness'. For Parsons, empirical deviance from the theoretically expected is to be explained in terms of a theoretical concept of 'deviance', and subsequently, a resort to psychological and structural elaborations of that concept. Dahrendorf provides another example of this position.

Aspects of the method and theory of traditional sociology indicated that action is itself rational and based on a full understanding of the situation. So, a rational model of such action, and the actor implied by it, became the basis for relating theory to particular empirical situations. But structure was equally ideally conceived by this approach and incorporated the view that shared ends, and the activities of others, fit smoothly with the rational conception of action. Such a view merely becomes the rational equivalent of the congruity which is argued by role-status advocates.

Role-status congruity implied and overtly contained the assumptions of methodological collectivism. So too does this rational equivalent. It is only on a combined philosophical and empirical level – that of the actual form and meaning of action and structure – that differences emerge. But neither approach logically recognizes the possibility, noted so forcibly in the empirical work and insights of Parsons, Marx and Weber, of a conflict between actual action and hypothetical or ideal structure. The point at which such tension is recognized in both approaches is not registered in their model of action, but in its distinction from 'reality'. The means by which they try to cope with this distinction is, however, important. The method behind the rationality model incorporates a means of explaining that distinction in terms of the 'irrationality' of real action and its misunderstanding of 'real' structural situations. That of role-status typically attempts to explain away the distinction by using such concepts as deviance and mal-socialization. In this sense, neither approach has any systematic empirical reference at all. The rationality approach does have one with reference to an empirical explanation of the deviance between its model and actual reality. This seems to be why many of its advocates oscillate between it and, in their more detailed work, the abbreviated description of actual action which we noted in Linton (Weber and Marx).

The 'facts' on which the concept of a 'social system' of unintended consequences logically relies are generated by its emergent, theoretically conceived, properties. So are the questions it poses. Examples include the relationship and compatibility between bureaucracy and the nuclear family, the relation between mechanisms of social control and social integration, the generation of conflict as a consequence of mal-social-ization, the embourgeoisement of the proletariat, the extent to which class explains educational institutions, etc. These are at once the problems and the designated areas for empirical work. But the resolutions of these problems are theoretical. They depend on the compatibility of abstract, ideal types of 'social system' whose reference to actual situations is obscure. So actual situations 'more or less' reinforce the resolution of problems and do not settle them 'once and for all'.

Actual reality must inevitably be in constant tension with such a theoretical over-view, for it is only the tangible manifestation of it. But its 'facts' are not the facts of everyday life. And so the theory cannot be falsified. In a very real sense such explanations owe more to the system of ideas and tradition of thought which conceive them than to the 'reality' they purport to explain. As such, they relate specifically to the currents of ideas, and philosophical and social concerns of a previous century, and the problems posed by empirical preconceptions about the shape of society at the time.

Related structural concepts : models of society
Having discussed the way in which the component structural concepts link to form an overall model of society or 'social systems', we shall now look at the model itself. Pictorially, it would seem to differ between Parsons, who concentrated on order, and Marx, whose concern was conflict. (See Fig. 2 p.125). Yet the model that Marx poses for the earliest form of society, and its most developed form, communism, equates in certain respects with the cohesion model that Parsons feels to be applicable to all

societies. Not only are the components of social structure which are used or implied in analysis similar, but so also is the basically cohesive and integrated picture of those models.

At all other stages of development between these first and last forms of society, Marx's model would seem to diverge very markedly from Parsons'. The latter poses cohesion at major points, while the former poses conflict between classes in all spheres of interaction. For Marx, classes and their basic opposition link directly with conflicts in educational, religious and occupational as well as political institutions, producing a social cleavage which divides the structure of society and the interests or goals of men at all levels. However, it is as though these classes were each internally related and cohesive – Parsonian social systems – though opposed to one another and contained within a wider system of conflict. This seems especially true in the most developed and overt forms of class struggle, where each class would have developed a complete set of separate institutions (of family, religion, education, political organization and culture). These two social systems are connected not only at the point of their interdependent relations to the means of production, but also, as a consequence, clash in the realm of political action.

For Marx, each of these two distinct but deeply related social systems, and for Parsons the one social system, were applicable to many forms of contemporary society. Each of the systems of class or status socialize their children in terms of their common interests, or, if you like, their ultimate and common values. The structure of relations of the family and the institutions of education are faced by the child as objectively given, set, structures which he cannot change. He can only learn to respond to them, becoming what is expected of him by others and, ultimately, by that related set of structural concepts, the model of society. The socialization process is, therefore, developed to explain the means by which the child comes to share the common values of his social system and the necessary ways of acting in that system. This reinforces the solidarity of the whole, whether unified, or polarized into classes. So, in interpreting Weber's authority-status hierarchy, Parsons makes him say that 'for one who holds' a social 'order to be legitimate, living up to its rules becomes . . . a matter of moral obligation. Thus Weber has arrived at the same point which Durkheim reached when he interpreted constraint as moral authority'.[6] It is precisely this view of authority that is implied in Marx's view of classes as systems. It is overtly developed by Marcuse, Rex and Dahrendorf, becoming a central feature of their analysis of modern societies. Indeed Marcuse and Dahrendorf could be mistaken for Parsons in many of their assertions about the incorporation of all people into the values and normative way of life or institutionalization of the dominant authorities. In a word, the dominant grouping of actors does not retain its rule by power, but by the exercise of legitimate authority alone.

It would none-the-less seem that there are two differences which are of vital importance despite these profound similarities between Marxism and Parsonian thought. The way the two theorists discuss power and change may be thought to be incompatible. For Parsons, power, or rather authority, is diffused throughout the social system. Where it accumulates in the hands of certain industrial or political groups it is legitimated in terms of common values, which are themselves shared and internalized by all members of the social system. Such clashes of power which do arise are then only temporary, and control mechanisms arise which limit their effect. At many points in the development of his theory Parsons saw the distinct possibility of that power-clash becoming very deep-rooted indeed. This applied especially to his discussion of fascism in Germany and his comments on the Russian revolution by means of the concept of charisma and its routinization.

Marx, however, saw each social system as clashing not just in terms of their separate common interests, but in their organized expression in the realm of political power. The power within each social system was diffused (as legitimized authority) in the way Parsons recognized for society as a whole. But Marx saw a basic clash between these classes and, therefore, a focusing of power within the actual structure of society as a whole. As economic and other relations between the class systems developed, so that power clash would change and develop. At first the bourgeois class would have almost total power. Then as the social system of the proletariat developed it would challenge that power and its legitimacy. At first, as in 1848 and 1871, the proletariat would be beaten. Finally, it would be in a position of such organizational and political strength as to overthrow the ruling order. Rex distinguished three separate models by which to explain these changes. But Marcuse shows how close Marx's model can be pushed into Parsonian shape when examining advanced industrial society. His was a model of order.

Once again, though the differences between Marx and Parsons appear to be great, they are vastly reduced both by the similarity of the component concepts and even by the nature of the model itself. It is only when those models are applied as explanations and descriptions of particular historical circumstances that apparent differences show up.

These comments have already shed some light on the usual assumption that while Parsons' model of the social system is static that of Marx is dynamic. If we examine this assertion now, we find that it too does not stand up. We have already noted how Marx's abstract model of the development and change of society was such that certain steps in those changes had to be reached and then transcended. This was inevitable, because of the rational logic which the abstract actor would follow in the situations he successively occupied. Each class then had to develop in a particular way and, in the process of struggle, had to assume certain inevitable interests or goals. The distribution of power had to alter as the development of the class system altered, as a result of the accumulated consequences of the innumerable rational acts of 'real' people. Though certain variations were possible in intermediate stages, the overall framework of change was determined, not just by this rational logic of unfolding action, but also because of the determining development of class situations, and with the force of economic 'laws' that had the same status as natural laws. Actual people in groups, classes, parties and the state then had to act in entirely predetermined, one might even say functionally determined ways. For such action and relations are functionally necessary for the structure and needs of either class or society, or both, at any one stage of development. All these elements, about which Marx was often hesitant, became more rigid in the hands of Marcuse.

There is nothing fluid in this conflict and change. There is nothing open or undetermined about it. So, when measured against Parsons' or Dahrendorf's model of the 'stable equilibrium' of society, and whilst Marx recognized a process of conflict and rapid change, his view of the forms through which that conflict and that change would necessarily have to go is just as static as theirs. It is then more correct to argue even in the field of social change that Parsons, Marx and those whom they or their interpretations influenced, (Marcuse, Rex and Dahrendorf) show crucial similarities. All, in a word, have rigid views of the abstract form which societies must take, how they develop, and of how their abstract actors in these societies must act.

Weber never reached this position. Nor, as is often alleged, is his use of 'ideal types' static. Nor, as a consequence, was he unable to handle change. If this allegation had been true, it would certainly have also applied to Marx. For, as Weber himself pointed out, his ideal types were identical with Marx's 'laws', 'trends' and 'concepts'.[7] Despite Weber's refusal to 'reify' his 'types', his refusal to relate them in particular ways made the models he constructed of them more flexible than those of Marx. Equally, because he retained a greater distance from any unicausal model of change it can be said that he incorporated Marxism within a wider and more open-ended scheme.[8] He was at once able to look at the effect of social life on economic life and to consider and explain the potential of different types of change.

Yet he increasingly focused on rationality in modern societies. To that extent, he did approach mono-causality and inflexibility and, as a matter of fact, opened up the possibility for Parsons to recognize in his work exactly that deterministic methodology of collectivism which we have analysed. All the same, Weber's method of individualism remained quite clear. It even coloured his prose. He was for ever qualifying his statements with such terms as 'perhaps', 'more or less', 'in general', 'as a rule', 'frequently, but not always'. His 'sense of caution', say the translators and compilers of *Economy and Society*, 'became a stylistic mannerism'.[9]

It is possible at this stage to indicate the kinds of conceptual models of society with which Parsons and Marx worked:

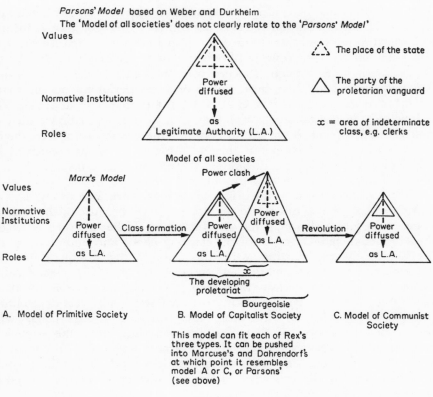

Fig. 2

Voluntarism and Determinism

It is only at this point that we can place the distinction between the terms 'voluntarism' and 'determinism' in their sociological context.

At the very centre of the sociology of Parsons, Marx and Weber resides the idea that actors act voluntarily with respect to the expectancies of others and the demands of the social system. That is, actors are not typically coerced or forced to behave as they do. On the contrary, they positively want to do what they do.

Yet our whole analysis of human nature, of the process of socialization, of social structure, of interests, and of the state and authority have led us to the understanding that the individual is allowed no real choice but to do as he does. His personality is formed and his motives are shaped for him. These mesh with the social structure, and in turn with the ideology or value-system. If the actor should step out of line then there are internal and external mechanisms to ensure that he adjusts very quickly, again submitting voluntarily but deterministically to the authority he disregarded. The 'system' may even have been changed as a consequence.

As such, the conscious individual as we know him in everyday life has no choice in his social situation and does not control either it or his own future. Yet naked force is only rarely used to compel him to act against his own given inclinations. The concept of power may be invoked here. In Marx's hands this signifies a major concern with the control and choice which real men exert over their lives, but it becomes peripheral to the main weight of sociological analysis. On that point all three analysts are agreed.

It is only in the area of power that we can use the ordinary idea of constraint. However, if we are to consider the possibility of free choice as we normally understand it, then all human action as conceived in sociological terms excludes it. Simply, there is no such thing, except as a liberal illusion.

This was not the case at the origin of Parsons' work. For an ambiguous margin of choice was offered to the actor exactly because of the tension between the Hobbesian man and social structure. If the structure 'relaxed', the Hobbesian man burst through, creating chaos and anomie through his choice. Marx, starting with the self-fulfilling co-operative and optimistic view of rationality, had to constrain it within class-divided society. But he was certain that man, especially in periods of social revolution, would burst the normative confines of his class-determined position, rationally overthrowing the previous ruling class, who represented an aspect of that class position. But, after the empirical creation of such new socialist societies, Marcuse was forced to concur in Weber's pessimistic view of rationality. Rex and Dahrendorf quite explicitly came to disavow their earlier dependence on Weber as well as their own political optimism.

With Marx the 'choice' is a collective one, with Parsons it was individual. But, in each instance, it was only fleeting, was not fully built into their methodology and their finished concepts logically deny it. Marx tended to avoid the problem by pushing it to the end-point of history, while Marcuse tries to come to contemporary terms with it by rejecting it altogether.

The Modern Consenus

Intermediate note

In passing to the second half of this chapter we should define what we mean by the 'cohesion' school and the 'conflict' school of theory. For, in the remainder of this chapter, we will refer to both schools while discussing the modern extension of the convergence which we have discussed in the 'founding fathers'.

Weber's and Parsons' view of Weber's concept of status, its application to so many spheres of life, and its ranking into hierarchies, has had certain consequences for sociology. Many contemporary sociologists have come under his influence, and that of anthropology, and have developed a similar view of the structure and form of society. This view has, on the whole, developed at the complete expense of Weber's and Marx's view of 'class'. This way of seeing society has sometimes been called 'cohesion theory'. In future, we shall refer to it as such.

Equally, many sociologists – fewer in America than in Britain and Europe – have developed Marx's and Weber's view of class. A school of thought has developed which is by no means united. While its exponents have not necessarily amended Marx's view of class very radically, they have at least tried to come to terms with the many empirical difficulties which are posed by the application of Marx's model to the modern world. But these sociologists all retain class as a central concept and, in particular, as a means by which to explain conflict. For them, conflict, class and power are at the very centre of the structure of society.

These sociologists have often sought assistance in Weber's concept of status, and some have found use for his concept of authority. As is the case with the 'cohesion' school, these and others have come under the influence of Freud and have tried to append a view of personality to Marx's model of man. This broad school of thought is sometimes referred to as 'conflict theory'. We shall use that term when we refer to any one, or all of its advocates.

The two schools of thought, conflict and cohesion theory, which Marx, Weber and Parsons influenced are commonly thought to be at opposed poles of the sociological axis. At least those who adhere to one approach view the other with varying degrees of hostility. This partly relates to what are thought to be the political and moral biases which append revolution to the conflict approach and conservatism to the cohesion approach.

There is also a shared hostility between these modern theoretical schools and those who engage primarily in empirical sociology. They charge that 'fact-gathering' is pointless and uninformative without a theoretical perspective to guide the empirical research. The empiricists often return the contempt. Though they too, as we shall see in later chapters, inevitably search for their information and interpret it through an implicit if not an overt or well-defined theoretical framework.

It is not this quarrel with which we are concerned in this chapter, but that between the cohesion and conflict schools themselves. It seems, on closer inspection, that the similarities between the two schools override their distinctions. To discuss what has led to the development of this convergence in any detail is beyond the scope of the argument. But, clearly, it relates to those similarities which we have discerned in the major figures from whom they take their point of departure. Because Parsons is still very much alive and his influence is continuing, though it is by no means always direct, we shall have to refer to him fairly frequently. We shall have to do the same for Rex, Dahrendorf and

Marcuse. But we shall mainly look at a cross-section of sociological opinion in the two schools of thought in an attempt to add substance to the claim that the basic concepts which they use to build their apparently opposed explanatory models are now fundamentally the same.

The individual and socialization

First of all we must ask how both schools view the individual, the way he acts, and how that action, and the individual, relate to the general fabric of society. In response to these questions Gerth and Mills, two conflict theorists, have written that 'the concept of role, the key term in our definition of person, is also the key term in our definition of institutions. It is, therefore, . . . the major link of character and social structure . . . Just as role is the unit with which we build our conception of institution, so institution is the unit with which we build the conception of social structure'.[10] It is not possible to see here any point with which any cohesion theorist would wish to take issue. For example, Biddle and Thomas were able to write that the perspective of role theory is 'a limited, social determinism that ascribes much, but rarely all, of the variances of real-life behaviour to the operation of immediate or past external influences'.[11] The 'role' concept, explaining the reality of action by external determinism, links the individual with the social structure in terms of institutional expectancies, which are themselves patterned according to 'cultural systems'.[12]

Berger uses a slightly different emphasis when he argues that 'institutions are embodied in individual experience by means of roles . . . By playing roles the individual participates in a social world. By internalizing these roles the same world becomes subjectively real to him'.[13] That is to say, 'the role represents the institutional order' which is objectified to and then internalized by the individual.[14]

Gerth and Mills take their argument a step further when they begin to suggest exactly how the person acquires these roles in terms of which he acts. 'A person is composed of an internalization of organized social roles which are embedded in the institutional structure.' A person internalizes new roles through a 'learning' process in which language is vital and where the 'expectations of others . . . become the self-expectations of' the person.[15] The process whereby the person does internalize the roles, the expectations of others which are held out to him and into which he must fit, has come to be universally accepted, and is called the socialization process.

The problem with which these theorists are faced is this: how do children when first born come to perform in these institutional roles as they mature into social adults? What is the process by which the blank screen, which is the child, slowly becomes patterned into socially accepted conduct as he matures, so maintaining, or causing change in, the institutional social structure?

In response to this problem Berger suggested that 'the reality of everyday life always appears as a zone of lucidity behind which there is a background of darkness'. This lucidity or certainty, which roles and role expectations provide for the individual, has the 'quality of an instrument that cuts a path through' an 'impenetrable forest'.[16] To the child life is this impenetrable forest. Socialization is the process by which he acquires lucidity, by which the trees assume names, and the paths become signposted. But this process involves the internalization of those trees and paths, those ways of behaving, which are already socially acceptable to adults and which have become defined institutional roles.

Role theory, as we have discussed it, is thought to be an integral part of this socialization process. For example, like Gerth and Mills, two cohesion theorists have argued that 'role behaviour is in large measure learned behaviour; and, as such, the learning process pertaining to the acquisition, maintenance, and extinction of behaviour become the proper subject of interest' for the sociologist.[17] These processes are subsumed under the theory of socialization. And this process itself is 'concerned particularly with the learning of socially relevant behaviour at various stages of the life cycle'.[18]

The theories which disciplines other than sociology have developed about how people learn have increasingly been influenced by the concept of role and related categories, just as Parsons first developed the concept from social anthropology. In its early years, psychology had concentrated very much on the individual, separating him from his social environment, even explaining that environment in terms of the extension of the individual personality. Indeed, such a criticism can be made, with some fairness, of Freud.

In rejecting this simple, psychological reductionist argument (as a result of cross-cultural comparisons) neo-Freudians (such as Erich Fromm) recognized a two-way process between the person and social structures or culture. Each, they came to feel, influenced the other. This means that they do not attempt to reduce the explanation of the one solely in terms of the other. This development in social psychology has become deeply influenced by the development of the role concept in sociology. It has become accepted by both disciplines as the vital linking concept between the two approaches. Since the early 1950s, learning and socialization theory has extended this link.

It was in the light of these developments that such a sophisticated commentator on human action as Goffman was able to argue that 'in entering the position, the incumbent finds that he must take on a whole array of action encompassed by the corresponding role. [Hence,] role implies a social determinism and a doctrine about socialization. We do not take on items of conduct one at a time but rather a whole harness load of them . . . Role, then, is the basic unit of socialization. It is through roles that tasks in society are allocated and arrangements made for their performance'.[19] Goffman thinks that this view applies to much, but not all, human conduct. Generally, 'a self . . . virtually awaits the individual entering a structurally defined position'.[20] Later we shall return to Goffman in some detail to examine some of the more basic criticisms which can be made of the concepts and approach we are discussing. But now we must turn to Parsons so that we may get a more precise view of the link he gave to the three systems of personality, structure and culture, by developing his theory of socialization.

Parsons assumes 'that the maintenance of the complementarity of role-expectations, once established, is not problematical . . . that the tendency to maintain the interaction process is the first law of social process'.[21] Parsons establishes even more firmly the idea of complementary role-expectations, not by any resort to empirical study, but by reference to the problem of social order as he originally stated it. It must follow from this that to have social co-operation, of any sort, people must have similar expectations of each other, and that they must force or encourage their children to adopt similar normative standards. It is only 'deviation' from this 'complementarity' which is problematical.

Parsons goes on to ask how this complementarity is acquired by the developing child. 'The orientations which an actor implements in . . . roles, are not inborn but have to be acquired through learning'[22]. Before this learning process is completed, however, the child would act so as to destroy the 'equilibrium of interaction'. The 'acquisition of the requisite orientations . . . is a learning process . . . [This is] the process of socialization'. The mechanisms involved in this form the 'processes of normal functioning of the social system'.[23] One such mechanism is in fact 'deviance', which is exhibited before the role has been learned. There are, then, mechanisms which the social system has to acquire and by which this deviance is controlled, so that the equilibrium of role-expectancies may be maintained.

Parsons spells out what is involved in learning. To do this he shows how the same concept (role) is equally vital for both the personality and the structural system. He argues that the 'allocation of personnel between roles in the social system', which is stratified by the division of labour in complex societies, 'and the socialization processes of the individual are clearly the same process viewed in different perspectives. Allocation is the process seen in the perspective of functional significance to the social system as system. Socialization . . . is the process seen in terms of the motivation [in role orientations] of the individual actor'.[24]

Whilst again asserting the direct link between the two processes Parsons also introduces social division in terms of strata, each of which contain a series of roles geared to the differing needs of the institutionalized social system, which are also linked by the culture system. Stratification theory, which accounts for the mechanisms by which individuals, irrespective of their overt beliefs and goals, are allocated to social positions, follows quite logically. The relation of this to empirical reality is again in doubt, but it does involve a particular view of what, when, and how, the individual learns his role.

What is learned or internalized when young forms the 'stablest and most enduring . . . major value orientation patterns' and is predetermined by the social structure. These resulting 'value orientations' are 'not, on a large scale, subject to drastic alteration during adult life'.[25] How any alteration may occur at the empirical level can be accounted for, and what this might imply for the socialization process as Parsons develops it, are not qualified.

Indeed, almost at the birth of the infant, 'a role is ascribed to him which includes expectations of his behaviour' and which he learns. In this process of learning there are five mechanisms at work. These are 'reinforcement-extinction, inhibition' of the 'id', 'substitution, imitation, and identification'.[26] From the point of view of the personality, these five mechanisms either involve unconscious reactions, or direct responses to the social structure, which have to follow a path in which there is no choice in terms of 'voluntary' acceptance or 'identification'. The result, the acquisition of specific roles and expectancies, neatly gears into the actions and expectations of other and related sectors of the social system.

Identification, Parsons insists, 'is obviously the most important' of these five learning mechanisms 'for the acquisition of value patterns'. Learning by means of 'identification' involves 'internalising the values of the model' of *alter* (parent, then others, all of whom reflect 'society') which the child uses.[27] Because the model of the parent reflects the values of the dominant sections of society, the values are also internalized, learned, and acted in terms of. 'Alter *is* the model and this *is* the learning process'[28].

This argument clearly involves a view of the complete determination of the individual by the joint effect of the personality and the external structural systems, mediated through the process of identification. Indeed, it is openly admitted that the individual is the plastic plaything of these conditioning structural forces and pressures. It means that 'value-orientation patterns can only be internalized from the outside'.[29] They may not be developed by the individual against these social constraints. Once internalized, they have become an integral and almost unchanging feature of the person, who now wants to fulfil the structural expectations which are held out to him.

Parsons continues with his own developing logic: it follows that 'certain broad, fundamental patterns of "character" are laid down in childhood . . . and are not radically changed by adult experience'.[30] The exact degree to which the 'plasticity' of the very young child finally 'becomes . . . diminished, are not at issue here'. It is quite consistent to argue from this that the 'combination of value-orientation patterns' which the individual acquires 'must, in a very important degree, be a function of the fundamental role structure', which is an institutionalized reflection 'of the dominant values of the social system'.[31]

There is an intimate link between the role concept at personality, structural and culture levels. Each of these sets of concepts relies heavily on the analysis of the socialization process. Parsons argues that socialization is 'the internalization of the value-orientation patterns', that is 'the role-expectations for ego of the significant socializing agents, which constitutes the strategic element of the basic personality structure'.[32] The vital mechanism is one of 'identification', which crucially develops the person from his 'childhood' and individual state of 'plasticity'. This forms the individual's outlook on life, and results in his action, if not always his ideas, meshing with what is expected of him by his relations in the social structure. Once formed, his ideas and actions may not change. Marcuse would not depart from this analysis.

In discussing this problem of socialization, Berger also accepts much of Parsons' thesis. However, he distinguishes two aspects of the socialization process, thus dramatizing a problem of which Parsons was aware: namely the possibility that the adult may adopt slightly different ideas and ways of action from those 'internalized'. This same problem is raised even more strongly in conflict theory. The probability is posed of at least two opposed and openly clashing cultural systems. Yet, it is argued, each system will have been internalized by people in the way Parsons has outlined for the one ordered system. In the development of such conflict between these systems, ideas and situations, and consequently roles will also change. How can the concept of role and the determined individual account for this?

Berger argues that 'this internalization of society, identity, and reality is not a matter of once and for all. Socialization is never total and never finished. This presents us with two further problems: First, how the reality internalized in primary socialization is maintained in consciousness, and second, how further internalizations – or secondary socializations – in the later biography of the individual take place.'[33]

Many societies, Berger notes, actually mark the dividing line between primary and secondary socialization by means of the rituals of adolescence and transition to adulthood.[34] The secondary aspects of socialization are less rigidly laid down. Though they mesh with those acquired earlier, they are more readily changed. In this slightly more fluid situation, Berger continues, it is only possible to maintain one's 'self-identity . . . in a milieu that confirms this identity'.[35] He goes on to insist that it is not difficult now to propose a specific 'prescription' for alteration into any conceivable reality . . . for, say, convincing individuals that by 'eating fish' they can 'communicate with Martians'.[36] This returns us to the view of the infinite manipulability of man. It occurs even in conflicting situations, and even after the stage of 'primary socialization' has passed. This is quite consistent as long as the concept of role is held in conjunction with its allied approach to socialization whereby man is sustained only by the interrelation of the personality with the structure and the culture systems.

That is, where 'society determines how long and in what manner the individual . . . shall live'.[37]

One further problem is posed by Berger. Socialization is seen as a never-ending process, of which the later or secondary part is more open to change than that in childhood. This is especially true of complex societies. It is then necessary to 'develop procedures of reality-maintenance',[38] before our determinate concept of man can be maintained. It becomes necessary to extend the theory of socialization in order to outline how the structural concepts of legitimation and authority are developed. They are as vital to the 'procedures of reality-maintenance' to which Berger referred, and of social control, which Parsons thought so necessary for 'successful' socialization. And both are concepts common to all orthodox analysts of both conflict and cohesion schools.

Institutions, Berger feels, are 'experienced as possessing a reality of their own, a reality that confronts the individual as an external and coercive fact'.[39] Marx was very aware of this point and used the concepts of 'alienation' and 'false-consciousness' as means to explain it. Durkheim was led initially to use the idea of social facts being external to the individual, and so constraining him to act in socially predetermined ways. Later, he developed the idea of an internalized moral constraint. Weber used the ideal type of rational legal authority, which he saw as prevalent in modern society, and traditional authority, for non-modern societies, as a means of explaining social order in terms of its moral and obligatory acceptance.

All these structural features, the argument continues, must be made reasonable to the individual or his personality, for, to the extent to which he experiences frustration in his situation he has scope to act against them. This means these constraining institutions must be made 'legitimate' to the actor.

'These legitimations are learned by the new generation during the same process that socializes them into the institutional order.'[40] These legitimations 'produce new meanings that serve to integrate the meanings already attached to disparate institutional processes'.[41] It is only where this process has not been adequate that Berger feels it necessary to argue for new legitimations, which will unite disparity or conflict at the lower structural level. Thus, 'the material out of which universe-maintaining legitimations are constructed is mostly a further elaboration, on a higher level of theoretical integration, of the legitimations of the several institutions' which make up society.[42]

Structure: the cohesion school

Weber's particular and subjective concept of status, as distinct from that of class, has been developed into the theory of social stratification. As each actor's or group's status is understandable subjectively by the scientist, then 'the point of view from which we approach the analysis of stratification prescribes that analysis should focus on the common value-pattern' in society.[43] This not only allows us to understand the subjective interests of each status position without consulting the 'occupant', but also the way these different positions link up in terms of the common value-system.

It is important to realize that such an abstract system of structural stratification 'relates to the system of [status] positions, not to the individual's occupying those positions'.[44] How actual individuals themselves see their life-style is not as important for the scientist to uncover as is the need to derive a view, a rational view in Weber's case, of what that style might ideally be expected to be, given an abstract type of dominant value system. In each case the particular status position, its expectations and the typical role which should flow in that position, are constructed by the scientist with a main eye on the value system, and also, in some cases, though not necessarily, the functional requirements of 'the system'.

It is in this context that it is possible to account for what writers feel to be the visible inequalities in the social system. 'Social inequality' becomes viewed as 'an unconsciously evolved device by which societies ensure that the most important positions are conscientiously filled by the most qualified persons'.[45] It will be recalled that Weber saw status as involving a positive or negative estimation of social honour. This aspect of his concept has been taken up in the context of the discussion of inequality. It is argued that 'some set of norms governing relations of superiority and inferiority is an inherent need of every stable social system'. Indeed, 'such a patterning or (normative) order *is* the stratification system of society'.[46]

Once the argument has reached this point it is possible to insist that the theory of stratification '*is* general sociological theory'.[47] But such a view involves far more than just the ability to conceptualize the abstract status hierarchy of one particular society. 'The theory of social stratification should not refer to a specific society, but should be general enough to apply to various social structures.'[48]

Perhaps it is clear at this point that the status position of, say, priest, teacher or politician can be outlined only in terms of the theory, and not by any reference to what particular priests or teachers do or are expected to do in any particular situation in any one society. Rather, there are general prescriptions which the abstract idea of the social system involves for such status positions and, indeed, for the roles which are attached to them. Such positions are subjectively understandable by the scientist *only* in terms of his theory. Though still formally involving subjectivity the relation of this theory to any empirical grounding which it attempts to explain is not only not spelled out, but would seem by definition to be irrelevant in the initial formation of that theory.

In each concrete society the normative framework is divided into separate spheres of institutional activity. This division of function is equally built into the abstract model of social systems. So the religious institutions are seen as stratified by an internal hierarchy. It is also thought to exercise a 'powerful control over human behaviour' generally, 'guiding it along the lines sustaining the institutional structure' of all other spheres of activity and so 'promoting the ultimate values and ends' of society.[49]

Similarly, labour and work are seen as being divided into different occupational groups, rather than into economic classes. So, 'the primary structural emphasis', it is argued, rests with 'the structure of occupational roles within the system of industrial society'.[50] As occupational status has to be ordered about scarce resources it 'becomes convenient for the society to use unequal economic returns as a principal means of controlling the entrance of a person into positions and stimulating the performance of their duties. The amount of the economic return therefore becomes one of the main indices of social status'.[51] It is, of course, a similar belief which has allowed some empirical sociologists to do work on the structure of society using income and similar 'objective' factors. G. D. H. Cole and, perhaps, the Registrar General would be examples of this approach.[52]

Political and legal life, as with religious and occupational life, is stratified by status. Its major importance lies in the structural fact that government gives legitimacy to the authority system and the dominant values of society. In a word, it 'organises the society in terms of law and authority' and so provides positive and negative sanctions to reinforce styles of conduct already determined by the socialization process.[53]

Weber argued that, in modern society, legitimacy rested on 'a belief in the "legality" of patterns of normative rules and the rights of those elevated to authority under such rules to issue commands'.[54] This carried the expectation that those in subordinate positions would feel the moral obligation to obey. This was taken only to one possible conclusion in the work of stratification which we are discussing. As we saw, Weber discussed power as lying in the province of political parties, acting in the interests of classes and or status groups. As such, it was entirely possible for him to examine conflict. But his view that legitimacy was attached to the State apparatus in terms of moral obligation (because it reflected the dominant value of society) in Parsons' hands strongly implies a view of structural cohesion.

It is to this view that the stratification theorists have adhered. They have developed it further. For them, authority is seen as a quality which is dispersed throughout the social system, accumulating at only certain quite legitimate status positions. Authority is attached to those positions, and so to those actors who occupy those positions and who have learned to accept the value system. These actors then strive to bring back to legitimate action (by means of control mechanisms) any who 'deviate' as a consequence of the strains and stresses of secondary socialization.

Authority may break down or be disputed in terms of a different set of values, and thus of different legitimations. Here we have, in embryo, the kind of conflict models that Parsons, Berger, Smelser and Coser all develop in different attempts to deal with the 'class', 'generational' and 'institutional' conflict which they have observed in modern societies.

At this point 'power' might become a key concept in developing a cohesion model into one of conflict. Very frequently, however, there is a failure by these authors clearly to distinguish any differences between 'authority' and 'power'. Though critical of the more vulgar aspects of cohesion theory, Lewis Coser is himself prey to this mistake.[55] But, then, so are many writers who focus more on conflict. Daniel Foss, for example, whilst asking for a ' "sociology of horror" in which social science tries to be honest with the industrial work and with itself',[56] fails to distinguish the two concepts.[57] Indeed, the major exponent of this approach argues that power can be seen as 'an attribute of the total social system'. It is made up of several variables which are 'the support that can be mobilized by those exercising power [and] the facilities they have access to . . .' The 'control of the productivity of the economy' is particularly important. Other variables are 'the legitimation that can be accorded to the positions of the holders of power and the relatively unconditional loyalties of the population to the society in its politically organized aspects'.[58]

Structure: the conflict school

Marx himself saw why it was necessary to treat the individual as if he were 'dependent', having 'no individuality'.[59] In the same way, Gerth and Mills regard the individual as 'composed of an internalization of organized social roles'.[60] We are involved in treating the individual not only as abstract, but as being analysed in terms of the roles which articulate with the class position which he occupies. In this way the very 'definition of the person' depends on the concept 'role', just as does the definition of institutions.[61]

Laing and Cooper, interpreting Sartre with approval, argue that 'the most immediate and brutal aspects of our objective reality', the class relations into which we are born, are our 'predetermination in general'.[62] This is exactly what Marx meant when he maintained that each concrete individual enters into 'definite and necessary relations which are independent of . . . will', and which he must accept.[63] It is possible to argue that roles 'await a person' in the positions to which he is allocated in the social structure. He must play them, and he must learn or internalize new ones as he develops. It is because of this that the scientist must see 'the life course of [say] a worker . . . even down to the fantasies of the machinist', as being 'predetermined in general. The factory girl in her sexual relations, pregnancies, abortions, realizes by herself what she is already' as the abstract bundle of social roles delineated by the scientists. That is to say, she passes against herself the sentence already passed by the whole nexus of socio-economic conditions into which she has been born.[64] This view, involving a psychological, structural and cultural perspective, is exactly what Rex means when he argues that the actions of the individual 'become integrated with' those of another 'through the cultural patterning of the elements . . . The ends which the individual seeks may be set for him by his cultural conditioning [and, in striving to these ends his conduct is] directed along common lines by learned culture patterns'.[65]

This conditioning occurs through the socialization process. So, the 'picture of the world [which the individual has] may be the same as that of his fellows because the process of getting to know the world is governed by norms which come to him as part of the cultural patterning'.[66] Norms are both a part of role and of the institutional structure of society. That institutional structure itself is merely the normative patterning which is ordered in terms of the cultural system. It is through this ordered system and by the process of socialization that the individual internalizes these cultural beliefs. It is for this reason that role is 'the key term in our definition of institution' and it is therefore 'one major link of character and social structure'.[67]

Cooper puts it in a slightly different way when he argues that 'by the time we leave school, we have become so conditioned to being in a box', or role, 'that from then on we erect our own box . . . around us'.[68] Reacting with even greater moral force to these structural pressures, Laing argues that from birth the 'baby is subjected to . . . forces called love as its mother and father have been . . . These forces are mainly concerned with destroying most of [the child's] potentialities'. So, by the 'time the new human being is fifteen or so, we are left with a being like ourselves'.[69] What is effectively being argued is that 'long before birth, even before we are conceived, our parents' and, by implication, the class into which we have to be born 'have decided who we will be'.[70]

We find the concepts of role, norm, institution, authority, legitimacy, culture, system, socialization, are indeed similar to those used by cohesion theorists. However, they are used to construct rather different pictures or models both of how the structure of society looks and how it works. This is mainly because they use class and not status as a key concept and, with it, the implication of necessary structural conflict.

The conflict model of society provides a picture of society as stratified. Fundamentally this division takes the form of two main classes. Each of these classes then takes the form of an independently observable, abstract social system, on its own, but crucially related to the other. An abstract view of the whole social system then incorporates a view of these classes, and also of the relations between them. These relations may pass through different stages, as the classes themselves develop in conflict with each other.

Rex argues that what is necessary to understand this total social system is 'a theory which finds a place for normatively oriented action' of the sort which is understandable when we look either at an ordered society or at the relations within one class. At the same time, in order to understand the relations between those two classes, 'we also need to recognize that some of the ends which the actor in our system pursues may be random . . . from the point of view of the [social] system' of the dominant class or may actually be 'in conflict with it . . . The behaviour of actors towards one another may not be determined by shared norms but by the success which each has in compelling the other to act in accordance with his interest'. It is in this context that 'power then becomes a crucial variable in the study of [total] social systems'.[71]

There is no great divergence between this approach and one which the cohesion theorists could adopt, or towards which their concepts could be pushed. To give an illustration, Robert Merton is deeply aware of the possibility of conflict arising between different groups within society. He argues that 'it is not enough to refer to the institutions as though they were uniformly supported by all groups and strata within society. Unless systematic consideration is given to the degree of support of particular institutions by specific groups we shall overlook the important place of power within society'.[72]

Dahrendorf, a conflict theorist whose articulation of role and socialization theory is almost more exact than that of the cohesion school itself, concentrated on the place of authority in group conflict rather than power. In the process, he, like Rex, merely developed concepts capable of explaining order.

Most conflict theorists, Marx included, have of necessity spent more time discussing what Rex has called the ruling-class situation, or something approaching the truce situation, than any other stage in Marx's continuous picture of the development of the class struggle. During the many stages of this ruling-class situation the oppressed class is regarded as hardly more than a class-in-itself. It has only nascent institutions, and no ideology of its own. The ruling class dominates not only within the economic sphere but also in the State, the educational and religious institutions, all of which they control. In this sense, the ideas and the culture of this class are the values which are predominantly institutionalized in the normative structure of the whole of society. It is, then, the class values and norms of the ruling class which are socialized into and internalized even by most of those who occupy positions in the working class. That is, the 'norms' and 'values' legitimize the class structure of society.

It is this process of legitimation and voluntary acceptance which Marx was describing when he said 'of this world [bourgeois] religion is the general theory . . . its logic in popular thought . . . its enthusiasm, its moral sanction, its solemn completion, its universal ground for truth and justification'.[73] It was functionally necessary for that stage of development in the evolving 'social system'.

Equally, Laing and Cooper, echoing Sartre, now argue of a later stage in this evolutionary development that the 'possessing class has found a new stratagem of mystification . . . by way of neo-paternalism, and human engineering'.[74] By various means of mass communication and social benefits the ruling class not only seek to keep the working class relatively content but also seek to define their situation for them, to legitimize their own rule by more sophisticated means than religion. In this sense modern Marxists such as Marcuse depart from Marx's optimistic interpretation of social democracy. It is within this context that Halsey argues that the 'basic function of education is . . . the preservation and transmission of culture', the culture of the ruling class.[75] The point is also argued at the empirical level by those who see the members of the working class as having become embourgeoisés.

The more the ruling class succeeds in encouraging this process of socialization, the more the naked power of the ruling class becomes transformed into legitimate authority in the eyes of the whole society, the more also the model which the conflict theorist has to construct approximates to that of the orthodox cohesion theorist.

Eventually, it seems to make sense to argue that the 'social system' or 'society needs lunatics in order that it may regard itself as sane and therefore society needs mental hospitals. But, because society needs hospitals, hospitals need patients. To satisfy this need system the passivity of patients is strictly enjoined on the day of their admission and subsequently reinforced by all the resources of that institution'.[76] We can see here that where the ruling class control even the definitions of sanity and madness, as well as the institutions of state and education, it is possible for conflict theorists to employ a model of society which directly reflects a naïve or vulgar structural functionalism. Society or, rather, 'bourgeois society', needs lunatics, so there are lunatics, just as for Berger it was possible to manipulate men into communicating with Martians by eating fish.

Marcuse has developed the most pessimistic of all the Marxist models. In his view the proletariat still exists as an objective class-in-itself. But its members have become almost totally submerged by and socialized into the system of 'repressive tolerance' by which the 'élite' of the bourgeois class control their destiny. However, it is crucial to recognize that even Marcuse retains Marx's original ambiguity when defining class. The workers have 'true' interests, which can be derived by the scientist from the objective class situation, and which are defined without reference to them. But, at the same time, their subjective relations with the bourgeois class are recognized as important in that class situation. So too are the subjective but 'false' interests which they actually develop and which render them impotent as agents of change. It can be argued that almost all of the 'English empiricists' use this formulation to the detriment of their work.[77]

It remains possible for these 'objective conditions' to be laid bare. All Marxist theoreticians are convinced that in certain circumstances the workers could recognize their 'true' interests, and come to act in the relevant revolutionary manner. So it is only when increasing numbers of the working class challenge the legitimacy of the ruling class, where 'law, morality, religion' become to 'them so many bourgeois prejudices, behind which lurk in ambush just as many bourgeois interests', that the 'conflict' model comes to look widely different from the 'cohesion' one.[78] Yet it is exactly in this conflict model that each class, rather than just the ruling class, can be seen as a cohesive 'social system', and, as such, be analysed in terms of the concepts which apply to the cohesion model. Equally, thanks to Merton's formulation of power along the lines used by the conflict school, it is quite possible, as we suggested was the case even for Parsons, to develop the 'cohesion' model into one which resembles the 'revolutionary' situation that Rex, Marx and others describe.

Conclusion

The areas of convergence in sociological theory may be seen to be far more extensive than say, Lockwood has recognized. Conflict theories have *not* 'failed to relate their interest in social change to the problem of system integration'.[79] Nor have functionalists failed to make inroads into the theory of change and conflict. Parsons, Coser and Smelser are good examples here, in addition to Merton. Dahrendorf, like Lockwood, having drawn the 'Marxian' and 'Parsonian' schemes at their most extreme, felt that any convergence between the two approaches did not seem 'feasible'.[80] He, like Lockwood, has been shown to be mistaken. It is, perhaps, ironic that he, a self-declared conflict theoretician, eventually came to summarize and develop the consensual conceptions of role, socialization and normative structure most articulately.

In outlining his view of man, his fundamentally sociological view of man, Dahrendorf expressed surprise that some should worry about the fact that it is so different from the actual men we see around us. In formulating their equations and laws the natural sciences produce explanations of matter which look in no way like the trees and mountains, whose composition depends in some way on those laws. Why then, the argument goes, should 'sociological man' look anything like the real men and women whom the sociologist knows in his 'out of office' hours? In the interests of scientific abstraction, in the need to forge ideal types of relations, actions, structures, we must be prepared to ignore the detail and variety of reality. Naturally the picture of man and his relations to society which emerges will bear no obvious similarity to the humble, empirical facts of life. For, to the sociologist, 'the individual *is* his social roles, but these roles, for their part, are' the structurally predetermined facts of society.[81] These are not the facts of one actual society, but of abstract society in general. It is exactly because of this that at last sociology can be seen as a science. Man's actions can be seen as rule-governed, as uniform, just as is the case with the inert world with which the natural sciences are concerned.

This finally means adopting a value-laden view of 'sociological man', artificially created for the purpose of explanation. Dahrendorf's socio-logical man articulates so exactly with the structural relations and expectations which surround him that he must mirror their values and structural norms with precision in his own personality and action. 'By observation, imitation, indoctrination, and conscious learning, he must grow into the forms that society holds in readiness for him as an incumbent of positions.'[82] This view of the socialization process must involve the rejection of any basic or initial view of human nature involving creativity or freedom, and must replace it with the abstract 'constraint and generality of social roles'.[83]

This view of sociological man, MacIntyre feels, is so obvious a standpoint that 'in America the reaction has been to suppose' that what Dahrendorf 'was saying was so obviously true as to be almost boring'.[84] In a more perceptive criticism Rex sees the outlook as displacing the basic idea of social action and the 'centrality given it by Weber'.[85] Yet, as we have seen, it is certainly 'no accident that in the course of time, sociology lost sight of people as human beings; rather, this development was inevitable from the moment that sociology emerged as a science'.[86] Or, rather, this occurred as sociology emerged as an academic discipline in universities.

We have suggested that there are real, deep and irreconcilable differences between aspects of the work of Marx, Parsons, and Weber. Yet their work converged. The similarities are not to do with an underlying convergence dictated by the needs of empirical and voluntaristic explanation, but due to the logic of the assumptions, ideas, and problems of their age to which they responded.

The origin of the explanation of this fact first began to emerge when we examined the nature of the kind of social problems which Marx, Parsons, and Weber were confronted with. We gained further insight when we looked in detail at the use of 'role', and related concepts. Finally, when turning to 'structure', we found that the works of Marcuse, Dahrendorf, and Rex, whose convergences with the later Parsons were significant, gave the final clue. Exactly because their approaches were different, and were still passing through different stages in their move to a common position, their work illustrated the point. Their differing view of man, or of rationality, or of the structure of situations, all failed to coincide with reality – the way real man interacted – and with the flexibility and variety of life. But, precisely because they retained their different starting points for a sufficient period of time, it became necessary to adopt similar structural concepts, and a similar view of man, in order to explain the deviance from that 'reality' of their models. Firstly, man himself had to be seen as determined, as socialized, and as infinitely manipulable, as being and as playing a role. Therefore, second, 'structure' had to be seen as determining in order to sustain that view of man. This made possible the explanation of why man deviated from the preconceptions of the initial theory concerning his expected action and relationship. It was a normative explanation.

In maintaining their initial position the concepts which developed to account for man were of necessity deterministic, in order to account for the otherwise inexplicable: the deviation of reality from the empirical starting point.

Such convergences as we have examined involved the gradual rejection of distinctions between Marx, Weber, and the early Parsons. These distinctions sustain a second tradition in sociological thought, to which we shall presently have cause to refer. This tradition, which was submerged in the work of the founding fathers, has been effectively removed by the advance of sociological theory in modern times. We have examined a range of modern writers who are almost exclusively concerned with, and are partly responsible for, this orthodox convergence. They have not always recognized this fact, and heated disputes still exist between consensus and conflict approaches.

We have offered some explanations of the original, classical convergence in sociological theory. But why has it been sustained and consolidated by subsequent generations of sociologists? The historical, sociological, political, and logical factors are manifold and far beyond the scope of our argument. The intention has been to present the convergence as a disquieting fact of life, not to explain it. Explanations of it would have to take into account the enormous impact of Parsons' own mammoth work *The Structure of Social Action* on succeeding sociological thought. In Britain it owes much to the influence and dominance (in the political sense of the term) of the London School of Economics over the teaching of sociology. So, alas, the struggle for academic recognition which sociologists are still fighting has contributed to its defensiveness, and its reliance on particular interpretations of the founding fathers. A contribution has moreover been made by the use of archaic teaching methods and the ruthless competition of examinations which successive waves of students have had to undergo. Similarly, there is a self-fulfilling aspect to the selection procedures of staff and student appointments. Indeed, a vested sociological interest has emerged as the discipline itself gained established recognition. This vested interest, despite claims to the contrary, is shared by the sociologists of the left.

John Rex and Ralf Dahrendorf both intended that the sociology they offered (and are still developing) should be seen as part of an alternative to the functionalism which Kingsley Davis defined as being sociology itself. They, like Marcuse and other representatives of the Frankfurt school, recognize the inadequacy and political bias of orthodox sociology. But their own work has seriously contributed to the general acceptance and establishment of the orthodox.

That these critics and dissenters, the advocates of an alternative, radical, sociology should in fact be part of the orthodox consensus is a measure of the crisis facing sociology and students of sociology. The first task for any student who cannot accept the orthodox consensus is to demonstrate that it does exist. Very few, including the advocates of convergence, recognized the extent to which it has already been achieved and institutionalized. One recent contribution to modern social theory has, in fact, attempted to draw several previously disparate strands together. The highly illuminating introduction to the work was written by Professor Donald MacRae. He felt that Dr Cohen's contribution 'puts the answer to the central question of all social theory, "How is society possible?" on a firmer footing than . . . will easily be found elsewhere'. This, precisely because it draws on the 'complementarities and convergences in the work of the sociological "classics" '. It shows us that a genuine unity 'is possible and, indeed, largely achieved'. In the face of such unity we must expect 'a comparatively long period of quiet . . .' Indeed, we are 'fortunate in' the timing of the work, because of its contribution to unification', and because of the lull that must for some time be expected and in which the newest generation of sociologists can and will be educated.[87]

Part II   The Concept 'Role', the Actor, and an Alternative

6: Problems and Possibilities

Introduction

This part will be as exclusively concerned as is possible with the way sociology does, and might, look at the individual person, and groups of people who seem to have similar characteristics. That is, we shall be concerned with only one half of the sociological equation. The other half, social structure, will be examined, criticized, and an alternative indicated in Part III. Of course, it will not be possible, or indeed desirable, to make no reference at all to 'structure' in our discussion of people and what they do.

If we are to argue that the orthodox and dominant theme is unsound and unexciting, then we will have to do so more objectively than is implied in a claim stemming only from a moral or value standpoint. Sociologists and other people have expressed dissatisfaction with sociology from exactly this moral standpoint. Those few sociologists who have done so have mostly been within the conflict school. It seems likely that this is as a consequence of their belief in the self-fulfilling side to human nature with which, we noted, Marx himself started out. But these complaints do not just relate to a moral view of man's potential. They are intimately intertwined with an important theoretical theme in the sociological tradition. It is precisely this theme which has been submerged by the 'modern consensus'.

It is astonishing that so very few have expressed any disquiet with the subsequent reinforcement of that convergence in orthodox modern sociology and the gradual omission of the distance which each of the major authors we have discussed retained from that consensus. Almost all the attacks which have been levelled against Parsons have, for instance, been aimed at later and insignificant additions to his main work: his conservatism, his organic and equilibrium analogies and so on. But these very attacks have been made by men who have come under his influences, who use the same basic concepts and who, like Rex and Dahrendorf, later recant many of their earlier doubts, and accept a functionalist or collectivist perspective.

The convergence omits much of what was radical in the original Marx, Weber and even Parsons. All three are and will remain intellectual giants. But the life and times which invigorated and challenged them are no longer with us. Their solutions are not necessarily solutions for the people and events which surround us today. It may even be that concepts and visions once revolutionary have become conservative in so far as they now mislead us and blunt the incisiveness of our action and understanding. This is especially the case when the original visions are stripped by later interpreters of convergence. The distinctions between these men remain. But we are not accustomed to them today any more than we are accustomed to the similarity between Marx and Parsons.

It seems that Robert Nisbet had the contemporary conservatism of our concepts in mind when he argued: 'It becomes even more difficult to extract new essence, new hypothesis, new conclusion', from such concepts as those we have discussed. 'Distinctions become even more tenuous, examples even more repetitive, vital subject matter even more elusive.'[1]

'The process of "moulding of still ductile forms" cannot go on for ever. Sooner or later the process of revolt, of abandonment of such concepts and methods must take place.'[2] Indeed, it is to become part of our argument that new social problems face us and that new concepts are required before we can get to grips with their explanation. In order to understand these problems and the concepts required to explain them, assistance can be sought in re-reading the giants and can also be found in the doubts which sociologists of both schools have had, especially if it lies in those empirical insights which most strongly indicate that our conceptual inheritance must be denounced.

The first chapter of this Part searches for the basis for an alternative to the consensus in two submerged strands which remain in the sociological tradition.

By way of introducing these strands we will first indicate the existence and nature of the disquiet that symbolizes their existence. Then we shall examine the submerged theoretical theme which we have underemphasized in our discussion of Parsons, Freud and Weber.

This theme concerns the relationship between theoretical and empirical work. We noted in Marx and Parsons a number of empirical observations which failed to fit with their theoretical formulation. In the third part of the first chapter we shall therefore examine the work of three contemporary sociologists who have attempted to bridge the gap between their theoretical dispositions and a close empirical observation of actual people.

These two, related, but submerged theoretical and empirical themes within the sociological tradition will then be used as a basis for the construction of an alternative style of analysis to that developed and institutionalized in the 'modern consensus'.

The second chapter of this section will then lay the foundation of this alternative, specifically addressing itself to an alternative to role analysis. In turn, this will lay the foundation for Part III, in which an alternative to structural analysis will be constructed.

The arguments concerning the alternative that we recommend in the second chapter of this Part (Chapter 7) and in Part III will not make any specific reference to authors and strands of thought that have influenced it. Rather, it is intended that their introduction in the first chapter of this section, and the critical questions and problems raised in the whole of the discussion so far, will make such reference unnecessary and indeed, cumbersome to the development of the argument.

Points of concern

Some sociologists, including several of those we have already referred to, have not felt happy with the approach to role theory which we have described. It is important to note what has concerned these writers.

Dahrendorf complained that in conceptual analysis the human individual, 'in the fullness of his expression, figures *only* as an incumbent of such positions' as those to which the structure has allocated him. As such he is a mere 'player of roles'.[3] Rex's work is shot through with exactly this concern but, like Dahrendorf, he suggests only orthodox solutions.[4]

In attacking Smelser's sociological analysis of industrial change in England, Edward Thompson feels an outrage at the way the individual and the part he plays in history is robbed of blood and passion.[5] But Thompson is writing history and he does not have to face the task of constructing more general sociological concepts. When he does so he falls into the approach for which he criticizes Smelser.[6]

MacIntyre, a 'Marxist', in criticizing C. Wright Mills, a 'Marxist revisionist', accuses his analysis of erecting a structural 'machine in which individuals are trapped . . . There is no picture . . . of the resistances that man can and does offer to such pressures. The only independent power . . . is [for Mills] the independent reason of the social scientist of integrity . . .'[7] Parsons on the Right and Mills on the Left are both accused of being submerged 'by the deterministic image of man'. MacIntyre insists that any sense of freedom, of choice or variety is generally 'lost to the contemporary mind. The view that human activity can be reduced to the stimulus of conditioning, this is the view which is continually fed to us'.[8] Unfortunately, the alternative we are offered is a sophisticated form of 'Marxism' which does not break out of the categories that MacIntyre himself condemns as inadequate.

These deep concerns have, perhaps, been expressed most clearly by Homans[9] and Dennis Wrong.[10] The titles of their essays are significant: 'Bringing Men Back In' and 'The Over-socialized Concept of Man'. 'Let us bring men back in and let us put some blood in them' is Homans' plea. He distrusts the approach which uses that cluster of 'structural norms', called roles, and 'the cluster of roles, called institutions', in order to explain life, movement, and variety. Yet the alternative which he suggests is one which is self-admittedly based on a 'psychological explanation' of man. He recognized that this cannot explain everything, merely because it does not yet have enough 'information' and thought that 'computers would help us'. But psychological reductionism cannot assist us in our search for sociological alternatives and the reliance on computers that he commends might make us wonder why he criticized the role analysts for being bloodless.

Dennis Wrong's criticism is more sophisticated. He insists that the orthodox approach oversocializes the necessary explanation of the individual, that 'structural expectancies' and 'social pressures' on groups and individuals give us an entirely deterministic account of action, which ignores the factors of variety and individual choice. He points out that learning is a two-way process and that in certain respects the individual can both be thought of as unique and, as a consequence of this, may affect the environment in which he acts. He finds both role and learning theory inadequate. At the same time he criticizes the overdeterministic view of social structure with which role theory works. There is no need, he suggests, to start from the problem of order. Man is a social animal, and the problems this poses are very different from the simple way Hobbes saw things. He wants to pose the question: how are 'conflict' and 'variety' possible when man is already basically social?

To help us answer this, Wrong points to Freud, who argued that people with the most developed super-ego, that is, the people who had 'internalized' and 'conformed' the most, were also the men who were most 'racked with anxiety and guilt'. This suggests an implicit assumption that there is no direct link between the person and the surrounding structure and culture, and that different concepts may be needed if we are to surmount our problem. Indeed, we noted that this side of Freud's work was ignored or misunderstood by both Parsons and Marcuse.

In searching for alternatives Wrong, like Homans, turns to psychology. He suggests that if only we make our assumptions about man explicit, not implicit, then he can be knowingly dehumanized and determined and we shall succeed in our explanations. He is not arguing for a dualistic view of man, part instinct, part social. On the contrary, 'the drives or "instincts" of psychoanalysis far from being dispositions to behave in a particular way, are utterly subject to social channelling and transformation and could never reveal themselves in behaviour without social moulding . . .' There is in this argument both a further untested assumption about human nature or instinct and the plastic view of the 'social moulding process' with which orthodox theory works. How Wrong would solve this dilemma is not suggested, and we are merely left with a greater doubt about the orthodox position.

The theoretical assumption of rationality and the place of subjectivity
The question which we must now ask is: are there any theoretical equivalents to those empirical insights of, say, Marx, which failed to fit with those theoretical and conceptual constructs which led to the orthodox convergence or which provided them with a methodological reference to empirical detail? The problems these questions raise are in some ways reminiscent of a few scattered references which have been made concerning the conception of 'situational logic'. Who has used it, and what have they meant by it?

Karl Popper discusses this problem in his sociological writing. He claims that it originates from the economists. He is himself, however, an important contributor. Indeed, were we to trace the history of the idea it would be difficult to find any major sociologist who does not implicitly use it in one form or another.

Popper maintains that 'there is room for a more detailed analysis of the logic of situations'.[11] As early as 1945 he had said that situational logic 'plays a very important part in social life as well as in the social sciences'.[12] He did not tell us any more than this. Unfortunately he has not expanded his idea in any later work.[13] Nor does von Hayek, with whom Popper is in close sympathy.[14]

Jarvie, who may reasonably be described as a disciple of Popper, puts forward much the same argument in his book *The Revolution in Anthropology*. He maintains that the advantages of analysis by situational logic over that of anthropological structural functionalism are 'substantial'.[15] Unfortunately, it is only the weakest support for functionalism which comes from the earlier anthropologists. It is not enough to assert the superiority of situational logic over the functionalism of R. Brown and Malinowski. The later functionalists have seriously met many of the criticisms of the theories which people like Jarvie rather belatedly expose. As an unfortunate consequence of this, Jarvie is not forced to examine in detail the method of analysis suggested by his use of the term 'situational logic'. It is not sufficient to insist on its supremacy. It must be shown to work in practice. Though Jarvie insists that his explanations use 'situational logic' he does not take the formulation of it any further than Popper's assertions.

Along which lines might the idea have developed had Popper and Jarvie carried it further? Popper argues from the 'assumption of complete rationality' and, perhaps, the assumption of the possession of complete information 'on the part of all the individuals concerned, and of estimating the deviance of the actual behaviour of people from the model behaviour' in situational analysis.[16] Jarvie kept this particular emphasis in suggesting that situational logic might be 'based on the rationality principle' and that appeals to 'irrationality give up the possibility of any explanation at all'.[17]

Were Popper and Jarvie to mean by 'rationality' something like 'common sense', the problems raised by our previous references to rationality might be avoided. However, as Popper wishes to estimate the 'deviance of the actual behaviour' of the actor from the 'rational norm', which is itself based on a complete understanding of the situation, we must assume that his meaning of rationality is rather more strict than that of common sense. Popper seems to share this methodological assumption with Weber. Both he and Jarvie recognize this debt, relating it also to the classical economists.

Let us recall that Weber insisted that in action is 'included all human behaviour when and in so far as the acting individual attaches a subjective meaning to it . . .'[18] He went on to distinguish four kinds of action. Action can be rational or directed to absolute beliefs, where the situation is often ignored. Separated from these two rational types are those of emotion, and tradition or habit.[19]

Weber's main work concentrates very much on the first two, whilst insisting that any one concrete act may contain elements of all four types. The main distinction between rational and irrational action, however, is most important in Weber's explanatory scheme, where he exclusively uses that concept of action which is geared to 'discrete individual ends'.

> For the purposes of typological scientific analysis it is convenient to treat all irrational, affectually determined elements of behaviour as factors of deviation from a conceptually pure type of rational action . . . In analysing [say] a political . . . campaign it is convenient to determine in the first place what would have been a rational course, given the ends of the participants and adequate knowledge of all the circumstances. [Having constructed this pure type and] by comparison with this it is possible to understand the ways in which actual action is influenced by irrational factors of all sorts, such as emotion and errors, in that they account for the deviation from the line of conduct which would be expected on the hypothesis that the actions were purely rational.[20]

The vital factor in this analysis is a concentration on a course of action rationally geared to the achievement of a meaningful end, with adequate or scientific knowledge of the situation within which the action takes place. Actual action is then compared with this and the deviations noted. They are explained in terms of irrational factors in the actual action. These include 'such emotional reactions as anxiety, anger, ambition . . . enthusiasm'.[21] In other words, Weber excludes from his scientists' model of action a very great range of conscious and subjectively meaningful features in the conduct of real people and their interaction with others. But action based on them cannot be explained in terms of a rational model. It can only be identified. Clearly, real people usually use a quite different logic of procedure, which, measured against a rational model, is likely to be distorted from the point of view of the scientists' understanding. The problem remains: how do we explain the great variety of action which is not rational in Weber's strict terms? It is clearly no solution to argue that 'error' or 'lack of effort' explains why this action is not rational. He argued that we must 'assume that the hypothetical actor has the sort of complete knowledge of the situation which a scientist might have attained [and] . . . that having this knowledge of the means and ends in the situation the actor employs the sort of logical reasoning which an applied scientist might use in carrying out his action'.[22] But, contrast such a model with the action of actual men, and considerable discrepancy must always occur to a greater or lesser extent. The explanation of this action must be introduced by accounting for the discrepancy between the actual and the rational in terms of the irrational or non-rational. Whilst this approach emphasizes the ends which people pursue, it must involve a departure from the meaning the actual actors ascribe to their particular actions. This meaning is itself subjectively meaningful, and as such is available to the scientist. But what help is a scientist's rationality in this? How this logic, as well as the end of action, is analysed is of tremendous importance. If we are to solve this problem, we must avoid the rational bias of Weber's method and analysis, and of those whom he influenced.

It must be noted that our discussion of Marx seemed to have little to offer in this direction. Indeed, he too used a highly rational means of explanation. He not only seemed to be sure that the ideal actor would operate with a full scientist's understanding of his 'objective' situation, but that he would also be able to intuit the same rational end as others in that situation.

We noted that Marx was not so formal as this in his explanation of particular empirical events. He argued 'that life is not determined by consciousness, but consciousness by *life*', that is, the process of acting, of producing, of making one's life. It is necessary to begin with 'the real, living individuals themselves, and [to] consider consciousness only as their consciousness . . . [The] premises are men . . .' in their actual, empirical, observable process of development under determinate conditions. It is vital to take into account the fact that 'men, who, in developing their material production and their material intercourse, change, along with their real existence, their thinking and the products of their thinking'.[23] From this point of view, the course of human action is bound up with the end, not just a rational pursuit of it. Perhaps this point is put most profoundly in the theses on Feuerbach: 'in practice man must prove the truth, i.e. the reality, and power . . . of this thinking . . .'

'It is' vital to recognize that it is 'men that change circumstances and . . . the educator himself has' to learn through his action. 'Materialism . . . does not understand sensuousness as practical activity . . . Philosophers have only interpreted the world in various ways; the point however is to change it' by exactly this action, which seems to involve ideas and, at the same time, changes them.[24]

Marx insisted that 'history is nothing but the activity of men in pursuit of their ends'.[25] And, when writing 'history', Marx generally adhered to these principles. Unfortunately the methodology of explanation which is involved was not worked out, and though the history he wrote often contradicted his theoretical models and presuppositions, he did not modify them. If we do develop this definition of action, then we might make some progress. For it suggests not only a flexible approach to 'structure', but also a means of showing how men change social circumstances and, to an extent, control their own lives. This was of course, a central concern in Marx's sociology.

Concern with action implies a consideration of the way actors give meaning to their lives. In turn, this implies an interest in the way they shape and control social situations. Even when Weber was closest to conceiving a 'social system' in control of man, this theme broke through.

Already now, rational calculation is manifest at every stage. By it, the performance of each individual worker is mathematically measured, each man becomes a little cog in the machine and, aware of this, his one preoccupation is whether he can become a bigger cog . . . it is horrible to think that the world could one day be filled with nothing but those little cogs, little men clinging to little jobs and striving towards bigger ones . . . It is as if . . . we were deliberately to become men who need 'order' and nothing but order, who become nervous and cowardly if for one moment this order wavers, and helpless if they are torn away from their total incorporation in it.[26]

This is not a statement about the controlling effect of a social system, for immediately Weber insisted that 'it is in such an evolution that we are already caught up, and the great question is therefore not how we can promote and hasten [these developments] but what we can oppose to this machinery in order to keep a portion of mankind free from this parcelling-out of the soul, from this supreme mastery of the bureaucratic way of life'.[27]

This question immediately leads back to situational analysis and the meanings of actions. For concepts of, say, the State or rational associations 'designate certain categories of human interaction. Hence it is the task of sociology to reduce these concepts to "understandable" action, that is, without exception, to the actions of participating individual men'. Simply, this is because the individual is 'the upper limit and the sole carrier of meaningful conduct'.[28]

We must understand why men 'need order' before we can 'keep a portion of mankind free'. But the sociological approach to both free and unfree action involves a recognition of how each kind of action generates the structure of interaction which surrounds men, even when in turn they force a 'parcelling up of the soul'.

This concern with human control mirrors that of Marx. The emerging proletariat were destined, in Marx's view, to liberate themselves, and so men generally, in a determined effort to control their own lives and the kind of society they lived in. The analysis of such free action was not to be postponed until after the revolution. For the whole of human history was the creation of man. Alienated men in class society may not know how they made that society, but they made it none the less. To ask the question 'how' takes us straight to an analysis of action and meaning or, as Marx put it, of 'sensuous activity'. The analysis of action, the pursuit of meaningful ends in rational ways, does not preclude the view that men can be constrained in certain circumstances. The question merely becomes, by which other men are they constrained?

These submerged aspects of Weber and Marx find an affinity with the second feature of Ralph Linton's definition of role which we discussed in the development of Parsons' work. Linton described role as the actual action of the actor. This definition was taken up momentarily by Kingsley Davis, but was very quickly dropped in his later work. Regrettably, none of these references outline in any detail the component elements which might be involved in such a view of action.

We have seen that Weber, Popper, Jarvie, Rex, Marx and Parsons all contributed to the seeds of a different approach which focused on action and meaning. Its development has been precluded by features of convergence in their work which we analysed in Part I, and which led to the modern consensus.

The dominant theme gave rise to methodological problems concerning the relation of explanation to real people and their activity. Consequently, for Marx and Parsons, empirical insights often contradicted theoretical concerns and models of society.

To help us to clarify some of these problems, it will be most useful to note theoretical and methodological implications contained in the work of some contemporary empirical writers. They, unlike Wrong and Homans, have either explicitly or implicitly challenged the validity of the role concept and socialization theory through their empirical work. This despite the fact that in many aspects of their theoretical work such authors still fit firmly into the consensual position which we are criticizing.

Neal Gross, Ward Mason, Alexander McEachern

Neal Gross and his collaborators conducted a very detailed study of certain features of the organization of and politics within a number of American schools, the relations between school superintendents, school boards, and representatives of outside organizations, parents and the like.

These writers felt that role theory had concentrated far too much on an assumed consensus between role and those status expectancies which are embedded in the social structure.[29] They felt that one unfortunate consequence of this was that the role concept, and those concepts related to it, had been so generalized that they had lost sight of any empirical grounding for which they were intended as factors of explanation.[30] They were able to conclude that the role concept in fact 'has yielded few significant hypotheses of theoretical importance'. This allowed them to argue that if the 'value of [a] concept is measured by the degree to which it is involved in significant theoretical propositions that are capable of empirical examination, it must be said that in current formulations the role concept has not proved its worth'.[31]

It followed from these points, and the nature of the actual relations which they uncovered between the people they studied, that they had to abandon the idea of conformity of role expectancy in order to explain the situation and relationships in that situation.[32] This fact poses questions for socialization theory. For if there is no consensus between the expectations of action which are held out to a child or adult as to how he should act, then it follows that it is not possible for simple 'identification' or 'internalization' to lead to role action. Either a choice has to be made between two or more structured role definitions, or some amalgamation of those differing definitions has to be made by the individual concerned.

Gross makes this point forcefully. 'The assumption that there is consensus on role definition on the basis of which socialization takes places [*sic*] is untenable for the occupational position we studied. We would suggest that it deserves to be challenged in most formulations of role acquisition, including even those concerned with the socialization of the child.'[33] This challenge is again directed by 'the empirical complexities of degrees of consensus' and conflict on 'role definition that we have examined'.[34] It would seem reasonable to assume that if on some occasions status congruence does not exist, then the degree of consensus or conflict in the expectancies which surround action would always be a matter for empirical investigation. It should not even be possible to approach any empirical study with the assumption of either congruence or conflict. And this, it seems, holds true for conflict and congruence between role and status, as well as within status expectancies themselves. But does this hold for children as well as for the adult groups whom Gross studied?

To take Gross and his fellow workers to the logical conclusion of their research, a point to which they themselves do not go, we could argue that parents, sisters, relations, teachers, and peers might all act differently towards and have different expectations of each other, as well as of a very young child. How that child establishes his identity and comes to act socially then becomes entirely problematic again. We shall have to look at work done on the family and the child in order to find if the conflict in expectancies held out to the child does exist in a similar way to that found by Gross and his collaborators in their adult population.

In attributing crucial significance to the conflicting expectancies which confront actors in the same situation, how can Gross explain differences in the consequent actions of these actors, a fact previously explained by deviance from the norm, unsuccessful socialization, and so on? He did not develop any new concepts with which to analyse the individual or his action to cope with this question. His solution was to refine and add to the existing concepts within role theory.[35]

Gross did find it necessary, however, to introduce one important factor, which we found has usually either been omitted, or dismissed as of minor significance. He felt that the *actual* action of the actors he studied, and the *meaning* given to it *by them*, was of crucial significance. Gross' emphasis on this followed mainly from his empirical observation that he could not assume (as an observer) consensus between what was structurally expected of the actor and what the actor actually came to think or do. Nor could he safely predict action without understanding the meaning given to it by the actor himself. When faced with these empirical problems Gross had to focus on the 'perception of actors, rather than the observer' before he could make sense of the actual action.[36]

Unfortunately, the possible consequences of these steps were not fully worked out. None the less, Gross and his collaborators assume there are major problems when attempting to account for action 'in roles' when that action is faced by more than two conflicting sets of expectations. These writers also note that a person may at once be acting in several or 'multiple roles' and that others may have 'multiple expectancies' of him. In these situations a person may be seen as teacher, parent, member of an association and writer at the same time, and may indeed act at the same time in terms of these different aspects of himself.

Role theory in fact typically separates out roles, only one of which is normally assumed to be activated at one time. This means that conflict can be contained between contradictory roles and relationships, so that no interplay between different areas of a person's conscious life need be supposed. Gross and his fellow workers discovered 'empirically' that actors 'may be activating multiple roles' at the same time. They suggest that this 'may be of major importance not only for a theory of role conflict but also for a general theory of interaction'.[37] Again they do not in fact make suggestions as to how we might proceed to cope with this important fact.

Their main conclusions, which are all derived from their empirical analysis of role theory, are that more subdivisions of the concept should be worked out.[38] These concepts should apply to all levels: personality, structure and culture. 'That is, the ideas to which role refers, if treated as a family of concepts instead of in a holistic manner, may be available for theoretical hypotheses' in psychology and sociology.[39] In this sense, they accept the assumption of a significant relation between the three systems of personality, structure and culture. But the three together should not be seen as a total system.[40]

It might be possible, on the contrary, to focus on the particular action of the actor and the meaning he gives to it. This may not be contained within the concept of role, especially in its psychological dimension. This suggests that the 'lack of fit' between the actor and structural expectations cannot be analysed in terms of the same concepts. If this is so, the part which psychology is thought to play in explanation must be re-examined.

Often unintentionally, these writers raise empirically several of the problems which we only indicated at the theoretical level in our previous discussion. They do not seem to provide solutions however.

Erving Goffman

Erving Goffman has written extensively about the relationships between people at what seems to be a very low level of theoretical abstraction. Often unintentionally, like the writers just discussed, he raises serious objections to role analysis in his detailed work. At the same time he is able to assert that much of the everyday social action of actors fits quite readily within the orthodox concepts.

By means of participant observation or informed and subjective 'thought experiments' Goffman frequently studies those people whose relationships and situations are not thought to be within the mainstream of 'normal' or 'typical' social life. Drawing evidence from his empirical work, he argued that 'any group of persons', from prisoners to mental patients and the disabled, 'develop a life of their own that becomes meaningful, reasonable and normal once you get close to it'.[41] His way of 'getting close' was to go and live on the Shetland Islands, to live in an asylum, and to intuit and question his way into the situation of a person with a social stigma. By these means he found that he could experience these lives almost as they were lived by the people themselves.

The point about studying such action and relationships in such a way and in such situations

> is not that some traditional role concepts can be applied in this situational setting, but that the complexities of concrete conduct can be examined instead of by-passed. Where the social content of a situated system faithfully expresses in miniature the structure of the broader social organization in which it is located, then little change in the traditional role analysis is necessary, situated roles would merely be our means of sampling, say, occupational or institutional roles. But where a discrepancy is found [between this and normal or expected conduct], we would be in a position to show proper respect for it.[42]

We can see that in many respects Goffman accepts the usual distinction between 'normal' and 'deviant' action. The former is explicable in terms of the orthodox concepts. But Goffman recognizes that their relevance breaks down in connection with 'deviant' forms of action. It is on these 'devious' areas of social life that he concentrates his attention. At this stage in his work he does not apply any of his findings in this area back into areas of 'normal' social action or its explanation.

Later on, Goffman does make these connections. He looks at people in 'more normal' situations: doctors, healthy children and their parents. He then becomes worried about the extent to which the dichotomy which he originally drew between normal and deviant is really valid. Following detailed study of such groups and their inter-relations he draws important conclusions.

'Whether a social situation goes smoothly or whether expressions occur that are in discord with a participant's sense of who or what he is, we might expect' – according to the usual deterministic implications of role analysis – 'that he will fatalistically accept the information that becomes available concerning him. Yet when we get close to the moment-to-moment conduct of the individual we find that he does not remain passive' in the face of action, experience and the conduct of others. On the contrary, the person 'actively participates in sustaining a definition of the situation that is stable and consistent with his image of himself'.[43] This image does not necessarily accord with the wishes, hints, or actions of others. This, of course, is exactly what Gross and his collaborators found in social life that they had thought to be highly ordered and consensual.

Goffman first observed this point in 'deviant' situations and action and then became convinced that it applied right across the social board. He came to feel that no type of action was free of these implications. He finishes by accusing the concept 'role' of allowing sociologists to avoid the private, the sacred, the unique and to discuss only the public, the profane, the uniform. We need a new concept, he argued, which, if developed, would 'help us to combat this touching tendency'.[49]

Goffman then develops his main theoretical alternative, 'role-distance'. What he means by it and whether it allows him to avoid the problems of role theory we shall endeavour to discover. What Goffman sees as his main point of disagreement with the dominant approach is not to 'ask how a chief surgeon, *qua* surgeon, is expected to act during surgery, but how those individuals who are designated chief surgeon are expected to act during surgery'.[45]

Unlike the Gross study, Goffman does not discern the fact that there is usually some clash of opinion as to what should be expected of a person by others. What he does observe is that despite the structural 'consensus' which exists on what is expected of a person, that consensus is in many small and sometimes almost invisible ways disputed by the person himself. As Goffman puts it, through his action within the stipulated role the person actually and intentionally distances himself from that role. This fact, and the concept 'role-distance', which Goffman suggests may be used to analyse it, implies a further important concept.

Goffman starts by criticizing the orthodox view that the actor is no more than a bundle of roles which have been internalized, which are ordered only at the unconscious level into role orientations, and which are only activated separately, so never causing realignment or new action. In place of this Goffman uses the idea of an ordering, conscious, 'self', and he went on to write a book which was actually called *The Presentation of Self in Everyday Life*.[46] What does he mean by this?

A person's words, gestures, and actions, which Goffman calls role-distance, and by which people leave a space between their action and their 'role', are really subjectively indicating: whatever I am, I'm not just someone who merely does what is expected. Whilst playing the role the person does just enough to publicly affirm his own self and individuality behind that role.[47] Goffman even discerned this type of action in steeply hierarchical and ordered organizations, where the person in the subordinate position does just enough by facial expression and by slowness to obey to show that, 'for any who cares to see', he is not quite what he is thought to be by others.[49] Goffman recognizes this conduct in children. The only observer of this fact may be the person or child himself. This is sufficient for the person to gain and retain an identity which satisfies himself, but which is not the predicated or expected one.

This has major implications for socialization theory, as we noted the Gross study did also. Here too, Goffman does not spell out these implications or, indeed, make explicit the scope of the problem he has tackled. But we must ask how such action can indeed be discovered by the scientist. If it is a response to a situation, but is not contained within it, then how can a structural model explain that response? Is it, perhaps, an area of unpredictability and thus of creativity, which might, in its accumulated affects, add up to significant social change? If so, what concepts might be used to account for it?

For all the virtues which we have so far noted in Goffman's work there is a major confusion which we must tease to the surface. It is diffused throughout his studies. So far we have noted Goffman's concern for role-distance and the concept of the conscious self which is implied by this observation. However, in freeing the variety of previously obscured action, and in noting the crucial importance of the particular self of the actor, Goffman gives his explanation a particular twist which, even in his own terms, is not necessarily acceptable.

The 'person who is subordinate', Goffman argues, is careful not to 'threaten' his superior in distancing himself from what is expected. The child is careful to show other, slightly younger, children, or his parents, that he transcends their belittling expectations of him. He chides them; he rides above them; he is aggressively superior. There is at once compliance and a calculating contempt in the people Goffman describes.

'The practice of resolving something of oneself from the clutch of an institution is very visible in mental hospitals and prisons but can be found in more benign and less total institutions, too. I want to argue that this recalcitrance is not an incidental mechanism of defense, but rather an *essential* constituent of self . . . If we find . . . that in all situations actually studied the participant has erected defenses against his social bondedness, why should we base our conception of self upon how the individual would act were conditions "just right"?'[49] Goffman is indicating something beyond those innovations which we have already discussed.

Joseph Bensman has suggested that Goffman tends to choose areas of life for analysis in which it can be argued that the features of fear and masochism have developed as defences to aggression and sadism.[50] In these areas Goffman has managed to limit the richness of real life by this simple dichotomy into which he tends to squeeze that reality. Goffman chooses to study hospitals, asylums, prisons, stigma, gambling, and even competitive games amongst children, where it is plausible to argue that 'it is . . . *against something* that the self has to emerge'.[51]

Goffman shows how the relations between people and groups build up pressures which belittle and constrain the 'patients' in asylums, how they force these people to be subordinate, to deny their selves in a 'self-alienating moral servitude, only indicating or hinting that they are other than "mad".'[52] The picture he paints of the life of the institution before drawing these conclusions does not fully justify the strictures of his own superimposed, one-dimensional, view of relationships. And, certainly, it would be difficult to extend this feature to other areas of interaction, even those which Goffman himself examines where, nevertheless, his simple dichotomy of emotions still applies. Though he tries to fit the child, the nurse, the parent into his implicit scheme, they constantly jump out of the categories of 'role', 'role-distance', and the sadistic or masochistic, competitive self which the scheme demands. Whilst Goffman realizes this fault when looking at orthodox role theory, he is blind to his own, albeit more sophisticated, repetition of its mistakes.

A further step is taken, which results in the avoidance of diversity and diminishes the fullness of the person, by the acceptance of a further assumption of role analysis. Though hardly explicit, this step pervades his work. The individual is an actor, half playing a role or part, which is not necessarily anything to do with his own conscious self. For Goffman, the self is introduced as central, but in a manner which suggests that social relations are in fact a game played out on a stage. The actor comes on stage to perform in relation to cues and hints. He displays the public 'part' of a 'character', only indicating to the 'audience' that he is somehow different from the 'part' they expect of him and which he is 'forced' to 'play'. He has to do this for fear of revealing himself to a hostile world or audience. This is why the actor has to employ hints which he, and others, then treat as 'claims and promises' that have 'implicitly' been made about how others will act. It is as if the individual says 'I am using these impressions of you as a way of checking up on you . . .'[53]

Though Goffman seems to realize some of the distortions and problems which accompany this style of approach, it fits so closely into the other, one-dimensional, aspect that he tends to use it despite this. The cumulative effect on his analysis is a severe impediment, allowing the real characters to speak for and reveal themselves too infrequently. In the end we are not shown openness, honesty, sincerity, idealism, any more than we are shown friendship, courage, brutality, compassion, love or hate. These qualities do not exist in Goffman's world.

Goffman is concerned with change and development, not just with relationships and interaction, but also with the individual. When two people meet for the first time they may, even in tightly 'institutional' settings, have very little information indeed about how they should, or could, or want to react to one another. In the gradual and subtle process of mutual discovery, which may or may not follow Goffman's hints, cues, and gestures, people may come to see one another very differently. As they discover that they went to the same or a very different school, belong to the same political party, meet out of work with their wives, share similar or have opposed feelings, they form developing or different views and expectations of each other. Their action changes accordingly. Over a period of time this experience will not only result in their own relationships and actions towards others changing and continuing to change. It can also lead them to change their own ideas about themselves. In turn this will lead them to act differently in situations in which they act quite separately, or where they might have originally been, say, in open conflict.[54]

Certainly no one role or set of roles could accommodate and explain these changing actions or their repercussions for social change generally. This has important consequences for the process of socialization, and the development of the individual's perception of himself. The point links exactly with that made in our discussion of the Gross study. It is likely that any alternative to socialization which accommodates these points will not find even the idea of role-distance to be adequate. We must know when a person acts without restraint, with sincerity and spontaneity, just as we must know when he is diffident, uncertain, tense, aggressive or fearful; or indeed, when there are no roles at all.

Goffman rarely discusses the social structure explicitly. He is too concerned with the lives of individuals in particular institutions to spend much time on general aspects of the theory of structure and society. Yet his particular analyses would seem to have considerable implications for this general area of analysis, which has been the central concern of so many of those whose work we have examined. Goffman himself draws no definite conclusions. Indeed, he generally assumes that 'occupational and institutional structures' are areas of more normal action, where the role concept can be applied without too much damage to reality. The assumption, therefore, is one of order and reciprocity. He argues that 'the individual must be seen as someone who organizes his [action in situations] in relation to [roles in situations], but that in doing this he uses whatever means are at hand to introduce a margin of freedom and manoeuvrability, of pointed disidentification, between himself and the self', which is made available for him by the cohesively structured situation.[55] The social structure would not only seem to exist and to be ordered but also to be unchanging and unchangeable, despite the fact that it is made up of the interrelations of others acting by similar means. It is, perhaps, in this assumption that we can see Goffman's need for the concept of role-distance. Is there, perhaps, a 'public' and a 'private' self? If so, what is their relation? Are they to be described by dissimilar concepts?

Had Goffman developed a different view of social structure where, as with Gross, he could have recognized the possibility that it was less structured, where different and clashing expectations might be held out to the person, then it would not have been necessary to develop the role concept in this way. It would follow quite reasonably that the individual and his view of himself need not involve such a dimension of aggression and submission, of fear and terror, where the person developed 'against', and in spite of, the constraining structural pressures.

It is because of these structural pressures, which are cohesive and so present only one set of expectations to the individual, that Goffman is able to argue that 'we must start with the idea that a particular definition [or logic] is in charge of the situation'.[56] But this logic must be the role, which in turn must stem from the social structure. There are no conflicting definitions except, marginally, those of the individual. And he is powerless in forming that situation. All he can say is 'this isn't me, not really, not the way I'm having to act'. It follows quite consistently from this that the behaviour of an individual while in a situation is guided by 'social values or norms concerning involvement'. But how do these norms and values arise, and what maintains them? Goffman deduces, perhaps, from such a question, that both roles and structure (as contained in 'norms and values', and role-distance) are functionally useful for the maintenance of the present system.[57]

The only hint that these problems remain unresolved in Goffman's mind is when he admits, contradictorily, that 'role-distance is not a part of the normative framework of role' or, therefore, of the institutional framework either.[58] By what means can the 'private' be described? What concepts can contain it? Can they be sociological concepts?

If every individual in a situation exhibits role-distance, is there no normative structure to that situation, or is it maintained only by that aspect of action which can be explained by role alone? If so, what is the origin of role action if no individual is concerned to maintain it? Could it be a public myth which is 'functionally' necessary to keep society from disintegrating into an anarchy of sado-masochistic war of all against all? Or could it be a myth of the sociological tradition? If it is merely other people who make up situations and structures, why is the individual always opposed to them, what is the significance of their clashing action and opinions, and how can these be accommodated in an explanatory set of concepts?

Goffman's work raises many questions which take the focus of attention further from role-analysis than he would admit. Moreover, as we have only indicated so far, they raise important problems concerned with socialization, change, process, and development. Finally, they cause us to wonder whether his conception of the self of the person is an adequate or a rich enough one and, at the same time, if it is even a sociological concept.

Whilst freeing the person and his self, Goffman ties variety up into a new view. It is that of fearful, but hardly perceptible opposition to the weight of social structure. With his limited view of motivation and the individual's control over his situation Goffman traps him at the very point of release. But it would not be just to focus on this theme without laying stress on the force and humanity which emerges through his work.

Goffman argues that patients in asylums are treated in ways which fit only a 'sane' definition of 'madness'. Some patients come to accept this definition and feel they must act in terms of it. Their selves are crushed and strained in the process. Equally, he shows how many, comprehending their situation in peculiar ways which in fact have reality to them, fight back, using anything which is to hand. They bang on locked doors, they tear or set fire to their clothes. They destroy their few sticks of furniture. Through their impotent action, they succeed only in unintentionally confirming the definition of them held by those in authority. They are then seen not only as mad and bad, but as incurable, and their guard is doubled. They are driven more and more into a hopeless situation from which there is no escape but to accept the authoritarian and structured definition of reality which their self would deny, or to retreat into a total and silent withdrawal.

Power, implicitly, comes into this analysis as it does elsewhere in Goffman's work. But it is a power between particular individuals and a structured group, not between groups, or diffused throughout a 'social structure'. Here, in hospital, it is an experienced reality, wielded by one group in solidarity and with shared values against particular, frightened people. Goffman does not spell out the possibilities of this observation, and we are left only with a moral indictment. And if, in applying the overt aspects of this type of situation to other, more normal, areas of social interaction, he distorts even further the quality and variety of belief, emotion, and action, his work still stands as a constant revelation of the shallowness of the more orthodox approaches.

R. D. Laing, Cooper, Esterson and others

Goffman's work is at some points very close to that of some American psychiatrists who have been involved in something of a 'breakthrough' in the study and explanation of some people who have been diagnosed as 'schizophrenic'. These workers have developed the concept of the 'double bind'.[59] This concept in fact involves an essentially sociological explanation of this form of 'madness'. In England, Laing and Cooper (with a few other collaborators) have taken these ideas rather further forward and placed them within a framework related to the conflict school. In earlier references to the work of Laing and Cooper we noted that the structural concepts and theories which they use vary very little from those of the dominant theoretical position.

Their empirical work deals with particular people, particular families, and the relationships between them and others in the medical, social, legal, and political sectors of action. From Laing and Cooper's examination of these relationships we find many examples which in fact conflict with their theoretical assumptions and conceptual apparatus.

Laing and his collaborators start from what they call the position of existentialist psycho-analysis. A perspective is developed which 'enables us to study at one and the same time (i) each person in the family (ii) the relations between persons in the family (iii) the family itself as a system' and (iv) the way these individuals and their relations in turn relate to, form and are formed by, other institutions.[60]

Rigorous empirical study is undertaken in the course of 'psycho-analysis', which demands that each person in the family should be interviewed so that his subjective view of himself and his relation to others in the family can be built up by the scientist. No previous definition is held or deduced. This indicates that the person's view of the others, and his view of their view of him should all be seen as having crucial importance.[61] Laing concludes from these studies that 'without exception the experience and behaviour that gets labelled schizophrenic by the family, the teacher, the doctor, and those in the hospital, is a specific strategy created to deal with the situation.'[62]

This specific strategy is a response by the individual to what he believes to be, and what actually is, an untenable situation in the family, which focuses on that person. Such a person has a unique definition of that situation, and it involves facing the 'double bind'. We should explain what this means.

The child is told by his parents, say, that he is good, that no son of theirs could do anything bad, but that every action of his is bad. The son concludes that he is and is not their son; that he is bad and good; and his own opinion of himself as their son, etc. is denied or made ambiguous.

His mother may tell him time and again that she loves him. But her response to any show of affection on his part may be to freeze. This is as if to say, 'I love you. I don't love you.' The child is presented with two mutually exclusive views, either of those who are important to him, or of himself, by these others. Laing sees this as an 'untenable situation'. It is a 'double bind' because the person cannot be himself without also disconfirming himself in the eyes of others. If he is as others would have him be, then he disconfirms himself to himself.

We know from our own personal experiences, and from the work of novelists and playwrights, as well as from Goffman and other workers in the field, that this type of relationship is not confined to 'deviant' families. (Laing is currently engaged on an examination of 'normal' families in an attempt to discover whether the difference is one of substance or only, if at all, one of degree.)

The point which Laing makes in relation to the child's actual response to this 'untenable situation' is that while apparently 'illogical' and quite 'mad' to those involved in relationships with him, it is in fact subjectively understandable to us if we can only intuit our way by subjective understanding into the texture of the family relationships and the child's situation, as he sees it himself. Such action then becomes not only meaningful, but also quite sensible, if we understand the maze of relationships which is unintentionally erected and through which the child has to pick his way.

Of course, others in the family have a different definition of these relationships and a different interpretation of the child's reaction to them. From their point of view the child's action is, say, at first 'odd' and emotionally disturbing. Then it becomes seen as 'bad' and perhaps 'shameful' as the child continues to act against their continued expectations, and strictures. Only at a later and more desperate stage does it come to be seen as fitting the accepted definition of 'mad': 'It is not our fault, it's his, and it's not even his, really; after all he's our son; you see he's mad, well, he can't help it you know. He was so different before.' Yet *he* is the same person who does, or at least feels the same things.

Laing's main point is that it is the texture of relationships within the family, not the child, which are in fact what is called 'schizophrenic'. In public 'fact', however, it is the child who has to bear the label, not the family relationships. This label affects the child. Such a process of interaction and definition involves the question of power; Laing does not use the term 'authority'. This power, and who wields it, determines which particular person in the schizophrenic situation comes to bear the public label. It could have been, and sometimes it is, either parent. Generally it is the child.

Representatives of other institutions who come into contact with the family accept this definition: the teacher, the nurse and doctor, the magistrate, finally those in the asylum, and often the child himself. It is, of course, at this point that Goffman takes over and extends the analysis in his study of asylums, which is approvingly quoted by Laing.

We can conclude that there is 'no such "condition" as "schizophrenia", but the label is a social fact, and the social fact is a political event [which involves] . . . a coalition [a 'conspiracy'] of family, G.P.', etc. to get a person committed. The label is only removed, the person is only released, when the child or adult comes to conform to what is expected of him. Such a person is 'degraded from full existential and legal status as human agent and responsible person . . . his time is no longer his own and the space he occupies is no longer of his choosing'.[63]

We have already suggested in earlier discussions that Laing and his collaborators seem to see no contradiction between this analysis at the empirical level and their comments and concepts concerning socialization and social structure. They use a Marxist, two-class, conflict model of society. Laing argues that we have to understand not just the family and hospital but also the 'meaning of all this within the larger context of the . . . political order of the ways persons exercise control and power over one another'.[64] We noted that Cooper even argued that 'society' needed mental hospitals to prove that it was sane. It needed patients, and required that its families should produce these 'half-crazed creatures'.[65] Any child is a product of his class and is socialized in terms of the values and attitudes of that class. The power which is wielded over the one class by the other is the same kind of power and contains the same kinds of contradictions as that which is wielded over the individual child who comes to be labelled schizophrenic. Even his least 'fantasies' are 'pre-determined in general by his class' situation.

At another level of analysis this means that the class which wields power and controls the means of communication and education has managed to socialize the 'working class' into a state of false consciousness. The worker, like the schizophrenic in his individual revolt, merely reflects the contradictions within a degenerate and crazed capitalist system. If this argument is pushed a little further, the schizophrenic become the new protesting vanguard of the proletariat.[66] Even without this particular twist, we can see the determinism of Laing's and Cooper's structurally constraining view of the conflicting 'social system'.

This contradicts Laing's existential approach, where the person is seen not only through his own eyes, but also in terms of the degree of conscious *choice* which is felt to be a characteristic of that person in that situation. There is a constant tug between structural determinism and the subtlety and range of feeling with which Laing approaches the particular family and individual.

We must note one further feature of the deterministic side of this equation. Laing states that 'undoubtedly' his analysis of particular families' relations 'are mostly unknown to the persons themselves'. We must be prepared to attribute to the agents involved phantasies of which they are themselves unconscious.[67] Whilst Laing has moved further from Freud than such sociologically disposed neo-Freudians as Fromm or Karen Horney, he retains a view of the 'unconscious' which cannot be tested and into which any observation which does not square with his subjective explanation can be fitted. This closes the possibility of seeing that the 'mistaken' definitions of the family relations may be equally explicable in fully sociological terms.

Laing moves some way towards this position when he discusses the person's development, and the general formation of a view of 'self'. It allows him to avoid the more obvious crudities of the usual 'introjection of outside reality' approach to which, in these other aspects of his work, he subscribes.

> Self identity . . . and . . . my view of your view of me are theoretical constructs . . . Self identity is constituted not only by our looking at ourselves, but also by our looking at others looking at us and our reconstitution and alteration of these views of the others about us. At this more complex, more concrete level, self identity is a synthesis of my looking at me with my view of others' view of me. These views by others of me need not be passively accepted, but they cannot be ignored in my development of a sense of who I am.[68]

This view, gained from reflections on empirical work, coincides with aspects of Goffman's work and suggestions which were made when discussing Gross's work.

It involves a sociological approach to the definition of the person and people whose relations and activity require explanation. This definition must rely heavily on the person's own opinions and the way he sees situations in which he is involved. The way he feels he relates to others who make up these situations, and the way they interpret and react to his action, become important for understanding his action. As situations and other people who, in a real sense, are these situations can be understood by this subjective approach, this raises the possibility of an alternative view and analysis of structure to that which Laing and Goffman adopted. It was Gross, it will be recalled, who stated that structural expectations could either diverge or cohere. As such, it was a matter for empirical investigation as to how any particular situation should be explained. Laing demonstrates this through innumerable empirical examples, and accepts it in his view of the individual's development. He discounts it only in theoretical explanations of social structure and the general mechanisms of the socialization process. Thus, an empirical view of both the individual and those who interact with him and have expectations of him seems to be essential. This again contradicts the view that either action (role) or situation (structure) can be derived or predicted solely in terms of an abstract, theoretical, model.

We are now in a position to see why Laing feels the child can only react to the 'double bind' in a 'mad' way. Two mutually incompatible logics are presented to him. He can accept neither. Had only one been presented to the child, Laing would evidently have been happy to feel the child would accept and internalize this structural pattern. That, he feels, is what 'normally' happens. The child would become a normal worker or member of the bourgeoisie, depending on which class his family came from.

As the child cannot do or take what is given, for it is contradictory, he has to innovate action of his own. This, of course, is exactly what Gross observed, though at a less intense and passionate level, for his school superintendents. But the actions of the superintendents in response to conflicting expectations were innovatory for, at the time, they felt they had to act in a way which did not have the consequence of open conflict. The same implication is contained in Goffman's concept 'role-distance'.

Laing feels that whatever action the child innovates in a 'schizophrenic' family must conflict so greatly with the parents' expectations that the parents *must* finally bring in the doctor to reinforce their definition. But this is not the only possible consequence of a double bind. It is not necessary to see this third way as in any sense predetermined by a logic of 'madness' which is dictated by the family situation.

The child may succeed in finding a way of behaving which both satisfies the parents and maintains the child's 'integrity'. Similarly, as Goffman suggested for development in other relationships, the parents may come to modify their view of the child and their own expectations of him. There would, indeed, seem to be far more alternatives to the 'double bind' situation than Laing suggests, as many as the child or parents and others may innovate. It is simply not true that the child must of necessity become schizophrenic in 'schizophrenic' situations, as the opposed concept of 'normal' families would imply. It may well be that 'normal' families have 'double bind' situations. Such families may only be defined as 'normal' because the child invents ways of avoiding the 'schizophrenic label'. Or, such parents may develop a new and 'normal' definition of their child as their relationships with him develops.

Laing encountered this difficulty in the first place by seeing a too simple division between 'schizophrenic' and 'normal' families. Secondly, he felt the child in a 'normal' family simply introjected the family and the class patterns of action. As children in each type of family may innovate entirely new ways of acting, this challenges both Laing's view of 'normal socialization' and his view of social structure. For, structure and the structural concept of class must of necessity be altered if the child, and others like him, come to act and feel in new ways.

Thirdly, we must consider Laing's view of psychological constraints which invite the child to act in ways, and experience consequences, of which he is not aware. Either those unintended or unseen consequences of action are social, and are to be explained in sociological ways, or they are 'unconscious' and to be explained in terms of an untestable psychological concept. This latter alternative is challenged by Laing's own existentialist view of the individual, and the social explanation he himself gives of particular individuals in particular families. Here, situations which are subjectively understandable could in fact be built up through the accumulation of unintended consequences of intentional interaction. Laing's view of the relevance of the 'unconscious' is also questioned by the account which he himself gives of how the individual develops in terms of his view of himself, and his view of how others see him.

Conclusion

It is important to note that the empirical and not the theoretical work done by these three writers has finished by pointing in similar directions. The Gross study looked at certain features in the organization of and relationships within an adult population which can be considered to have no marked or unusual features. The Goffman studies predominantly looked at what might be thought of as unusual kinds of people in unusual situations. Each of these studies raised points about the socialization process in general. In looking at the work which Laing and others had undertaken, much of which involved discussing family relationships and the development of children, we found that the indications of the other two sets of empirical studies were reinforced.

It is vital to recognize that each of the workers we studied raised problems which seemed beyond the scope of role theory to explain. The writers concerned did make various attempts to amend and reform these concepts, but the facts of people's lives and activities had an obstinate habit of breaking beyond even these adjustments. In interpreting the factual information which was revealed it was not possible to avoid indicating paths which might be pursued. This meant criticizing not only the theory itself, but also the very kind of structural analysis and concepts which constituted the orthodox approach.

Finally, this chapter started by returning to a submerged theoretical theme in the sociological tradition. That theme was concerned specifically with the explanation of social action in terms of the meaning which people themselves gave to that action. It was also concerned with the extent to which that action could be seen as directed to the goal of controlling situations and of shaping life chances. It was the very opposite of the dominant, converging, theme which became fastened within orthodox sociological theory. Crucially, it links with those problems raised by the empirical studies examined in the second half of this chapter.

The basis of an alternative approach to the means by which the orthodox consensus explains social life has, therefore, been laid both in theory and empiricism. It will not be necessary to revert to a discussion of or detailed reference to them. This is not to say that they do not require further elucidation in general. Rather, that task is beyond the scope of our argument.

7: An Alternative

The Theoretical Assumption of Rationality Redefined

It has already been suggested that the initial problem facing sociology has been misstated. Man is social. It is not his sociality as such which has to be explained in opposition to some pre-social existence. Nor are we primarily concerned with how the person becomes social in the first place. We are faced with people who are already and unalterably social, and whose social action is meaningful to us exactly because we share that sociality with them.

The question then becomes: what features are there which seem to be common to the sociality and social action of men, which may be analytically distinguished? These separable elements, which on the level of reality are intimately related, must be individually discussed in some detail before we can see how they relate in real life. Then we may be able to explain and generalize about action in real life with some degree of clarity.

Subjectivity and social reality

If we are to talk of the actor, his subjectivity, and the logic of his action, we must first of all ask what we mean by the 'subjective meaning of social reality'. To ask this question involves asking what we mean by man being basically and at all times social. The main exceptions to this rule include autistic children and the few instances of feral children who for various reasons have been 'brought up' by animals without any human relations at all. What is known about these children does raise problems, but they are ones which need not concern us here. In all other instances, everything that man sees, hears, feels, does, or says, is social in that he interprets these experiences to himself and to others by means of signs, pictures, and, above all, words and emotions. These experiences are always meaningful by virtue of man's social existence.

It is exactly because we are all social that we can have the possibility of understanding the actions and feelings of others. Such understanding is more difficult for us the more we are removed from those we study, in terms of our own language, ways of looking at things, and experience. But, in principle, we are capable of understanding, and of articulating, what *any* other human being is doing and feeling, whatever that may be. In this sense, as opposed to any judging sense, no one is capable of doing anything which can be described as inhuman, or non-social, or anti-social.

It is in this context that it seems to have been a mistake for Weber, and

171

others after him, to have excluded human action from being social when it is not oriented to the existence of other people. This definition implies an important distinction between social and individual action, which, in turn, suggests that individual action can be non-social, and so not understandable. It further implies that it is of little significance in explaining subsequent social events. Yet we are fully aware that the most individual and solitary acts can have the most profound personal and social consequences, even though these may not have been intended.

The second feature which is involved in this approach to the actor is that all 'reality' is 'social reality'. Sociologists have often distinguished between, say, material and ideal interest; between empirical and non-empirically, testable ends, or means to those ends; between what is merely social myth, and what is concrete reality. Such distinctions may on occasions be usefully made. But, for the sociologist, it is important to recognize that there is no sphere of human knowledge, whether that knowledge be scientific or religious or political, which is not crucially coloured by our social existence and our awareness of that existence.

Karl Popper, among others, has shown that no theoretical or law-like feature (even of the most strict natural sciences) can be said to be true or correct. We may, perhaps, approach the objective truth about non-social reality, though it may be useful to forget this, for we can in the nature of things never know what that 'truth' is. It is important to remember, by the same reasoning, that we can never know social reality in any final sense. There are many different versions of it. They all have their significance.

In redefining the scope and problem of the sociology of knowledge Berger has illuminated this problem which we are discussing. The orthodox sociology of knowledge concerns the dominant ideas, religions, philosophies, and political theories of epochs, societies, social groups or classes. As such it makes a similar distinction to that which orthodox sociology makes when it separates out the culture system of a society from the institutional or normative system of that society.

Berger quite correctly sees the sociology of knowledge as having been misdefined through making this arbitrary distinction between internally consistent theoretical creations of particular men and of groups and the knowledge which all men use in their everyday life. The former are then treated as having an existence almost independent from the social knowledge by which ordinary people make sense of their everyday lives. It ignores, therefore, the fact that all men live, act and interact with their own understanding of social and natural reality. Berger suggested that the sociology of knowledge should be regarded as the sociology of everyday reality; that is, the beliefs about reality which men have in their everyday social existence. Though Berger himself did not follow through all the consequences of his definition, it is in fact useful to do so.

It involves recognizing that the most mundane and the most private beliefs or knowledge of men are as significant for understanding human action as those which are incorporated in philosophical, political, or ideological systems on the one hand, and in the cultural systems of sociology on the other. Later we shall see how this approach severely questions the usual distinctions which are made between value and norm, between culture and institution. We shall note that it has relevance to the way the scientist defines situations, and questions whether the scientist can regard these definitions which he makes as objective, true, or more true than those of ordinary people. Here, we must stress the fact that material interests and ideal interests are not as separate as Marx or Weber thought. What do we mean by this?

It should be, but evidently it is not, an elementary point for a sociologist to assert that, say, money only has the social value it 'has' because people believe it to have that value. An ounce of gold is 'worth' 35 dollars, and £1 'is' approximately equal to 2.4 dollars, because people act as if they had these values. An ounce of gold could be 'worth' 100 dollars or 'nothing at all' if enough people believed that to be so. Similarly £1 could be thought to equal 8 dollars as it once 'did', or 1 dollar, as it might in the future. Indeed it would be socially important if only *one* person had such beliefs, for they would influence *his* economic action.

The same, of course, applies to property ownership. Mr Clore or Mr Rockefeller do not in some 'absolute' fact 'own' the property which is generally alleged to be theirs. They (and many others) merely believe this to be social reality. So, their ownership of property makes sense, and has social significance. In this sense, and in this sense only, ownership is a social, but also a subjectively social, fact. If, say, Jim believes that gold is not worth anything at all, and that Mr Clore has no property, then this too is a social fact. It must be taken into account in any actions and relationships in which Jim may engage in the stock exchange or with Mr Clore, or in his political life.

Suppose there are large numbers of people who earn £10 a week, and large numbers who earn £40 a week. Also suppose that these two groups of people believe that there is no important difference between them on that account. Indeed, they may all believe, say, that the H-Bomb should not be manufactured. They also believe that this fact unites them to a far greater extent than the difference in their income can disunite them. Are we to consider them as two separate, or two similar, groups, or even as one group? Does the 'material' affect the 'ideal', or the 'ideal' the 'social'? The point is that a false division has been driven between the two. For both are equally *social* by virtue of the subjective meaning imposed on them by actors.

What seems to be crucial here is that most sociologists think some phenomena are more 'real' than others, so 'real', indeed, that they actually affect or even determine the more 'ephemeral' reality of other phenomena. For both Marx and Weber, economic 'reality', irrespective of people's beliefs about it, could determine many features of status.

The argument can be separated into two points. Firstly, the 'ephemeral beliefs' of people in non-economic situations can be of equal or of greater significance for social analysis, than apparent material or economic reality. Secondly, material and economic reality are themselves ephemeral. They are only made up of people's knowledge and beliefs about what they think that economic reality really is. As such, apparently separate areas of study can be analysed in the same way. The significance of people's beliefs concerning reality in one as against another situation would be determining for any one social situation only if this could be shown to be so by a resort to the empirical evidence contained in that situation. Ideas, now about religion, now about politics, now about private life, now about economic activity, now about education, on different occasions and in different situations can each be predominant or secondary in effect.

We can now see why the empirical work and the submerged theoretical theme to which we referred earlier implied an alternative to the 'social system' approach. Such an alternative involves building a model of actual actors, their action, their goal towards which that action is intentionally directed, and the logic which they themselves derive to account for, and to form, their action. While there is nothing intrinsically new in this, it is necessary to spell out the component elements of this approach in further detail. In the course of doing so, we shall find that further components will become necessary additions to this brief statement before we can fully explain action in situations or, indeed, before we can finally see why the problem of order and the definition of social reality has been so misleading.

The Component Concepts of Social Action

Situational logic

In discussing and analysing the component elements of action in situations, and situational logic, two things must be noted. We are distinguishing only those elements which are common to all social situations, and which are vital for the sociological understanding of those situations.

Secondly, we will not develop these elements by way of making classifications within them or in the different forms which they may take at the level of reality. We will, however, illustrate them by reference particularly to certain features in modern Britain. To suggest possible classifications with the same elements would not aid us in the task of suggesting a new approach to the analysis of situations as such. Indeed, as we shall have occasion to point out, it may even hinder the construction of theory and the task of explanation.

The immediate problem is contained in the meaning of the phrase, 'the logic of the situation'.

In the course of everyday life people who are apparently faced with the same situation often act very differently; it seems, so inexplicably differently that we may say that one or the other person is acting 'irrationally'. Action, particularly in different countries, regions, walks of life, is also often thought to be 'impossible' to understand. It may be regarded as meaningless or, again, as irrational and illogical. Clearly it is not the case that each social situation has a logic of its own. It does seem however that every situation, seen from the point of view of a particular type of actor or actors involved in it, has a particular logic which makes sense to that actor. The way the actor sees his situation is what we would call his 'perception' or 'definition' of the situation; a slightly different concept.

All action, whilst not necessarily proceeding in accordance with the laws of classical logic, can be regarded as being within the bounds of reason and common sense when judged from the point of view of the actors involved. The same action viewed by other actors may indeed be termed quaint, unreasonable, illogical, and so on. The social scientist must not regard action in these ways. But he must often take such views of others into account, for the judgement of some other actors involved in the same social situation who find the action we are considering meaningless or illogical may be important for a fuller understanding of the situation.

It is clear that such action does not proceed in accord with the rules of classical logic or rationality. Such distinctions have been recognized as of major significance by most sociologists. Some action has been recognized as being non-logical, not illogical, non-rational, not irrational. Indeed, all four terms have been used by sociologists. We may use them only in so far as 'logical' and 'rational' action are regarded as special or particular types of the more general concept of 'the logic of the situation'. It would, however, seem wise to use only the one term ('situational logic') so as to avoid confusion with the everyday meaning, and the specialist but non-sociological meaning of these words. We must then be very clear how we are to use the overall term – the logic of the situation.

There is a reason or a logic which any actor gives to his action in each situation even though that action be vague and unarticulated. This logic differs according to the type of actor and the type of situation. (Later we shall see how even 'neurotic' and 'psychotic' action is quite logical to the actor involved. It is often tightly calculated and purposeful, given the concrete and constraining conditions of the neurosis.)

Classical deduction, induction and rational action in general are, then, only particular types of this general element of situation logic. They are not to be measures by which other logic and social action is to be judged. This important fact for sociologists says nothing about the way rationality is used by professional logicians.

In the term 'situational logic' the word 'logic' refers to the reason and meaning for acting given by the actor in a particular situation which forms his action, and which is assessed by the scientist from the actor's point of view. It may motivate or satisfy no one else, or it may coincide with the reason for action of many other actors. Involved in it are the actor's goals and the way he orders them in priority. We shall refer to these aspects of the situation later.

It must be made clear that the reason for action and its consequent explanation is not a simple description of the logic which the concrete person uses. Rather, it is an individual hypothetical type especially constructed by the scientist for the purpose of explanation, but with detailed reference to the concrete person or persons involved. Thus, the logic for any one situation is itself a hypothetical type and assumes explanatory or predictive power only in conjunction with other elements of situations, and with empirical reference to actual events.

It should now be clear that for any social action to be understood, the scientist is required to understand subjectively, and from the point of view of actual people concerned, the logic which they give to their action. Such action itself, and the logic of that action, are two sides of the same coin. It is not possible to describe, or understand, or build a model of the one without the other.

It should also be clear that we are recommending an approach that differs from those which have started by devising a typology, or classification of action. Some have suggested that the following distinctions may be made within this element in the analysis of situations:

1. It is possible to distinguish between strictly rational action, in terms of classical logic, and apparently irrational and illogical action. An example of the former might be the pursuit of science in Cambridge, and of the latter, a political protest in Grosvenor Square.
2. It is possible to distinguish between action which has some empirical reference and that which has not. An example of the former might be a political protest which we were able to demonstrate could, or could not, achieve its stated goal by appeal to the 'facts'. An example of the latter would be prayer at a religious meeting. Here, it would not be easy to show that the desired end of the prayer could be achieved by that form of action.
3. We could distinguish between action whose logic is internally consistent and that which is not. An example of the former might be the actions of a Marxist group, and of the latter might be that of a group of hippies or teenage gangs in Glasgow.
4. We might distinguish between action whose logic appears closed or dogmatic, and that which is open-ended, which seems capable of changing or developing into new forms. Clearly we might again include forms of Marxist action in the former and of hippy behaviour in the latter.

We could make more distinctions than these. But it is important to make certain points in connection with these classifications within the element of situational logic. Firstly, while seeming to fit the classification, each example in fact breaks down on closer examination. Thus, the logic pursued by those scientists at Cambridge which led to the discovery of the 'double helix' was only on occasions in any close accord with the forms of classical logic or rationality. In its other aspects it fits into any one of the other seven polar types. The same applies to Marxist action. It may be empirically testable, or it may not. It may be logical on occasions, or it may not. It may be dogmatic or it may not.

Consideration of this point only indicates that classification of this kind has several harmful consequences for analysis and explanation. Firstly, it not only fails to fit the actual complex logic which people apply to their action into clear categories, but also actually constructs classes into which that action can be squeezed only by overlooking certain vital features of it. Such classifications therefore owe more to the philosopher of science's view of logic than to the way most people conduct their lives. It is this latter view with which the sociologist is concerned. Thus it cannot be possible to predict action at a concrete level by applying any one of the traditional classifications of action to it. When derived from such classification action will always diverge, often considerably, from the ideally predicted course.

Secondly, to distinguish between types of action in this way invites a similar classification of ends, and a confusion between ends and the logic of action. So, love, which was for Weber, Rex and others an irrational or emotional type of action, was distinguished from the rational pursuit of economic ends. But love, for most people, can be an end which, for those of us who are calculating, is often 'rationally' pursued. For others it can be pursued by more traditional methods, or even by a complex combination of the two approaches. Similarly, an economic end may be pursued by emotional, traditional or rational means. The highly 'rational' action of some Labour Ministers proved in certain respects less empirically 'successful' in attaining their goal than, say, the use of matchsticks by Lord Home, or astrology by many industrialists. Weber and others, in confusing ends with types of action, then, linking types of end with types of action (say, rational ends with rational action, empirical with non-empirical), accentuated even further the bias contained in the scientist's classification which uses his own logic rather than the actor's.

A further problem in this kind of classification is the temptation to see certain classes of action as developmental. So, rational action and rational ends, for Weber, and the rationality of the ideal type of worker, for Marx, in conjunction with their objective or ideal interests, indicated certain consequences for the development of society: complex technological society in the case of the former, revolution for the latter.

It would seem more reasonable to accept that most forms of action, and of the logic which actors apply to their situation, are created at the level of reality by aspects of all or at least some of the possible types of action which the scientist or logician might distinguish. As such it not only becomes difficult to type action but it is also undesirable, because it is misleading when we adopt the actor's viewpoint. It is misleading because 'reality' would always have to be treated as 'deviant' from, and only explicable in terms of, the scientist's model which, for the sake of classification but not for explanation, has excluded many other features of the reality of the action.

Model building in relation to the logic of action follows as closely as possible the actual action, and the logic applied to that action by the actors themselves. As a consequence of such a procedure, our model will only have a constant empirical reference, but it is indeed constructed in the first instance by empirical reference to actual people. It is not deduced from some theoretical model, or from a set of classificatory types.

For explanation we shall have to construct two kinds of model of the actor, of his logic and of the situation. Firstly, how is the situation defined through the actor's eyes, and secondly, how is it defined from the point of view of the scientist, that is, from the point of view of our knowledge of the 'institutional situation'. Far from attempting to build a model of action which is rational, we clearly distinguish between the actor's view of the situation he is in and the scientist's assessment of the situation. We do not then amend the one in relation to the other. We do not define the one in relation to the other as irrational or as a deviation. All the information which the scientist possesses from this position is that of the factors in the 'real' situation of which the actor is unaware or in which he is uninterested but which may, nevertheless, act as means or conditions for the realization of his goals when he attempts to achieve them. Explanation and prediction follow from the expected differences when they are related to the type of action upon which the actor then engages.

Having made our estimation of the actor and his logic for that situation, what are the consequences of it being proved wrong by an appeal to factual evidence, i.e. that the actor acts differently from the way we expected? We do not immediately say that our ideal type is wrong, that it has been falsified. Nor do we ask to what extent deviation has occurred from a model of rational action. Rather we say that there may be a further empirical variable affecting the actual outcome on the level of reality of which we were previously unaware. That is, an empirical variable of which we, the scientist, but not necessarily the actor, were unaware. It may be that with further empirical investigation we can uncover such a variable. In this case our situational model is amended to incorporate it. We do not explain the reality in terms of its 'deviation' from the model. Should no such variable be forthcoming, then our model of the logic of the situation may have to be amended by further empirical reference. If in doing either of these things we impose a strain on the consistency of our theory we should have to regard it as inadequate, and consider ways of altering it so as to include the new evidence.

We shall encounter similar problems with those other components of action to which we must now turn. It is clear that a consideration of situational logic implies both an actor, and the ends which that actor pursues. Involved in this is not only the situational logic which he constructs in terms of his ends, but also the situation in which the action takes place. We are therefore going to have to distinguish ends, situations, and actors. Firstly we shall discuss the social actor.

The actor
Social ends, and a course of action designed to achieve those ends (which are both involved in the logic of the situation), cannot usefully be discussed without coming to terms with the concept of the actor. We now know quite clearly (from comparative and empirical studies) that 'man' has not one nature, but can develop in a series of very different ways. While it is true that there is very considerable scope for variation, and that this variation is deeply affected by the social environment into which individual man is born, it is equally true that there are severe limits to that effect. As the individual develops so he gains a distance and an independence from those around him. In small but significant ways the situations through which he acts and gains knowledge differ from those which form the experience of others. Each man is in certain respects, and to greater or lesser extents, unique. This uniqueness expresses itself in his way of understanding himself, the world, and his desires. So also, his scale of values, the relative importance of his ends and the way he orders those ends take on unique qualities.

Man's understanding of himself, his self-awareness, begins to form very early in life. From that point he himself enters as a vital determining factor in his own action and beliefs and, in a complex way, into the future formation of his own personality. As such he not only becomes resistant to whole ranges of possible types of structural and psychological pressures, but actually participates in the formation and the alteration (whether intended or not) of those structures and ideas. In a word, man becomes resistant to social manipulation. Even the most compliant personality we can think of is resistant to such social 'pressures'. This is especially true if those 'pressures' tend to force him to rely on his own resources, or to change in certain ways which he recognizes and which no longer accord with his previous way of defining the world. He may seek to oppose such 'trends' by searching for others who wish only for the security of their own mutual identity. These factors (of uniqueness and resistance) of separation from certain social surroundings and, thus, of variation of personality, have four vital consequences for sociological explanation and for the kind of concept of the social actor with which we seek to work.

The first of these features relates to the nature of the effect which the actor can have on the situation around him. Just as he and his beliefs are affected by the social situations he experiences, so, through that action and those beliefs, he in part affects that social environment. We will return to this question when we have discussed all the elements of situational analysis, including aspects of how different situations relate and change through the interaction of men.

The second feature relates to the first and also concerns the 'socialization process'. Clearly, if the actor is not determined as fully as role theory would have us believe, then its assumptions about socialization are also wrong. The work of Gross, Goffman and Laing indicated all kinds of discontinuities between the apparent socializing agencies and those they were thought to socialize. It follows that it becomes just as problematic when we find actors with an identity of ideas and actions as when there is not. These problems will be returned to only when we have discussed the whole question of social structure as well as social interaction.

The third feature concerns the fact that we have no immediate need to suppose a particular view of the rigid constraints which were found necessary when sociologists started from their particular assumptions about a specific human nature. It also means that as sociologists we need no 'scientific' view of 'sociological man'. There may be as many natures, dispositions, and personalities as exist at an empirical level. It is the task of sociology to uncover the particular nature of the particular actor in so far as that nature affects his social action.

The fourth point concerns the empirical grounding of sociology. It is clear from the three previous points that the actor is a concept which only takes on meaning in relation to the real person of whom that actor is a hypothetical abstraction. But the only way that abstraction can be built is by reference to, and check with, real people themselves, their beliefs and their actions.

We are suggesting that the model of the persons or people, which we call the actor, is not only built by empirical reference, but that such a model should always contain the features of uniqueness and self-determination which, we argue, are common to all men, irrespective of the actual form their natures and actions take. The importance of this is more clearly seen if we put the argument slightly differently.

We have argued that the way the actor sees himself, the situation in which he is acting, his goals, standards and priorities, are important determining features in his action and for that situation. If the actor is to be seen as shaping himself, as well as in certain respects being constrained, it is clear that we cannot intuit from these other constraining factors alone what the action of the actor will be. Herein lies the need for the empirical reference. For, we can only discover by a subjective appeal to the actor what the content of his action, and what the content of the components of that action, will be. We should stress this argument.

Although new ideas, new ways of seeing things, and new actions, are always arising, especially in changing situations, it can be argued that in a sense everything which makes up the actor already exists in the social environment. They do so exactly because of the prior interconnectedness of situations into which man is born. Man is born into social situations and relations of whatever type, over which he can have no immediate control, and which he must react with, rather than internalize, in order to become social. All his ideas and ways of behaving must relate crucially to what already exists. In certain respects this may, on a superficial level, indeed be true. Even in such cases, the way these existing ideas and situations combine in the new and developing individual must take entirely original forms. Actors may indeed be exposed to nothing original, to nothing which is not already thought, perceived or done, by other actors. Yet, now only marginally, now significantly, they always combine in new and entirely original ways within his experience and person.

In stable societies there is a firm tendency for actors to inhabit only the same social situations which others have inhabited. Even here, subtle distinctions can accumulate to have dramatic social consequences. This is far more often the case in rapidly changing societies and situations. The developing individual is exposed to a series of situations which no one person has ever been exposed to before. The connections between them which he draws, albeit in terms of pre-existing ideas, and the effect of this on his own developing ideas and actions, has a uniqueness which it is vital to understand before sensitive analysis and explanations can hope to proceed.

In one sense there may be periods of which it is almost true to say that there is no new conduct, there are no new situations in social life. Yet it is also true to say, even in the most stable societies, that the way these existing features focus on and combine in the developing individual are entirely extraordinary. This is a fact which sociology must be ready to take into account.

It is a vital consequence of this argument that the actor must always be treated as irreducible. That is, he cannot be intuited from past experience, from social structures, or from a determining socialization process. He cannot be hypothetically split up or divided into cultural ideas, a social structure or, even, a personality system and, thus, a 'human nature' independent of their combination in him. So, he can only be discovered (using any one or all of the techniques already used by sociology) by appeal to his own self.

We will explore many of the consequences of this viewpoint when we come to discuss the analysis of social situations. Here we are only concerned with the conceptual distinction that can be made between the component elements of situations, which are vital prerequisites for situational analysis.

It is relevant at this stage to question whether the existing concept of the 'actor' can fully contain the meaning which we wish to convey by that conceptual element of situational analysis that is to refer to actual men. What is the point of retaining the term? It may at first glance seem reasonable to suppose that what activates a course of action is an activator, an actor. It follows reasonably from the supposition that what 'plays' a 'role' should be an 'actor' posturing on a make-believe 'stage'. But it is exactly the mechanical aspect of the first assumption and the theatrical implications of the second which impregnates the term 'actor' with non-human, or very particular human qualities which we would not wish to attribute to all men. This was especially obvious in the case of Goffman, for whom the 'humanity' of man and of individuality was only indicated by an ability to peep round the stage curtains after the show is over, so exhibiting a 'role distance'. We want to know what goes on behind the scenes. The very term 'actor', as well as the general theory in which that concept is embedded, tends to preclude the possibility of this.

A further supporting argument for the term 'actor' might be that it reminds us that we are dealing with abstract concepts, not with real men. Sociological men are typifications, polar extremes, and it is as well to remember this by referring to them as 'actors', not as people.

These arguments merely combine to give sociology the sanction of departing further from the realms of human variety and individuality than is strictly necessary. The term 'actor' originated in its sociological use with Weber's schema, where ideal types of actor were not meant to come close to the people whose action he was trying to explain in any way. For the very purposes of his explanation they had to be extreme polar types. Explanation was to begin only with the measure of the irrational deviation of people from this sociological standard. All role theory, and the actors lying behind that theory, implies this kind of usage. Now that we are recommending a far closer approximation of the concept to the people whose actions and interrelation it is meant to explain, a different method of ideal type construction becomes necessary and a new concept of the actor is involved. It would seem desirable to coin a new word to describe the freshness of that concept.

In proposing at this stage to replace the concept 'actor' with the concept 'person', and 'actors' with 'people', it is not assumed that this accomplishes the task of 'bringing people back into sociology'. It might serve to remind us of our ultimate point of departure, reference and explanation: real people. It might cause us to wonder when our concept departs very significantly from the forms people take at the level of reality or from what makes sense to the non-sociologists. They too, after all, operate with what might be called theories of life, however 'unscientific' those theories might be thought to be. Equally, they, perhaps especially the artist, use concepts which are in fact abstractions of the people to whom they relate in their everyday life, and which they use to understand the behaviour, expectations, and lives of these other people. If novelists, in creating their characters and archetypes, if people generally, in their theories, stereotypes and concepts of other people, find no problem in using the term 'person', there seems to be no good reason why sociologists should not do so also. The sociologist is only applying a particular, and relatively refined, method and set of standards, not necessarily used by ordinary people. There seems to be no good reason, therefore, why he should not be content to use the same term as people use to describe people.

Such scientific terms as electron, atom or molecule, let alone 'people', are being used in everyday language, and with varying degrees of approximation to the way the natural scientist uses them. The natural scientist feels no insecurity or obligation to invent new terms in order to speak to his fellows with objectivity and in a way which others cannot readily understand.

Ends-values

We are already working with an assumption that what drives a person to act in particular ways is, in addition to the situation in which he acts, the end he pursues in and through that situation. Such ends, which have subjective meaning to the actor, are as understandable to the scientist as the logic the actor gives to the course which his action takes. Indeed, that logic is meaningless without a consideration and knowledge of the end to which it is directed.

These ends are only what the actor himself feels they are. They are not what the scientist derives from the culture system. Nor do they relate to the objective situation in which the scientist may feel the actor is placed. They do not relate to any rational ends which it might be thought should be associated with that situation were the actor only a little more rational or clear-headed or like the scientist.

It has been pointed out by many writers that ends may be classified into different types. It seems, however, that there are certain features that they all have in common, which it is important to illustrate. The arguments are similar to those we suggested in the case of action itself.

Ends or goals have real value to the actor. They have great significance and meaning to him. Whether the 'end' is the acquisition of £100, the experience of love, or salvation, it is the actual experience of the desired social feeling or emotions which is valued and in terms of which action is geared. The fact that one value, say, love, seems intangible and that another, say £100, seems, superficially, to be tangible, and that the attainment of the latter is more clearly verifiable, is irrelevant for analytical purposes.

Some ends are clearly more important than others for a person. He may sacrifice one of low priority for one of high priority, even though there may be little chance of attaining that end. So, love may be sacrificed for money, or money for love. The way ends are ordered into scales of priorities, like situational logic itself, need have no relation to the ordinary rules of logic. But they do have a pattern or logic, which may contain many discontinuities or contradictions. Three things follow from this.

Firstly, such a scale of priorities and the ends themselves are subjective, and only understandable to the scientist because of this. Secondly, and following from the previous point, they are only discoverable by empirical appeal to the actual people who have those ends, and whose action we are considering.

Thirdly, we can be sure that ends are intimately related to situational logic. A knowledge of ends helps us to discover the means by which the person decides to achieve his end both in connection with the situation which he feels he faces and because of the interrelatedness of the ends themselves as seen by the person. Ends, that is, are as vital to the formation of the logic for action as is the way the person defines the situation in which he is acting.

It is usual to separate ends from means. Means are then thought to relate to social norms and ends to social values. In turn, norms further relate to the institutional or structural system and values to the value or cultural system. It is possible, as a consequence of looking at ends and means in this way, to see them not only as separate from any one person, and having an analytical distinct life of their own, but also to insist that they have a kind of binding constraint over the person, as if they were not a part of him. We are attempting to look at ends and means rather differently.

Ends, or goals, are also often thought of in a very particular way. An economic aim is placed, without questions, in this component of action. Love, however, is often thought of as a psychological affect. Ends, it is argued, are discrete, unambiguous and tangible. When stated in this way it is difficult to deny the assertion that not all action is directed towards ends. But if all action which is subjectively understandable falls within the scope of action theory, then the only way of making it understandable is to assume that it is directed towards ends. This does not exclude ends from being vague, ambiguous, diffuse or even unobtainable. Love certainly falls within such a definition. But then so will passion, hate, spiritual feelings and desires, the satisfaction or terror gained from climbing a mountain or the questioning of a deeply held belief in a way which cannot quite be articulated.

Such aims and experiences towards which, or through which, action is geared are not tangible, discrete, so easily summarized or communicated as we, the scientists, might like for precision of analysis or the construction of a model. They inform and drive action none the less, and we would exclude much of the stuff of social life if we did not consider them as having the same kind of importance for people as a simply stated economic goal or political charter.

We might call the distinction which is made between such ends as one between tangible or material rewards and emotional experience. Others have distinguished between material and ideal interests or ends. The desire for particular kinds of emotional experience, the scent of a flower, an expression of solidarity, are then classified as affects, as non-logical, psychological or irrational assumptions of which people are not aware. They are not regarded as conscious ends, and are not open to subjective interpretations in terms of situational logic and the analysis of action in situations. They then have to be explained by psychological or structural features of social systems, rather than from the standpoint of particular people. This excludes a great deal of human action from the possibility of any but an entirely deterministic explanation, leaving choice only to the realm of economic or strictly rational action.

If we look at the ends of action in the way we are suggesting we bring all action into the scope of situational logic. We may do so exactly by seeing it as enriching to interpret non-discrete or diffuse desire, experiences, and ideas by the same means as we use in approaching, say, exact economic action. Even political or economic action can owe as much to a person's feelings of anger, love, anxiety, security, as any strictly rational calculation. But this does mean that it does not make as much sense to speak of these experiences, their resolution or fulfilment, as ends. It would seem more reasonable, indeed, to speak of all such desired material, emotional, and ideal experiences as values.[1]

To define this component of action in this way clears up a series of previous muddles concerning the need which some feel for concise specification of ends. The standpoint for which we are arguing avoids both this problem and the problem of placing certain types of values for which people strive into other components of analysis, such as psychological conditions, situations themselves or, even, types of action.

The approach which we are recommending links, incidentally, with that field of research which has tended to fall into another discipline; that of 'situational ethics', or the 'ethics of relativity'. Not only do we have to see action as making sense only in so far as it is directed towards the experience of values and, thus, of being cloaked and guided by the morality of the person, but we also have to see that value, that morality, as being understandable only through the actual situations in which people find themselves and as they define them.

A person may or may not feel uneasy about using a certain action, say, the manipulation of a friend, or a valued object, say, his wife's wedding ring, to achieve another value, say, solvency, or to pay for his child's schooling. He may in a later situation feel anxiety, and that feeling may be related to a psychological condition. This may lead him to believe, on reflection, that he acted wrongly. The one action, and the value related to it, is then questioned by another value, namely the desire to escape the feelings of anxiety.

Such later recriminations merely suggest that other values, which were thought not to apply or be significant in the previous situation, now take precedence in the person's scale of values. This only confirms the fact that, especially in societies where men are pressed into or faced with many and changing situations, they operate with varying degrees of contradictory, discontinuous, ambiguous, and fluctuating scales of values. In this sense, all action is not only always geared to values, but at the same time all action is moral, when viewed from the point of view of the person in his situation and with the values with which he operates.

At this point we must raise a further point of divergence from orthodox action theory, which sees 'norms', or the standards of conduct by which action is directed towards 'values', as being distinct from and possessing quite separate qualities from those of 'values'. There are two points to be made here.

Firstly, a person's action always relates directly to his values. Indeed action is a part of values, the person feeling it morally right to act as he does in that situation. Such action is, within certain limits, a matter of choice, and, as we shall see, of the creativity of the person. It is as if in the orthodox terminology norms were seen as ends, which, in their turn, were means to higher-level ends. But all these 'norms' should be regarded by this terminology as ends. This confusion provides another reason for changing the terminology, for we might otherwise mistake the distinction which we are making from the previous position. As such we must regard all action as involving, and being partly explicable in terms of, values in situations. In turn these are adjusted to accord with values on which the person places a greater priority. It becomes of only classificatory, but not methodological, importance to define some values as ultimate when no other values lie beyond them.

Secondly, action with a moral value attached to it by one person may be treated as a condition of action by another person. For example, John may be indifferent or opposed to the need felt by Jim to cross himself before an altar. He may none the less cross himself because of his respect for Jim or because of Jim's power over him, or for some other reason. John does not value crossing himself, but does so for entirely different reasons. He values Jim's friendship or respect. To the casual observer, it might be thought John was constrained to act as he did by an 'institutionalized' and 'internalized' norm which related to a religious end.

We can, however, only distinguish between the two people and their action by knowing their values, their definition of that situation, and their logic of action in that situation. We may well discover in the course of the necessary empirical enquiry that Jim too crosses himself more through his definition of John, whom he values, than from any direct religious value being attached to the act itself. Such action, which is based on one or more people acting more or less as they believe others expect them to act without valuing the action in itself, has a potential for rapid change when the expectation is broken or found to be without substance. It would seem that there is a great deal of action based on such expectations in modern, technological societies. It creates the superficial impression of order and cohesion. It is then difficult to explain subsequent rupture and conflict, unless the suggested consideration is taken into account. The case of the student revolts and the French national strikes of May 1968, are cases in point. But we shall return to this point only when we discuss situational analysis itself.

We have been arguing three separate, but related, points. Firstly, we are suggesting that in a real sense 'means' and 'ends' should be treated by the sociologist as indistinguishable by virtue of their shared moral value from the point of view of the person. However, the priority of the value attached to particular acts will vary considerably – crossing yourself may not be important, but, sometimes, it must be done before stealing from the collection box. It would, however, be merely arbitrary to call one act a norm, and another a value, depending on where it comes in the person's scale of priorities, or the defined situations in which he is acting. So to regard John's crossing himself as a 'norm' when it is a 'value' for Jim is a further confusion. For both are acts designed to implement values. Simply, the acts relate to different values, not to different elements of action.

Secondly, values are discoverable not by appeal to the normative structure or value system of a society, but by empirical appeal to the particular people whose action we are attempting to explain. This applies equally to the value attached to any one act as to the scale of values with which the person is acting in several situations, or, indeed, in his life situation. The fact that such scales of values may apparently be contradictory, or are often diffuse, or may pay no regard to classical logic, is of no significance to us. The point is to understand the logic which the person himself gives to his action in particular situations, in relation to the way he conceives his values and their relation to one another.

Thirdly, because the separation between values and the logic of action which we make is an artificial one we must stress that we make it only for explanatory purposes. In a real sense action is value, and value is action. Thus, as action changes so at least some values may change. As values change so at least some actions of the person must change. Because of this we should regard each value, and the scale of values with which the person operates, as being to a greater or lesser extent in a constant state of flux. It is clearly not the case that each action is never to be repeated in reality in exactly the same form. But this comes nearer to the point in many circumstances than the assumption of static values or norms. What significance has this for our understanding of the form which action takes?

At this point we shall have to recall our arguments concerning situational logic. In an important sense the person decides or *chooses* the logic and his action for the situation in terms both of his definition of the situation (including psychological, physical and social conditions) and of those values which he feels apply to that situation. Even where the action seems identical in similar situations it can in this sense be seen as a constantly *creative* process, deriving its focus from the person himself. Even when the person's action and that of other people in similar situations is sufficiently similar to be treated for explanatory purposes as identical, it must still be treated in an important sense as chosen or re-created by the people. From this point of view action can clearly be altered, given only minor changes in a person's or people's definitions or values. In a word, the person develops anew his action and his logic for that action each time he engages on it, even where that action is similar on different occasions, or for different people on similar occasions. Such action is only superficially assumed to be conditioned or determined even when, say, church ritual or military conduct is being considered. Crucially, this view of apparently repetitive or ritual action gives us insight into its potentiality for change as well as into its empirical grounding. We shall return to these controversial points later in this chapter and when we come to discuss social structure and possible alternatives to analysis at that level.

Social situations: definitions

1. *Psychological factors.* There are, of course, other aspects to situational analysis and the component elements of situations than the person and those features which the person himself thinks important. It is important to discuss one of these now: the psychological factors. Other factors, including physical objects, and other people, will be discussed in the next sections of this chapter.

To put the conclusion before the argument, we suggest it is necessary to regard the psychological as against the sociological aspect of the person as a personal and situational condition for his action. In defining his social situation the person may see aspects of his personality either as important or as not significant for the action through which he strives to reach his values. It may be, however, that such features which he regards as insignificant or does not define at all do affect the course which his action takes. In either case such limitations or conditions are important features in the general situation, for they can nevertheless affect the course and the consequences of action. As such, the sociologist must take them into account in the way he, the sociologist, defines the situation of the person. So, psychological factors must enter into analysis in the same way as those factors which are external to the person (such as physical objects and other people).

It is accepted, especially for rapidly changing societies and situations, that people are frequently faced with new ideas, new ways of acting and new possibilities. Such new alternatives imply values and courses of action that do not fit readily with the personality of the person, which, of course, developed in a period that has been superseded. The same applies in 'static' societies for the person who enters, say, adulthood from childhood situations. Such a person is likely to come to see himself in new ways, to become aware, as it were, of new features of himself, of his limitations and his possibilities.

A person may previously have thought of himself as timid, shy, or nervous. Bearing this in mind, he may, quite deliberately, have avoided all kinds of social situations in which he felt these qualities would be exposed. If, however, he is forced into such a situation and finds, contrary to his expectations of himself, that he 'makes out', he will not feel the same necessity to avoid such situations in the future. Here, the possibilities of a whole new range of values and activities may be opened up to him. In each case (before and after so to speak) his own awareness of himself would have been a vital factor in determining the course of his action. Let us now look more closely at an instance of a limiting condition which is important for the sociological explanation of a particular act in a social situation.

A person, Tom, is walking with two friends who are taking him to meet a girl in whom he has expressed great interest. Tom is talking with them about her, and says that he feels he could spend hours with her, as he thinks they have the same interests. They all arrive at the girl's flat. Tom is introduced and is shown by her into her living room. No sooner has Tom sat down that he leaps to his feet, mumbles an excuse about a forgotten appointment and rushes awkwardly from the room, leaving his two friends staring in amazement and irritation after him. The sociologist is tempted to regard this as irrational conduct, perhaps explicable only by the psychiatrist.

We can immediately understand Tom's action, however, if we are told that he has a 'phobia' about telephones, such that he feels he cannot stay in a room where one is visible. There was a 'phone in the girl's living room and, quite simply, Tom had to leave to avoid the tension and anxiety which was building up in him, and which he knew from experience would become unbearable for him. The desire to avoid that expected feeling of anxiety was of great value, though conflicting with the value of meeting and impressing the girl.

This not only means in general that Tom has to go far out of his way to avoid 'phones, but, when he inadvertently encounters one, he must also risk losing all except his closest friends. This further curtails his freedom of movement and his choice. His 'phobia' is a psychological condition on his action. His definition of it limits, but does not totally determine, his range of action. In explaining Tom's subsequent actions it is sufficient for the sociologist to know of the existence of that condition, but it is not necessary to be able to explain it. That may be the job of the psychologist. The sociologist has only to know of its existence, and of Tom's subjective interpretation of it, to begin to explain Tom's social actions.

There are many apparently more trivial examples than this one. A person might be prevented from speaking in public because he does not feel he has the ability or self-confidence to do so. Yet, as is often the case, if large numbers of people are prevented from speaking in public because of this definition of themselves, then such a condition can have considerable social consequences concerning the outcome of social situations. It is also possible to think of people whose psychological make-up limits their action far more severely than these people, or even Tom, though they may not always have such widespread social consequences as the previous example. For example, a 'catatonic schizophrenic' may be almost totally immobilized and speechless. It is hardly possible for him to act in a social way at all. Even so, his action may be understandable and open to sociological explanation if we regard his 'problem' as a condition for his social action.

It is possible to imagine a line reaching from one end, where the conditions on the choices which people would like to make are not significant for their action, to the opposite extreme, where the person has almost no scope for choice at all. An example of the latter might come with some 'schizophrenic' people. At any point along this line, we explain a person's action partly in terms of the way he sees or defines these limitations. They form his choices, limit his values, and constrain the possible courses of his action, in so far as he is consciously aware of them. Though we will deal in a later section with instances where a person's definition of his personal and social situation seem to contradict the definition the sociologist draws, it is important at this point to stress one feature of such psychological conditions.

When a person engages in the action of his choice, and he feels no constraints on that choice, psychological factors are generally not significant (except in terms of their absence) for the explanation the sociologist offers. Where such psychological conditions do intrude on the course of action, even when the person did not think them to be important, then, in the very course of his action, and the intrusion of those conditions into the course which his action takes, he does become aware of them and attaches significance to them. It is generally the case that there are no psychological conditions that affect action of which the person does not have, or does not quickly come to have, a definition which he takes into account in forming the logic of his action. As such, the vital factor for analysis is the subjective impression or definition which the person has of these conditions, or, as we saw, the possibilities and choices which he feels are open to him.

We are not suggesting that sociology has need of an explanation of the origin and growth of these conditional psychological features: such a thing may not even be possible. Rather a person's action is of psychological significance only in so far as he has a definition of his psychological conditions and takes them into account in the course of his social action and the formulation of his values.

This approach leaves in question the actual explanation of such psychological factors. Explanations of them may have no significant relation to a person's social development but, rather, to hereditary and biological factors. They may, as psychoanalytical theory suggests, be understandable to, and explicable by, the scientist in subjective terms. The person may himself come to accept these explanations during the course of analysis, or therapy. As such, they will help shape his action, and be important for analysis. In general, however, such explanations of the origin of psychological conditions need not affect adequate sociological explanation, simply because they do not affect the course of social action.

It is useful to summarize this argument. We have agreed that all social action is based on the existence of the possibility of choice and alternatives open to the person. We have envisaged a continuum, at one end of which almost no choice exists for the person. This is where the person is almost entirely constrained by powerful psychological factors of neurosis and psychosis. In extreme cases such people are not able to enter into human contact at all. They have no choice. They are not open to interpretation by the sociologist through such concepts as we have developed, unless, in attempting to understand their situation and action, we have had subjective access to them before they entered this state. Such people, and those only one stage removed from their condition, mark the closest point to which our method will allow us to approach the idea of psychological determinism.

We may now envisage moving along this line towards complete freedom from restraint by psychological conditions. In doing so three things must be noted. Firstly, the idea of such a continuum is only a useful device to help us envisage different levels of constraint by and freedom from the psychological conditions that people face. It does not necessarily mean that the particular person is completely unconstrained in all the situations he faces. He may be so in only one, or in a few of his situations. In the others he may be completely free, in the sense in which we are speaking of freedom. A person may be totally constrained from speaking in public meetings and from staying in rooms where there are 'phones. Equally, that same person may be free to act as he chooses in private debate, in rooms where there are no 'phones, and in many other situations. Such people may occupy situations in which they wield great power and have wide significance for other people, and for the development of society. There are no people who are fully constrained or fully free. All people are in varying degrees partly constrained and partly free.

Secondly, the incidence of these combinations of freedom and limitation must not be thought of as appearing in direct relation to certain types of social structure. Given our state of knowledge at the moment the relation must be treated as a random one. As far as we know, 'schizophrenia', say, is equally distributed throughout the social structure, irrespective of class, status, and the general social background of the population. The same seems to apply to some kinds of 'neurosis'. It is thus important to regard the incidence and type of psychological conditions as being discoverable only by empirical appeal to the actual people acting in particular situations. When these conditions are found to be significant they will be treated as *conditions*, not to be explained in themselves, but only to be taken into account in so far as they are subjectively defined by the person as important for his course of action.

The third point incorporates this last argument. Sociology has been fatally attracted to the integration of personality systems with structural and cultural systems, in an attempt to develop abstract and total systems of interaction. This is largely due to the influence and development of psychoanalytical theory, which interprets the development of the personality in relation to structural and cultural phenomena. However, behavioural psychology is equally capable of explaining personality development, often, but not necessarily, in non-subjective, and non-social terms. For sociology to take sides in this unresolved psychological dilemma may be tempting, but, to say the least, it is premature. To do so would be and has overwhelmingly been prejudicial to adequate sociological explanation. This tallies with our arguments that psychological phenomena must only be taken into account in situational analysis when empirical work requires it for explanatory purposes. Further, and fundamentally, it means we must note a sharp and absolute break between psychological and sociological phenomena. The two must remain, at least for the moment, as entirely separate fields of enquiry. The problem of such features which affect action, yet which the person does not define, will be discussed in a later section on the analysis of social situations themselves.

2. *Physical objects*. A vital element in situational analysis is the way the person defines his situation. There may be, indeed, there frequently are, very great differences between the way the person and the scientist defines the situation.

There may be any one or any combination of three features in his situation from the person's point of view. Firstly, there is, as we have already discussed, his own definition of his personality, or his psychological conditions.

Secondly, the way the person defines physical features of his situation is important. These physical features may involve either personal or external factors, or both. For example, a person or, for that matter, groups who make up a demonstration or an army, will have to take into consideration both of these factors were they to find, say, a river separating them from their valued objective. The river itself, their estimation of its width, depth, and whether it might be more easily forded lower down, constitutes an external physical factor. The person's or group's own definition of their physical ability to swim such a river, or to carry a sufficient number of large stones to make a ford, constitutes the personal physical factor in determining their action.

In earlier discussion we stressed the social nature of the way people defined reality. This applies just as much to such physical objects, the physical construction of people included, as to more obviously socially relevant facts, like those of chemistry, technology, agriculture and so on.

Imagine that a boat is tethered to the bank of the river. It may seem irrational to an observer that the observed person not only does not use the boat but does not even seem to consider the possibility of using it. This becomes understandable to us if we know, say, that he feels the boat must 'belong' to someone, and that it would therefore not be permissible for him to use it without 'consent'. Similarly, a tramp may be starving, yet hesitates to take and sell the objects on the altar of a church because he feels they have a certain spiritual significance. The social definitions of such objects are perhaps obvious, as is the way a person defines his own body, for there are many things which we will or will not do with our bodies. But the same applies to apparently quite neutral objects like rivers, trees and stones, coal, uranium or the moon. It is not only 'savages' who have socially significant ways of seeing such objects.

3. *Other people*. The third, and usually the most significant factor for the sociologist in situational definitions is the way the person sees or defines other people. In striving to live in accord with his values, the person has, of necessity, to take other people into account. Usually he positively wants to do so. Other people may be defined as objects to be manipulated, as physical means to an end. Soldiers are often used by generals and games theorists in this way. Usually, however, even in economic situations, the very act of relating to, and acting with or against other people, is a value in itself which militates against simple, rational, calculation. In either case the way other people are seen, the way they are expected to behave, the significance they have for the person in living by his values, are all socially defined by him. It is as if the person has a theory of how other people behave, of how they will react to his own actions: a theory from which he is able to make predictions and in terms of which he conducts his own actions in that situation. Some examples of what we mean are required.

Tom, anxious to assuage his hunger, might go into a shop to buy a bar of chocolate. He tells the person behind the counter what he wants and offers him a coin. Tom expects the other person to give him both some chocolate and some change. These expectations may be more or less fulfilled, and Tom will leave the shop happily. But, suppose the person behind the counter offers Tom some toffee and no change. Tom may redefine the person as mad and rush from the shop, or he may think the person is deaf and repeat his request in a louder voice. If in this latter instance his expectation is still not fulfilled he may simply give up, or try some other tack until he gets what he wants. If he does not he may even doubt his own adequacy.

When Tom has need to go into a different shop he is likely to expect no such bother, and is not likely to start off by shouting or by assuming that he or the shopkeeper is 'mad'. In effect Tom has a theory or set of expectations about shopkeepers in general, and in terms of which he relates his own action. He is prepared to amend his action within certain limits which he sets, depending on the particular action of particular shopkeepers. This amendment happens very frequently, but in less dramatic circumstances. Tom is only likely to deliberately change his general theory about shop-keepers if very many of them start giving no change and commodities other than those for which he asks.

There are many situations in complex and changing societies where some people will tend to meet and react to other people in terms of generalized expectations, not in terms of their own individual idiosyn-crasies. Bus-conductors, policemen, schoolteachers, managers, workers, aristocrats, and demonstrators might be examples of these as well as shopkeepers. There are two things of importance to note in connection with these general expectations.

Firstly, different people will have different general expectations of these categories of other people. For example, Tom may expect policemen to be nice, co-operative, impartial, and to arrest bad people. Bill, however, may expect them to be nasty, aggressive, partial, and to arrest only good people. Though it is not necessarily important for sociological explanation to ask how Tom and Bill came to have these different expectations of policemen, it is vital to know what definition they are using if we are to understand their action in relation to policemen.

Secondly, it is important to recognize that when Tom or Bill meet a particular policeman they may alter their expectations of him, while retaining their definition of policemen in general. So, through personal contact and interaction Bill may actually come to treat one policeman as a friend, saying 'but he lives just across the way from me, he's different; I mean, he thinks'. Many white people say similar things of the black people they know personally, while holding a theory that black people are gener-ally not congenial.

These features of discovery, of change from the general expectation to the particular expectation are more usual in certain types of relationships. These might be called personal as against formal, though no absolute distinction can apply, for there will always be elements of the formal in the informal and vice versa. Take, for example, a relationship between the sexes.

Tom has certain expectations about girls in general. When he first meets Jean he sees her merely as a girl. He invites her out, they talk, meet again, make love. In a word they gradually and painfully and happily get to know each other as individual people as if by a trial-and-error process. It is doubtful, though possible, that this personal relationship will reach the stage where Tom entirely drops all features of his general expectations of girls in his understanding of Jean. His intimate knowledge of her may, however, cause him to change in various ways his understanding of girls in general.

Just as it is true that both in formal and in personal relationships the person has a general expectation of how the other will behave, so it is also true that he has an expectation of how the other person expects him to behave. Tom expects a director of his firm to expect him to obey his command. Tom expects Jean to expect him to ask her out, pay for the meal, and not make sexual advances to her at their first meeting.

A person may or may not take into account these predicted expectations of other people. If Tom is not too worried about staying in the employment of a particular factory he may choose not to obey the command of the director. If on the other hand he values Jean's friendship he is likely to conform to his predictions concerning her expectations by not requesting her to sleep with him on their first date. Of course, Tom may get his predictions wrong. In which case his action based on them will create, from his point of view, unintended consequences.

We have already noted that people do not always have rigid or closed definitions of other people. They do not always see them simply as policemen or managers, and different people have different definitions, with differing degrees of closure or openness, of the same people. The same applies to their predictions concerning the expectations which these other people have of them.

When we look at action, interaction and relationships in this way we can see that a very great range of possibilities arises. To understand any one relationship and the situation in which it occurs will consequently demand a subjective understanding, based on a direct reference to the people concerned and of the two types of expectations which people have of other people, which have been discussed above. Two important considerations follow from this.

Firstly, through the actual process of interaction, relationships, and definitions of other people, we can begin to understand how action will change and develop, so taking widely differing forms. This occurs as the person moves from his general definition of other people, through interaction with some people, to a fresh understanding of them and, possibly, to a redefinition of people in general.

A crucial point arises from this. Tom and Bill both have different but general, theories about or definitions of policemen, shopkeepers, busconductors and so on. These theories are constantly being challenged by the way particular policemen, shopkeepers, and so on actually do behave to them. At times expectations may be more or less fulfilled as Tom and Bill *see* it. At other times, they may be dramatically challenged to the point where Tom and Bill have to consider changing their theory or definition. They may do this by a quite deliberate choice. They may do it over a period of time. So, Tom's relations with the policeman in his street or the black bus-conductor whom he meets on the 68 bus route may more subtly result in Tom changing his mind. It may be of surprise to him when he finally 'admits to himself' that policemen can be nice.

It is in this personal interchange, which we find more often in friendship, or close political, religious and family situations, that people's definitions of one another change. At first, and by and large, people meet one another as individuals. In the process of the encounter, their general stereotypes and theories may change.

As these 'learning processes' go on at most levels of society and in most situations, and as they affect both the person and other people and their interaction, so a whole series of slow and cumulative changes are constantly taking place. This applies not just to the way people see other people, but the way they see themselves. It applies to fashion, to dress and hair styles, as much as to 'personal' and 'impersonal' relationships. None of these phenomena can be understood without placing subjectivity, and the concept of the person and his definition, at the very centre of our analysis.

The second consideration relates to the way the scientist must view and define other people. So far we have seemed to concentrate on the person, while seeing other people, as well as psychological and physical circumstances, only through his eyes. In looking at how situations work, how people interact, and the consequences of that interaction, we must treat other people exactly as we treat the person. The scientist, then, searches for their values, their definition of the situation, and of other people (including our original person) before he can understand their action and the logic which they apply to it. And, all this has to be done before he can really get to grips with an explanation of, say, Tom's action and interaction in social situations.

This means that we, as scientists, will usually operate with a rather different definition of the situation and the elements of that situation from the ones which all the individuals have who make up that situation. These differences are important and have caused sociologists many problems. Before we discuss their consequences we must indicate three features of situations as we are now coming to see them.

First, as with psychological conditions, it is possible to imagine a continuum, at one end of which the person expects that he has an open range of choice of action from his point of view. At the other end he feels that only one course of action is possible because of others' expectations of him or, even, that he may not act at all. Such a continuum may be thought to parallel a movement from 'uninstitutionalized' action to the most rigidly 'institutionalized' action. This would be false, for we are questioning what is typically implied by institutional or normative action. So, freedom from constraint of the person by others might occur in situations where all the people have similar and fairly rigid definitions of others; that is, where they all accept as a value their expectations and the values behind those expectations of each other's conduct. In this sense there is no constraint in those who conform with church ritual, taking tickets on buses, or using money in a shop.

Constraint may apply in superficially open situations. Tom and Jean may have none of the Victorian values concerning sex and marriage. But they may actually get married when Jean becomes pregnant in order to protect their child from the expected reactions of other children and parents. Constraint in our sense would only apply when people *feel* prevented from acting in ways which they feel right by the actions, or the defined expectations of other people; that is, expectations and actions which, for whatever reason, the person feels it necessary to take into account in forming his own action.

In this sense it would seem best to talk of 'institutionalization' as occurring in those situations where most people in a situation share certain definitions and styles of action in common, because they also share the same values. Such situations are, however, rarely found in practice. In most situations most people, if only marginally, will have different definitions and values and so perform different actions. Thus, all situations are to some extent 'institutionalized' and to some extent 'uninstitutionalized'.

The second feature of situations involves the unintended consequences of action. The leaders of a religious, industrial or political organization may feel that some of those in their organization are questioning too freely what they feel the aims of the organization to be. To restore a desired unity they may redefine the rules of membership or implement certain means of discipline. Russia may put troops in Czechoslovakia, and the Pope may issue a document on contraception or on his own infallibility. These acts may have the unintended consequence of creating a situation which is defined by even more members as undesirable, so leading to a direct challenge to those in authority or an increased withdrawal of interest in the organization.

The same applies on the personal level. It is easy to think of many things which Tom might do to gain Jean's approval, yet which might have the reverse, and undesired, effect. One of these might be to conform with what he expects her to expect of him, when in fact she wants him to be 'independent'. We have spoken only of instances where the instigators of action are likely to recognize the unintended consequences of their action, so attempting to 'rectify' their initial action. There are, however, more instances where these consequences are not apparent but, in their accumulation, may drastically change the shape of social situations, and, as a consequence, the definitions and actions of other people.

This leads to a third point. The way people interact in situations, the intended and unintended consequences of that interaction, and the ways these set the social circumstances for future action, is the matrix of which 'social structure' is composed. Having discussed the elements of social situations, we shall shortly have to look more deeply into what constitutes this 'social structure'. It will clearly involve asking how situations link up, what makes them change, how cohesion and conflict may spread. From this initial formulation, and in order to highlight the fluidity of this 'structure', it is necessary to focus on 'its' dynamism and process. At the very centre of this is the person and his social action.

It may now be more obvious that replacing the concept of role with that of situational logic and action determined by the person implies the need for a reinterpretation of the way we look at situational or structural analysis. If the person can, as it were, stand on his own feet, constantly forming his own action, then the need to pose a rigid, static and constraining situation or structure over him becomes redundant.

The person's and the scientist's definition of the situation

We have discussed several factors which it is important to distinguish in any situation. In each situation we considered the person, his values, and his definition of the situation, which includes his beliefs about other people, as well as his own personality and capabilities. We have also argued that it is important for the sociologist to look at those 'other people' who may be involved in that situation, by distinguishing exactly the same elements in *their* actions. Further, we have argued that, depending on the kind of situation and action, we must on occasions make our own assessment of the psychological, physical lay-out of the situation, in particular those physical features to which the people have already reacted or may in the future have to react. All this means that we may see, indeed usually will see, the situation in which people act in a different way from the way the person or people themselves see that same situation.

It is usual at this point for the sociologist to assume that his definition of the situation is the 'objective' one, or the one which is closest to objectivity. It is then usual to argue that the observed person has an 'incorrect', 'incomplete', 'irrational' or 'false' awareness of the 'objective' reality of his situation. We know better than he what dangers or advantages lie in his adopting a different definition, in formulating different interests and values. In turn, we feel capable of applying a different, more rational, logic and way of acting in that situation.

It is only partly because of the different way we build our model that we do not treat as problematical the fact that the person may define his situation differently from the way we, the scientists, define it. Or, rather, we may see it as problematical only for our model. It is our model which may be wrong, not reality. We are not only concerned with the significance of this problem for our model-building. What does matter is whether it is important to see the person's definition of his situation as incorrect, partial, or ignorant. It follows from the general line of our argument that such a view is not only not important for explanation, but may be positively dangerous. There are two reasons for adopting this position.

Firstly, however peculiar we may think the person's definition of his situation is, it is nevertheless crucial in determining the decisions that he makes for action. That action is only comprehensible to us when, amongst other things, we understand the way he sees the situation he is in.

The second reason concerns the nature of sociological explanation itself. For the purposes of explanation we ignore certain features of reality, because of the nature of the problem we have set ourselves. We feel certain features of reality to be relevant, others possibly to be irrelevant, and we are almost certain that others are not significant at all. In a real sense, just as the novelist creates an archetypal character, highlighting some features, omitting others, so do we. Our definition of him, and of other people in that situation whom we feel to be important are all of significance to us, given the explanatory purposes we have set ourselves. In a word, we as scientists have set ourselves the task of explaining and defining reality in a highly particular and, in some respects, a very peculiar way. In reality the person sets himself different problems, only some of which in some ways resemble those which we face. It would therefore be very surprising if he saw his situation in the way we did. Not only might it be a surprise but it would also in some respects be a little gruesome. Imagine only the possibility of everyone being a sociologist, or the assumption by the sociologist that people should somehow see the world as he does.

Two things follow from this way of looking at the difference between the way sociologists and other people define situations; one of these concerns explanation. New ideas and new ways of seeing things are always arising in society. As Popper has pointed out, it is not possible to see or predict such ideas in advance or they would already be with us. Such new ideas affect the way people act. The way people act, especially when those ways are new ways, can, and very often do, change situations. Indeed, old or existing ideas, in so far as they influence people's actions, can change situations in their intended and unintended consequences. If we, the sociologists, are not acutely aware of this, our definitions of situations as objective are likely to give them a permanence, and hence a determining emphasis, which they may turn out not to possess.

The second consideration which arises is really a moral or political problem. When a natural scientist feels he understands features of, and laws governing, the physical world, he can argue with some reason that he has a more 'correct' view than the lay person, though he can never finally prove this. The application of his theories affects social life (say, in the form of rockets and bombs, as well as medical services) and is very properly thought not to be entirely his own concern. It is a social matter, though the scientist feels, or is sometimes made to feel, that he has social responsibilities in such applications of his theories.

The sociologist's problem in these matters is almost more acute than that of the natural scientist. We are more likely to be careful about the applications of our theories and explanations if we are aware that they do not stem from objective concepts which can be demonstrated to be true, and are somehow superior to those of ordinary mortals. We are all aware of the problems which Stalin encountered while trying to fit the Russian people into the 'objective' Marxist model of reality, and of those that

Johnson and Nixon have had in fitting the Vietnamese peasant into their less well-defined thesis. Stalin did damage both to the Russians and to aspects of the Marxist standpoint, while Johnson and Nixon have strained the idea of social democracy and changed the face of Vietnam. Exactly the same problems arise with piecemeal human engineering, a point which Popper did not seem to be aware of. The consequences may not be so all-embracing, but they are just as real and dramatic for the people concerned. The approach which we are suggesting for explanatory purposes should, as it happens, be of assistance to us in recalling our moral obligations in applying our theories. It might also suggest to the lay person that economists, amongst others, have fortunately, if unintentionally, helped to warn people against placing too great faith in the social sciences in general.

Situational analysis and social structure

We have considered the most significant elements in situational analysis. It is now important for us to indicate how situational analysis links with, and indeed constitutes an important part of, the analysis of social relationships in society. First we must consider how situations link together in real life, for they rarely occur in isolation.

There are two important considerations which vitally affect the person and his relation to any one situation. Firstly, he is always involved in many situations at any one period of his life. He may be married with children. At the same time he will possibly earn his living as a clerk. Moreover he may also belong to a tenants' association, a church, a political party, or a golf club.

Secondly, he will be involved in different situations in different periods of his life. As a child he may have parents, go to school, and belong to a gang. On leaving school, he may work as an office boy before becoming a clerk. This pattern, too, will change as his life develops further.

All these situations are linked either at any one moment, or over a period of time, because of the person's present, past, and future involvement in them. The way such a person defines one situation may affect the way he defines and acts in another. The values with which he operates and the priorities that he ascribes to those values may also affect action in different situations. A person may feel that there is no relation between the church he attends on Sundays and the factory where he works as a clerk on the other days of the week, or between either and his home life. But it is almost inconceivable that he will not link (through his own values, definitions, and actions) most of the various situations which we might for analytical purposes divide into his general work situation, his general home situation, etc.

Though there may be some discontinuities, or even apparent contradictions between some situations and others, what we are saying is that there will always be many others which are linked directly by the way the person himself sees those connections because of the meaning he imposes on them. Further, even the discontinuities which we may observe between a person's actions in different situations are always in principle capable of alteration by virtue of the fact that such action is, ultimately, the choice of one person.

Not only are a person's values likely to suggest such connections to him, but so are his perceptions and definitions of physical objects and other people. If the people with whom he shares religious or political views are the same people with whom he works, then at least some aspects of his relations and interactions in both types of situation will bear comparison.

One apparent advantage of the type of analysis which uses the role as its central category is that the importance of each role is clearly delineated against that of the others. Thus, one takes precedence over another and, should conflict arise, it is 'solved' by social-control mechanisms. However, in new and changing circumstances (that is, where new situations face the actor) a new logic is called for. This may, but not necessarily, involve his reordering the priorities of his action, and the type of his action. It is difficult to see how role analysis can cope with an explanation of how roles change in content, or how new roles are innovated, or how their relations to one another are redefined. These problems are additional to those which were raised when we discussed the work of Gross *et al*. If we approach these problems from the point of view of situational logic, not only can we see how a fresh logic may be innovated by the actor to deal with the fresh situation, but we can also trace the effect of this innovation through the situation to the way it affects and, perhaps, changes the experience and logic of the situation for other actors. Equally, we should see how it affects the action of the same person in other spheres of his life. Whereas for role analysis the actor is a simple collection of roles, in situational logic the person is far more than the simple sum of his actions. He has particular qualities of his own which are irreducible. It is in conjunction with this concept that we must examine how change and cohesion may spread from one situation to another.

In one sense we have been discussing the intended consequences of action stemming from one person, which link those situations in which he acts. Just as there may be discontinuities between a person's actions in different situations because he sees no connection between them, so there are many other discontinuities exactly because no one person, or group of similar people, acts in all the situations which exist in any one society. Despite this, it is still possible to see why there should be connections between such situations. These relate to the unintended consequences of action.

Such unintended consequences will tend to create similarities in situations for different types of people. Such people may or may not define these social conditions similarly. If they do, then their action will tend to appear the same because of these shared elements of their definition, even if their values are initially quite different. Examples of this might be drawn from looking at the effect on different kinds of people of a prices and incomes policy, or the effect on the different kinds of children who experience the same school situation, say, of a comprehensive school.

In such a school, children who might previously have been divided between two quite different schools (secondary modern and grammar) are now put together in the same building, and the same framework of organization. The extent to which 'other people' for each different child can be seen quite independently by them as similar, yet without their necessarily defining this, introduces a common element in their situation. This common element exists, and may be fostered by the personal relationships and interchanges of the children, irrespective of the initial differences between them. These would include their values, their home situation, and the way they define their future prospects, as well as the different classes, teachers and courses which enter more specifically into their educational situation. The common element, to the extent that it is commonly defined, is a factor which, despite the other differences, begins to explain why in certain respects the children develop a similar logic for action. This in turn, and over time, results in the children altering their values (again not deliberately but in a cumulative way) and thus their action in other situations, and, indeed, in the way they define those situations. But the common element may focus around the harsh competition by ability, which merely induces a different kind of segregation from that of family background.

We have, of course, only emphasized the possibility of the development of common elements and a common logic. It is equally possible for the initial distinctions of values and definitions between children to override any identity in the activity of others in the school organization. Indeed, as we shall discuss later, it is wrong to suppose that there need be such identity in the interaction of, say, teachers and children. For the children may have different initial ways of reacting to the teachers. The net consequences of these differences may, through interaction, merely produce new conflicts and discontinuities.

If we look at the prices and incomes policy introduced by the Labour Government of 1964-70, including with it a whole range of deliberately induced incentives and disincentives with which members of the Government hoped to influence the economic activity of those employed in commerce and industry, this too can be seen to have had unintended consequences. Let us suppose, as with the school situation, that it introduced a common feature in the situations facing and between trade unionists. Their different actions in response to this policy constituted one factor which led the Government into the situation where it felt it had to devalue the pound sterling. The loan which the Government then felt itself obliged to accept also carried with it the stipulation, or rather the interpreted stipulation, that certain cuts in the public spending of the Government should be made. A range of educational, medical, and other social services, and the people who operate and implement them, were in turn affected. Equally this affected the situation of those who use these services. If we take only one example here, that of the decision not to raise the school-leaving age to 16, we find that a great number of children who would otherwise have had an extra year at school are forced, by their common situation, to leave and seek an occupation.

They are forced to seek such employment because they have in common at least the desire to eat, have shelter, and enough money to enable them to buy records, clothes, and pursue other leisure activities. There are only certain kinds of occupations open to them in view of their particular educational qualifications. Despite many differences in their own aspirations, dreads, hopes, and intentions, they are gradually forced, at an identical physical stage in their development, into a work situation which, at least in its economic remuneration, its stipulated days on and days off, and perhaps, in the kinds of pre-existing relationships on the shop floor, can for certain purposes be regarded as having key features in common. That is to say: whatever the differences in the personalities and values of these children, they are forced into situations which have certain fairly impersonal features, other people, and expectations in common. As was the case with the comprehensive school, this does not mean that in every respect the children face a common situation.

The differences in the values of these children and trade unionists, the ways they define their situation, certain of their consequent actions, and the ways they relate those actions to other situations may be widely different. So may be the response of others to them. But, so to speak, in a trial-and-error process of interaction it is easy to see why certain actions and logics will be chosen by, say, the school-leavers, which may come to be regarded as similar. Many will not feel the desire, having lost interest in school long before their leaving date, to attain any technological skills. The pleasure of listening to records and other leisure activities, and the expectation of marriage, may be sufficient in their minds to counter-balance the boredom of work. At the same time, the cumulative effect of these children's activity in work will be to slow down the rate of technological development by which members of the Government hoped to achieve a steady annual growth of four per cent. This is an unintended consequence of the incomes policy, which has had many repercussions, only one of which we have indicated. We can also see how the decisions which the children took to leave school have unintended consequences for their own lives.

Through these examples we have a clue to the problem of how cohesion may spread or be induced. They suggest that the actual dynamic of change is focused on people themselves. It may flow from people who are not directly concerned with the specific situations which their action alters.

Equally, it may flow from the action of people whose altered definition of those situations results in their formulation of a different logic of action.

In interaction with other people, physical objects, and psychological conditions, the person may often not achieve the experience or value for which he was striving. This may be because one or more of these other elements in his situation do not fulfil his expectations of them. In these circumstances there are five general ways in which response is possible to this failure to gain the desired value. The examples, for the sake of simplicity, will assume the intervention of other people, not personality and physical factors as well.

Firstly, the person may continue in a changed situation as if nothing untoward had happened. He keeps the same definition, holds to his value and applies the same logic to his action. This very fact may cause those who previously frustrated his action to change themselves, to comply with his 'expectations' or to oppose them more deliberately. Of course, this may not happen, and the person may simply continue hoping to fulfil his values.

Secondly, the person may continue to hold to his definition and his values, but devise a fresh course of action, believing, say, that he merely miscalculated the best course of action first time round. This may or may not produce the desired results. But it can lead to change in three directions. It may lead to the person changing his values or his definition. It may equally lead others to change their response to him.

Thirdly, the person may alter his definition of the situation, whilst keeping the same values. This will lead to a change in his action. In turn, this will both affect other people and may, over time, affect his values.

Fourthly, the person may change only his values. He may 'lower his sights'. To do so will be likely to cause his definition to change. Whether or not it does, his action will change. Again, this is bound to affect other people and their response to him.

Fifthly, and more radically, the person may change both his values and his definition. This would seem to be the more likely consequence of our third and fourth point than an immediate decision.

There are other combinations of possibilities, especially were we to include personality and physical objects. The point to note is that in each case change must result, even where value, definition and action remain more or less the same. Depending partly on the response of other people, but also on the person in our last four possibilities, that change will have greater or lesser consequences within the situation itself as well as, possibly, for other situations. Finally, it should be noted that those changes may involve the spread of either conflict or cohesion, depending on the kind of interaction and the interpretation of it which the people have.

Prediction would not be too difficult if we only had to consider the way the person saw and acted in his situation. But we have just seen five possible ways in which simple interaction may have unintended consequences following from the perceived failure to achieve a value. The possible manifestations of changes for the person, other people and for situations beyond the one we are discussing are considerable. It is less easy to imagine predictions in such circumstances.

In defining the situation in such a way as to include all those involved in, and who have significance for, the situation, the scientist has a certain advantage over the person who is directly involved in the situation. Using situational analysis the scientist will look at all those involved in the same way. He will look for obstacles which the intentions and expectations of some may place in the way of the intentions of others. He will have some idea, given a knowledge of those involved, of how each individual or group is likely to react to such an obstacle, or even if the individual or group is likely to perceive it as important. Similarly, he may consider how this reaction will in turn affect the action of others, so opening up the possibility of further response from them.

The first tentative steps have been taken towards an understanding of social interaction, based on a study of the analysis of social situations and social action. A major problem immediately arises: do the dynamics of interaction, and the analysis of social relations, transcend situational analysis or merely extend it? In a word, does interaction, and, especially, the unintended consequences of action, the fabric of social life, assume an irreducible quality of its own? Are the dynamics of social action to be explained by new concepts, developed to explain interaction in linking situations?

These were the key questions facing those who moved towards the orthodox consensus, and we are now familiar with their answers. The key to the alternative answer is provided if we return, for a moment, to the central feature of situational analysis and the elements of such analysis.

The living, active person strives to make sense of his social existence. He has a definition, a theory, of who he is and where he is going in life. That vision may be a reactionary, static or revolutionary one. Whichever it may be, it is crucially related to the central values and meaning that the person sees in his own particular life, and the definition he has of the social reality and social situations that surround his life and through which he lives.

We can be confident that actual social reality (comprising physical, psychological and social factors) never conforms in fact to the particular view which the person has of it. But the 'facts' of reality itself have no subjective meaning. Even the laws and concepts of the astronomer, physicist, and the systems of the engineer do not 'exist' in reality. They are given meaning only by the beliefs, the philosophies of science, with which the social person operates. The person *imposes meaning*, beliefs and patterns on to external reality as well as his own life. In that life he lives out his meanings in practice. So, the person imposes such meaningful patterns of ideas on to the universe, geographical contours, his own body, and, in particular, on to social life. Simply, because the person acts in terms of these meanings and values, he practically imposes meaning through them – he controls and shapes reality. He shapes the land which he tills, the seawater which he distills or utilizes as a means of transport, the technical innovation which he creates, and his social relations with others. Whether he intends to do so or not, his life-long interaction leads him to control, to shape, that life and the satisfactions which he gains from his activity in so doing.

At the same time, there is always a tension, a distance, between the actual facts and the meaning which man seeks to impose on them. This distinction is similar to that which exists between 'subject' and 'object', between 'idealism' and 'materialism', between 'free will' and 'determinism', between 'ought' and 'is'. In so far as social interaction is made up of relations with other men and not with psychological and physical factors, the distinction becomes that between personal meaning and control on the one hand, and other people's meaning and control on the other. It is a tension between different kinds of meaningful activity, the one personal from each particular person's point of view, the other external to each particular person.

In one sense both areas of interaction are subjective, for both are made up of people. In another sense the person is subjective, whilst the external is objective. But the 'objective' does not have a fully independent existence. It is being acted upon by the subjective, the personal. So, it is partly being controlled and patterned by the individual (in intended and unintended ways). The 'objective' cannot, therefore, be analysed objectively in the same sense that physical systems can be analysed objectively. Its meaning and pattern is crucially the meaning and pattern of subjective meaning that is acting upon and shaping it. As the external, objective, social factors are not the sole creation of the personal, they cannot be analysed simply as the direct, intended consequences of personal action. But, by the same argument, they cannot be analysed without reference to the fact that they are the personal and subjective action of other people. Such action may be partly shaped, hindered encouraged, constrained by the external objective, but is not controlled by it. The external consequences of interaction have no fully emergent properties or life of their own.

It is exactly this irreparable human fracture between external social factors and person action which renders all attempts to inject a systems analysis into sociological analysis irrelevant, distorting or harmful. To do so involves rejecting a crucial factor of social life. Our concept of the person as unique, creative and irreducible also ensures that the alternative analysis by which 'structure', 'external social life' and 'unintended consequences' are to be explained must develop from and may not transform the analysis of situations by situational logic. In the process, the vital empirical grounding of such analysis is retained in the actual person and the subjective social act by which he seeks to impose his meanings onto reality.

The elements of situations as abstractions

We have begun to see how the elements of situations which are involved in situational analysis link, through a constant focus on the individual person or groups of similar people, with considerations of interaction, conflict, cohesion, change, and the way in which situations themselves relate to each other. Situational analysis, it seems, is a vital beginning for the analysis and explanation of 'social structure'. Before discussing 'social structure' (to which the third part is devoted) in greater detail it is necessary to conclude this chapter by considering the nature of abstraction in the approach which we are developing.

The person whom we have been discussing must be regarded as an abstraction from social reality. We have not just been discussing one actual person, his values, priorities, definitions and action. Nor have we been discussing any one actual situation. We have been discussing those elements which cover all action and all situations and in terms of which they may be analysed and explained.

When illustrating these elements by reference to Jim or Tom, behaviour in rooms where there are also telephones, or Tom's relationship with Jean, we may be selecting certain features of one real person, one real room. We would do the same in the actual analysis of situations. This means using people like Tom as models to account for the actions and interactions of one or of many different people who may have never personally encountered each other. The concepts of situational analysis are to be filled out with sufficient content by empirical reference to subsume this range of sufficiently similar people and situations. It is as if we explain the action of many people by the action of one person and his relations with others. This allows not only explanation, but also a limited prediction. If we find other real people who seem to have similar values or psychological conditions to those of Tom, then we can predict to a limited extent what the logic of their action and what the consequences of their interactions might be. That is to say, we explain their action and situation as if it were the same as that of Tom's in all important respects.

There will always be differences between our model Tom and the real Toms and Jeans. The point is to judge when those differences are significant from the standard of adequacy of explanation. Such divergences may seem to be solely due to local variations. The point at which a 'local variation' becomes important enough to include in a new or altered model is a delicate one. Adequate explanation would seem to involve the recognition that 'local variations' should always be treated as potentially so significant as to require modification of the original abstract model, or the division of that model into two new aspects, one of which is capable of incorporating the variant and one the present information. These variations may occur in any one or any combination of all of the situational elements, or in the way situations themselves cohere or conflict and change.

Even though we are only talking of situational models of action and interaction, and not of societies, it would seem better to use such abstract models as a heuristic device, a starting point or a perspective, from which we may move by empirical reference to the creation of a particular model which is able to take these variations into account. We might compare this process with that which Jim adopted when he moved from his picture of policemen in general to an understanding of his local policeman.

It would seem quite possible, however, to move in the opposite direction. That is, say, from an interaction model of students, staff, and administrators at one college to one including other colleges, and finally to one cutting across social frontiers and including American and French as well as English colleges. With such a general model it might be possible to apply it to yet another particular situation, say, in Germany. In so doing, we would have to amend and alter, rather than refute it, by altering its content when we seek to explain the German college or the American college in any detail.

The extent to which we can approach an explanation of reality by means of our abstract models of situations and components of action can best be seen as involving a relativistic method. We can indicate this by two models, the one highly abstract, the other taking the form of only a low-level abstraction. These are only two polar types, and it is possible, indeed desirable, to imagine a whole scale of intermediary possibilities of different levels of abstraction.

First let us take an instance of high-level abstraction which is applicable not only to many situations in one actual society, but also to situations in many different societies. We may construct such a model of the militant student, or his values, of the way he defines his situation, of others in that situation, their interaction, and of its consequences. We may do this while drawing from our knowledge of Japan, Britain, America, France and Germany. We may feel the abstract models of people and their situation assist explanation and understanding to the point where local differences need not be seen as significant. They may indicate problems for which we must search when we come to look at the East European or Latin American student, even if we do not finally believe that we can contain them within the same model.

At the other extreme we may feel that the situation and activity of the militant student in England are sufficiently different from those in other countries as to render it essential for the detailed understanding and explanation of particular events (say the occupation of a college or a demonstration) that we construct rather different, localized and separate models from those we build of their 'equivalents' elsewhere. The abstract model from which we may or may not start, by focusing our attention on certain problems, becomes split up into two or more models, each of which have only relatively local application and explanatory power. But, and this is vital, because of the empirical detail and variety of the 'low-level' model it is not possible to deduce it from the 'high-level' one. Nor is it possible to move by induction in the other direction. The one model does not, in any strict sense, contain or logically derive from the other.

It was necessary to conclude this discussion of situational analysis by references to the nature of abstraction in sociology for several reasons. To counter the deterministic bias of orthodox sociology (in its use of concepts such as role, status, and the actor) we had to lean almost too heavily in the opposite direction, so as to liberate the individual from the abstractions we make of him. In doing so we found that for every element of situational analysis it was necessary to have an empirical reference. To discover a person's values, his logic for action, the way other people expected him to behave, even the unintended consequences of his action, it was always necessary to be in close touch with actual people themselves. To see why conflict or cohesion spread from one situation to another, to see how situations relate into complex patterns of interaction, it is necessary to have our concepts filled out with a content drawn from the lives of real people.

We now face the task of extending situational analysis to include the analysis of several situations and many different kinds of people. We have noted that the problem of order led to the solution of constraint and external control. A series of structural concepts followed logically from this problem. However, a different series of concepts are implied by the problem of personal meaning, action and control: that is, the problem of how people shape, sustain and alter the circumstances in which they act. We have examined those elements necessary for an analysis of any one situation. But situations rarely occur in isolation. We have already gone some way towards indicating how these situations are linked in actual societies, both by intended and unintended action. What kinds of concepts, additional to those of situational analysis, are required to translate the analysis of one situation into the analysis of many situations? The answer to this question is attempted in the last part of this book.

Part III Concepts of Social Structures

8: An Alternative to Social Structure

The objective-subjective dilemma

Sociology is by no means solely concerned with the social action of the individual, but with the way that his action links up with that of others, who may in his eyes be means to or conditions for the achievement of his beliefs, or both. It is exactly here that the question of external facts, posed so starkly by Durkheim, is involved. They may be external from the point of view of the individual person. But they are not external from the point of view of others. Indeed, they are the very ideas and the actions of others. This is all, basically, the structure can be from the point of the individual – nothing more than the actions and beliefs of others.

The view maintained in situational analysis was that the person with whom we start is self-contained, and because we do not have to sustain him with any particular sort of constraining structure, we can suppose that 'structure' may take any possible form. What it is like is essentially a question of empirical discovery. However, there is a certain method of analysis that we saw had to be followed in each case before the model of the social situation was constructed. There was no need to suggest an integration between person and structure. Indeed, it became possible to see that what the person does is actually a part of the total situation with which he and we are concerned. To take him out of that situation would be to change the situation, as well as the person's actions and relationships. It is exactly his action, the consequences of his action whether intentional or not, and the expectations that others have of him, which help to make up the social situation in which he is taking part.

Whilst to an extent the person can be separated from the situation, the situation in which he acts cannot be separated from the person, and those others who go to make it up, without radically altering that situation. The question is, how do we define those situations which are common between, and have equal significance to the person or to people whose beliefs are similar? The suggested way of defining such situations is by seeing that what the person *does* in such situations is vital, not certain 'objective' features which the scientist thinks they may have in common by virtue of the similarity of situations, apart from the person's place in them. This means that situations are defined not by objective factors which they may appear to have in common, but by subjective, active ones. In this sense we may speak of structure as being defined by men as they continually live their own separate, common and interdependent lives.

This argument can be put slightly differently. The person and the situation cannot be treated separately in the analysis of situations or structure. That is, while the person can exist and be discussed without the particular situation, the situation cannot be thought of without the people and their definitions of the situation and their actions, for all these in fact constitute that situation. Only when the two are separated in structural analysis, and the structure is afforded a determining part, or when the 'role' is subsumed within and created by the structure, does the subjective-objective dilemma arise.

Once we accept this point it becomes clear that the scientist's definition of the situation or structure must crucially involve the person's, and other people's definitions of that situation or structure in his analysis. In a word, the definitions which people have become an integral part of the way the scientist defines the situation. Two things become clear at this point.

First, we are treating situations as dynamic. We are concerned with the way people's values, definitions, their consequent action, its relation with and effect on the action of others, form and change the situation. This must form the viewpoint of the scientist.

Secondly, it is possible to see that when people have the same values in, and definitions of, a situation we may speak of them as belonging to the same grouping or class, despite the fact that the scientist may have previously felt their objective situation to be very dissimilar. This would still hold true if people within this class situation found themselves in different classes in other spheres of their lives. An example is necessary.

Tom and Jim may share the same political values, define the political parties in the same way and, say, vote for the Tory party. That is to say they believe and act in the same way in their political situation and we may place them in the same class of people. It may equally be true that Tom is a skilled non-manual worker in an atomic station, and Jim, an unskilled building labourer. Tom is satisfied with his wage and his work, except for the fact that his supervisor does not allow him sufficient scope for initiative. Rather than join a union he considers moving to another part of the plant, or taking a course which would make him a supervisor. Jim has the same wage and is satisfied with it, though not with his work. However, it is all he knows, and he does not see the possibility of changing to anything else.

The beliefs and actions of these two men in their work situation may be so different that we may not include them in the same class. We are really suggesting three quite simple things.

First, people who fit into one class in one situation may fit into separate classes in other spheres of their life. Secondly, we must not assume that one situation, or one class, determines the class and thus the situational action of the same people in other situations.

Thirdly, in further clarifying these points, we might take another example and ask what reason there would be in classifying Bill, a refuse collector or unskilled manual labourer, along with Fred, an electrician or skilled manual labourer? Both men may have an income of £15 per week and both may be liable to be dismissed at a week's notice. Equally they will have no property, and are employed by the same agency, say, the local Council. They may be conceived as believing in the same religion and voting for the same political party. There is nothing here which suggests that they will define either their work or their economic situation similarly. So, while we might fit them into the same class when discussing their political and religious situations, we would now hesitate to do so in the case of their work and economic situation until we actually know how they themselves define and act in them.

We may find that Fred gets on well with his mates, and thinks that the hours he has to work are reasonable. While being dissatisfied with his wage, he may feel, like Jim, that there is no possibility of improving it.

Bill equally may like his mates. But, dissatisfied with his income, he may perceive the possibility of improving it by going to night school and gaining additional skills. Thus he may be dissatisfied with the hours he has to work, requesting and being denied the right to take time off for further training. He develops an attitude to those in authority over him which distinguishes him from Fred.

Despite the common and 'objective' income, lack of property, agency of employment, hours of work and so on, we would have to recognize that the way these two men see and sustain their work and economic situation differs. Consequently, so will their action. So also, in a very real sense, their work and economic situations will differ for the scientist who seeks to define them. For those definitions will partly depend on the actions and relations of the people who compose them. That is, we place Bill, a refuse collector, and Tom, a skilled worker, in the same class in their work situation. We put Fred, a skilled worker, and Jim, an unskilled worker, in the same class in their work situation.[1]

We should now take this argument a stage further and ask if we should ever put all people who have the same occupation in the same work and economic situation. To exemplify this we shall take two teachers, John and David, who work in the same school, who joined it at the same time, and with the same qualifications.

John is quite satisfied with his post as a secondary-school teacher. He likes the head teacher, but feels the children are rather ill-behaved. He aspires to promotion and hopes, over a number of years, to get it in the same school.

David is dissatisfied with his job, though he wants to teach very much. He prefers to talk with the children rather than with the head, and disagrees with the prevailing manner of and equipment for teaching.

Any serious examination of the school at which they work, or of schools generally, would have to separate John, David, and those who think like them, into two quite distinct classes of teacher.

Their income, and all other 'objective factors', might suggest they should, on the contrary, be placed in the same class; perhaps into a non-

manual, against Bill's and Fred's manual class. So also might the reaction
to them of their fellow teachers and the children. Yet not only do we see
them as distinct, but also perceive the possibility of classing John with
Fred and Jim, and David with Bill and Tom, for certain explanatory
purposes.

We can do this in so far as each of these two new groups have certain
features in common: in the way they define their job and regard their
income, and have future aspirations for change or stability. Crucially,
this would affect the way they acted in their work and, indeed, would have
consequences for change and stability, for others besides themselves.
Again, we are fundamentally concerned with action, process, and the
shape which people give to their situations, rather than with the activity
which their 'objective' situations might rationally encourage or dictate.

We are now in a position to summarize six related aspects of the
allocation of people into classes by scientists. Some of these points will
require further development, for they relate to other features of structural
analysis. We shall develop them later.

1.   In the course of their everyday activity people can usually be said
to act through many distinct life-situations. These would include their
family, educational, work, economic, religious, political, and leisure
activities. Later we shall have to look at the way in which such qualities as
authority, power, cohesion and conflict will further complicate the way
we discuss any one, or all, of these situations.

2.   It is the way people define each of these situations, and those values
which they apply to them, which crucially, but in part, determine their
activity in these situations. These subjective qualities, and the consequent
action flowing from them, allow us to distinguish between people in these
situations, thus placing them in different groupings, or classes. As we
are classifying people into similar groups it is reasonable to call them
'classes'. Of course, this term has a very different meaning from that
usually implied by 'class'.

3.   If we were to take any one of these general situations, say, education,
we would have further to distinguish the situation, and the active classes
of people within that general situation. A person who goes as a new
teacher to a comprehensive school will meet a different situation from one
who goes to a public school. Each in turn can be distinguished from a
person who may have been teaching for several years and who may have
reached a position of 'authority'. Again, both will be distinguished from
others who start teaching at the same time as they do but who have
different beliefs, definitions and values. And needless to say all will
differ from the child who in facing the teachers meets a totally different
educational situation. Later we shall have to come to terms with the
problem so far omitted, of people who define and act similarly in situations
where others act very differently towards them. The same problem arises
in classes of people who face similar physical or psychological situations.

Can people in the same class 'occupy' different situations?

4. People who may be in the same class in one situation may be in another class in a different situation. We have already exemplified this. Here we must note, however, that this vital fact is important for consideration of change and the spread of both conflict and cohesion. For a person who has close or hostile relations with another person in one situation and yet entirely different relations with the same or similar people in another situation may reconsider the validity of his definition and hence his action in one or other or both of these situations.

5. People's definitions of their situations usually do not take into account all the features of the situation which affect the outcome of their actions. We saw in our discussion of the alternative to role analysis how a person's own personality, physical objects, and especially the actions of other people can prevent the person or the class of people from achieving their desired values. In this case one of the five possibilities which we raised in situational analysis can occur:

(a) The person may continue to act with the same definition and the same set of values. Fred (the skilled manual technician) may assume that the 'class war' is out of date and that he will have little trouble in securing 'time off' to increase his skills. It may be that defining his situation as he does, he will continue acting in this manner whilst constantly being frustrated, for, it will be remembered, he was refused this leave of absence by his supervisor. It may be, however, that his definition of reality has caused him to act in a way which has the unintended consequence of altering the supervisor's definition of him and, hence, the action towards him of those who generally hold positions of authority over him. He may, that is, achieve his end without ever recognizing the obstacle, which some believed to be an 'objective fact', and which the scientist had originally placed in his own definition. Or, it may be that Fred is dismissed, though he may still retain his value and definition.

(b) Fred may retain his definition, but may change his value when his action is first frustrated. That is, he will lower his sights from improving his skill to accepting his present position. However, it would seem likely that over a period of time he would also come to redefine at least some aspects of his situation in order to explain why he had to alter his values.

(c) Fred may stick to his values, but alter his definition. It may be that Fred comes to feel that there is some personal weakness in his character which prevents him improving his skill. He still values the possibility of improving his skills but blames himself for not doing so. On the other hand he may come to feel that his supervisor, manager, or managers in general, are to blame for his not being offered the desired opportunity. A great many possible consequences, intended and unintended, may follow, not the least of which is that Fred may search for allies in an attempt to remove what is by now a perceived obstacle.

(d) The fourth alternative is that Fred may redefine the situation and the value at roughly the same time. This, as we suggested, is in any case the most likely long-term outcome of redefining the value alone. But it could also follow from changing the definition of situation.

(e) It is important to note that in each of these alternatives the situation changes because of the response of people like Fred to that situation, and owing to the reaction to this change by others in the situation. In all cases Fred's action is likely to further affect other people in that situation, and so to further change it. The ramifications of these consequences of Fred's particular definition of the reality of the situation are very great. They merely add weight to our previous argument that it is in fact unwise to regard people's definitions of reality as being either correct or incorrect. It is exactly because they themselves believe in them or change them in certain ways, that their action takes the form it does. The effect of other people's actions, and of physical conditions, on the outcome of this action, only highlights the complex question of the unintended consequences of action.

6. One final and general feature to note, which arises from each of the previous five points, is the nature of the empirical reference in discussing class action which forms situations. It is not possible to understand or build models of class values, definitions, actions, or the reactions of other people whose interaction we are attempting to explain, without empirical reference to real people. This point was made forcibly when we discussed the alternative to the 'role' concept. The arguments which were offered then apply here in exactly the same way. This is the only way by which models of classes in situations, their actions towards and relations with others, can be constructed and understood.

We must now turn more particularly to the significance of those features in situations apart from people's similar values, definitions and actions, which affect our classification of them.

We considered John and David, two young teachers in the same school, and supposed others acted in the same way to both of them. John and David had very different definitions and actions in this situation. We place them in different classes.

Their different actions, based on their differing views, are in fact likely to affect the way other children and teachers react to them. It is likely that John and David will come to be defined differently over a period of time. Different actions towards, and interrelationships with them will develop.

The consequence of this may only be to reinforce and develop both John's and David's different suppositions and actions. Their division into different classes will be upheld. The class which they form will change and develop as they respond in this escalating process of interaction with others. In this sense both the similar and dissimilar subjective perceptions of people, and the reactions of others in their situation, will affect our definition of the classes into which we place them.[2]

We must now consider the case where two or more people who form a class because of their subjective definitions and active values in a situation are, nevertheless, defined differently by the people with whom they interrelate.

Peter and Paul may both have the same views of their work situation. They are civil servants. Both believe in innovation, professionalism, and being as informal as possible while at work. But they are defined differently by those who work with them. Because Peter has an Oxbridge accent and a public-school and 'well-to-do' family background, his professionalism and progressive ideas are forgiven as a permissible eccentricity. His work and decisions are not frustrated. Paul, however, is seen as having a grammar-school education and 'poor' parents. Those qualities which were forgiven in Peter are not forgiven in Paul. His work is frustrated and made difficult. His decisions are implemented only slowly and he does not receive promotion.

This may come to affect Peter's and Paul's initial ideas. They may come to act very differently. Equally, they may act in unison against these different situational reactions to them, merely confirming in their minds the need for change in their situation.

Whichever course of interaction develops, change will also take place. Though in one sense their situations can be defined as different, because of the dissimilar reactions to them, they can still be regarded as being the same class for as long as their action and definition and values remain sufficiently similar. This remains true, however great the difference in the reaction of others to them becomes.

So, identity of class can be reinforced or developed by dissimilar aspects of response from other people. Equally it can be challenged and broken. In either case, the person's own definitions of these dissimilarities are vital determinants which indicate whether we do or do not keep them in the same class. Similarly, if the differences in 'other's reactions' to their situations are great we are tempted for this reason alone to put them in different situations. Yet the identity of class action still places them in the same grouping. Here we recognize only the possibility that these differences may cause a change in a person's class or a difference in the intended and unintended consequences which his action produces. This may merely harden Peter's and Paul's identity over time, or it may split them up. In either case it will be the subjective reaction to them, in conjunction with their own definitions, values, and actions which determines their class location and the shape of their class action, but not all its consequences.

These points support our earlier arguments. They merely make class determination by the scientist a complex, empirical and subtle task. It means that classes must be seen developmentally, in terms of people's reactions and interactions and the five constant possibilities of choice which we personified in Fred's decisions.

Class and status

We have already seen how the development of the objective-subjective dilemma led to a distinction being made between class and status. However, the style of class analysis for which we have been arguing, and which links with situational analysis and logic, suggests that such a distinction between class and status is not tenable.

When the artificial distinction between objective and subjective factors in analysis has been dropped, the need to distinguish between class and status in this way no longer holds. In our view, classes are only classes when people have a common definition of their situation and common values, even when, as we saw, other features of their situation may appear to the scientist to be dissimilar. Class action need not necessarily be corporate or lead to political action. In this sense classes may, and do, occur in all areas of society. This means of distinguishing classes of people allows us to separate classes not just in economic work and market situations, but also in educational, family and all other situations. It is these latter situations which are usually analysed either in terms of status, or in terms of the formative influence on them of the person's economic class. Against this view, it is possible to see people in all these different kinds of social situations as being meaningfully grouped into active classes with specific values and styles of action. This view solves several problems.

Firstly, it allows us to see class at all times as an active, formative, phenomenon through which people are always and inseparably involved in shaping the situations through which they act. This avoids the static implications of much class analysis. It further avoids the problem of predicting class action as passing through certain necessary and deterministic stages. That is, there are no objective class interests apart from those interests or values which the participants themselves have at any one time, and which are crucial for understanding their class action. It would seem quite undesirable, therefore, to talk of latent classes, interests, or classes-in-themselves, etc.

Secondly, it avoids the need to distinguish between material and ideal interests, as if material interests were more tangible and important than ideal, ephemeral ones. Interests are not concrete or testable, except by reference to the actual people who have them. Not only may we not speak of latent or objective interests, but also we must regard all interests as equally important for the analysis of action and, consequently, of social structure. This leads to the third point.

The class interest or values which people feel in their educational, political, or family situations can either be quite independent of, or able to affect, class action in economic or work situations.

Finally, our approach to class enables us to deal with the categorization of people into action groups when, in countries such as Russia, the State has taken over all property, implying that 'the people' have formally taken over the ownership of the means of production. Using the old definition of class, all people in these countries had exactly the same objective relations to the means of production, so there could be no classes. Yet, as Djilas has clearly shown, distinctions exist between people in the Party, the State apparatus, educational and other situations, which are vital for an understanding of the relations of people, groups, and the active 'structure' of the society.

Classes cannot be defined by their relation to objective phenomena. This is only obviously so in Russia. Action groups or classes could prove to be as central an element in the understanding and the explanation of development and dynamism of structure in both Eastern and Western kinds of society as, previously, objective ones were thought to be.

The effect of the action of others on class formation
Because people are a part of their situation we have argued that it is not possible to define that situation apart from the people who make it up. It is not possible to define a class of people without the people who make up that class having some similar, but not necessarily common, awareness of themselves and their situation. What we must stress is that the features which these people have in common, and which are vital to our analysis, are not to be seen in objective terms by the scientist as residing in the situation which the people occupy or as binding over them. They are to be found in the way people respond to, interpret and act in their situations. To proceed in this way means we must see the structure and form of relations in a society in very different terms from those against which we are arguing. It will be useful to give examples.

The impersonal conditions of the market may well seem at first glance to place many people in an identical situation. Similarly the activity of the owners or management in one firm, or in many firms, may seem to reinforce the communality of the situation in which the consequences of these actions place the employees of these firms. But other employees may define their situation very differently. Some are quite content with the money they receive and the goods they buy with it, and regard the management either with neutrality or with co-operative feelings. Others, say, the typical union member, have some dissatisfactions in both areas but are content to leave the satisfaction of these grievances to union officials. Still others are dissatisfied not only with income and management, but also with their union representative. This small group of people may or may not define their situation in similar terms to those of Marx.

We have distinguished three groups in terms of the subjective content of their action (though we could have suggested more), each of which are easily recognizable in contemporary English society. We might further make distinctions by looking at different types of occupation. Those employed in the building trade, those in the cotton industry, those in the car industry, can be separated in terms of the way they see their economic and general work situation. We might do the same for those who are normally thought to fit into the 'middle class'. Civil servants, teachers, doctors, social workers, might be distinguished in the same three ways that we found applicable to the 'worker' especially if, in most cases, we were to substitute the 'State' for the 'owner' or 'manager' of the firm and, in some cases, the professional association for the union. Some of the 'middle-class' radicals whom Frank Parkin discusses might well be linked with the 'working-class' radicals who are dissatisfied with their trade union representatives.[1] For certain explanatory purposes there could be far more in common between the two groups than between either group and their fellow workers. Two otherwise similar types of people would have to be distinguished, because of their different response to the reaction to them of others in their situation. Of course, just as we might link these two groupings together, so we might link other 'middle'- and 'working'-class people who are satisfied with their work and economic situation, and react co-operatively to those in authority over them.

Each one of the many types of class which we have here distinguished, or suggested, define themselves in terms of the way their members act: in terms of their values and the definition they have of their economic and work and leisure situations. Were we to engage in the task of erecting a model of these class activities and interactions, it would both be a complex empirical task and would take a form very dissimilar to that which is usually drawn.

Let us for a moment consider these classes in relation to the general political situation as well as to their work situation. Here we have to link those few people in manual occupations with the rather greater number of teachers, social workers, students and others who all have a deeply critical view of the action of groups in authority in contemporary society and who engage in radical activity as an attempted means of changing that society. Similarly, we have to link people in many different occupations and with widely different incomes whose political attitudes and actions are authoritarian and conservative. Were we to paint an adequate picture of the general political situation we would, of course, have to distinguish very many such political classes.

To attempt the joint analysis of work and political situations and the various classes which combine, conflict, and generally form these situations, is an important, if complex, task. We would have to include trade unions, management, professional and other classes of people in addition to those other action classes which we have discussed so far.

It should be clear that in producing intended and unintended consequences the interaction of classes would be constantly re-shaping the classes, groupings and alignments which we had drawn at any one time. Partly because the interaction of the classes would be constantly having the effect of changing class aims, definitions and actions, our model would have to be a very fluid and temporary affair. We shall say more about this shortly.

It should be clear that the action of one class does not produce another class automatically. Nor can it be said that it even produces in any meaningful sense a latent class or class-in-itself. Such concepts are misleading. In fact the same actions by one group may have the consequence of stimulating the formation of several classes whose interests are quite different. Further, it is not possible to predict in advance what these interests will be, or how the people will act. The same applies to historical classes and their formation in the same way as it does to the contemporary shape of social reality. There must always be an element of chance in the formation of class values, definitions and actions, for the people within the class could have chosen differently, as we saw in discussing situational analysis. These elements of accident and choice must always be taken into account, though reference-group theory will be of use in partially explaining past and present developments.

As the kind of classes we are discussing are forming through the interaction between similar people, and between them and others in a changing situation, there will be an interaction between them and other classes whose values and aims their own interests may contradict. The way people in one class define the interests and activities of those in another class are vital to class relations, whether they be of co-operation or of conflict. Because of the effect of intended and unintended consequences, there will be an intensification of relations in which new situations will develop. Under these circumstances the classes are likely to take on both new forms and new aims, and so take in new members. At the same time, others will leave. This continuing 'entry and exodus' will itself change the form of the class, for it is crucially made up by the activity of those who are conceptually placed within it.

Types of action classes

We must distinguish between several kinds of class activity, and of people within a class, a problem which we have so far ignored. It would not be accurate to assume that people 'in', and who make up, say, the Labour Party, the Methodist Church, the Consumer Association are acting as if they were one similarly constituted group of people. We must look within these general contexts of political, religious and economic activity. It is possible to distinguish many classes acting within, say, the 'Labour Party'. It is essential to create models of them before understanding the 'Labour Party' or 'its' relations with other classes. The same is true of any other organization.

So far, we have only discussed classes as if their constituents have some feeling of common identity and values. But there are many classes whose members cannot be defined in these terms.

People who make up *atomized classes* have similar definitions of their situation and similar values, but they do not usually feel that there are others like them. If they do, they do not feel any need to relate to them in special ways. It follows that there are no relations between, or peculiar to, these people. Their actions are individualistic and isolated, though they relate with other, different classes. They form important action classes none the less, and they have significance for those who are in them. Because of the accumulated consequences of the action of individuals within them they may affect other individuals and classes in other situations. They are often as important for understanding development and class formation as other kinds of action classes.

Atomized classes might comprise the members of a church who do not attend its organized functions, the readers of a newspaper, unmarried mothers, the clients of a solicitor, formal members of a trade union, schoolchildren, and so on. They must have similar definitions, values and actions, and they cannot be separable in terms of the different reactions of others to them. Similarly, it must be stressed that an apparently common situation does not necessarily produce a common atomized class. So, pregnant unmarried women may react to their situation very differently: one searching for an abortionist, another wishing to marry the father of the child, yet another wishing to have the child and not get married. Each course of action on which these people independently engage will place them in dissimilar situations, to which it is likely that they will respond in further and unlike ways. Equally, other women and men who are neither unmarried nor mothers may share definitions, values and actions in common with one or other class, obligating us to link them with 'unmarried mothers'. Such differences and similarities may be further escalated in terms of the differing reactions to them of parents, social workers, boy-friends and others in their situation.

In some circumstances, and depending on the way these people react, they may form themselves into *co-operation classes*. For example, unmarried women in a hostel may unite in objecting to certain features of their environment. This may lead them to further common action. The same might be true of many other atomized classes. A clear case in point is illustrated by the differences between the way students behaved in the early nineteen sixties and the way many of them behaved in 1970.

A movement in the opposite direction may be illustrated by a comparison of church or local Labour Party attendance at the moment with that of pre-war times. In each case, the movement is not from passivity to activity or vice versa, but from one kind of class activity to another kind of class activity. Each kind of activity, atomized and co-operative, is vital for an understanding of the relations between people and the form and development of situations.

The movement from atomized to co-operative class activity does not necessarily follow (though it may) from the activity of another class. For example, no one class behaved very differently towards the students in 1971 than they did in 1961. Students simply began to redefine their educational situation for reasons which partly relate to the unintended consequences of their experiences in school. Similarly, the reverse movement, from co-operative to atomized class, does not follow, though it may, from the alteration of the action of others in their situation.

Within and between the old 'working class', 'middle class' and 'ruling class', are many classes of the kind to which we have referred. They include solicitors, clerks, dentists, dockers, journalists, gipsies, and so forth. Their action, in addition to those individuals whose action apparently cannot be fitted into a class at all, would seem to be constantly shaping and re-shaping (through their interaction with others).

To discuss the third kind of class it is important to look once again at the place of the individual in relation to our alternative view of social structure. We have been at pains to stress the uniqueness, individuality and creativity of the person – qualities which we argued it was essential for sociology to retain in its explanations and the way it perceived the person. In this changing activity of society all individual people in varying degrees stand apart from all others. For certain purposes we place the same person now in a co-operative class (say, in his professional situation) now in an atomized class (say, in his political situation) now in an *individual class* (in, say, his home, religious or educational situation). What do we mean by this?

It is quite clear that the values and actions of certain individuals, and the reactions to them of others, cannot be classed with others in certain spheres of their activity. Examples might include Harold Wilson, Mary Whitehouse, Jack Dash, Bobby Charlton, David Watson, Richard Hughes Rita Tushingham, George Brown. Their activity as individuals cuts them apart from all others. (For instance, else George Brown demonstrated that there was no Foreign Secretary 'role'.) We may place such people in atomistic or co-operative classes in their family, leisure or any other situation. But we must create another class, of which they are the sole members, to conceptualize the activity by which they are known to us.

When we argue that every person has qualities of uniqueness and creativity, we are not referring to Weber's concept of charisma, for that is concerned mainly with authority. We are suggesting that it is as if everyone has 'charisma' in one or other sphere of his life. It would be quite mistaken for the sociologist to ignore either the Harold Wilsons or the Jim Smiths of this or any other society in these important respects. Change may start in a palace, or it may take first root in a stable. So may reaction.

Clearly we have not gone far enough if our approach is to be contained solely within individual, atomistic and co-operation classes. Such classes will certainly conceptualize and help to explain much social life. But that life would remain flat, would not pulse with the full jostle of the activity we recognize in everyday life if we did not consider how such classes related to one another.

In subsequent sections of this chapter we will continue to discuss how classes do affect and are affected by one another in intended and unintended ways, and how the qualities of control, acceptance, power and authority are important considerations in such relations. One such relationship, which has very wide relevance to social life, concerns the possible combination of individual, atomistic and co-operative classes, into another, more complex, kind of class. This class is defined by the close relation of two or all three classes into a fourth class: *the combination class*. Examples of such classes may be drawn from any organization, and will, therefore, include aspects of political parties, churches, bureaucracies, protest movements and, say, such industries as television and such small groups as the family. They will, however, not necessarily contain the whole of such organizations, when defined from a popular standpoint.

The life of the Labour Party comprises several co-operation classes: the ex-Gaitskellite M.P.s, the remnants of the Bevanite M.P.s, the active trade unionists (though they can be divided into more than one class according to their values and definitions), and the local party activists (who can similarly be further divided). A few, very few, 'voters' might also be included; also some industrialists, advertisers and others.

There are moreover many classes of individual people who must be distinguished before the Party can be understood. Harold Wilson is an obvious example, but so are Ray Gunter, Michael Foot, Anthony Crosland and many others. Equally, there are several atomized classes. Most of these will comprise different kinds of people who vote for the Labour Party at elections, but who do not relate to one another by virtue of this common aspect in their lives. Others will come from the trade unionists who, by their subscription to the Labour Party, help to sustain it financially, but who may not have a strong commitment to it.

The Labour Party, the extra-parliamentary opposition, the Church of England, schools, the Civil Service, etc., only begin to breath and live for sociology when the distinct activity of all those who live within them and their mutual relations are taken into account. Even this is only the beginning of the story, for we must take into account the relations of classes one with another.

In discussing the individual person we also talked of situational analysis and situations. We found that our view of the person was a vital and inseparable part of our view of the situation in which he lived. Precisely the same is true of classes of people. Whether we are considering individual, atomized, co-operative or combination classes we cannot discuss the concept of class situation without recognizing the intentional activity of that class as a formative feature of that class situation. But that situation is also made up of other classes. These may be any one or any combination of all four kinds of class. In this sense, class situations are more complex phenomena than classes because they include other classes. But, like classes themselves, they cannot be discussed objectively or apart from the class or classes which create them.

For this reason class situations have no logic or interest of their own. The only interests or values that exist in class situations are those which the classes creating the situation articulate. There are, therefore, as many possible values in a class situation as there are classes which make it up. So, also, there are great ranges of activity within one situation, let alone between several situations.

As most combination classes comprise several individual, co-operative and atomistic classes, they are never self-contained entities. This is true for two reasons. Firstly, the individuals in these classes always live through several situations and their experiences in one influence and shape their experiences in others. Even 'total' institutions, such as asylums, prisons, submarines, and concentration camps have crucial links with other areas of life. They do so because the individuals in them have affinities and shared experiences with other people who may even have no knowledge of their present existence.

Secondly, combination classes are never unified. There are always dissensions, discontinuities, rough as well as smooth edges within them. So a political party or an educational organization never has 'aims' or a 'situation' in the way that individual or co-operation classes or individuals in an atomistic class do. Rather, they are 'made up', sustained and changed by the interaction of these component classes, which always retain distinct aims and situations, even though they may do so in changed form. If their aims and situations were the same they would not be a combination class at all, but, rather, a co-operation class.

There is constant interchange of people and interaction between the four kinds of class. So, as soon as people in a co-operation class begin to organize to achieve a common value they must make distinctions between themselves. This immediately leads to the formation of individual and, often, atomistic classes. Together they form a developing combination class. Similarly, the interaction of classes within a combination class must lead to the development of new kinds of any of the other three types of class. The number of possibilities is as infinite as the range of human activities itself.

Before we turn to the next topic in this chapter it is important to recognize certain features which are related to, and flow from, the concept of class which we are developing. Power, authority, acceptance, and through them, control, are exercised intentionally and unintentionally by individual, atomistic, co-operative and combination classes. We shall later discuss the fact, and the reasons behind the fact, that these qualities do not simply rest in the hands of political parties, though they do reside there as well. For our purposes, political parties are merely special combinations of classes which, for various purposes, are organizing and co-ordinating together in a special kind of situation or set of situations in an overt attempt to exert power and authority over others so as to change or preserve social situations.

The concept of 'action class' can be applied to groupings of men in all the different spheres of social life. But these groupings may be quite distinct and autonomous. So it is possible to refer to educational classes, to political classes, to family classes, to work or leisure classes, as well as to a host of others covering almost all social activity.

Further, it is possible, indeed necessary, to distinguish different kinds of classes within each of these settings. There may be many distinct classes within, say, the general educational sphere of activity. Just as educational and political classes are distinguished not by the concept 'class', but by the empirically determined subjective content of the social activity which the concept is designed to accommodate, so we also distinguish classes within one particular sphere of activity. For example, in education, children who tend to believe that teacher is right are distinguished from those who have different beliefs and definitions. So too are teachers and administrative staff distinguished by their activity and the subjective content of that activity.

There is, therefore, no disadvantage in having only one overall concept, subdivided into four types, by which to indicate significant active groupings within the fabric of society. Rather, a great diversity and, consequently, an important flexibility is implied which is capable of covering a great variety of empirically different forms of activity. It is crucial to recognize that it is this very diversity, and the subjective content of that diversity, which gives meaning and sociological import to the concept we have developed. Action classes are not designed to abbreviate that variety so much as to explain it.

We should emphasize that there is no necessary relation between the classes which form and act in, sustain, and change the various situations that make up society. At the same time, their action can and will crucially influence aspects of the development of other classes in both similar and widely dissimilar situations.

In this sense, the whole of society is made up of a variety of active classes of four basic kinds, in each of which every individual both lives his life and thereby forms those classes. 'Action class', then, is a key sociological concept, but it has assumed a very different shape in our argument to that given to it either by orthodox class theory or by the concept of status.

Though we will take up the problem of the concept of 'institutions' at a later stage, it will be useful to conclude this initial discussion of class by suggesting that the alternative concept of class also begins to replace the concept of institution. We have already noted that families, schools, political parties, etc., which are usually referred to as institutions (with particular accumulations of roles, status positions, ends etc.) are in fact constituted by class activity of different forms. As such they are in a constant process of movement, development, reshaping and conflict, engendered by the activity of the classes which combine within them and between any one or all of these classes and classes in other areas of social life. At this stage we can only suggest that the concept of institution seems to add nothing to this concept of class, and in particular to that of interrelated combination classes.

Our discussion of class activity is far from complete. For, just as individuals try to control their life situation by exerting power and authority over objects and people who make up that situation, so do classes. Before we can discuss such problems of control we must investigate further the significance of intended and unintended consequences in class activity and the relations between classes.

The significance of intended and unintended consequences
In the chapters on situational analysis we discussed briefly the significance of the unintended consequences of the person's action for those with whom he relates, as well as of their action for himself. Firstly, we recognized that the person could not achieve all, or even most, of the values by and for which he lived. He tried, but could not fully impose his will on reality. There were psychological and physical obstacles to such attainment, irrespective of whether the person, or class, defined them as significant. Of far greater import for sociological explanation and the person's own actions were the actions of other people, which facilitate or prevent him from achieving these goals and desires.

The person's definition of the reality of the situation does not and cannot take into account all the features of that situation, nor is it designed to. This not only renders unlikely the full realization of his desires, but also makes likely, through his action, the reaction of others involved in that situation who are striving to impose their different meanings on reality (including him). The reaction of these others will further affect his chances. By this means there are chains of consequences to each act which may have few or very considerable ramifications for the relations between people, and the form of social life. While engaging in his original act, our person may have some definition of these ramifications and consequences. But it is very unlikely that he will have a definition, or even feel he should have a definition, of all of them. The definition with which he may operate, though helping to form his action, is unlikely to coincide in every respect with that which those who react to him have of him or of themselves.

In this sense, there are always areas of intended and unintended consequences to *every* social act which involves more than one person. But the unintended consequences from one person's point of view are intentional action from that of another. Now that we are mainly discussing the action of groups or classes of people, the area of significance of unintended consequences is dramatically increased. This forms a major part in any sociological explanation. It is useful to look at some examples. Firstly, we shall take instances which would seem to be confined within one general situation.

One class of teachers believes that schoolchildren 'misbehave'. That is, pupils do some things which these teachers think are 'wrong', and which must be discouraged. These teachers operate with a belief, or theory, that the child can and must be deterred from doing wrong by making him do something unpleasant, or by forbidding him to do something which he values. He may be made to write lines, or be caned, or, perhaps, be forbidden to go on the next school trip.

Many parents accept a similar belief or theory or definition in relation to their own children and, as such, constitute another class. Again, with significant exceptions (who may be placed into a separate class), most people who are involved in legal relations believe that people who break the law should be deterred from doing so again. (Those who make up these three classes may well form different classes and engage in different kinds of action in, say, their work or political situations.)

What are the unintended consequences of the interaction of these three classes of people who believe this theory and act in terms of it towards, respectively, their own children, schoolchildren, and criminals?

First, it must be recognized that some children and criminals may redefine their situation in response to these three active classes, with the possible consequence that their action conforms more closely to that which is desired. Equally, we are all familiar with instances where the very opposite results. The child who is smacked by his parent or detained by his teacher may for the first time come to question the infallibility of these people, or to have previous doubts reinforced. He may in future trust his own opinion rather more, so coming to think more independently. Future acts of deterrence are likely to have even less effect on what he thinks, even if he bends for a while to what he believes to be their superior power over him.

Similarly, the criminal who may be imprisoned for an act which he knows many others, who are not caught, engage in, may next time merely be more careful or seek assistance. Meanwhile, his stay in the prison cell can introduce him to people whose techniques and attitudes he finds sympathetic. Far from being 'cured', he may only be induced into a whole new way of criminal life.

In each instance the action of the parent, teacher, and legal officer has precisely the opposite effect to the one intended. Their theory and definition would seem to be proved 'wrong', for they have not achieved their aim. It does not follow that they redefine their situation, or, if they do, that they should do so in a way which takes into account the way others in that situation define it. The parent, teacher, and legal official may come to think that the deterrent did not work because it was not strong enough. Or, they may redefine their child, pupil, criminal as even more wicked than they had at first thought.

In the cases which Laing examined he recognized how children often came to be defined as 'mad'. There is an escalation of interrelated and changing definitions, values and actions. This whole sequence of unintended consequences may end up with the development of situations very far from those with which we started. The child may end up in an asylum, the pupil in a special school or borstal, the criminal as a professional thief being chased by police and obtaining a gun to protect himself, when violence, hatred, and conflict were the last things any of those involved intended in the first instances and in the first situation. In this sense, it can be assumed that there is an escalation in the unintended consequences of action by which people unintentionally place themselves in successively different situations through interaction with others. In this way the three classes of people develop, so altering the situations and, consequently, the fabric of society.

This escalation starts from a situation in which the actions are at least marginally different. Almost of necessity, it is filtered through the different definitions of social reality. As the process of interaction and unintended consequence of that action escalates, so the filtering of communication becomes further exaggerated. This is clearly of importance for communications theory. Logic and action changes as a consequence of altered situational definitions and consequences. It is innovated, not shaped by external norms or values.

The developmental process which we are discussing has a dramatic effect on the lives and relationships of the people involved in the three situations. It does not necessarily affect other social situations through which the parent, teacher and legal official act, though if it goes far enough it will clearly affect those of the child, pupil and criminal. There is nothing inevitable about this process of escalation. We cannot predict with any certainty how the people involved will define their new situation and relationships at any one stage, or what the next stage of the interaction process will be. So, we cannot predict with any certainty what the end-point of escalation will be, or how many other situations will be affected.

It is therefore difficult to construct models of unintended consequences, let alone of future responses to these consequences. What structural analysis, as well as some historical explanation, has tended to omit, is the fact that the patterns which the past has taken have always, at any one time, been those of the present or future. That 'past present' has always had a future, which was and should remain as difficult to explain as the present future. Yet in retrospect that future, now the historic future, has seemed to follow certain inevitable paths of development. It would seem desirable for sociologists to bear in mind the unpredictable nature of that future when it has become the historic future. For, at any stage, people and classes of people could, in varying degrees, have always defined their situations, held values and acted in ways which were different from those which they in fact chose. As such, the pattern of the present or of the past must be regarded as to some extent accidental and discontinuous. Further, it must always be viewed dynamically. That is, it must be seen in terms of the activity, the interaction, the process, the escalation and development of situations through the effort and beliefs of the people who make them.

Relations between situations and classes
Situations are linked because people act and develop relations with others in several situations. It follows that all the situations through which any one person acts are related by having at least this one individual in common. The significance of this link is not, however, automatically apparent. For example, if one person sees two situations in which he is involved as quite separate, say, his family life and his interest in golf, it would seem that this involvement in both may not be vital for a consideration of his activity with either one. Often it will be significant, as men who play golf frequently find out from their wives. Whether this is so or not in any one case depends on an actual investigation of the circumstances. We may find, for example, that the business associates whom a person meets on the golf course and in his other leisure situations are more closely linked together than each taken separately is linked with his family situation. Equally, golf and other leisure activities may deeply affect family life in a way which could be quite unintended.

Whilst not all the people who can be placed into one class (in, say, their educational situation) can be placed into the same classes in their other situations, the fact that some can be is of similar significance to the fact that the same person lives through several situations. The same applies, of course, for classes of people in religious, political or other situations. Clearly situations are linked by the fact that people, and classes of people, occupy several situations in which their action and relations with others are in some way intertwined, and by the way people, and people in classes, define and act in terms of their connectedness. It is also important to recognize the inevitable discontinuities between situations. These breaks between situations can occur when people in two or more situations do not recognize connections between them. They also occur when people in one situation (say, religion) are not involved in the other situation (say, certain types of political or work situations). The same applies where people who occupy the same class in one situation (say, in work) do not all occupy the same class in another situation (say, in their political or family life).

In all societies there are continuities and breaks of these sorts between situations. In small, 'closed', tribal societies the continuities can be more frequent than the breaks. In complex technological societies the continuities and discontinuities would seem to be of roughly equal significance.[2]

There is a second means by which situations are linked. To do so we have to take into account the unintended consequences of the actions of people and classes of people. In pursuing their interests or values, people set in motion chains of consequences which they do not and cannot foresee. They do so by changing the situations of other people, and so changing their own situations. We have already offered examples of this feature. Let us look again at the instance of the parent using the deterrent theory to prevent his child from behaving in a particular way.

The parent chastises the child who in fact responds by repeating the deed or even engaging in more 'reprehensible' actions. The parent, following his logic, is likely to see his child as being quite irrational for otherwise he would have behaved 'differently', that is, 'correctly'. The parent tries again, only to find a more 'extreme' response. Say, the child hits his father back. The mother might come in at this stage . . . 'your father loves you, that's no way to behave to your father'.

To the child, however, his father can't love him, as he has just beaten him. So he rushes from the house. This only confirms to the parents that the child is becoming 'uncontrollable'. Such scenes might be repeated over a period of time, and with an increasing intensity. This affects the child's concern with the things which his parents 'want for him', such as school attendance, good reports and so on. Late hours, spent in cafes and with friends to get away from his parents, further affect his school work. So, when his parents tell his teachers of his behaviour they merely confirm to one another that the child needs some 'special treatment'.

A social worker or, perhaps, a doctor, is brought in who, hearing the combined evidence of parents and teacher, suggests a course of 'treatment'. The child may end up in a borstal or mental home, or he may be resilient enough to avoid these institutions. Laing's work has shown that many do not. We are only interested in two facets of this story.

Firstly, the child was quite unintentionally placed by a number of successive people into situations against which he felt he had to react in particular ways. The experience of living through these situations was sufficient to mark both his personality and his social values. Whether he 'becomes' a 'criminal', a 'schizophrenic', or an 'ordinary' person, is not relevant. What is important is that these formative experiences distil through his life aspects of the way he sees social reality. This view forms his future actions. These actions in turn further affect the situations in which he lives, whether they be prison, hospital or grammar school. So do the reactions of Home Office and Local Authority to such situations.

It must be noted that there is nothing inevitable or necessarily constraining about this process of connections, or the resultant view of reality. Many who have the same experiences react in different ways and sustain different kinds of future situations. The fact that many do react in this kind of way confirms only two things. There are quite a lot of parents, teachers, doctors, and so on, who define this sort of child in these sorts of ways.

There are quite a few children who draw from such situations a logic which can be treated, for explanatory purposes, as similar. From this it becomes understandable that the escalation of response should take a similar direction in these instances, while it would be quite misleading to see this process of developmental relationship as laid down, 'out there'. It is only when this mistake is made that it can be alleged that the 'Teddy Boy' is the same thing as the 'Hippy', is the same thing as 'Morgan'.

The second important feature to recognize from our story is the way the child's action also sustains, and unintentionally shapes, the situations and, consequently, the reactions of the parents, teachers, and doctors to him. To them, his action partly confirms their beliefs about 'this type of child' and, perhaps, their desire to 'help cure' that sort of child, and also their belief that places like borstals or mental homes are necessary and that they should continue to be staffed. Partly it does not confirm their reaction. Attitudes to and beliefs about 'madness' and 'asylums' are changing. Now that so many people are defined as 'sick', most of us know someone who 'suffers'. We are, therefore, more likely to 'want to do something' to change the circumstances of 'sickness'.

To sum up, both the child and those who affect him are caught up in an actively developing series of relationships and situations which are not directly intended by either the person's or the class's activity. Though this first example covers more than one type of situation, it is certainly not universal in society. Indeed, many make deliberate attempts to control this and other kinds of activity within certain limits. The extent to which these attempts to control others can fail might be indicated by measuring the intentions of the people who killed Martin Luther King and Robert Kennedy, against the consequences of the acts. We can now look at consequences of actions which have extensive, but often 'invisible' effects in linking situations and classes.

We have already remarked that no one person occupies all, or even nearly all of the situations in any one society. This fact accounts for both continuities and discontinuities. So also no one situation is filled by all or nearly all of the people in a complex society. But there are some general kinds of situation, like education or the family, which can each be divided into many different types of situation, and which are lived in by many people. There are other situations which have far fewer people within them (like the 'state bureaucracy', the 'political parties', or the 'mass media') but which nevertheless are similar in the extent of their influence on very many other situations in which many people live whose lives are affected by them.

Various people within the British Government and Civil Service worked out a 'Prices and Incomes Policy' during the Labour administration (1964–1970). This itself was a compromise between various interested class groups, and was later amended as a consequence of further pressures and debate. It gained the formal support of both the Unions and the Confederation of British Industries (CBI) – or, rather, of a majority of people within each of these bodies – who in turn attempted to interpret the policy in a way which, as they saw it, would be more favourable to them and their supporters. The policy was, then, a developing thing, existing more in terms of the interpretations and efforts of those who supported or opposed what they believed it to be, than as a written document.

The mechanism of implementation which developed to put this policy into effect comprised, in the first place, those people and groups we have already referred to. But it also involved other Government officials and Civil Service departments which, like the Department of Education and Science, and the Treasury, were engaged in action that was felt to affect or be affected by the policy. Similarly, we may not ignore those who were involved at the more local level of policy implementation, such as particular trade union officials and the management of public or private industry or profession. The interaction of all these groupings of interested classes of people would seem to constitute the actual, practical, implementation of an economic policy which no one group could itself wish, or fully foresee.

Let us suppose for a moment that such a policy were applied uniformly to each section of the working community. This would not, of course, be the case in practice, because of the different kinds of wage and salary agreements negotiated by trade union and professional associations, because of the different negotiating powers of the larger and the smaller unions and so on. But the hypothetical assumption of uniformity will add substance to the point we are to make.

How will the people who have had nothing to do with the implementation of the policy (the people in offices, on the shop floor, and in the home) interpret its effects, in their work-place, and in their economic and family situation? First, people will actually be confronted with its effects at different times, depending on when their representatives submit a wage or salary claim. The granting or refusal of the claim will depend in part on what 'the state of the economy' is considered to be at that particular time. Similarly, a nil or a three per cent norm, if adhered to, will affect a ten-pound wage differently from a thirty-pound salary. Again, the press, radio and television, as well as personal associates and friends, will all place definitions on the general and particular incomes situation of the people concerned. The wives and other dependents, and the particular purchasing power of the particular income, will be further sources of definition in the person's economic situation.

It can now be seen that the same policy, that is, the same set of accumulated consequences of many people's decisions, will in fact create different situations and definitions for many classes of people. In addition to the different general values of these people there will be several competing definitions of that situation from which the person will derive his particular definition and his particular reaction. This reaction will be one factor in the wives' and other dependents' economic situation. It will affect what is bought, whether books are purchased for a child, whether a holiday is taken, and so on. In particular, both the prices side of the policy and the wage-earner's, if not the whole family's, attitude to the political situation will be affected. Here we have turned full circle. For these last two factors will have to be taken into account, defined, or estimated by the interested Government and the Civil Service Departments. And, on their estimations, further policy decisions will be made, and further effects will result in the economic situations of the majority of the people in the society.

If we add to this chain of events the differential application of the original policy, we can see how complex, how unpredictable and often unintended will be the consequences of the policy for people's economic, family, consumption, educational, leisure and political situations. It might lead, in part, and as one consequence, to an 'economic miracle', or to a rise in racialism, or to student protest, or to the Government losing the next election. Which of these consequences actually follows will depend very much on the connections which people define.

A similar approach would be necessary for any one of the many situations through which small and large active class-groupings of people engage in acts which visibly and invisibly affect many people by virtue of their personal involvement in situations far removed from the initial acts. The reactions of these people in these different situations then further complicates the equation. To imagine only the State bureaucracy, which administers the social services, education, technology, and nationalized industries, as well as local authorities and those who control such leisure industries as the cinema and theatre, is to see how complicated these interconnections are.

Consensus, conflict and change

We must continue our discussion of class, intended and unintended consequences of and relations between classes and situations to see what bearing they have on change. Such consideration is of immediate importance to the problem of order and conflict in society generally.

Consensus. One type of consensus is clearly involved in considering co-operation classes. They have definitions, mutual recognition, values and styles of action in common in at least one situation. Atomistic classes are unlike co-operation classes in that their members do not have mutual recognition as a significant feature of their situational definition. In so far as their activity is similar, however, another kind of consensus is involved.

Individual classes are distinguished by their uniqueness and, therefore, do not encourage the kind of consensus which is involved in either co-operation or atomistic classes. But as all three kinds of class may unite to form combination classes a further kind of consensus occurs, in which individual classes may play a vital part.

We may call the kind of consensus which flows from the activity of a co-operation class a 'consensual unity', and that of an atomized class a 'consensual identity'. But the consensus involved in a combination class clearly involves both forms and relates them into a third kind, which we may call 'consensual co-ordination'. Other classes who, together with the class we are considering, make up the total situation (formed by class action) need in no way share beliefs in common before we can accept that consensus within the class constitutes a part of that situation. When consensus actually does exist between classes and people in the situation, it would seem reasonable to regard this as a further and special form of consensus. This kind of concensus may actually exist in two or more related situations. In such instances whole sections of society would seem to be defined by this form of consensus. But the frequency of such instances would seem to be rare. Such consensus may be referred to as 'consensual acceptance'. It is only one of the forms of consensus which are found within combination classes.

A further type of apparent consensus may exist in areas of society where the only connections between situations are entirely unintended ones. Here, people or classes may be common to the two situations, but their effect on one another is either defined by them as unimportant, or is not recognized by those involved. In the latter instance the relations between the people in the two situations is such that they do not, in effect, have to form a definition of one another upon which to base their action. As with the second type of consensus this may be more stable than the first. It may be referred to as 'unintended consensus'. It is very distinct from situations in which people have a close and mutually dependent relationship, for such people can 'fall out'. When they do, ensuing conflict and changes of attitude can be far greater than that between two groups who have previously had no mutual relations.

It would be wrong to regard any of these types of consensus as 'stability'. The kinds of consensual situations we have so far described are in a continuous state of action and interaction between those who compose them and other sectors of society. Seen from this perspective, consensual relations within classes, and between those classes involved in the 'unintended consensus' and those involved in yet other areas of society, are bound to imply the constant possibility of breakdown. This is more clearly the case when consensus takes a different form.

People and classes in one or more situations may not share the same values, or definitions. But their definitions of the situations in which each are involved may be compatible, not leading to conflict. This is especially the case when these definitions suggest to the participants that change in their situations is not possible, or that it is only possible in certain specific ways. Here, it is best to regard the framework of interaction and, therefore, consensus, as non-existent. Simply, there is neither consensus nor conflict. Such situations may on occasions be more stable (in the sense of unchanging) than those contained in any of the previous kinds of consensus.

Each kind of consensus could be further distinguished by its specific content, or by its relation to other areas within a society. But it is sufficient to note that each can exist, indeed must exist, in a complex society. However, its location and area of effect within the fabric of society are not predetermined and may take many forms. They are matters for empirical investigation.

Conflict. Though all people and classes live through one or more of the different aspects of consensus, it is not possible to find the occurrence of consensus without conflict also being present. As with consensus, conflict takes several different forms.

A class, and that aspect of a situation which is formed by that class, is internally consensual in one way or another; but, at the same time, it might contain overt or covert aspects of conflict within it. It will usually also encourage conflict with another class in that or other situations. For this reason, the situations as well as classes comprise aspects of both consensus and conflict.

People and classes of all kinds may have some similar values but different definitions of their situations, and will engage in differing actions. This will lead them into conflict with one another, which may or may not lead to their distinguishing between their values, or to any combination of the five possible alternatives that we have outlined. For example, people may retain similar definitions while having different values. This leads them into 'internal conflict' which, in turn, may affect other elements of their action in that situation.

Even co-operation classes may develop internal conflict. They may do so because the individuals who comprise them may apply experience gained in other classes and situations to this particular class. Or it may arise owing to the unintended repercussions of the activity of other classes, which change aspects of the class situation, which are then reinterpreted by some members of the co-operation class.

Both inter- and intra-class conflict may be the intentional result of activity. In these circumstances the class concerned must have some awareness that the action designed to achieve its values will conflict with the activity of other classes. Equally, conflict may be the consequence of unintended consequences.

'Unintended conflict' may have wider and deeper consequences than intended conflict. For quite often people deliberately engage in conflict only when they know they can limit its effects. So, a father may punish his child with the intention that the conflict between them will be confined to the one act. Similarly, a protest movement may engage in activity designed to change only one set of situations in society, say concerning nuclear weapons or abortion. Such limited intentions may have unlimited unintended consequences for conflict.

'Unlimited conflict' is rarely engaged in intentionally. Even acts of war (since Clausewitz), or revolution are not interpreted as intending to change everything, certainly not, for example, the revolutionary organization, with the possible exception of those seeking 'permanent revolution'. 'Unlimited conflict' is, therefore, usually the unintended consequence of action which may have been intended to produce either consensus (punishing a child) or limited conflict (a single-issue protest).

In the sense in which we speak of it, conflict, like consensus, exists in all situations. All people and classes experience both kinds of activity throughout their existence. For almost every action has facets or repercussions of both kinds. But which specific kind of conflict or consensus exists in one act, or for one person, class or situation is not determined, and can only be discovered by means of empirical reference.

Conflict has usually been highlighted by 'conflict theorists' who only fasten on 'intended and overt conflict' between two classes, as defined in the orthodox way. Similarly 'consensus' has been distorted by 'cohesion theorists' who define it in terms of complete reciprocity of act and expectation, due to the determining influence of shared, dominant values. Both approaches are equally misleading simply because they only fasten on one of the many possible forms of conflict and consensus. Equally, they mislead by failing to recognize forms of conflict where consensus is felt to exist, and vice versa. In fact no situation can be adequately understood or explained without taking both aspects of social life and the various possible manifestations of them into account. We have abandoned the view and analysis of cohesion and conflict offered by both these theories, and we have shown how it is possible to adopt a different perspective of the place of both cohesion and conflict in societies.

Our more complex view of cohesion and conflict enables us to look at one or several related situations from a combined perspective. Further, this means that process, development and change can be seen in the same light. There is sufficient flexibility in this approach for us to recognize not only that there is no one form of order or of conflict, but also that there is no one form of change.

Just as all action and all situations involve different kinds of conflict and consensus, so all action involves at least one of these kinds of change. In this sense, social life is never static or stable, but is always in flux and motion.

Change. Because the person or class which has one form of consensual relations in one situation may have conflicting relations with the same or similar people in the same or in another situation, the possibility of development and change exists. A person or class, or grouping of classes, that is defined as an opponent in one situation may come to be defined as an opponent in another, previously consensual, situation. In this way conflict may spread from situation to situation, gathering in intensity and in impact on people's lives. The same development of conflict may also occur through the repercussions of unintended consequences.

Similarly, cohesion may spread, so diminishing or, at least, confining the area and intensity of conflict. In this way it is quite possible for people who make up one class in their work situation, and yet who are in separate and opposed classes in their political situation, to dissolve that opposition. In this way classes may become aligned in certain areas of society, at once causing the development of consensual relations between them, and also relations of conflict with those classes to which they are opposed. This may force those opposed classes to align, seeing areas of common ground in their mutual opponent which had not previously been perceived. Exactly the same effect can be produced by the spread of changes in aspects of the situations of people which flow from the unintended consequence of other people's actions.

This perspective includes a view of consensus and conflict which may involve the spread of either or both types of action or the alteration of their form. For this reason itself, class action, definitions, relations and values are always changing. It is possible to define change and distinguish between different forms of it by its cause or its effect, or its content and degree of intensity. It is most useful, however, to distinguish different forms in terms of the composition of situational elements within them.

Change may develop where two individuals, say, Stalin and Trotsky, or Kennedy and Johnson, conflict in the means of defining a certain situation, or the logic for action in that situation, or a whole range of situations. The same is true of conflict between two co-operation or combination classes or between similar classes. Change flowing from conflict between an atomistic class and any of the other classes is of a different order, because the atomistic class cannot reciprocate intentional conflict. Just as change is involved in all the possible forms of conflict – we have not even mentioned change flowing from unintended conflict – so change is involved in all the possible forms of cohesion and between all possible groupings of people and classes.

As combination classes represent the most complex kind of class they involve complex and different forms of change. These changes occur both within them and as a result of their influence on other areas of society. Though the number of elements which such change involves is great, and their effect is widespread, they do not necessarily produce the most severe form of change. The death of one man – Martin Luther King or Tom Mboya – can have the most profound consequences for change. So also the unintended effect of an atomistic class can be enormous – as when prospectors discover oil or uranium. It is easy to see that death or discovery alters the situations and consequent activities of other people or classes.

The same is true of all forms of change. Less dramatically, almost every act has unintended consequences for change. Indeed, the very notion of class and class action is inseparably involved with the concept of change.

It is difficult to discuss class, let alone the different concepts of conflict, consensus, and change, without introducing a set of concepts which are distinct from all these. So far we have omitted the different elements of control – authority, power, acceptance and legitimacy – in our attempt to build the foundation of an alternative perspective. We need only think of the four kinds of class in conjunction with 'power', 'authority' and 'acceptance' to see how the points we have made so far immediately become more complicated.

In attempting to implement their aims by intentional action all four kinds of class will be attempting to control one or more features of their social situations. The phenomena of 'acceptance', 'power', 'authority', and 'legitimation' are intentionally or unintentionally involved in the general concept of control.

Control of situations
When discussing situational analysis we were continuously faced with the point that people attempt to control the reality of situations as they see them. This involves an attempt to control the psychological and physical environment, as well as their relationships with other people. This is only more clearly the case, with, say, politicians, scientists, trade unionists and industrialists than with other people, or even with these people in other aspects of their lives. The argument hardly needs stating for those people who are in co-operative or combination classes, such as students who advocate 'student power', negroes who advocate 'Black Power', nationalists who advocate their countries' 'independence', or doctors, nurses, teachers, as well as trade unionists, who attempt to control their work and economic situation. But what about the 'loner' in the big city, the girl in the bed-sitter, the young child, the lover, or the many people whom we earlier indicated should be seen either as individuals in some aspects of their lives or as people who make up a common, but atomized, class?

All these people must not be seen as passive or inert. In attempting to live by their values and achieve their desired experiences, they act according to a logic which is at once moral and reasonable in their eyes. Theirs is not necessarily a calculated or deliberate attempt to manipulate other people. Sometimes that is what rationality suggests, and sometimes it is what is actually done. But through the limits prescribed by their definition and values, the logic which everyone develops is designed to enable them to live by and to fulfil their values. This means doing some things and not others, saying some things and not others, which now slightly, now dramatically, change their situation and give them a margin of control over it. The ever-present possibility of the interaction of other people's actions and of unintended consequences flowing from such actions means that the control will always be less than complete, though equally it will sometimes be more than was predicted.

The lover, in suggesting new forms of love-making, may only frighten his friend. The child, in crying to gain attention, may make the parent angry. Even the person who is compliant to the wishes of others may incur hostility, not affection. But the feature of control is for ever present in the person's attempt to achieve by action the fruits of what he values. It is only more overtly present, perhaps with a definite theory of control and change to accompany it, in combination classes in economic, work, or political situations.

Control implies the existence of the means by which control is exercised. If control is exerted through the actions of each person and class, and in each situation through which they act, then this presupposes the elements by which they attempt control. The concepts which become involved at this point are acceptance, power, authority, and legitimacy.

People may recognize that their hopes for changing their situation in a way which will make them approach more closely to the meanings and values they attach to life are bound up with those of others who share their interests. At the same time, they may intentionally or unintentionally deprive others of fulfilment, and may cause the spread of conflict if this is perceived and objected to.

The same is equally true of the individual, of small and of large atomistic or co-operation classes. It will often be the case that in pursuing their values, these classes will invoke the common action of others who would be deprived should that value be attained. Control, then, is intimately bound up with class action, conflict, cohesion and change in situations and society.

The significance of controls by people of their situations is especially acute at all levels of social life in technological societies such as that of modern Britain, where change is rapid and widespread. For many people in such societies situations are constantly taking new dimensions. To retain a previous way of life, or to develop a new one through these changing situations, suggests the need to gain at least an element of intentional control over their definition of what is producing the changes in these situations. Because other people are a key factor in these changes (as are psychological and physical factors), this means that in some sense people seek to control, intentionally or not, the direction of aspects of the lives of other people, as well as of their own. Exactly because action is directed by the person, though the consequences of action may not be the predicted ones, the person attempts to give that action a certain legitimacy. The purpose of this may in certain circumstances be solely his own satisfaction, and legitimacy may be in terms of his own values. But, in so far as he is attempting to influence the action of others it is often, but not always, the case that he will attempt to legitimize his action and values in their eyes also. This is as true for a combination class as it is for the solitary individual.

No person or class is likely to wield intentional control over another for very long without attempting to make his position of control more secure by making, or trying to make, that control both credible and acceptable to that person or class. Control is not always or, even usually, developed in a highly deliberate way. It may be spectacular and associated with major and rapid change. More usually, people and classes try to control their situation by more delicate attempts to legitimize not only their situation, but also their intentions and activities for extending and changing that situation. This may not be spectacular, but its effect may be enormous. Legitimation is concerned with the change from power to authority, and not with either concept alone. The third form of control is the least spectacular of all and is to do with acceptance.

Acceptance, power, authority and legitimacy

Acceptance. Acceptance distinguishes a relationship in which people or classes accept the other's right not only to exist, but also to live in the way he himself chooses in the situation or situations in question. This must hold true even where the values and activities of one person may jeopardize the activities and values of the other. The acceptance must be complete. If it is not, then other defining qualities have entered into the relationship. These will involve either power or authority or both.

In historical societies acceptance occurred not only within co-operation and atomistic classes, but also between them. So, serfs and barons often lived in close, if distinct harmony. Acceptance can, therefore, involve and consolidate enormous distinctions between people. But, it can also involve the idea of equality. Jesus Christ argued: 'love your neighbour as yourself'.[3] However, it must be said that he did have difficulty in persuading people to accept this logic. People have usually wanted to know who their neighbours were before accepting or loving them.

In modern times, especially in social democracies and as a consequence of Marx's extension of the cry 'liberty, equality, fraternity' from its application to one group of people to all people, the possibility of people relating to one another in that form of mutual acceptance which involves equality has gained some limited respectability. However, whilst on the one hand its general application is as much in doubt as ever – witness only the situations of race, Vietnam, poverty, madness, crime, power, authority and, say, Nixon and Brezhnev – on the other hand, its particular application in personal relations, even between classes of people, is spreading. This point has been taken a little further in the popular debate about 'permissiveness'.

The point to note for our purposes is that in their attempts to control their situation and live by their values some people will not exert power or authority over others, but value them as important in themselves. If this definition and value is reciprocated, the relationship is one of acceptance. But the relationship need not be one of similarity or of strict equality, for the relation may exist between a man and a woman, a boy and an old woman, a black and a white. However, the more people's experiences and values are removed from one another, the more it becomes unlikely that such a real relationship of acceptance will exist. But it is not impossible. For relations of acceptance can and do exist between different classes of people, not just within them.

As people's experiences in classes and situations change, so their relations with others change. Thus a relationship of acceptance, say, between a girl and her mother, may become one of authority. But, equally, relationships of authority or power may become ones of acceptance.

Power. Power, like class, is not an objective quality of a situation. For example, a State, army, atomistic class or person does not wield power simply because of the quantity of its armed forces, the quality of its armoury, its numbers, or personal physical strength. These material phenomena may be important, especially if that power is put to the test. But the subjective estimation of that power is a vital determining feature of a power relationship. That estimation has to be made either by the person or group which wields that power, or by both, and by those against whom it is used.

In the end, power is merely the ability of people to persuade other people against their will and values to act as they are commanded, because these other people believe they do not have the power or ability to resist. So it is quite possible for a person or group to be held in subjection despite the fact that the scientist feels the person or group has superior power. Or one person may take on a Goliath or a whole army and gain a victory. This is because people's view of reality partially determines their effective possession of that power.

Power need not reside simply in the possession of military or fighting strength. Examples of alternative power might be the ability (used by Gandhi, Martin Luther King, trade unionists, and students) to disrupt certain services which are considered essential by other people. Such people need not necessarily be those classes of people who are most directly involved in the power contest. So also, moral force can take the shape of power by which people may hold out against others: the ability to shame or to disgrace in terms of relatively consensual values are examples. These instances more clearly demonstrate the fundamentally social definition of the reality and quality of power, and the importance of the subjective meaning which contending and other groups have of it.

Needless to say, there can be unintended consequences to actions which are based on definitions of available power. A government which prepares for or declares war simply because it feels the other side has inferior weapons may be in for a sharp surprise. So also, the management of a firm may be shocked when they believe (wrongly) that the men on the shop floor would not react adversely to a given act, or that they could persuade the public in any ensuing strike that the strikers were 'wrong'. So far we have spoken only of the more visible and obvious kinds of power and conflict.

A wife who cries, a child who sulks, an associate who has knowledge of your past, a teacher who has a stern expression, those who set examination papers, or those who hire and fire you can all, by these defined qualities, wield power over you. That power may be wielded quite deliberately to achieve given ends, or it might be used quite unintentionally. There are other, and often quite cohesive features to such relationships as those we mention. It would be quite wrong, however, to underestimate the extent to which this kind of power pervades many facets of the fabric of social life. It is often missed by the observer only because of the more glamorous use of what we might call the formal symbols of power between the larger combination classes in society, for example the actions of and between States. But it does not seem helpful to distinguish between forms of power simply by the criterion of scale.

First, it may not be recognized by those who wield it. The State, a manager, or a wife may, respectively, issue an order, specify a production target, or cry, without any awareness that others may interpret this as a form of domination. So also, those who are forced to act in ways which they would prefer to avoid may believe that they do so because of the unalterable limits of their situation. In fact such 'limits' may be drawn by the alterable actions of others. State laws, the instructions of an organization, school hours and crying wives may be seen as undesired but given features of the criminal's, clerk's, child's, and husband's situation, which have to be reluctantly accepted. Indeed, these people may not even identify the class of people who make those laws, edicts and rules, etc. But when both the 'dominator' and 'dominated' do not have some definition of domination or subjection then it cannot be said that power or domination or subjection exists in their relation. One, or both, must have such a definition for power to exist. Otherwise there is merely social fracture or discontinuity.

Concepts of inequality and exploitation, of domination and subjection, are often misused by sociologists. The value judgment, which is not necessarily explicit, becomes overt when it is applied to situations where neither party in a situation has a subjective definition of domination or subjection. For example, 'inequality' is often used interchangeably with the concept 'class'. Power, and hence exploitation, subjection, or inequality, must in part be recognized and felt by those directly involved before power can take on a sociological rather than an ethical meaning. If we do not recognize this, then the action of those involved and the consequences of that action are likely to be misunderstood.

Power is not a stable thing, for people's definitions of it change, because of the unintended consequences which follow its use, and because people may slowly accumulate what is thought to be a new source of power – say, arms or moral force. For example, in the late 1960s students in Britain had only a very diffuse power, which they used, if at all, in an unco-ordinated manner. That situation had clearly changed by 1970. By co-operative action they disrupted the previously accepted styles of college life. In turn, staff and administrators began to search for and find sources of power which they did not feel they previously possessed, in order to counter that student power.

Similarly, the man who feels he has the right to behave towards a woman in various ways which she once felt she could accept may no longer achieve his intended aim, because she may now define her relationships with men in a different way. So also, children, partly because of the unintended consequences of an earlier economic independence and the 'teenage consumer market', have now forced their parents in many subtle and often unintended ways to begin to behave rather differently towards them. These facets of relationships which develop from consensual if differential, relations and which now turn along the axis of social power, are only one feature of most of these relationships. Another facet is that distinguished by the concept 'authority'.

Authority. Authority, unlike power, is usually, but not always, a source of consensus. Like power, it is a quality which depends on people's subjective estimations of one another in social situations. Weber distinguishes between three different types of authority: charismatic, traditional, and rational-legal. Others have argued that the idea of charismatic authority – the personal qualities of an individual – is not a sociological concept, precisely because of its individual reference. The other two concepts are qualities of office or defined status, irrespective of the quality of the occupant. Therefore, it is argued, they are fundamentally sociological: that is, structural.

The distinction which is drawn by these critics and, to a certain extent, by Weber's original formulation, seems to introduce a misleading dichotomy. Let us first look at what is usually thought to be charismatic authority.

Che Guevara, Lenin, Jesus Christ, Daniel Cohn Bendit, and Billy Graham have all been nominated by sociologists as possessing charisma. If, however, we take these people out of their social settings by a feat of imagination and place them in a quite different social setting, it is easy to see that the 'personal' quality is, in part, dependent on the way other people define it. For example, place Cohn Bendit in the Conservative Party Conference, Che Guevara in the French Assembly, Billy Graham in a meeting of the March 21st movement, and Lenin in the John Birch society.

No doubt other individuals who in every respect had the same ideas as these people and lived in a similar setting would have differences in effect because of the difference in the way their personal qualities were perceived. This would only relate in part to the personality differences they 'really' had. It is not in doubt that these people's charisma would be of no avail in these alien settings, or that others in the same setting would have different relations with others.

Simply, middle-aged conservative ladies and gentlemen would see Cohn Bendit or Lenin in a very different way from the kind of view which, respectively, certain kinds of students have or Bolsheviks had.

The aura which Cohn Bendit's presence, words, gestures evoke in fairly like-minded people in one social situation (say, a packed meeting in the Sorbonne) simply evaporates in a different social situation with people who have a different view of social reality. Charisma, then, depends in part on the 'actual' person, but also, and of equal importance for the sociologist, on the definitions of him which other people have. Finally, it also depends on the general situation that both the person and those who are influenced by him are in at the time. And this situation can, in part, produce a range of unintended consequences: in Cohn Bendit's case the action of the police, General de Gaulle, the press and, very probably, mothers. Charisma, then, is only in small part a personal quality. Largely it is an interpersonal quality of authority.

We must ask if there are different components at work in what is usually distinguished as traditional authority. The Pope, or, say, the Archbishop of Canterbury, would be examples of office-holders in a traditional setting, who wield authority by virtue of their elevation to that office. Imagine the difference in attitude on the part of even people sympathetic to these two men as individuals if they were only ordinary priests. It would, of course, be very marked.

Part of the explanation for this would be in terms of the way people subjectively defined and expected differences between the office of Pope and priest, Archbishop and vicar. But this would be only part of the explanation. Religious people reacted in noticeably different ways to Pope John and Archbishop Fisher from the ways in which they react to Pope Paul and Archbishop Ramsey. Has the office changed, or have the occupants changed?

People do not fully distinguish the 'office' from the 'man', and those personal qualities which they feel he possesses. Though the social situation and the man have a greater degree of definition in cases of traditional authority than in those of charismatic authority, these two aspects of authority are equally important for analysis in both types of authority situations. Both types of authority develop through, and are the product of, unintended consequences as well as overt values and morally defined public 'rules'. There are such moral and public 'rules' for Cohn Bendit. They are only less obvious than for Paul and Ramsey. Cohn Bendit's 'position' would be in danger if he said or did certain things, for those who were previously influenced by him would, probably, alter their definition of him if he said, say, that he liked the police. The difference lies in the defined limits and the defined rigidity of those public rules.

This has been another distinguishing feature of charisma. The charismatic person can break and create ways of behaving because of his charisma. But Lenin, Jesus and Che could create action in one direction, but not so easily in another, because of their subjective relations with others whose beliefs and actions tended to impose limits. If these limits are broken then the authority can diminish and power can enter into the relationship. For example, when Judas Iscariot came to believe that Jesus Christ was primarily interested in an other-worldly kingdom their relationship changed. Exactly the same point is true, albeit on a different scale, with Ramsey and Paul and those with whom they have a religious relationship. It is also the case that these rules can be broken and new ways innovated by the person 'in authority' appealing to certain groups whose support he feels he can count on at the expense of others. The 'success' of this depends in part on the definition of the situation which the person uses. At the same time power is again involved, say, in the deliberate suppression of conflicting ideas, or of their advocates.

Exactly the same arguments apply to what is called rational-legal authority. We have only to imagine the difference between General de Gaulle as head of the French State and the present incumbent of that office or, even, the difference between de Gaulle's occupation of that office in April, May and June of 1968. Imagine again the difference between Sir Edward Bridges and Sir William Armstrong as head of the British Civil Service. The personality of the occupant of office is important, as is the kind of subjective affinity people feel for that personality. So, of course, is the way people define the limits of office or the situation of the charismatic person. The former may be the most important feature in the analysis of rational-legal authority, and it may be more important than in the case of charisma. But it is still only *one* feature, none the less. And as with the other 'two kinds' of authority, personality, the way it is perceived, and the general alignment of groups in the social situation within which authority is wielded, may not be left out of analysis.

In summary, the actions and qualities of the person who wields authority are important, though in different degrees in different social settings. The ways people who are influenced by authority see the person and the situation of the person who wields authority over them are all-important analytical factors. Similarly, the particular social situation through which the person influences by means of authority and is influenced by it is important.

The way all three features interact produces what we call 'authority'. Because situations are constantly changing, as are the ways people define and act in them, so the form which authority takes changes. In this context it does not seem particularly helpful to retain the Weberian classification. We have separated the different features of authority which are of necessity always present in differing degrees. Because of the subjective reference of these factors we can only construct a model of authority, or of its development, by empirical appeal to the values, definitions and actions of people. The fact that these features will always combine in differing proportions and with differing subjective content suggests that it would not be helpful to operate with a classification of three, or any other number of types of authority.

The proposed view of authority allows us to see it as being located, like power, in many areas, and at many levels in the fabric of social life. 'Power' comprises the ability, or the attempt, to force people to act against their values because of the nature of the situation and the way it is defined by those involved in it. 'Authority' becomes the ability of people to issue commands or make suggestions in a given situation with which others will comply in a way in which they would not otherwise have conceived or wished. But acceptance is voluntary and does not involve conflict within the relationship.

A superficial view of the more orthodox attitude to authority, as to power, suggests its location only in specialized areas of society: the leaders of political, radical or religious movements, the topmost officials in large bureaucratic organizations, industry or the state, a feudal monarch or the officials of an orthodox religion. But relations of authority exist in family situations: between parent and child, child and child, friend and friend, man and woman, and a great range of other forms of 'informal' as well as more 'formal' relationships which people create. In particular, it is at this less formal level of relationships that the advantage of an absence of classificatory types of authority can be seen.

Having pointed to particular aspects of the three different kinds of control it is necessary to comment on an aspect of their analytical significance. 'Acceptance' involves the criterion: 'live and let live'. Those involved in a relationship of acceptance may have different values and different definitions of their situation. So, also, they may engage in different actions. But their action may not deliberately intervene in or seek to control the action of others in the relationship of acceptance.

Those who wield power and authority in relationships specifically seek intervention in order to bend the action of others to their will. But (as with acceptance) those who wield power may share neither values nor definitions with those against whom they wield it. They merely wield force with the specific intention of gaining the response of particular forms of action which are beneficial to them. It is possible, however, for power to be wielded against people who more or less share definitions or values in common, but not both.

Power may be wielded against superior, equal or independent classes, and seeks to subordinate those who are not subordinate, or to maintain a position of subordination amongst those who wish to change their position and who do not feel subordinate.

On the other hand, authority can only be exercised where feelings of subordination already exist. That is, those who are dominant in an authority relationship have no need or wish to resort to force in order to encourage the desired response of those who are subordinate. For those who are subordinate feel themselves to be subordinate and, therefore, comply with the request. In a word, they control themselves as much as they are controlled by others. This vitally distinguishes them from those who are controlled by force and power. Yet those who are controlled by power may feel subordinate in the sense that they feel they have no power to resist. This definition may be 'inaccurate'. But in so far as it guides action, it means that those involved would resist or act otherwise *if* they felt they possessed power to do so.

Those involved in an authority relationship do not act with similar definitions. But their definitions do more or less *complement* one another. For the dominator feels he has the right to dominate, and the subordinate is subordinate precisely because he does not feel he has the right to act otherwise than to respect the command of the dominator.

Those who are subordinate often want to act in ways other than those which are commanded of them. They obey or comply simply because they feel that the dominator has superior scientific, intellectual, technical, legal or spiritual awareness of what it is right to do. We have already noted that this right is partly vested in the dominator as a person as well as his situation as defined by the dominated person. This may, but need not, imply shared values. Indeed, shared values are not even the defining feature of authority in spiritual situations. Imagine only the distinction between the values of a Spanish Catholic peasant and the Pope.

For this reason we can recognize that authority takes the form of a continuum, one end of which involves partial choice on the part of the subordinate person. Most authority in modern societies takes this pattern. Such authority is relative and contingent. The right to dominate is respected, but within limits. The subordinate can and does question commands. So courses of action stemming from such authority relationships are often based on consultation and compromise. They are not the absolute prerogative or choice of the dominator. But the dominator, for whatever reason, is given a major right and therefore also a major duty: the duty to advise or command and lead.

At the other pole of the continuum, authority involves the choice of abdication of choice by the dominated. Commands and course of action are chosen by the dominator. For it is crucial to note that the subordinate can entertain no sense or definition of autonomous action on his part, and so also no sense of criticism of the authority relationship in order to control his situation and achieve his values. Abdication of control therefore is merely a special form of control.

If we were to resurrect for a moment the three kinds of authority (traditional, charismatic and rational-legal) we would note that the two polar types which we have distinguished are applicable to each in turn. Which form becomes manifest is dependent on a variety of factors, some of which are quite independent of the concept of authority (for instance, psychological conditions, the specific form of rationality, or charismatic situation).

The limits of authority are flexible. Authority can be envisaged as a continuum, at one end of which it merges into power, that is, where the right of the dominator is exceeded either by the nature of his command, or by his action, or by a change in the situation as defined or perceived by the subordinate. At the other end of the continuum, authority merges into acceptance.

It is particularly important to note that none of the relationships or forms of control between classes need imply either shared values or shared definitions, though both may be more or less shared. Within atomistic and co-operative classes shared definitions and values do exist. But only one special kind of authority relation between classes involves full compliance and a voluntary abdication of choice. Only this kind of authority equates with Weber's concept of rational-legal authority and Durkheim's concept of moral obligation. It can lead to a conception of the 'social system'. In fact, only a cursory glance at the facts and forms of social relationships is needed to show that it is not common in society in general, and certainly not in industrial societies.

Any one actual empirical area of control, of domination and subordination, and of acceptance, is a complex phenomenon (say, the Civil Service, a school or industrial organization). All three forms of control will exist in it, but in differing degrees. So, also, different kinds of any one form will exist in it. In what sense can there really be 'networks of control' which have any overall integrated meaning like, say, that of rational-legal authority? For in reality such networks comprise different people and classes seeking to impose their values by acceptance, power and authority. Equally, others will resist, compromise and ignore, by seeking acceptance, and wielding power and authority over other people. The actual, empirical outcome of all these different relationships and activities will not be the intended creation of any one class or of any one form of control. Indeed, the unintended repercussions of such action will be both considerable from any one group's point of view and in many cases discontinuous as well as cohesive, or conflictful. It would be most surprising for such a heterogeneous, empirically distinct, assembly to bear any relationship to an internally consistent, patterned, controlling system.

Because such a 'network' is not under the total control of any one person or action class does not mean it is under the control of something else. It is in a literal sense both in control – in so far as many different people and classes are striving for control and to impose meaning on it –

and out of control. In so far as it is out of control, its overall shape is accidental. This fact does not prevent us from giving it meaning with a label, say, a 'school' or a 'political democracy' or a 'totalitarian state'. Such a label will mean one thing to a political philosopher. For the sociologist, the emergent meaning and significance of relations in any one particular situation or society will not closely resemble the philosopher's meaning, or the meanings imposed by those involved. On the contrary, he will impose a new meaning, a new label. We should, therefore, be careful in our use of such classificatory labels, which signify particular forms of overall control.

Legitimization

We have argued that all human relations are to a greater or lesser extent unstable and discontinuous. That is, they may change either slowly or dramatically. Even the most apparently stable relationship (say, that between mother and child) will, over time, change in fundamental ways. So, at another level, we see the Catholic Church, the Communist parties of the modern world, and the MCC shuddering with internal dissensions and taking on new and unpredictable forms.

Relations which are based on power, and to a lesser extent those based on authority, are particularly unstable and liable to rapid change, of smaller and greater consequence. This is partly because of the fact that they involve people or classes who impose conflicting definitions or values on situations. Though these differences may apply in all the situations in which these people are mutually involved, they may equally apply only to one particular situation. It is partly along this line of mutual involvement in one or many situations that the degree of instability of the relation and of its repercussions for other situations is measured.

A power relationship can move in two directions. It can grow in intensity, and spread to other situations where the conflict becomes more open. Or it can develop into an authority relationship. One way of describing how this happens is to say that the power inherent in the situation becomes 'legitimized'. On the other hand, it is quite possible for an authority relation to break down into conflict and dispute, that is, into power. Here, in a certain sense, we can speak of 'illegitimate' authority, before the 'power' becomes 'transparent', that is, before some people discontinue their respect for those with whom they had a relation of authority.

To speak of either power or authority in these ways seems in itself illegitimate, for it involves a word which is far from being value-neutral. The danger is that we might speak of class, or a combination class, with 'its' related organization, as wielding legitimate power or authority, when from the point of view of others that power or authority is the subject of dispute. Such a criticism will, however, not apply if we speak of an individual or combination class (say, a State) which attempts to control its situation by making 'its' power legitimate in the eyes of other groups within immediate and more peripheral situations. If such a class begins to succeed in persuading these other people that their power is fair, just, right or necessary in terms of consensual definitions or values, what they are really doing is attempting to establish an authority relationship where there was once a power relationship or no relationship at all. That is, an area of consensual agreement is reached, by whatever means, concerning what relations must exist between different classes, where other kinds of relations previously existed. We can speak of the power in a relationship being legitimized into an authority relationship between two or more contenders. But as soon as the power becomes legitimate it is no longer power. The previously subject people, for whatever reason, now voluntarily do what they were once forced to do or did not do at all because either their definitions or their values, or both, have changed.

By definition power is always illegitimate, in the sense that it is under dispute from the point of view of those against whom it is wielded. At the same time, it is legitimate from the point of view of those who wield it and those who accept their authority and right to wield it. Exactly because in most circumstances those who wield it are aware of, and have a definition concerning, the discontent of those over whom they wield it, they attempt to change the nature of their domination and the quality of their power. In a word, they try to change the social definition which the dominated people have of them and of their mutual relationship. As with all social relationships, there are unintended consequences to this process of attempted legitimation, not the least of which involves either a compromise of aims and values on the part of both parties or a greater dispute between them.

An example of the latter would be the class of people in the legal situation who attempt to change the 'criminal's' definition of his life and activity by using the deterrent theory. The Russian OGPU managed to produce similar unintended consequences, as did the Novotny regime in Czechoslovakia. The husband, or the friend, or the child, might have similar difficulties in their relationships. So an attempt at legitimation might well produce the opposite effect to that intended. Equally it might succeed, but in an unintended form. In either case an alteration in the definition of those in power is inevitable. So also, a change in their values may ensue.

The change of power into authority might itself follow from the intended consequences of action, or take an unintended form. For example, African negroes felt oppressed by the power of the white slave-traders who first took them to America. Gradually, and through a host of situations including religious and domestic ones (such as the birth of children who had not experienced the same kind of disruption as their parents) these negroes came to accept in terms of authority what had previously been a power relationship. In some cases, of course, it would not even be regarded as an authority relation, for where the negroes shared most of the values and definitions of some of their white 'employers' they actually wanted to act exactly as the white master would have them act, and vice versa.

This example is useful, for with a changing situation the relationship between many whites and negroes has once again become that of power. The example also suggests the very delicate balance which can exist between power and authority, and how very rapidly the one may change into the other. It is unlikely, however, that these new lines of cleavage, conflict and change will copy previous ones. A further example is called for.

As trade unions developed in England their members came up against resistance by industrialists and politicians. In this sense the industrialists wielded power against the trade unionists, and authority against other workers who respected their positions and 'rights'.

During the period of their growth the power of the unions, which was partly based on their internal acceptance and authority, became such that they could effectively challenge the power of the industrialists. For various reasons, including the mutual attempt to increase their power and control over their situation, both sides sought allies, and built central organizations, which led to the formation of complex combination classes. The trade unionists encouraged their members to enter Parliament to protect their interests and to legitimize their values in the eyes of others. Perhaps at this point the power relation reached its zenith within the industrial and political situations. But equally, authority and other relations remained and indeed developed, in Parliament as well as in many other spheres of life, where divisions and conflict occurred at different points. Incidentally, it is important to note that these two combination classes or alliances affected only a limited number of situations in society. Certainly many situations were untouched by them, though others were affected unintentionally.

At the same time, and because of the roughly equal power wielded by both sides, the conflict came to be fought out by representatives within the parliamentary setting and that of industrial negotiation. Yet in searching for allies (in terms of their social definitions of change and stability) each 'side' made compromises with the other. This affected (often unintentionally) other classes in other situations as each side tried to legitimize its significance and values in the eyes of others whom it hoped to recruit or, at least, influence. Such compromise meant that new values emerged and new definitions and actions developed. Such actions imposed situations in which it made sense to some Conservatives to appeal to 'working-class' voters, and to some Socialists to appeal to 'middle-class' voters.

In the process of these developments and actions many of the original lines of cleavage which crossed the axis of power and authority disappeared. New ones emerged. The consequence of each side attempting to legitimize its power position was unintended by both sides. The authority and power which is now recognized by many people and by new classes bears little relation to the aims and values of the original contenders.

Conflict may or may not have been 'institutionalized' or localized, as Dahrendorf suggests. What is certain is that most of the old conflicts have disappeared. New authorities, new powers have developed which are wielded and respected by new and changed groupings.

These would include the New Men who gave their title to C. P. Snow's novel: technologists in industry and commerce, the experts who are being consulted by central and local government, or being drawn into the Civil Service, those who at once oppose tradition and background and yet fear the excesses of change. They include the doctors who now value the Health Service, the managers of the steel industry who recognize that it is most efficiently organized at a national and not at a private level, and those who want to enter the Common Market.

These men, whose similar values affect their activity in a range of different situations, are not unlike Weber's rational actors. But, they are rather more rounded and complete than that, and they have not had all the success that Weber reluctantly envisaged for them. What is certain is that they do not fit into the previous conceptions of a 'ruling' or 'bourgeois' class, nor are they advocates of a 'working class', for they feel that such a class no longer exists. Some of them have reformed the 'magic circles' of the Conservative Party. Others, like Gaitskell or Wilson, have helped change the shape of the Labour Party. Still others have carried this style of politics further, and formed a distinct pressure group of industrialists and technocrats.

It would be difficult, though tempting, to analyse this heterogeneous assembly of men as a new combination class. Certainly it has the makings of one. Even so, the effect of those individual, atomized and co-operation classes which are formed by these people is having a profound effect on the shape of many situations in modern Britain.

It is, however, not simply due to their effect that large sections of the fabric of society have changed and are changing drastically. But their existence is sufficient to allow us to assert that Rex's 'truce situations' cannot under any circumstances cleave along the 'old lines'. These lines have not been 'papered over' or been 'submerged'. They have disappeared. Let us return, for a moment, to our American example. In challenging first the authority and then the power of the white racialists the negro integration movement, led by Martin Luther King, created a new situation. It was one in which the whites had to compromise. So did many of the negroes in turn. A new authority began to emerge around 'respectable integration', and the 'white liberal'. This is now challenged by the power of those who retain their values of 'white supremacy' and of those who support 'Black Power'. The power, the authority, the lines of conflict have all changed in such a way that a return to the previous situation is inconceivable. This latter point – the impossibility of return – is a vital feature of change which many interpreters of, say, the French May 'revolution' omitted to observe.

It will now be helpful to turn from the simple distinction between worker and industrialist, or black and white, to the more complex question of some of the main action classes that wield power and authority in a modern society.

Marcuse believes that 'the state', or the 'ruling class', more or less deliberately and rationally sets out to incorporate the 'working class', and other exploited people within their definition of order. Some have called this process 'mystification'. Marcuse calls it 'repressive tolerance', and applies it to both Eastern and, more especially, Western industrial societies. What makes this essentially similar to other 'radical' theories is not just the 'two classes-as-systems' model of society with which they all operate, but their attribution of the specific intention to the ruling class as a unity of altering the definition of the working class in such a way that its members accept the legitimacy of their rule. That is, the 'rulers' are consciously and rationally attempting to change a power relationship into one of authority and, thus, into one of complete agreement at the level of shared values, as well as definitions. The process is more complicated than that. And, if our argument is correct concerning the extent to which legitimation does occur, whether intended or not, then the 'mystified' lines of cleavage have simply disappeared, and cannot reopen.

First, we have argued that society is not made up of two such classes. There are indeed many classes of different kinds whose members may, in different situations, occupy different relations to one another. Suppose we accept that a certain clustering of individual, atomistic, and co-operation classes does occur, thus forming combination classes. Industrialists, civil servants, politicians, educators and those who attempt to control the means of communication, may have similar family and educational experiences. Partly because of the subtle differences to which they were exposed in family and school, they have occupied ever more distinct situations and entered into different relationships in adult life which have affected old relations, and caused new ones to develop. Their activity in those situations which we describe as 'clustering' because of certain common features in some of their lives is in fact likely to be quite different from that expected by the orthodox model. Even if we could speak of the industrialist, the educator, and the mass media expert as acting in unison, and even if they were to feel the need to combine their mutual interests in an attempt to redefine the situation of those whom they control, they would first have to agree amongst themselves on a definition of society and a transformation of it, so as to control it more effectively. To reach agreement they would have to compromise, and the outcome would be rather different from that which any one component class of the combination class would actually wish. Such attempted compromises are made in centralized states. They are made, often unintentionally, in social democracies.

If we now consider the effect of this hypothetical compromise definition on those who are controlled, it is possible to anticipate some further unexpected consequences. In the field of education there are, for example, many different situations. There are those of the secondary-modern, grammar and comprehensive schools. There are those of the 'top' and the 'bottom' stream of any one age-group. There are those of children from different home backgrounds, which to a certain but changing extent coincide with these other situations. Even if the educators were united in intention amongst themselves and with the combination ruling class, the definitions by which they were attempting to induce this variety of children into acceptance would be interpreted in as many ways as there were classes of children. We can only predict that the final definition which the children developed would have widely different aspects from those intended. We discussed this feature earlier in rather greater detail.

The same is of course true for any other group. Apart from the fact that the State, the politicians, the industrialists, the press and television did not manage (whilst some did not attempt) to reach a compromise definition concerning, say, the Prices and Incomes Policy, it is difficult to see how 'workers' and 'consumers' and 'viewers' would have been persuaded to accept such a definition, in view of the different complexes of situations through which they live. As with the schoolchildren, or 'official' attitudes to race, it would have been interpreted, rejected, and accepted in many different ways.

In addition there are other groups (trade unionists, religious organizations, families, radical intellectuals, and students) who are attempting to persuade these 'exploited' groups to accept a variety of quite different definitions of their social and power situation. Perhaps all we can say is that the picture is becoming very complicated indeed. For the attempts of some classes or combinations of classes to define other people's situations for them are always bound to lead to unexpected consequences. This merely happens more visibly in Hungary, East Germany, Poland, America, South Africa, etc., than it does in England. These consequences will change the situation which those within the dominant and subject combination classes were attempting to redefine, and the task of legitimation will become even more difficult for them. Whether classes do redefine their situation, and in what way, will depend as much on the accumulation of unintended consequences as on the intentions of the definers and the defined. To the extent that Marcuse and Rex have seen these processes they have attempted to redefine Marx. But partly owing to the nature of the component concepts of their theoretical models, they have very seriously failed to provide a radical contemporary alternative.

Rex argued that radicals and conservatives compete to define the situation of the clerk. But if the clerk were initially persuaded by the conservative he would presently be shocked, by the 'objective' reality of his situation, into accepting the definition of the radical. Rex was being optimistic in terms of his own political perspective and misled by his sociological presuppositions. For the clerk who accepts the conservative definition will act in terms of it. In the process and even if Rex's original definition was correct, the clerk will actually change that definition. So will all those who are 'mystified' or 'repressed' in any society. The clerk is only one instance of such a person in this society. Imagine, for a moment, the 'new generation' for whom all the 'old divisions' were, in Rex's terms, merely a 'folk-lore'. What further differences are there in their definitions, and hence in their actions, from those of the clerk, schoolteacher, or television producer? They have fresh and perhaps more subtle views of their own situation, of class conflict, of the place of industrial disputes and union activity. Many, as in fact was always the case, are conservative, have nationalistic feelings, and so act in ways which, unintentionally, further remove the vestiges of what might once have been a 'two-class' society by defending a new *status quo*. At the same time, the views which, for the sake of hypothetical argument, we called those of the combined dominant classes, are constantly being compromised by the trade unions, Labour Party and other interested classes. There is a constant attempt to legitimize this changing compromise for many people. But this legitimacy and these authority relations are both widely different from what a nineteenth-century industrialist or socialist might have hoped for, and are disputed by quite new groupings of people. The whole tension of society in the area we speak about has changed and cannot revert to its earlier form. The future is being shaped by these fresh areas of overt and covert action, of conflict, cohesion, power, authority and acceptance.

This discussion has only indicated the great complexity of the process of legitimation, of the nature of change and conflict, of the nature of power and authority and of the kinds of class action and control in society.

The discussion of legitimacy has tended to focus only on certain situations and classes within society. But legitimacy, like acceptance, authority and power, does not only exist in the more glamorous or tangible situations. It can develop or dissolve in any relationship and in any situation.

Consequently, any discussion of legitimacy and the forms of modern British society could not be confined to the areas we have so far mentioned. It would have to include the family, leisure, the church, the distinctions between urban and rural life, and so on. Just as they may be affected by developments in political or industrial power and legitimation, so they may affect them.

Social systems—social kaleidoscopes
We have finally reached the point where a consideration of those concepts involved in situational analysis has led to a consideration of those concepts concerned with an analysis of activity and interaction in many situations.

The explanation of the activity of Tom as a person has been translated into an analysis of action classes. These classes had to be divided into different kinds of class. There are individual classes. But there are also atomistic, co-operative and combination classes. Whilst the analysis of the first three kinds of class closely follows and uses the situational analysis of Tom, that of combination classes is different. For they do not act as one person. They are made up of various possible relations between the first three kinds of class.

Any situational analysis of the first three kinds of class, therefore, involves the use of the following elements of analysis:

1. (a) the person or people
   (b) the meanings and values which these people seek to impose on reality
   (c) definitions of the situation, which include:
       (i) other people
       (ii) psychological factors
       (iii) physical objects
       (iv) the situational logic employed by the person(s)
2. A similar analysis of other people
3. The sociologist's definition of the situation, its interaction, including intended and unintended consequences.

Analysis of combination classes is based on these elements. But it crucially involves the repetition of such analysis for each of the classes whose activity makes up the combination class. Such analysis, as we noted, means that a combination class cannot have aims or values in the way that individual or co-operation classes have values. On the contrary, its impact on and relationship with others are the intended and unintended consequences of the activity of those classes which comprised it. So it is possible for such a class to have a policy or a charter, which is a compromise acceptable in different degrees to all its constituent classes, and which each has sought to control and influence. But this policy is the 'value' of no one class. The Church, the Labour Party, the State relate with other classes and individuals via these policies. But they also relate with others via the values and activities of their constituent classes which are, to some extent, independent of the combination class.

The analysis of activity within and between combination classes, is, therefore, most complex. For it is difficult to analyse the jostle, activity, compromise, conflict, anger, hope, and all those aspects of control which are a constant and changing feature of real-life situations. Such analysis replaces the analysis of the 'institution' of the orthodox terminology. For what is meant by 'institutions' can be made up of one or more combination classes (government) or of a combination class and one or more of the other three kinds of class (political parties), or of these latter three kinds of classes, which may well relate in other areas of their activities to different combination classes (schools, industrial organization) or of different individual, co-operation and atomized classes (many families), and so on.

This view of combination classes and 'institutions' makes it possible to see how indistinct the boundaries are between different aspects of people's lives. A man's family life is affected by his working life. His political life is affected by his family life, etc. So his action in any one area is crucially affected by his overarching conceptions of himself and the meaning he gives to his life in general. Though one person may modify and compromise these meanings in helping (often unintentionally) to form, say, a co-operation class or a combination class, the activity of that co-operation class is itself to be measured by the values of those who form it.

We noted that all people and all their actions could be fitted into one or more of these classes. So the way individual people live, interact, seek to impose their meaning on and control over reality became almost synonymous with the analysis of class. This advance only extends situational analysis. It does not transform it. Another area of analysis is immediately opened. It involves a scrutiny of those distinct, additional elements necessary for a consideration of control – of how classes act and relate with one another in their attempt to impose their values on their social situations.

Men seek to exercise control over their situation and the activity of others by the use of authority, power or acceptance. They equally seek to legitimize their activity in the eyes of others, so transforming relations of power into ones of authority, or their authority into acceptance.

These constituent concepts of the control of others specifically create relations and connections between people and classes. But these relations are not necessarily intended ones. Power can unintentionally be exercised by an atomistic class over a co-operation class. And authority can be exercised by one individual class over a co-operation class. Acceptance is more especially the property of relations within co-operation classes, but it may exist between two such classes, or between them and the individuals who make up atomistic classes. It may, therefore, exist between different classes within a combination class, or between a class within a combination class and classes in other combination classes.

Such interpersonal and interclass activity further leads to developments in situations which have properties of conflict and consensus. We noted that these concepts had to be further distinguished, because there were vitally different kinds of conflict and consensus which could exist independently of other forms.

It was difficult to discover either classes or situations which did not contain one or other of the forms of both conflict and consensus. Equally, there was no need, though it was possible, for either conflict or consensus to spread from one class or situation to another class or situation, or that it should be of the same kind in these cases where it did link. Indeed, there were many areas where no direct relations at all existed between one particular class and another particular class. But the number of instances where some classes, particularly combination classes, impinge on a wide range of other classes, has grown in modern industrial societies. In feudal and medieval times it was quite possible for local communities to live quite separate lives, uncontrolled or unaffected by the activity of such classes as kings or barons or churchmen or guildsmen or burghers.

The development in modern societies of industrial classes and, in particular, the development of the various classes which combine into forming what we know as the modern State, has changed the possibility of social isolation – as tinkers, witches and hermits have discovered to their loss.

Similarly some classes, particularly the combination classes such as trade unions, political parties, the executive and administrative classes involved in central government, either relate directly with many other classes or, through their action, affect aspects of the situation of many other classes. In these latter instances, the effect of, say, the Confederation of British Industries (CBI) is considerable. It even affects the situation of those housewives whose husbands are related to private industrial management in their work situation. Similarly, the educational situation of children is affected by the State, whose influence is mediated by schoolteachers and the organization of the facilities of the school. Their situation is also affected by the political parties, trade unions and industrialists. For these combination classes have relations with and partly shape the policy of the State. Their influence is, however, transformed through the State. For, as a complex combination class itself, the State reformulates these pressures into its own logic of action, which cannot be explained solely by relating that policy to those classes with whom the State has relations. Such complex chains of influence do not differ markedly in Communist countries.

These chains of interaction are disjointed and fractured. At each point influence is mediated and reformed and this calls for new responses. These responses change the aspects of the situation of these classes and, therefore, encourage changed activity on their part. The sphere of interest and attempted control of the State is still spreading, but an increasing number of people define its activities as illegitimate for different reasons.

In a relatively static society the exercise of control may be largely unintended. Where it is intended, its effect is usually localized. In modern industrial societies, however, whilst all people and classes still exercise some forms of intended control, some people and classes exercise it more extensively and effectively than others. Such classes, which are usually the constituent co-operation classes of combination classes that shape the policy of combination classes, specifically seek to impose their values on large sections of society. The Catholic Church is a case in point. It is a combination class, whose constituent classes include the Pope. He and other classes affect the policy of the Church. In turn this controls aspects of the lives of Catholic and other people in many ways and in many countries, though it does not determine all aspects of any one person's situation.

Similarly, such combination classes as the State, the ruling political party, the CBI, TUC, professional associations, etc., have enormous impact over aspects of the lives of millions of people in this society. Whilst all these people continue to seek to control their own lives, the situations, definitions and the consequences of their actions are crucially affected because of their direct or indirect relations with these combination classes. In such areas both authority and power are the vital concepts, rather than acceptance. Yet a key factor is the definition which people have of their situation. Do they see their relations with the State, etc., as constraining or as given factors of life, to be accepted, or as something to avoid or change? Some classes resist these relations and connections, defining them as unnecessary impositions. Some seek directly to control only aspects of their lives (professional associations, trade unions), others to transform their social situations (Black Power, workers' control, women's liberation, student power). They form new combination classes as a consequence (Black Moslems, the Communist Party, RSSF, etc.).

Neither power nor authority, nor, therefore, the ability to shape large aspects of the surrounding situations are generally dispersed in society. Whilst every person exercises them in some form, they are concentrated in the relations of particular, if changing, action classes. Such concentrated power, authority and control are then contended by other classes, including those mentioned above. However, the definitions of the situation which such groups develop also form their action and suggest the kind of legitimation by which they can attempt to seek alliances. So their understanding of the distribution and location of power is vital to the logic of their political action. Usually they define situations in such a way as to suggest that most people have no power or freedom in their lives. Shortly we shall consider the concept of freedom in society. Suffice it here to recall that as everyone attempts to control his own life in daily action this means that power, authority and acceptance are qualities in family life, school, golf clubs, as well as in the State or industry. They are crucial concepts in the analysis of any situation.

We can now more clearly recognize that change is an endemic feature of the analysis we are advocating. The opposition of static to dynamic, cohesion to conflict, order to change are meaningless dichotomies from this standpoint. For all these qualities, and the tools for their analysis, are incorporated in the general analysis we have outlined. They are not separate features to be analysed by one or another approach.

So far we have tried to show how these concepts involved in situational analysis are linked to and extended by all those concepts required by an analysis of many social relationships and social situations.

The following question must now be raised: do these different concepts order themselves or link into one further concept? When any particular sociological explanation is undertaken, is it possible to construct an abstract working, explanatory model of that social life and interaction involving not only those concepts we have discussed so far, but also an overarching concept, incorporating and ordering these lower-level concepts? In a word, can there be a concept of society which integrates all those concepts we have discussed so far? If so, does it bear comparison with the orthodox concept of the 'social system'?

Those concepts which are crucially concerned with the interaction of classes are of two kinds. Firstly, the elements of situational analysis, particularly the actors' or classes' definition of others, the logic for action, and the actual action, are all involved with an understanding of interaction.

Secondly, the concepts of legitimacy, power, authority, acceptance and several of the different kinds of consensus and conflict are concepts about relationships, and not just the activity of one person or class. They are meaningless without the separate acts which constitute them and which are analysed by the first category of concept. But they are also meaningless without a consideration of the quality of the relationship itself. And the sociologist may have a different definition of the relationship from that of the separate actors or classes involved in it.

Could it be that interaction networks of, say, power, legitimate authority and acceptance, in conjunction with other concepts (such as consensus), form relatively self-contained systems of interaction which develop their own identifiable dynamic? If so, these systems could be reinforced by consideration of the unintended consequences of interaction, so limiting the need to stress the prime conceptual importance of the person and class action.

There is a permanent incongruity between the meanings which men seek to impose on social reality and the outcomes of their interactions with others, between intention and the unintended consequences of men's relations, between, if you like, the 'ideal' and the 'real'. This distinction is at first glance similar to that which exists between situational analysis and the permanently escalating consequences of action. It is precisely because of this distinction that situational analysis cannot be conducted in terms of, or derived from, an understanding of permanently escalating consequences. For there is no immediate relationship from the latter to the former. The former cannot be derived from the latter. On the contrary, because the latter is formed as a consequence of the former it can only be approached in its terms or, as we advocate, by an extension of its terms.

The permanently escalating *unintended* consequences would seem to cover that complex feature of social life which sociologists, from the founding fathers onwards, have referred to as the structure of society, the 'social system'. Given their theoretical assumptions, it was easy to understand why it has been supposed that this structure should have the force of external constraint over and against any individual person, a class of people, or, even, all people in society; why Marx thought that it was not men's consciousness and values which shaped their social situations but, rather, men's social situations which determined their consciousness; why Durkheim was encouraged to feel that social facts were external to the individual and constrained his conduct, even in such private acts as suicide.

In contrast with these assumptions, we tried to show that social situations do not determine, but are crucially defined, sustained, changed, and controlled by the meaningful activity of people, and classes of people. The situations have no existence independent from the people who create them. Consequently, particular social situations can only be interpreted by employing these concepts which we spelled out when discussing situational analysis.

This means that the permanently escalating intended and unintended consequences of interaction are the changing, action-formed, situations which follow from intended and unintended consequences which are themselves created by the interaction of people and action classes.

Put one way, this indicates that particular social situations are not distinct from the escalating consequences of activity. The escalating consequences merely imply the embracing of several situations which are either unrelated, or related by the various concepts of interaction, such as conflict and consensus.

The intentional activity of individuals and classes creates the intended and unintended consequences which escalate, so affecting existing situations on which new meanings are imposed. This indicates that escalating consequences have no independent meaning or existence apart from the changing situational activity of individuals and classes. Escalating consequences, therefore, do not constrain people for two reasons. Firstly, people define ideals, forms, and patterns in their situations. They act in terms of these definitions so as to sustain and form their values, experiences and meanings. In part, people limit and pattern themselves, but in terms of meanings which cannot be derived from external patterns. Secondly, the intentional activity of people is affected but not determined by that of others. Clash of wills and actions leads to further escalating consequences. In turn this links in one or more of the various possible forms of cohesion or conflict or, simply, is discontinuous. That is, both links and discontinuities occur at the level of escalating consequences (unintended). But these are merely changing aspects of the same and developing and (or) different situations. Actual constraint is, therefore, a consequence of the interaction of the intentional activity of different people and classes, and can only be explained in its terms.

That is to say, having resurrected the resilience, uniqueness and passion of the individual we have also found it impossible to see the permanently escalating consequences of action as determining the individual or fully forming his action and its effects. In turn, this has implied an approach to social relations which relates to an extension of situational analysis. At the same time, and from the point of view of any one person or class (including such combination classes as the State), there are always escalating consequences which are beyond their scope and power to control fully. To this extent they are limited, but not by some system or structure external to them: rather, by the identifiable consequences of their own action as well as that of other individuals and classes.

In order to distinguish between this argument and the orthodox view of structure and constraint it is advisable to suggest a new term. The term must contain the sense of the concept: 'the permanently escalating intended and unintended consequences of interaction'. The most appropriate term which suggests itself is 'kaleidoscope'. So we shall refer to the social kaleidoscope when we refer to the particular juxtaposition of all those concepts which we have so far discussed in relation to any area of social life under investigation. As we have pointed out, there can be no one social kaleidoscope. The term must always be in the plural. As such, it can be applied to a wide area, covering several aspects of life, or to, say, educational kaleidoscopes when delineating more specific areas.

The place of the displaced person
It is necessary to indicate the extent to which the concept of the social kaleidoscopes and all the different concepts we have discussed demand an alternative view of what is involved in an explanation of the different ways in which people become social.

The person becomes social very early in life, even before the time when he first begins to speak. What is important for our purposes is the unique and irreducible self-image which comes with social existence. This image is unquestionably affected by the particular social kaleidoscopes which the person experiences. But the person also affects social kaleidoscopes because he, his values, his action and relationships are a part of them. Once the person becomes social he can be thought of quite apart from kaleidoscopes. But kaleidoscopes themselves have no existence apart from the individuals whose ideals and activity create them.

Any consideration of socialization must, therefore, take into account the way in which the individual shapes himself, and, at the same time, shapes the kaleidoscopes through which he lives. But it must also consider particular relationships which the person helps to sustain, because it is through them that, in part, the individual develops.

Such a study would take special steps to interpret the ways in which the individual develops his values and definitions in terms of his own previous experience, as well as his present social relationships. The means, therefore, by which the individual socializes himself are paramount. Equally, the intentional and unintentional control which the individual exerts over his social kaleidoscopes are important considerations for an understanding of the ways in which the person changes and develops throughout his life.

Social kaleidoscopes are made up of the continuing and changing attempts which men make to control and shape their own social life and that of others. So, all those concepts, including that of social kaleidoscopes, which we have discussed are prerequisites of any sociological interpretation of the socialization of particular people.

We may now return to the question: in what way, if any, does it make sense to speak of man as constrained, as unfree, in social kaleidoscopes?

The rational but relativistic position for which Marx argued suggested that it was possible for social restriction to be removed. All existing denial of freedom and control for a person or class was associated with the particular conduct of other people or classes within the confines of a social system. That is, Marx operated with a definition or theory of the source of men's unfreedom which extended to indicate the means of changing man's general situation in such a way as to remove that constraint. Indeed, the whole of Marx's, as well as Freud's writing can be seen in this light – as an attempt to demonstrate how people can come to control their own destiny, and master their social and psychological environment.

An equally common distinction is made between 'freedom from' and 'freedom to'. 'Freedom from' involves the liberation from particular constraints; hunger, prison, the State, capitalism, or the need to work. It is, then, a negative view of freedom. 'Freedom to' involves a more positive or active, if rather 'liberal', view; the freedom to do as one wishes: to paint, to fish, to attend school, or speak on political issues, to become cultured, and so on. Lack of freedom takes the two opposite forms of these two distinct qualities of freedom in social activity. Similarly, one theme of our argument has been based on a demonstration of the fact that the convergence in modern sociological thought has focused on an assumption, now hidden, now open, that sociology is only capable of dealing with the external constraints in people's lives which may, subsequently, have become internalized. The social system controls action.

Without attempting to deny the historical importance of either of these approaches, it does seem that they have combined to exclude that facet of man's life which at *all* times seeks to control his destiny. Whilst seeking this imposition of his will and, therefore, the exercise of both 'freedom from' and 'freedom to', man is inevitably involved in the perpetual creation of unintended consequences and the development of fresh obstacles to the expression and experience of his desires. Freedom, therefore, can never be total in the way that Marx and others have dreamed. But neither can the lack of freedom be total. Freedom is never completely absent from human activity. Nor is it ever fully present.

Against these two previous positions we are suggesting two alternative and related ways of looking at freedom. Firstly, the gulf which is drawn between the free person and the socially conditioned person obscures the issue, for the person has no choice but to be social. He is not even presented with such a choice. In this sense he is always within the boundaries of social life, and usually of social relationships and kaleidoscopes. The great leaps into freedom which are indicated by Marx or Sartre or Marcuse, and the idea of 'uninstitutionalized' action, are in this sense misleading and romantic. They suppose a non-social alternative which cannot exist. Yet, by the very virtue of his social life, the person is exposed to a great range of activities and experiences. These encourage a sense of value, vision and destiny which in turn give him an urge to shape his life. This holds whether his activity is highly 'conformist' or 'ritualized' on the one hand, or where it is quite unique and original on the other. Man's action is always volitional and involves elements of ideal control.

A man's actions are also always limited. They are constrained for two different reasons. Firstly, the different forms of contention for intentional control involve the concepts of acceptance, power, authority, and legitimation. Individual, atomized, co-operation and combination classes all seek to impose their will on others. This may involve brutal forms of control (say, war) or gentle ones (say, a committee manoeuvre). It may be extensive (say, the act of a state) or localized (the act of a parent). Whatever path is taken, it is visible, felt by the contenders, dramatic, and contains unintended consequences.

The second form more directly involves unintended control. A girl's declaration of love may place her in a new situation where she faces an unexpected proposal of marriage or a pregnancy. The wage-claim of a class helps to create an increase in food prices or school meals. A choice to attend a particular school creates a situation which contains no option for a professional or further educational career. Such constraint is the more pervasive because it is so hidden and unrecognized, though it may become defined. Equally, such constraining situations do not preclude all choice, merely particular choices. Such situations reintroduce the first form of constraint and, therefore, the various attendant forms of freedom and choice.

Any theory of constraint must take both kinds of control over men into account. Equally, any theory of freedom must recognize that one man's constraint is another man's freedom (intended control) or fresh opportunity (unintended control).

Sociology can ignore neither constraint nor freedom. But a sociology which involves an examination of constraint must locate the course, form and meaning of that constraint before it can explain it, and constraint is always located in the intentional activity of particular men and particular classes even when it is unintended. Similarly, for sociology to involve a consideration of freedom it must locate the form of freedom within an area of constraint and unintended consequences.

It is helpful to return to the orthodox sociological problem and its solution in order to contrast it with the alternative we are offering. For as soon as the orthodox problem of order is posed, the analytical significance of unintended consequences is elevated into the subject-matter of sociology. The problem of order entails the solution – external constraint.

Once a different problem is posed, the solutions also differ. If it is accepted that society is possible; once, as it were, we accept that society is actually with us, the problem becomes: how does *this* society work *now*. The solution to that problem presupposes the existence of social men, of diversity, where men have already placed themselves by their action in different classes, hold different values, engage in different ideas, wielding control and exercising choice in different ways. How this society works implies a sociology of personal control and constraint.

These two conflicting problems, of order, of how society is possible, and of control, of how this society works, imply different kinds of attendant areas of enquiry.

The existing orthodox viewpoint requests that this and that family, this and that bureaucracy, this and that state, be stripped of their distinction and meaning and be seen in terms of their common factors. It asks: how does the social system of industrial society generate conflict between bureaucratic organization and the nuclear family? Or between classes, etc., etc.,? The very problems that are examined are posed through the theoretical assumptions contained by the approach. The solutions are similarly influenced.

The key distinction between the orthodox and alternative approach is introduced in social life by the very factor of subjectivity and the relationship between subjectivity, social action, and social constraint. This interlocking relation between meaning and action gives the person a degree of voluntarism (in the commonsense meaning of the term). Man may perform this act, or he may not. And, crucially, he enters as a decisive, conscious, factor in the making of the choice. That choice cannot be predicted for two reasons. Firstly, action has no systematic relation with pre-existing social relations and, therefore, cannot be deduced from them. Secondly, new ideas, or formulations, or meanings cannot be predicted – or they would not be new. Tom, the individual, is, therefore, vital before analysis can begin. He is the empirical grounding for sociological theory and explanation.

Society, social circumstances, the social system, do not ensure that this person becomes a technocrat or that this society should develop a technology. Technology can take different shapes and meanings and technocrats can act in different ways and with different meanings. This variety is not explained merely by reference to necessary conditions, but, in addition, by references to action and meaning and control.

To argue that there is one set of necessary conditions, one kind of technocrat, one kind of technological organization, one kind of technological ideal, is to see man and society as system-governed, as controlled. It is also to avoid explaining and understanding this particular technocrat, this particular ideal, this particular form of organization and the way *it* is sustained (by and against whose concerns?), and changed (by whose pressures and with what consequences for which people?).

This is not to argue that necessary conditions and escalating unintended consequences fail to be of socially shattering proportions. We only have to think of the effect of wars, or family life, or those forms of urban activity and the application of technology which became manifest in the urban snarl of such cities as New York, Tokyo or London to see the extent to which we are in fact unintentionally affected by the consequences of a myriad actions. But we respond to this shaping, and London was built by men.

Two points remain. Firstly, we cannot understand these human constrictions without understanding the complex way in which people's intentional acts and unintended consequences created them (social history), and now sustain and change them (sociology).

The analysis of the present (or past-present) requires that previous development is taken as given. It is, therefore, unhistorical. An interest in how this society, or London, or Parliament, hold or do not hold together now is, therefore, a question of which people attempt to control London or Parliament, and by what means. How do their acts affect the responses of others? To what extent is their control unintended, accepted, resisted, balanced by response and the action of other classes, etc., etc.? So, to what extent are those shifting, changing kaleidoscopes of acceptance, conflict, tension, which go to make up London, the creation of any one class? To what extent is London out of control? Whose authority, whose power, whose acceptance, which definitions, sustain it whilst continuing to change it?

Such questions can equally be posed of the major kaleidoscopes which make up any society, say, that of modern England. When raised to that level they clearly replace those questions derived from the problem of order.

Secondly, it is clearly not necessary for unintended consequences or for the focused control of particular classes to shape and limit the situations and relations of as many other classes as they do at present. On the one hand, unintended consequences can be brought under a greater degree of intended control. Changed awareness and different definitions alter the nature and repercussion of response and may enhance the intended effects of action. On the other hand, the influence, power and authority of particular classes can be changed by removing their legitimacy, altering the nature of their power, or by increasing the power of others by changing their definitions, legitimacy, alliances, etc.

It remains the case that whatever form of control is attempted, unintended consequences cannot be removed. Only their nature and effect can be changed. Intentional control cannot be removed from human activity. Classes which control most extensively can be challenged and altered.

Finally, it is clear that just as the problems that sociologists have posed imply the nature and style of their solution, so, also, they imply the kind of activity in which the sociologist engages. In so far as the orthodox problem and solution are conservative, so they direct and imply conservative activity. The sociologist intervenes in his subject-matter. His theories affect social attitudes and social life. Therefore, and lastly, we must ask what stance the sociologist who adopts the alternative approach must take.

The social scientist – the active interpreter

It can be argued that the definitions which people apply to their situations, other people and society in general, are in a very real sense like sociological theories. People apply their definitions in action. Often, but not always, they change them when they are found wanting, and develop new ones. As such, they shape the approach which people have to their life and to their conflicting and consensual relations with others.

In the nineteenth century and even earlier some people tried to refine their definitions or theories of people and social situations in particular ways. Comte and Montesquieu were amongst the first to call these special definitions 'sociology'. The work of Marx, Weber, Durkheim, Parsons, and later sociologists have merely further refined and developed these historical definitions in continued, contemporary, attempts to understand people and society.

One of the themes of our argument has been to suggest that these particular definitions, which were created in and from the last century, were responses to current situations, problems and ideas. They have been inherited and accepted in this century. With the weight of the authority of their advocates, an increasingly consensual approach has been suggested to each succeeding generation of students. As an unintended consequence of the pre-conceived definitions the actual problems and actual peoples of this century have been made opaque to sociologists.

The complex definitions or theories of Marx, Marcuse, Dahrendorf, Rex and many others have focused in particular on a criticism of existing social relations, including those of power and the potential means of changing these relations. To this end they developed an almost exclusive concentration on class and, in particular, on the proletarian class. This was the only objective agent of change discernible within the theory which could overturn the existing economic and political relation between power and exploitation.

The defined application of this theory was itself fought over in the Labour Party, as personified in the Gaitskellite/Bevanite clashes, the nationalization and nuclear disarmament controversies. Similarly, the Communist Party, the New Left and other left-wing groupings have developed their own unique definitions within this general approach.

All these definitions have profound conceptual similarities. It is only the detail or the overall model that differs.

These groups are doing, in essence, what everybody else does. Even the humblest tramp or the most traditional aristocrat must be analysed in similar terms. So, as with all intentional activity, the consequences of these sociological and political theories or definitions have unintended repercussions. The first of these involves the emergence of an innate conservatism, which the theory itself contains.

So far, this point has only been partially recognized in practice in the developing disputes between the new radical left and the 'orthodox' communist parties of East and West. Yet, if our argument holds, it is the very concept of Marxism itself, and not merely the organized Communist parties, which is orthodox and conservative in application.[4] Some of the radical students are moving towards a recognition of this. Others are not. Those who are, argue for a more flexible approach, which might provide at once definitions that are more applicable to current and historical situations and a new prescription for radical action and change.

However hard sociologists or socialists may try, they are not capable of totally separating themselves from the destinies, fate, and formative processes of other people. They may merely do so in differing degrees. The rules and methodological considerations which are defined by these people are strict. But they remain tied to human situations and experiences. As such, they cannot be objective or true, or, for that matter, value-neutral. The least that can be done is to recognize this fact. For any kind of sociology, including the one we are advocating, is value-biased. It necessarily contains or creates sets of definitions, assumptions and views of reality. The very ideas of 'truth' and 'objectivity' have to be seen as merely one further set of definitions in terms of which some people live, and which have unintended and therefore unpredictable consequences. The unintended consequences of the everyday definitions of 'truth' and 'objectivity' obscure the fact that they are merely sophisticated definitions of reality. As such, they are of no greater status than any other definition, and may be regarded as rationalizations for value-laden positions. Here we are advocating one further alternative means by which to define or explain reality. This has status only in terms of current problems and radical issues. As such, its consequences are more revolutionary than those of any current aspect of Marxism.

To accept this argument involves recognizing that sociology as we know it is, like Marxism, merely one more form of secular ideology with a rhetoric, vocabulary, and set of concepts and definitions which relate as much to the lives and meanings of the people who use them as to those whose activity they wish to explain or change. A criticism of contemporary sociology is inseparable from a criticism of Marxism, even in its most sophisticated form. But a criticism of such revolutionary theory must also involve a criticism of revolutionary practice in so far as it is based on that theory. When the practice is not based or is only partly based on the definition and theory then those involved may be forced to question the theory. Lenin and Stalin discovered this through their own lives. Mao and Castro did so, and made rather different use of their discovery. But none of them made a decisive or radical break with the traditional definitions. Such a break may or may not be the destiny of students, or Black Power advocates, or any of these groups who overtly argue for increased and democratized control over and participation in the shaping of work and life situations.

The arguments which were presented in the section on situational analysis concerning models are as applicable to social events which involve many situations as they are to the most local or small-scale human situation. But certain points should be emphasized.

Those factors which we have emphasized in this section indicate the difficulty in creating abstract models which may adequately represent or explain the processes and dynamisms involved in the fabric of any one society. Consider only for a moment the differences between the USA, with its violence, its racial harmonies and conflicts and its peculiar historical development; Germany, with its Nazi past, its division into two different styles of political and industrial organization; France, with its history of occupation, its police, its peasants; and England, with, let us say, its own brand of 'repressive tolerance', its welfare state and labour movement. Or consider the England of 1926, of 1945, of 1968, or compare nineteenth- with twentieth-century England.

In this context, the task of constructing a model which, however, abstract, is capable of submerging these differences, would seem beyond the scope of the most or even the least imaginative of sociologists. Even so, orthodox sociology of both cohesive and conflict types consistently makes the effort to do so. The consequence of that effort remains at variance with the welter of empirical material, of greater and lesser import, which emerges about and from these societies and periods. Variety and, therefore, possibility and choice are obscured.

It is not, however, one of our arguments that such model construction is entirely without significance, but that at least four points should be borne in mind when such models, applicable to several societies, are constructed.

First, the eloquent point that Popper makes concerning the politically totalitarian implications of historicism can be levelled at this kind of model. The point holds, whether we consider the models for political or intellectual purposes. That is, and secondly, such models do such grave injustice to the great range of empirical variety in any one society that their relation to 'reality' and concrete events is too tenuous. Their explanatory power is not available to the usual scientific means of falsification. Thirdly, this means that change, the accumulation of intended and unintended consequences, and the reaction of individuals and classes cannot be predicted by the sociologist any more than they can be predicted by the lay person. Yet these models purport to do exactly that.

However, fourthly, these models can perhaps be used as orienting or heuristic devices by the sociologist, in exactly the way Weber suggested for the functionalism which, on all other grounds, he condemned. This feature should not be underrated because of the strength of the other arguments, for the kinds of problems and areas which it suggests for further elaboration and investigation are significant.

The conclusion which we draw from the standpoint of adequate explanation, despite the wide scope contained within that criterion, is that a total model of even one society, in one historical period, is not possible. However, dynamic models of situations and kaleidoscopes within that society may be constructed, which apply over a limited historical period and which may even cover a fraction of the future. Simply, the number of vital features which have to be built into these models is too great to allow further abstractions. We are now in a position to see that these features include:

A. *Situational analysis:*

    (1) The person
    (2) The values of the person
    (3) The person's definition of his situation including his view of:
        (a) His personality
        (b) Other people
        (c) Physical objects
    (4) The person's logic of action
    (5) Other people, analysed by the scientist as above
    (6) Intentional action and interaction, and the unintended consequences of actions; connections and discontinuities between situations.

B. *Situational analysis, widened to include kaleidoscopes of interaction:*

    (1) Action classes:
        (a) Individual classes: particular people
        (b) Atomistic classes
        (c) Co-operative classes
        (d) Combination classes: comprising any possible combination of this and the previous three classes.
    (2) The relations within and between classes and situations: intentional activity and unintended consequences. Including:
    (3) Conflict
    (4) Consensus } sub-divided into different types
    (5) Control in situations: involves conflict and consensus by means of

    (a) Acceptance
    (b) Power
    (c) Authority
    (d) Legitimation
  (6) Change: sub-divided into different types
  (7) Models of social situations, including all previous factors within one or within and between more than one situation: the scientist's definition of social kaleidoscopes.

As we are concerned with individuality and uniqueness in personal and class action, we will often have to be concerned with people and classes who have no recognized public name. Of course, such anonymous people and classes will have to have public labels. But the public labels will overlap, combine different classes, obscure crucial distinctions and, sometimes, make distinctions where none exist. This problem, so far unresolved, is contained in the problem of the identification of people, classes, situations and kaleidoscopes. We have referred to trade unionists, teachers, students, unmarried mothers, as if they were people or classes. We have also referred to economic, work, religious, political, and educational situations and kaleidoscopes. This involved accepting some of the assumptions of orthodox analysis.

In fact, the logic of our argument leads us to distinguish between people in terms of their own definitions and action. It is not correct to see politicians, students or bureaucrats as distinct categories of people or as necessarily important groupings for sociological analysis. For example, 'bureaucrats' do not have action or, therefore, class in common. Rather, they are defined in common by some other people in society. This fact need imply nothing about bureaucrats as real people or, indeed, about how we should group such people for the purpose of sociological analysis. So, when we refer to 'bureaucrats' we should refer to 'those people who are seen by some other people as bureaucrats'. But the main problem remains, for we do not want to refer to 'bureaucrats' at all.

The very fact that people do have definitions and theories of other people and situations makes their activity meaningful to the scientist. But other people are more complex than and are distinct from these definitions of them. So are situations and kaleidoscopes. The meaning and patterns imposed on other people and situations is partial, for escalating consequences create a fracture between the imposed meaning and the complex of reality. The sociologists' task involves a recognition of the unrecognized person beneath the label and other unrecognized kaleidoscopes behind or beyond the defined situation. In a word, it involves new definitions of people and kaleidoscopes.

If in fact we only take and refine other people's definitions, we merely build a series of particular biases into our analysis. These biases will relate to definitions of those who have publicly defined and imposed their categories on social reality. If sociologists simply study 'deviants', 'criminals', 'schizophrenics', 'drug-takers', 'blacks', 'students', etc., they will be engaged in politically biased research. Indeed, public labels (that is, definitions and theories about other people) do often affect the people who are labelled and, to an extent, they are controlled by them. As such, they are vital factors in sociological explanation. But for the sociologist to accept and work only with such labels involves admitting not only bias to his work but to actively intervening in a process of social control and constraint. This is only more obvious when the sociologist, or someone else, applies his research in social policy. The alternative is concerned with labelling as a factor of control. But how the sociologist refers to people becomes a new and unresolved problem.

The same problem arises when we refer to, say, 'economic' or 'educational' situations or kaleidoscopes; that is, when we distinguish areas of activity in social life. Just as, say, 'workers' are real live people who are also lovers, fathers, enemies and, in the final analysis, unique and nameless, so is, say, the 'work' situation or kaleidoscopes. It is also a 'leisure', 'political', 'educational' situation and, at the same time, spreads into other, distinctly labelled situations (the 'family', 'church' etc.).

Enormous questions are raised by this problem. Such questions include the very nature of adequate explanation, and require much further study before any alternative sociology can be regarded as having a firm basis. The immediate task is to consider the activity of the person who accepts the need for such an alternative analysis which will use alternative labels. For, as the problem of identification implies, neither existing nor alternative sociological theories can be free from value-judgements and political stances.

Each step in our whole argument has taken us further from the orthodox convergence, so that now the two positions are irreconcilable. With each of these steps we have advocated the need for a new terminology to contain the new concepts and the new style of analysis. We refer to the person, not the actor, to action, not role, to social kaleidoscope, not to social structure or social system. Almost all the central concepts for the alternative interpretation of social life have been constructed and related to one another. Only one concept has remained unchallenged, except by implication and until the above discussion.

Traditionally, the professional sociologists refer to their colleagues as 'scientists' and 'social scientists'. The assumption contained in this self-definition is that such people rationally and objectively pursue an impartial inquiry using a method which has the same status as that of the natural sciences. This traditional assumption is not only inadequate as a means of understanding what the sociologist does and the social consequences of what he does, but it is also potentially dangerous to social life and the individual people who, ultimately, are the subject matter of the sociologist. It is dangerous precisely because of the intended and unintended uses to which sociological theories or definitions are put and because of the act of theoretical explanation itself.

These uses of theory may be visibly politically charged. Stalin's use of sociological definitions is only one example. The use of our counter-insurgency definitions, specifically commissioned by Western Governments, is another. But so are the more piecemeal and local uses of such definitions, whether in the psychiatrist's consulting room or in the 'treatment' of a 'delinquent'. That such consequences are as dangerous to personal life, if they are believed to have objective impartial qualities, as are those of Marxism or any other orthodox form of theory should go without saying. In fact, it does not, and the uses of sociology needs further investigation and questioning.

In so far as they imply their use as a logic for action all sociological definitions are at the same time active interventions into social life. This holds true whether the particular sociologist is aware of this or not, whether he intends this or not. As a consequence of this fact we must regard the sociologist as actively intervening in social life. He does not just interpret or explain it.

Equally, as all social definitions are of similar status, sociological ones are no more or less true than any others. So also, they are only more or less meaningful and adequate from the point of view of some people. They are not impartial or objective or dispassionate, though, from the point of view of our argument, some are passionless. This simple fact is of great significance. The very act of sociological enquiry and explanation intervenes in and can affect its subject matter – real people. The very attempt to explain social life carries, therefore, a commitment. That commitment is merely obscured if the sociologist claims objectivity, impartiality, special expertise, access to truth. To invest commitment with such an aura is to engage in a confidence trick. Fortunately the subject of the trick is not so passive or so stupid. Part of the crisis in sociology is to do with the fact that the subject has called the bluff of the sociologist.

The fact that the act of sociological inquiry, irrespective of the deliberate use of sociological research and theories, is committed and value-based does not imply that we should throw up our hands in horror and retire to the study of, say, the objective natural sciences. Rather, it suggests that the sociologist should engage with his subject matter more directly and intentionally than orthodox theory allows.

Such contact will show the sociologist things about people that he never dreamed of in his detached, objective position. It will also show him emotional, personal, political things about the pressures on himself which already bias his work in countless ways. In the process he will become freer from and clearer about his own presuppositions and assumptions, but not fully free or completely clear.

That the sociologist should not be let loose on people without looking at himself is important. A few sociologists on the left are very belatedly recognizing this fact. But there is a tendency for them to look only at the sociologists of the right. They must look at themselves as well. Even the angels have a vested interest in a particular view of heaven and of whom Peter should allow through the gates, not to speak of how to get there in the first place.

As important as self-discovery is the discovery of who other people are and what they are doing. In fact, as suggested, the two aspects of discovery are deeply related. The one can not precede the other. But to discover and understand real people the sociologist has to recognize that he is merely one amongst many. To discover the many, he has to join them, to live with them, to accept and live with the fact that his interpretations and explanations and theories stem from and influence the many.

To see meaning in Caesar one does not have to be Caesar, but one has to have some grasp and experience of responsibility, power and vision in one's own life before that leap of creative imagination can be made, filled out and made meaningful. The closer one gets to the life of the subject, as Goffman illustrated, the more informed is the study, a fact to which any anthropologist will testify.

So, the sociologist must get closer to his subjects, and his explanations can affect the subjects' life. Does he then retire to his University Department, write up his research, publish and turn to his next enquiry? He can and traditionally does. But this does not recover the objectivity or neutrality he has lost, or rather, never had. On the contrary, it implies a more continuous engagement with his subject, indeed a more human relationship with him. It suggests that he must stay with the people, point out the conclusions of his work, be prepared to accept their criticism and so develop his work *with* them. He should also help them, as they helped him in his study by submitting to his presence, questions and theories. That is, he must point out the unseen consequences of their actions, help them in their appointed task, help them to achieve their values, and so to control their own lives more fully. In the process, he will be helped himself, as a person as well as in his sociological activity.

Clearly, the sociologist cannot do this indiscriminately. Because of his own values, he can not help those who hold other values to achieve a greater control over their lives and, therefore, over the sociologist and those with whom he sympathises. Simply, the sociologist has to make a conscious choice of whom he will engage with, a choice he makes at the moment without recognizing the fact.

This fact of engagement involves a self-conscious attempt to understand and change peoples lives. That is a political act. It is political whether it is intended or unintended. For this additional reason established academic sociology is politically biased and is not objective. If the fact is overtly recognized and intentionally accepted, then the sociologist cannot remain academic in the established sense. His home is not in the University so much as with the people he studies. He is not impartial, detached or aloof. He is partial, engaged and down to earth.

None of this suggests for a moment that objectivity and self-critical questioning of assumption and conclusion are to be dispensed with. Rather, they are to be practised as methods of understanding and techniques within the confines of commitment. Indeed as has been suggested, the sociologist will become more objective and professional in this sense exactly because such commitment will encourage him to become more aware of the ordinary day-to-day pressures which play on him in the same way they play on other people.

In addition to the opposed academic view which orthodox theory implies, its very acceptance and establishment has created extra pressures to ignore the view for which we argue. It particularly discourages the notion that the sociologist must recognize that changing the world is part of his intellectual task – this, despite all the connections, consultancies, grants and educational vested interests that professors undertake and accept and which imply particular kinds of change, or, rather, stability and social control.

This, then, is the final request, that the sociologist should look at himself and recognize what he is doing, that he too is human and exposed to human pressure. This can only be achieved by the sociologist if he takes part in social activities and intentionally tries to change the world along with others. In so doing he will not only discover more about himself, but he will learn more about other people, about the nature and limits of co-operation, the meaning of hate or power or exploitation, and about love.

If sociological definitions are value-biased and also take the form of social interventions it is not reasonable to see the sociologist as a social *scientist*. The style and content of the means of analysing and interpreting the person and the kaleidoscope of social activity implies a radically different definition for such a person. It is therefore, proposed to replace the term 'social scientist'.

The question remains, what should replace the existing term? Any person who examines social life from the perspective which we have outlined will not be explaining or defining social reality, for that reality does not exist independently from the beliefs and actions of all people. He will merely be offering another view, he will be reconstructing and reshaping reality and thereby creating the possibility for more active intervention, either by himself or by others, despite his own protests. It seems, then, that the social scientist is an active social interventionist, a reformer of reality, a person, like all others, who attempts to control and exert an influence over reality and social possibility. Either intentionally or not, such a person is engaging in the committed interpretation and transformation of social reality. Such an activity is reasonably contained in the phrase, the 'reformulation of social activity', or the 'active reconstruction of social realities' or by the terms 'active interpretation' or 'intervening interpretations'. We therefore propose to refer to the person who engages in this kind of social activity as an 'active interpreter' of social life and not as a 'social scientist', on the assumption that a distinctive and meaningful activity in this area of life remains possible.

The only question that remains is: what kind of commitments and to whom? That is a difficult moral and political choice. Any one active interpreter is as likely as the next person to make a choice to which others take exception. So, the subject of active interpretation should be warned. Not only may the active interpreter not understand you, but he may have a morality which is not yours. He may not be acting in your interests, and there, as in other things, you are as good a judge as he is.

9: Conclusion

Marx worked and wrote at fever pitch. He fashioned and created his concepts, ideas and assumptions from those who had gone before him and from the contemporaries with whom he debated fiercely. The concepts and theories were themselves revolutionary in content. Alone, as well as in the hands of such political and intellectual extenders as Marcuse, they have helped to change the world.

Writing and working in different social kaleidoscopes, Weber developed different concepts based on a different methodology. But then he was often responding to different problems. Some of these were exactly those which, at a later date, Marcuse faced when extending Marx's original scheme, relating it to the modern State. Just as with Marx, Weber's ideas were creative, prophetic, and revolutionary in content.

John Rex and Ralf Dahrendorf, responding to mid-twentieth-century problems, revised Weber's insights. In the process, they developed exactly those features of Weber's work which came closest to those of Marx and Marcuse. They illuminated, as it were, the latent collectivism and determinism in Weber's horrific analysis of advanced industrial societies. They advanced the thesis of the infinite manipulability of man and diminished the significance of the subjective features of social life. The rationality and concern for choice, central to both Weber and Marx, were distorted and their significance downgraded.

To this end Rex and Dahrendorf were helped on two separate counts. Firstly, Freud, who in many ways was responding to the same intellectual ferment as Marx and Weber, had a similar concern with the rational and irrational, as well as with man's effort to control his destiny. Freud's work was creative and revolutionary. It too has helped to shape contemporary thought. But these positive dimensions of Freud's work were often misunderstood. Only the deterministic implications of his revolutionary insights were seen. As a consequence the addition of aspects of his work sharpened the constraining, non-subjective and manipulative features of the revisions of Marx's and Weber's theories.

Secondly, Rex and Dahrendorf were helped by the work of Parsons. Though his first major work appeared in 1937 he, like Marx and Weber, was responding to social problems posed in the previous century. But while they were vitally concerned with revolution and change, he, like Durkheim, was concerned with the problem of how social order was possible despite such revolutionary change and chaos. Whilst Parsons, as a consequence, has been a politically conservative force, his work of sociological synthesis was none the less quite as revolutionary in its conception as was the work of these men on whom Parsons based his study.

We looked in detail at three intellectual and radical giants. We illuminated their uniqueness, but focused more on their similarity. Our disquiet was sharpened by noting that much of modern sociology had been influenced by and, indeed, has taken its starting point exactly from this convergence.

Right from the beginning of their endeavour sociologists were faced with what seemed to them to be a problem of the highest importance. How is it that the individual becomes social, and how is his sociality maintained? In a real sense; how is social order possible?

Marx and Parsons both confronted this problem with firmly held views of the basic nature of man. But this did not help them with the solution for, though very different, their views on man's nature contradicted the form which they felt existing society actually took. In developing concepts and theories with which to account for the structure of society, this dilemma was only resolved by posing a view of social structure which was almost totally determining in its effect on the individual. So, also, they had to assume or imply the infinite manipulability of human nature. This conception was the logical solution to the problem of social order.

In making the link with Freud both Parsonians and Marxists, such as Marcuse, ignored or amended that aspect of Freud's work which was specifically designed to free man as much as possible from unconscious and irrational controls. For Freud the 'normal man' was to a greater or lesser extent already free to exert some rational control over his action. It was the 'neurotic' personality which he sought to liberate through psychoanalysis to an understanding of these constraints.

The distorted reading of Freud's work was combined with that of Durkheim and Marx and had the consequence for modern sociology of completely submerging the individual within both structural and psychological concepts which allow him no choice, no originality, and no control over his own destiny. So the solution to the central problem of this dominant sociological concern was further consolidated, and a new view, a fundamentally sociological view of man, emerged.

In their turn, such solutions have generated new problems: the mechanisms of socialization, structural stress, and tension management, the pressure engendering class conflict and the mechanisms of revolution, and so forth. But the basic problems have remained outstanding, and continue to focus thought and encourage the direction of research. Whilst we tried to locate these problems in a particular historical period, we have also tried to suggest that new problems are presented by contemporary events, which in turn demand new solutions.

However, the cumulative effect of the modern consensus between conflict and cohesion theoreticians, as well as empirical work based on such theory, precluded the easy recognition of alternative problems and solutions. Indeed, the convergence has led a few to believe that the long-awaited 'golden age' of sociological agreement is at hand, if not already established.

In one sense, the emergence of this dominant theme in sociological thought is understandable when measured against the rational individualism which the thought of the seventeenth and eighteenth centuries proposed, or, indeed the problem of order as posed by the social conflicts of the nineteenth century. But the extent to which both cohesion and conflict sociology accepts this position as a finished product, requiring only future amendment, is highly disturbing from both an intellectual and a humanistic standpoint. Certainly a debt is owed by sociology to Marx, Durkheim, Freud, Weber, Parsons, and their various contemporary followers for putting man firmly in his social context and extending the arguments of the 'founding fathers'. But is the intellectual 'lull' which Donald MacRae predicts when faced with sociological 'unity' really to be accepted? Should we agree that we face a 'long period of logical refinement, and cleaning-up operations?'[1]

We saw that one or two sociologists, such as Wrong and Homans, have expressed a certain dissatisfaction with modern sociological theory, without indicating any kind of satisfactory alternative. Others, such as Rex and Dahrendorf, have at some time expressed disquiet but have later come to accept the same position as their contemporaries. Indeed, it was Dahrendorf himself who, in his essay 'Homo Sociologicus', expressed the orthodox position most succinctly.

Far from adducing proofs of the validity of the emergent view, we suggested some social explanations for its origins. It was not the purpose of this work to detail the social and academic political factors involved, such as the teaching of sociology, the influence of particular individuals, such as Parsons, kaleidoscopes such as the London School of Economics, or of movements and beliefs, such as those of Marxism. Fortunately, these factors are detailed in Alvin Gouldner's recent work *The Coming Crisis of Western Sociology*.[2] Yet, we must note that the pervasive, colluding and often escalating unintended agreement amongst contemporary sociologists carries with it an interest and value for those who concur with further consolidation and extension which, it is safe to predict, will not easily be rejected. In the intellectual 'lull' which is foreseen, some assert that they 'can and will' educate the next generation of sociology students into what is essentially a consensual dogma.[3]

We have tried to show that insights into views of man and his relationships, which, in the founding fathers, amounted to a revolution in thought of profound and creative importance have become, in the consensual development of modern sociological thought, a gross limitation on the possibility of adequate or constructive explanation of those relationships and of man. Variety, life, choice and individuality stares the modern sociologist in the face, but he makes nonsense of them by reducing them by means of his concepts, definitions and explanations to the dull, the grey and the lifeless.

We suggest that the consequences, now intended, now unintended, of the activity of men in relationships of power and authority have been partly responsible for the lack of certain kinds of major revolution and conflict of a socialist nature in contemporary society. To put it too smugly, social kaleidoscopes have been too complex by half, even for the Marxists who, of course, feel they understand the nature of society more truly than anyone else. But the very definitions and theories of the Left constitute another major reason for the lack of radical activity. It is, of course, a main aspect of our thesis that dominant elements in Marx and Marxism are as incapable of understanding society as are Parsons and the orthodox consensus of which they are a part. The concepts which they use and the actions are, as an escalating consequence, a conservative force. Marxism is, therefore, at least as responsible as those it attacks for the lack of conflict and radical activity in contemporary social kaleidoscopes.

It is, in part, the arrogance of certainty, and the terminology, which cut off from political activity all those who in modern societies hanker for some kind of alternative, for some personal extension of control over their lives. Mainly, the definition and theory are at fault and inform and sustain that arrogance and terminology. The Left has lost too many vital battles and political opportunities as a consequence of those definitions. It can no longer afford the security of hanging on to them. If it does, others will reign supreme by default. Because of this, socialists, like sociologists, are under an obligation to take a leap into the unknown; an obligation which is ultimately laid on them by the people with whom both are intimately concerned. The need is great, for it 'becomes ever more difficult to squeeze creative juices out of the classic antitheses that, for a hundred years, have provided theoretical structure for sociology . . . Distinctions become ever more tenuous, examples ever more repetitive, vital subject matter ever more elusive'. Simply, this 'process of "moulding of still ductile forms" cannot go on forever . . .'[4] Nor can the solution rest in technical adjustment of previous conceptions. For ultimately such historically situated concepts cannot relate to contemporary problems or people or values. So, definition, theory, and concern for the unique practice must be redefined if aspirations and visions of new or dissenting thought are ever to be approximated in the practice of future social kaleidoscopes.

This is not to suggest that technique is irrelevant, but only to argue that technique will not transform sociology, or understanding, or action. For sociological explanation is suffused with value and meaning. It imposes those values and meanings on those people and kaleidoscopes it attempts to explain. Technique can only aid it in its interpretations. It cannot change the nature of contemporary transformations of reality and social action.

The problems facing the active interpreter today are problems raised in the vortex of immediate social kaleidoscopes. They are new problems, quite unlike those which concerned the founding fathers. Technique is important, but subordinate to the *valued meaning*, to the will, to the problems it seeks to explain. So, as Weber argued,

> the cultural problems which move men form themselves ever anew and in different colours, and the boundaries of that area in the infinite stream of concrete events which acquires meaning and significance for us . . . are constantly subject to change. The intellectual context from which it is viewed and scientifically analysed shifts. The points of departure of the cultural sciences remain changeable throughout the limitless future as long as a Chinese ossification of intellectual life does not render mankind incapable of setting new questions to the externally inexhaustible flow of life.[5]

Such 'ossification' is indeed a danger if it is felt that only technical adjustment is required. But we have tried to argue that new cultural problems exist for which new explanatory solutions are required. Indeed, we have tried to locate such alternatives in a submerged theme of socio-logical thought.

Those empiricists whose work we examined all started by using concepts which derive from that convergence of two great schools of thought that originated from two separate formulations of the basic problem facing an explanation of society. In the course of their investigations, however, important features in the conduct of man were raised which would not be solved by the concepts with which they started.

These features linked with a consideration of the way individuals and groups attempt to control their situations, in conflict and consensus with other people and groups. We have stressed that this second dimension in the work of Parsons, Marx, Freud, and in particular, Weber, was intimately concerned with the nature of explanation involved in this problem, which was systematically excluded both by the other dimension of their work and by the later interpretations and theories of Parsons, Rex, Dahrendorf, Marcuse and the whole modern consensus. We have tried to reintroduce and redefine factors related to the way men shape and control their lives, and to suggest concepts capable of explaining this phenomenon, whilst excluding the peculiar rational bias in the original work of Marx and Weber.

The magnitude of the task of constructing an alternative, and the extent of its necessary divergence from the view of man which the established orthodoxy contains can, perhaps, be partly illustrated by the views of Edmund Leach. Every person, writes Leach, 'is astonishingly inventive and resourceful . . . linguistic behaviour demonstrates this quite clearly. Every time you engage in serious argument you can spontaneously invent huge chunks of brand new sound patterns which no one in the course of history has heard before, yet you and your listening audience can both immediately understand what is said'; or, in interpreting them differently, and in other terms, can react in entirely unexpected and apparently senseless or irrational ways.

> We must get out of the [way] of thinking that reason and imagination are two different [things], and that the truth of mathematics relates to one kind of fact and the truth of poetry to something quite different . . . The unique and astonishing thing about human beings is not their capacity to observe and analyse . . . but their capacity to create. Every one of us is an artist with words [and actions]. We create brand new sentences, we don't just imitate old ones.[6]

Even these assertions do not state the problem radically enough. For, as we speak and act, we take part in reshaping our own awareness, we take part in our own creation, and impose a meaning on our life and those around us. We, and the relationships we build, make up the active process of life; pattern the social kaleidoscopes and give them colour. Yet, just as we act, so we change ourselves and the patterns of the kaleidoscope. We create great and disjointed chains of activity, the multitudinous ramifications of which we cannot hope to foresee. So, we create a constant disjunction between the intended and the unintended, the ideal and the real, the meaning we seek to impose and the meanings the sociologist interprets, based on an understanding of our meanings.

Our analysis has led us to see social action as dynamic, changing, constantly forming and re-forming. Whilst our view suggests that patterns do form, they are recognized as man-made, imposed and sustained. So, our view is also unstructured when opposed to the orthodox view. The patterns are brightly coloured and in constant flux and can only be understood in terms of the action of men.

It is not possible to capture the view that men are constantly forming their own lives, shaping those of others and being shaped by them, without the new conception of social kaleidoscopes. These are patterned or formed only by the lives of men as they impose their values on reality, now with the need, now with the acceptance, now with the antagonistic hindrance of other men, from day to night to day.

It has been the task of our argument to build up the different components of these kaleidoscopes of social life. In doing so we have placed special emphasis on situational analysis and situational logic. This emphasis on the individual was later placed within the context of a new form of class analysis, where we distinguished four different, if related, forms of action classes. These classes became the basis of the form of social life. But so too did other concepts, which were of a different order. The control which men strive to exert through their lives, and over the situation of which they are a part, may take the form of acceptance, power or authority. These concepts helped us to understand that all men and all situations were constantly changing through different forms of conflict and consensus. If this is the stuff of social life, if these different kinds of concepts are of help in understanding and explaining the fabric of activity, then the prevailing consensus of modern sociology is indeed a danger to that social life, and not a hallmark of a golden age.

It is the alternative view which is the new problem for the sociologist, the active interpreter, who at once is required to interpret the social kaleidoscope and 'you, the individual', who are bound up with these kaleidoscopes and are part of them. It is a problem of depth, for, in explaining, the sociologist has to create concepts of a certain abstraction, so as to deal, in general, with the variety of the particular. These concepts must not do injustice to the variety of that particular uniqueness. These concepts, then, must relate to theories and models by which the general and the particular are interpreted. At the same time the particular may not be distorted simply to satisfy the ideal and internal consistency of the theory, or the problems which it was initially designed to solve. The theory and the concepts must both be drawn from and explain the variety of life, without distorting it.

The task of constructing an alternative is immense, despite the help which can be sought from the classics, and Weber in particular. Indeed, we have only suggested what may be one possible starting point, which certainly requires enormous additional work.

The sociological problems of today no longer cluster around those of rationality, order or conflict, but concern rather the means by which men seek to control their own destiny in the face of others, so shaping peculiar and new kaleidoscopes. What alternative visions are open to them, and how can they be achieved?

On both sides of the 'iron curtain' we recognize a reaction against particular forms of State control. Individuals and groups engage in activity which we immediately understand as concerned with their efforts to sustain a style of existence uniquely their own – Black Power, workers' control, student power, women's liberation. But the phenomenon is not specific to such organized groups or articulate frameworks of value and meaning. Rather, it is endemic in modern societies. If it were not so, it would be correct to assert that the alternative sociology for which we argue is, indeed, nonsense. Roger Pincott, a close friend who is a Marxist, wrote of an earlier draft of this book:

> I suppose if I were to come really clean about [your argument] I would simply refer to your concluding remarks in Chapter Five – 'But socialization invariably means depersonalization, the yielding up of absolute individuality, etc. . .' This is how life is, mate, and that's just tough. Or at any rate, that's how life is for ninety-nine per cent of all the populations of the world societies. Your alternative may provide a better way of looking at the action of the other one per cent (including certain hippies, a few privileged students, and the odd crazy . . .) but that's the way 'real' people live. Sorry to disappoint you, but this really is what it's all about.

On the contrary, that is what orthodox theory, one possible kind of interpretation, implies it is all about. Unfortunately that interpretation has assumed the proportions of established Marxist and élitist sociological truth. Another point of view, like the one we suggest, argues quite differently. Starting from a different value, a different faith, it develops a different kind of understanding and so sees different kinds of potential in ordinary 'real' people. Therefore, it sees different problems from those posed by the orthodox view. So, also, its solutions and prescriptions are distinct. Several sociologists have either overtly or covertly seen the need to work along these lines, including Gouldner, Garfinkel, Douglas, Laing, Gross, Goffman, Matza and others. The sociological consensus is no longer all-embracing. It has reached a crisis point. Too many ordinary people, students and enough professional sociologists recognize this fact for the orthodox consensus to survive.

Modern sociology, like Marxism, has become another secular ideology, a definition of what is and what is not possible. Its sociological definitions are fearfully loaded, bereft of feeling and colour, arrogant and élitist. They imply conservatism and constraint. Their scope for the radical change which they insist upon is as limited as their unfeeling criticisms of prevailing kaleidoscopes and their insensitive assumptions about what moves real people.

Contemporary social life is not like this. It can be understood as a variety of beautiful colours and forms, made grotesque only by the accumulating actions of particular men and particular action-classes. Brightly coloured patterns exist. The point is not just to construct an alternative means of interpreting them by recognizing their relation to the actions of men, but, also, to seek to shape and colour our future lives more vividly. The variety and beauty contained in such colours is like the rainbow. But, unlike the rainbow, they can be grasped.

Notes

CHAPTER 1   INTRODUCTION

1. GOULDNER, A., *The Coming Crisis of Western Sociology*, Basic Books, 1970.
2. COHN BENDIT, D., *Obsolete Communism: The Left Wing Alternative*, André Deutsch, 1968.
3. GOULDNER, A., *The Coming Crisis of Western Sociology*, Basic Books, 1970.
4. NISBET, R., *The Sociological Tradition*, Basic Books, 1967.

CHAPTER 2   TALCOTT PARSONS

1. PARSONS, T., *The Structure of Social Action*, Free Press, 1961, 81–82.
2. Ibid, 75.
3. Ibid, 732.
4. Ibid, 383.
5. Ibid, 384.
6. Ibid, 46, Parsons' italics removed.
7. Ibid, 45.
8. Ibid, 402 *et seq.*
9. Ibid, 43 *et seq.*
10. Ibid, 740.
11. Ibid, 747.
12. Ibid, 748.
13. FINLAY SCOTT, J., 'The changing foundations of the Parsonian Action Scheme', *A. S.R. XXVIII*, October 1963.
14. PARSONS, T., 'The Place of Ultimate Values in Sociological Theory', *International Journal of Ethics*, 1935.
15. PARSONS, T., 'The Place of Ultimate Values', *International Journal of Ethics*, 1945.
16. Ibid.
17. Ibid.
18. PARSONS, T., *The Structure of Social Action*, Free Press, 1961, 401, see also 385–6.
19. Ibid, 401.
20. Ibid, see also 886.
21. Ibid, 401.
22. Ibid, 402.
23. Ibid, 107 *et seq.* and 488-495.
24. Ibid, 107 *et seq.*
25. Ibld, 404.

26. Ibid, 492.
27. PARSONS, T., *The Structure of Social Action*, Free Press, 1961, preface to 2nd edition.
28. PARSONS, T., Introduction to Max Weber's *General Theory of Social and Economic Organization*, Free Press, 1947.
29. PARSONS, T., 'The Superego and the Theory of Social Systems', *Psychiatry*, 15.
30. PARSONS, T., Introduction to Max Weber's *General Theory of Social and Economic Organization*, Free Press, 1947, 26.
31. PARSONS, T., Introduction to Max Weber's *General Theory of Social and Economic Organization*, Free Press, 1947, 20.
32. Ibid, 20.
33. Ibid, 27, my emphasis.
34. Ibid, 27–28, my emphasis.
35. PARSONS, T., 'The Superego and the Theory of Social Systems', *Psychiatry*, 15.
36. Ibid, my emphasis.
37. PARSONS, T. with BALES, R. and SHILS, E., *Working Papers in the Theory of Action*, Free Press, 1953, 20–1.
38. PARSONS, T., *The Family, Socialization and Interaction Process*, Free Press, 1955, 104.
39. PARSONS, T., Introduction to Max Weber's *General Theory of Social and Economic Organization*, Free Press, 1947, 20.
40. Ibid, 21.
41. PARSONS, T., *The Social System*, Tavistock, 1952, 543, my emphasis.
42. PARSONS, T., in *Essays in Sociological Theory*, Free Press, 1954.
43. LINTON, R., *The Study of Man*, Appleton-Century, 1936.
44. Ibid, 44.
45. LINTON, R., *The Study of Man*, Appleton-Century, 1936, 114.
46. Ibid, 114.
47. LINTON, R., *The Cultural background of Personality*, Appleton-Century, 1945.
48. Ibid, 77.
49. GROSS, N., *et al*, *Explorations in Role Analysis*, Wiley, 1958.
50. SPROTT, W. J. H., *Social Psychology*, Methuen, 1960, 153.
51. GERTH, H. and MILLS, C. W., *Character and Social Structure*, Harcourt Brace Jovanovich, 1964.
52. DAVIS, K., *Human Society*, Macmillan, 1959, 88–91.
53. PARSONS, T., *Essays in Sociological Theory*, Free Press, 1954, 230.
54. Ibid, 230.
55. Ibid, 231.
56. Ibid, 230.
57. Ibid, 233.
58. Ibid, 233.
59. Ibid, 229.
60. Ibid, 229.
61. See, for example, 'Democracy & Social Structure in Pre-Nazi Germany' in *Essays in Sociological Theory* or his discussion of the absence of father in *The Family, Socialization and Interaction Process*, 23–4.

62. PARSONS, T., 'Voting and the equilibrium of the American Party System' in *American Voting Behaviour,* eds. Burdick and Brodbeck, Free Press, 81, emphasis changed.

63. PARSONS, T., *The Family, Socialization and Interaction Process,* Free Press, 1955.

CHAPTER 3   KARL MARX

1. BOTTOMORE, T. B. and RUBEL, M., *Karl Marx: Selected Writings in Sociology and Social Philosophy,* Watts, 1961, 169.
2. Ibid, 83–4, emphasis removed.
3. Preface to 'A Contribution to the Critique of Political Economy' in *Marx and Engels Selected Works,* Vol. 1, Lawrence and Wishart, 1962, 363.
4. MARX, K., *The Eighteenth Brumaire of Louis Napoleon,* Foreign Languages Publishing House, Moscow, 47.
5. BOTTOMORE, T. B. and RUBEL, M., *Karl Marx: Selected Writings in Sociology and Social Philosophy,* Watts, 1961, 97.
6. MARCUSE, H., *Eros and Civilisation,* Sphere Books, 1969, 24.
7. MARCUSE, H., 'Repressive Tolerance', *A Critique of Pure Tolerance,* by R. Wolfe, B. Moore and H. Marcuse, Beacon Press, 1965, 98–99.
8. MARCUSE, H., *One Dimensional Man,* Routledge & Kegan Paul, 1964, xv.
9. MARCUSE, H., *Eros and Civilization,* Sphere Books, 1969, 42.
10. Ibid, 161 and Chapters 2 and 4.
11. Ibid, 83–4.
12. See Chapter 1.
13. Ibid, 213.
14. Ibid, 203.
15. Ibid, 195.
16. MARCUSE, H., *Eros and Civilization,* Sphere Books, 1969, 195.
17. DAHRENDORF, R., *Class and Class Conflict in an Industrial Society,* Routledge & Kegan Paul, 1959, 12.
18. Ibid, 12.
19. Ibid, 13.
20. MARX, K., *The Eighteenth Brumaire of Louis Napoleon,* Foreign Languages Publishing House, Moscow, 123.
21. Ibid, 124.
22. DAHRENDORF, R., *Class and Class Conflict in an Industrial Society,* Routledge & Kegan Paul, 1959, 14.
23. Ibid, 14.
24. MARX, K., *The Eighteenth Brumaire of Louis Napoleon,* Foreign Languages Publishing House, Moscow, 47.
25. BOTTOMORE, T. B. and RUBEL, M., *Karl Marx: Selected Writings in Sociology and Social Philosophy,* Watts, 1961, 187.
26. MARX, K., *Das Kapital,* Lawrence & Wishart, 1954, Vol. III, 862.
28. DAHRENDORF, R., *Class and Class Conflict in an Industrial Society,* Routledge & Kegan Paul, 1959, 17.
29. BOTTOMORE, T. B. and RUBEL, M., *Karl Marx: Selected Writings in Sociology and Social Philosophy,* Watts, 1961, 8.

30. Ibid, 20.
31. Marx, K., *Das Kapital,* Vol. III, Lawrence & Wishart, 1954, 862.
32. Dahrendorf, R., *Class and Class Conflict in an Industrial Society,* Routledge & Kegan Paul, 1959, 17.
33. Marx, K., *The Eighteenth Brumaire of Louis Napoleon,* Foreign Languages Publishing House, Moscow, 48.
34. Ibid, 125–6.
35. Ibid, 51, my emphasis.
36. Ibid, 66.
37. Marx, K., *Das Kapital,* Vol. III, Lawrence & Wishart, 1954, 862–3.
38. Dahrendorf, R., *Class and Class Conflict in an Industrial Society,* Routledge & Kegan Paul, 1959, 22.
39. Marx, K., *The Eighteenth Brumaire of Louis Napoleon,* Foreign Languages Publishing House, Moscow, 66.
40. Quoted by H. Kelson, *The Political Theory of Bolshevism.*
41. Marx, K., *Das Kapital,* Vol. III, Lawrence & Wishart, 1954, 862.
42. Engels, F. and Marx, K., *Collected Works,* Lawrence & Wishart, 1962, Introduction, 125.
43. Ibid, 130.
44. Ibid, 134.
45. Ibid, 136.
46. Marx, K., *The Eighteenth Brumaire of Louis Napoleon,* Foreign Languages Publishing House, Moscow, 50–1.
47. Marcuse, H., *One Dimensional Man,* Routledge & Kegan Paul, 1968, xv.
48. Ibid, xv.
49. Ibid, xii.
50. Marcuse, H., *Soviet Marxism,* Routledge & Kegan Paul, 1968, 120.
51. Lefebvre, H., *The Sociology of Marx,* Allen Lane, The Penguin Press, 1969, 113.
52. Marcuse, H., *Soviet Marxism,* Routledge & Kegan Paul, 1968, 120.
53. Lefebvre, H., *The Sociology of Marx,* Allen Lane, The Penguin Press, 1969, 75–6.
54. Marcuse, H., 'Repressive Tolerance' in *A Critique of Pure Tolerance* by R. Wolfe, B. Moore and H. Marcuse, Beacon Press, 1965, 93.
55. Ibid, 83.
56. Ibid, 84–5.
57. Marcuse, H., *Negations,* Allen Lane, The Penguin Press, 1968, 207, emphasis removed.
58. Marcuse, H., *A Critique of Pure Tolerance,* Beacon Press, 1965, 95.
59. Ibid, 94.
60. Ibid, 94.
61. Lefebvre, H., *The Sociology of Marx,* Allen Lane, The Penguin Press, 1969, 64.
62. Marcuse, H., *One Dimensional Man,* Routledge & Kegan Paul, 1968, xii–xiii, my emphasis.
63. Ibid, xiii.
64. Ibid, xiii.
65. Ibid.
66. Lefebvre, H., *The Sociology of Marx,* Allen Lane, The Penguin Press, 1969, 75.
67. Marx, K., *Critique of the Gotha Programme,* last sentence, Foreign Languages Publishing House, Moscow.

68. MARCUSE, H., *One Dimensional Man*, Routledge & Kegan Paul, 1968, xiii.
69. Ibid, xiii and xiv.

CHAPTER 4   MAX WEBER

1. GERTH, H. and MILLS, C. W. (eds), *From Max Weber*, Routledge & Kegan Paul, 1948, 55.
2. WEBER, M., *General Theory of Social and Economic Organization*, Free Press, 1947, 88.
3. Ibid, 89.
4. Ibid, 115 *et seq.*
5. Ibid, 92 and 111.
6. Ibid, 111.
7. Ibid, 90.
8. Ibid, 92.
9. Ibid, 92, my emphasis.
10. Ibid, 101.
11. WEBER, M., *The Protestant Ethic and the Spirit of Capitalism*, Allen & Unwin, 1959, 27.
12. WEBER, M., *Economy and Society*, Roth, G. and Wittich, C. (eds), Bedminster Press, 1968, Vol. I, lxiv.
13. Ibid, 26.
14. Ibid, 27.
15. Ibid, 29.
16. Ibid, 30.
17. Ibid, 31.
18. Ibid, 32.
19. Ibid, Vol. III, 941.
20. Ibid, Vol. III, 945.
21. GERTH, H. and MILLS, C. W. (eds), *From Max Weber:* Routledge & Kegan Paul, 1948, 180.
22. Ibid, 182.
23. Ibid, 182.
24. Ibid, 182.
25. WEBER, M., *General Theory of Social and Economic Organization*, Free Press, 1947, 424.
26. Ibid, 425.
27. GERTH, H. and MILLS, C. W. (eds), *From Max Weber*, Routledge & Kegan Paul, 1948, 183.
28. Ibid, 183.
29. Ibid, 184.
30. Ibid, 184.
31. Ibid, 184.
32. Ibid, 186–7.
33. Ibid, 192.
34. Ibid, 194, and WEBER, M., *General Theory of Social and Economic Organization*, Free Press, 1947, 428.

35. GERTH, H. and MILLS, C. W. (eds), *From Max Weber*, Routledge & Kegan Paul, 1948, 190, my emphasis.
36. Ibid, 185, my emphasis.
37. Ibid, 194.
38. WEBER, M., *Economy and Society*, Roth, G. and Wittich, C. (eds), Bedminster Press, 1968, Vol. I, lvii.
39. Ibid, Vol. II, 928.
40. Ibid, 929.
41. Ibid, 932.
42. Ibid, 936.
43. Ibid, 937, emphasis removed.
44. WEBER, M., *Economy and Society*, Roth, G. and Wittich, C. (eds), Bedminster Press, 1968, Vol. II, 938.
45. Ibid, 930.
46. Ibid, 938.
47. Ibid, 939.
48. Ibid, 53.
49. Ibid, 53.
50. Ibid, 215.
51. Ibid, 33 and 36.
52. Ibid, Vol. III, 1002.
53. WEBER, M., *General Theory of Social and Economic Organization*, Free Press, 1947, 329.
54. Ibid, 329.
55. Ibid, 154, emphasis removed.
56. WEBER, M., *Economy and Society*, Roth, G. and Wittich, C. (eds), Bedminster Press, 1968, Vol. II, 903.
57. Ibid, 901.
58. Ibid, Vol. III, Chapter XVI.
59. Ibid, Vol. II, 905.
60. Ibid, Vol. III, 998.
61. Ibid, 999.
62. Ibid, Vol. I, 223–4.
63. Ibid, Vol. III, 991 and 1003.
64. Ibid, Vol. I, lxxvi, Vol. III, 1003.
65. Ibid, Vol. III, 999 ff.
66. Ibid, Vol. I, 245, emphasis added to.
67. Ibid, Vol. III, 1116, emphasis added to.
68. Ibid, Vol. I, 245.
69. Ibid, Vol. III, 1117.
70. Ibid, Vol. III, 1116 ,my emphasis.
71. MARCUSE, H., *Negations*, Allen Lane, The Penguin Press, 1968.
72. BENDIX, R., *Max Weber, An Intellectual Portrait*, Heinemann, 1960, 455.
73. Ibid, 455.
74. WEBER, M., *Politics as a Vocation* in Gerth and Mills. *From Max Weber*, Routledge & Kegan Paul, 1948, 126.
75. WEBER, M., *General Theory of Social and Economic Organization*, Free Press, 1947, 329.
76. GERTH and MILLS, *From Max Weber*, Routledge & Kegan Paul, 1948, 253.

77. NISBET, R., *The Sociological Tradition,*
    Basic Books, 1967, 295.
78. REX, J., *Key Problems in Sociological Theory,* Routledge & Kegan Paul, 1961, 180.
79. Ibid, 134.
80. Ibid, 93.
81. Ibid, 94.
82. Ibid, 94.
83. Ibid, 94.
84. Ibid, 87.
85. Ibid, 88.
86. Ibid, 85.
87. Ibid, 112.
88. DAHRENDORF, R., *Class and Class Conflict in an Industrial Society,* Routledge & Kegan Paul, 1959, 161.
89. Ibid, 162.
90. Ibid, 164.
91. REX, J., *Key Problems in Sociological Theory,* Routledge & Kegan Paul, 1961, 140.
92. Ibid, 141, my emphasis.
93. Ibid, 141.
94. Ibid, 142, my emphasis.
95. Ibid, 142.
96. LOCKWOOD, D., *The Blackcoated Worker,* Allen & Unwin, 1958.
97. REX, J., *Key Problems in Sociological Theory,* Routledge & Kegan Paul, 1961, 142.
98. Ibid, 144.
99. Ibid, 144–55.
100. Ibid, 150.
101. Ibid, 153.
102. Ibid, 153.
103. DAHRENDORF, R., *Class and Class Conflict in an Industrial Society,* Routledge & Kegan Paul, 1959, 71.
104. Ibid, 71.
105. Ibid, 152.
106. Ibid, 165.
107. Ibid, 169.
108. Ibid, 168.
109. Ibid, 169.
110. Ibid, 171.
111. Ibid, 172–3.
112. Ibid, 173.
113. Ibid, 173–9.
114. Ibid, 178–82.
115. Ibid, 183.
116. Ibid, 179–89.
117. Ibid, 182.

118. Ibid, 182–9.
119. Ibid, 189.
120. Ibid, 189.
121. Ibid. 174–5.
122. Ibid, 175.
123. Ibid, 176.
124. REX, J., *Key Problems in Sociological Theory*, Routledge & Kegan Paul, 1961, 117–18.
125. Ibid, 118.
126. Ibid, 124.
127. Ibid, 131.
128. Ibid, 131.
129. Ibid, 134.
130. Ibid, 123.
131. Ibid, 124–6.
132. Ibid, 126–7.
133. Ibid, 127–9.
134. Ibid, 128.
135. Ibid, 128.
136. Ibid, 128.
137. Ibid, 129.
138. Ibid, 128.
139. REX, J., *Race, Community and Conflict*, Routledge & Kegan Paul, 1968, 2.
140. Ibid, 3.
141. Ibid, 6.
142. Ibid, 7.
143. REX, J., *Key Problems in Sociological Theory*, Routledge & Kegan Paul, 1961, 102 and 85.
144. DAHRENDORF, R., *Class and Class Conflict in an Industrial Society*, Routledge & Kegan Paul, 1959, 166.
145. Ibid, 166.
146. Ibid, 166.
147. Ibid, 71.
148. Ibid, 169.
149. Ibid, 178.
150. Ibid, 120.
151. Ibid, 178.
152. Ibid, 179.
153. Ibid, 190.
154. Ibid, 169.
155. Ibid, 170.
156. Ibid, 170.
157. DAHRENDORF, R., *Essays in the Theory of Society*, Routledge & Kegan Paul, 1968, 79–88.

CHAPTER 5   THE CONVERGENCE OF CONCEPTS AND MODELS

1. PARSONS, T., *The Structure of Social Action*, Free Press, 1961, 492.
2. Ibid, 492.
3. Ibid, 739.
4. Ibid, 743.
5. DAWE, A., 'The Two Sociologies', *B.J.S.*, Summer 1970.
6. PARSONS, T., *The Structure of Social Action*, Free Press, 1961, 661.
7. WEBER, M., *Economy and Society*, ed. Roth, G. and Wittich, C. (eds), Bedminster Press, 1968, xci.
8. Ibid, lxxix.
9. Ibid, ci–cii.
10. GERTH, H. and MILLS, C. W., *Character and Social Structure*, Routledge & Kegan Paul, 1961, 22–23.
11. THOMAS, E. and BIDDLE, B., *Role Theory*, John Wiley, 1966, 17.
12. Ibid, 17.
13. BERGER, P. and LUCKMAN, N. T., *The Social Construction of Reality*, Doubleday, 1966, 91.
14. Ibid, 92.
15. GERTH, H. and MILLS, C. W., *Character and Social Structure*, Routledge & Kegan Paul, 1961, 83–84.
16. BERGER, P. and LUCKMAN, N. T., *The Social Construction of Reality*, Doubleday, 1966, 59.
17. THOMAS, E. and BIDDLE, B., *Role Theory*, John Wiley, 1966, 345.
18. Ibid, 345.
19. GOFFMAN, E., *Encounters*, Bobbs Merrill, 1963, 87.
20. Ibid, 87.
21. PARSONS, T., *The Social System*, Tavistock, 1952, 205. emphasis removed.
22. Ibid, 205.
23. Ibid, 205.
24. Ibid, 207.
25. Ibid, 208.
26. Ibid, 209 and see 211.
27. Ibid, 211.
28. Ibid, 211, emphasis changed.
29. Ibid, 213. Parsons adds in a footnote that 'there may . . . be creative modifications from *within* the personality'. But this fact has no place in his theory.
30. Ibid, 227.
31. Ibid, 227.
32. Ibid, 228, emphasis removed.
33. BERGER, P. and LUCKMAN, N. T. *The Social Construction of Reality*, Doubleday, 1966, 157.
34. Ibid, 159.
35. Ibid, 174.
36. Ibid, 180.
37. Ibid, 202.
38. Ibid, 166–7. (See also Goffman 'On Face Work' in *Where the Action Is*,

Allen Lane, The Penguin Press, 1969, part 1 and also 'Where the Action is'.)
39. BERGER, P. and LUCKMAN, N. T., *The Social Construction of Reality,* Doubleday, 1966, 76.
40. Ibid, 79.
41. Ibid, 110.
42. Ibid, 127.
43. PARSONS, T., *Essays in Sociological Theory,* Free Press, 1958, 393.
44. DAVIS and MOORE, in *Sociological Theory,* Coser and Rosenberg (eds), Macmillan, 1957.
45. Ibid.
46. PARSONS, T., *Essays in Sociological Theory,* Free Press, 1958, 325, my emphasis.
47. Ibid, 439.
48. SPIER, in *Sociological Theory,* Coser and Rosenberg (eds), Macmillan, 1957.
49. DAVIES, K., *Human Society,* Macmillan, 1959, 371.
50. PARSONS, T., *Essays in Sociological Theory,* Free Press, 1958, 324.
51. DAVIS and MOORE, in *Sociological Theory,* Coser, L. A. and Rosenberg (eds), Macmillan, 1957.
52. COLE, G. D. H., *Studies in Class Structure,* Routledge & Kegan Paul, 1955.
53. DAVIES, K., *Human Society,* Macmillan, 1959, 373.
54. WEBER, M., *General Theory of Social and Economic Organization,* Free Press, 1947, 328.
55. COSER, L. A. and ROSENBERG, *Sociological Theory,* Macmillan, 1957, 20 *et seq.*
56. FOSS, D., *Sociology on Trial,* Prentice Hall, 1963, 126.
57. Ibid, 112 *et seq.*
58. PARSONS, T., 'Voting and the Equilibrium of the American Party System' in *American Voting Behaviour,* Burdick and Brodbeck (eds), Free Press, 1959.
59. MARX, K., *The Communist Manifesto,* Foreign Languages Publishing House, Moscow, 73.
60. GERTH, H. and MILLS, C. W., *Character and Social Structure,* Routledge & Kegan Paul, 1961, 83.
61. Ibid, 52.
62. LAING, R. D. and COOPER, D., *Reason and Violence,* Tavistock, 1964, 119.
63. MARX, K., in preface to 'A Contribution to the Critique of Political Economy' in *Selected Works,* Vol. I.
64. LAING, R. D. and COOPER, D., *Reason and Violence,* Tavistock, 1964, 119-20.
65. REX, J., *Key Problems in Sociological Theory,* Routledge & Kegan Paul, 1961, 85.
66. Ibid, 85.
67. GERTH, H. and MILLS, C. W., *Character and Social Structure,* Routledge & Kegan Paul, 1961, 22-3.
68. COOPER, D., *Psychiatry and Anti-Psychiatry,* Paladin, 1970, 32.
69. LAING, R. D., *The Politics of Experience and The Bird of Paradise,* Penguin Press, 1967, 50.
70. SARTRE, J. P., quoted by Laing and Cooper in *Reason and Violence,* Tavistock, 1964.
71. REX, J., *Key Problems in Sociological Theory,* Routledge & Kegan Paul, 1961, 112.
72. MERTON, R. K., *Social Structure and Social Theory,* Free Press, 1957, 15.

73. Marx, K., quoted by Caudwell, C. in *Further Studies in a Dying Culture,* Bodley Head, 1950, 75.
74. Laing, R. D. and Cooper, D., *Reason and Violence,* Tavistock, 1964, 173.
75. Halsey, A.H., *Education, Economy and Society,* Halsey, Floud, J., and Anderson, C. J. (eds), Free Press, 1961.
76. Cooper, D., *Views,* no. 8.
77. Atkinson, M. R., *Education, Student Power and Social Change,* Chapter 3 forthcoming. See also Birmingham University Discussion Paper Series C, no. 15.
78. Marx, K., *The Communist Party Manifesto,* Foreign Languages Publishing House, Moscow.
79. Lockwood, D., in *Explorations in Social Change,* Zollschan and Hirsch (eds), Routledge & Kegan Paul, 1968, 256.
80. Dahrendorf, R., *Class and Class Conflict in an Industrial Society,* Routledge & Kegan Paul, 1959, 164.
81. Dahrendorf, R., *Essays in the Theory of Society,* 1968, 25.
82. Ibid, 57.
83. Ibid, 57.
84. Macintyre, A., *The Guardian,* 9 April, 1968.
85. Rex, J., *New Society,* 11 April, 1968.
86. Dahrendorf, R., *Essays in Sociological Theory,* Routledge & Kegan Paul, 1968, 77.
87. Macrae, D. G., in Cohen, P. S., *Modern Social Theory,* Heinemann Educational Books, 1968, viii. It must be noted that Professor MacRae also expresses 'hope' that the 'fortunate' lull which he predicts does not occur.

CHAPTER 6   PROBLEMS AND POSSIBILITIES

1. Nisbet, R., *The Sociological Tradition,* Basic Books, 1967, 318.
2. Ibid, 318.
3. Dahrendorf, R., *Class and Class Conflict in an Industrial Society,* Routledge & Kegan Paul, 1959, 120, my emphasis.
4. Rex, J., *Key Problems in Sociological Theory,* Routledge & Kegan Paul, 1961.
5. Thompson, E. P., Preface to *The Making of the English Working Class,* Penguin Press, 1969.
6. Thompson, E. P., 'The Peculiarities of the English', *Socialist Register 1965,* Merlin Press.
7. MacIntyre, A., 'Breaking the Chains of Reason' in *Out of Apathy,* E. P. Thompson (ed), Stevens, 1960, 224.
8. Ibid, 203.
9. Homans, D., 'Bringing Men Back In', *American Sociological Review,* 1964.
10. Wrong, D., 'The over-socialized concept of man', in *A.S.R.,* 1961, Vol. 26.
11. Popper, K., *The Poverty of Historicism,* Basic Books, 1966, emphasis removed.
12. Popper, K., *The Open Society and its Enemies,* first pub. 1945, reprinted by Routledge & Kegan Paul, 1962, Vol. II, 97.
13. Popper, K., *The Poverty of Historicism,* Basic Books, 1966.

14. VON HAYEK, F., *Scientism and the Study of Society*, parts 1 and 2, also *Economics*, Vols. IX and X.
15. JARVIE, C., *Revolution in Anthropology*, Routledge & Kegan Paul, 1964, 216 *et seq*.
16. POPPER, K., *The Poverty of Historicism*, Basic Books, 1966, 141.
17. JARVIE, *Revolution in Anthropology*, Routledge & Kegan Paul, 1964, 92, also 113 and 78-9.
18. WEBER, M., *General Theory of Social and Economic Organization*, Free Press, 1947, 88.
19. Ibid, 115.
20. Ibid, 92.
21. Ibid, 92.
22. REX, J., *Key Problems in Sociological Theory*, Routledge & Kegan Paul, 1961, 80.
23. BOTTOMORE, T. B. and RUBEL, M., *Karl Marx: Selected Writings in Sociology and Social Philosophy*, Watts, 1961, 75, emphasis removed.
24. MARX, K., *The Theses on Feuerbach*, Foreign Publishing House, Moscow.
25. Ibid.
26. Quoted in MAYER, J. P., *Max Weber and German Politics*, Faber and Faber, 1944, rev. ed. 1956, 127-8.
27. Ibid, 128.
28. GERTH, H. and MILLS, C. W., *From Max Weber*, Routledge & Kegan Paul, 1948, 55.
29. GROSS, N., MASON, W., and McEACHERN, A., *Explorations in Role Analysis*, Wiley, 1958, 161 and 241-2.
30. Ibid, 71-4 and 321-5.
31. Ibid, 320.
32. Ibid, 320.
33. Ibid, 321.
34. Ibid, 320-1.
35. Ibid, 324.
36. Ibid, 248.
37. Ibid, 323.
38. Ibid, 326.
39. Ibid, 324.
40. Ibid, 324 and 326.
41. GOFFMAN, E., *Asylums*, Doubleday, 1961, preface.
42. GOFFMAN, E., *Encounters*, Bobbs Merrill, 1963, 99.
43. Ibid, 104.
44. Ibid, 157.
45. Ibid, 144.
46. GOFFMAN, E., *The Presentation of Self in Everyday Life*, Anchor, 1959.
47. GOFFMAN, E., *Encounters*, Bobbs Merrill, 1963, 107 and 118, *et seq*.
48. Ibid, 114.
49. GOFFMAN, E., *Asylums*, Doubleday, 1961, 319, my emphasis.
50. Private conversation.
51. GOFFMAN, E., *Asylums*, Doubleday, 1961, 320.
52. Ibid, 386.
53. GOFFMAN, E., *The Presentation of Self in Everyday Life*, Anchor, 1959, 249.

See also Goffman's *Behaviour in Public Places*, Free Press, 1963, especially chapters 6, 7 and 8.

54. GOFFMAN, E., *Encounters*, Bobbs Merrill, 1963, 99 *et seq*.
55. Ibid, 132-3.
56. Ibid, 132, emphasis removed.
57. GOFFMAN, E., *Encounters*, Bobbs Merrill, 1963, 124.
58. Ibid, 115, see also 114.
59. BATESON, G., JACKSON, E., *et al*, 'Towards a Study of Society', *Behavioural Science*, Vol. I, 1956.
60. LAING, R. D., *Sanity, Madness and the Family*, 2nd ed., Basic Books, 1971, 9.
61. LAING, R. D., PHILLIPSON, H., and LEE, A. R., *Inter-Personal Perception*, Tavistock, 1966.
62. LAING, R. D., *The Politics of Experience and The Bird of Paradise*, Penguin Press, 1967, 95, emphasis changed.
63. Ibid, 100-101, see also:
   MACNAB, F., *Estrangement and Reality*, Tavistock, 1965.
   FOUCAULT, M., *Madness and Civilization*, Tavistock, 1967.
   ROSEN, S., *Madness in Society*, Routledge & Kegan Paul, 1968.
64. Ibid, 101.
65. COOPER, D., *Views*, Vol. 8, S. Segal (ed).
66. See the whole of *Views*, Vol. 8.
67. LAING, R. D., *Sanity, Madness and the Family*, 2nd ed., Basic Books, 1971, 12.
68. LAING, R. D., PHILLIPSON, H., and LEE, A. R., *Inter-personal Perception*, Tavistock, 1966, 5, brackets removed.

CHAPTER 7   AN ALTERNATIVE

1. cf. Alan Dawe's 'Central Meaning' idea, *B.J.S.*, Vol. XXI, 2, June, 1970. The article unfolds a new idea, which I adopt, of the problem of control, its implied sociology, and of the 'Two Sociologies' based respectively on the problems of order and control.

CHAPTER 8   AN ALTERNATIVE TO SOCIAL STRUCTURE

1. PARKIN, F., *Middle Class Radicalism*, Manchester University Press, 1968. See also ATKINSON, Dick, *Education, Student Power and Social Change*, Chapter 2, 'Empiricism and Class', forthcoming.
2. cf. COHEN, P. S., *Modern Social Theory*, Basic Books, 1968, 152-6.
3. cf. DEBRAY, R., *Revolution in the Revolution*, Pelican, 1962. Also ATKINSON, M. R., 'The Academic Situation' in *Student Power*, Nagel, J. (ed), Merlin Press.

CHAPTER 9   CONCLUSION

1. MACRAE, D. G., introduction to COHEN, P. S., *Modern Social Theory*, Heinemann Educational Books, 1968, viii.

2. GOULDNER, A., *The Coming Crisis of Western Sociology,*
Basic Books, 1970.
3. MACRAE, D. G., introduction to COHEN, P. S., *Modern Social Theory,*
Basic Books, 1968, viii.
4. NISBET, R., *The Sociological Tradition,*
Basic Books, 1967, 318.
5. WEBER, M., *The Methodology of the Social Sciences,* New York, 1949, 84.
6. LEACH, E., *The Reith Lectures,* B.B.C., 1967.

Index

DATE DUE